IN TWO MINDS:

IN TWO MINDS:

A KIND OF MEMOIR

PETER MORONEY

Peter Moroney Publishing

Published by Peter Moroney Publishing

ISBN 978-1-8383333-0-0

Typesetting services by BOOKOW.COM

Dedication

To Wayne, Simon and Lee for making me a man.
For Mam and Dad, who are always there for me
and to everyone who helped keep me alive. A
final mention to all those who tried to hurt me:
You can go to Hell.

Acknowledgments

I never thought that I would ever get this book finished, but I managed it, thanks to some very special people. I asked Hubert Murphy, the editor of the Drogheda Independent and Dr Paul Gaffney, an author and psychologist at Trinity College Dublin, to read through my first draft. Their comments and encouragement gave me the motivation to keep going. Simon Coury did a structural edit of the manuscript, and his recommendations and suggestions showed me what I had to do to make the book worth reading.

I would also like to thank my family, especially Noel, Madeline and John, for their encouragement which kept me going when times were tough. I want to give a special mention to everyone who has helped keep me alive, particularly Dr Paul Neary, who knows me better than I know myself.

Last but not least, a big thank you to my nephew, Jack Moroney, who did all the lovely artwork for the book and website. I love the image he came up with, and I think that it fits my story brilliantly.

I am sorry if I left anyone out; If I added everyone, there would be no room for the story.

Thank you all so much.

Introduction

I have been blessed in Life. I was born into a beautiful, loving family with the best Mam and Dad, and I was very fortunate to have three brilliant sons of my own. I had the great fortune of never living through a war. I never experienced Life as a homeless person or a refugee. I have not faced any dangerous natural events like earthquakes, hurricanes, volcanoes, or typhoons. I did not experience famine or extreme poverty or faced religious persecution or terrorist actions. I have been lucky in this regard, yet most of my adult life, I have been searching for something. Most people have it or can find it, but it remains elusive to me.

The story I tell here has been rattling around in my brain for decades. I have taken years to get it down on paper, but at last, I have something that I am kind of happy with, and hopefully, it is a weight off my shoulders. It is a kind of memoir but includes other information I feel I have to share, and maybe it makes this book more exciting and informative. I have a newfound respect for good authors as this project was not easy for me. How they can sit and write for long periods, and keep their story and details in order amazes me. I have read books where I was disappointed by the ending, which seemed rushed to me, and I often had questions in my mind, about what happened to some people or other parts of their story. I hope I don't make the same mistakes. The writing was hard because I am a two-finger typist, which means I am plodding. Yet, I still manage to make so many mistakes. I have also chopped and changed, edited, and re-edited this so much that I am fed up with it now. Maybe the time has come to wrap it up, but please be understanding and disregard any mistakes I missed.

Writing this also took so long because it was dependant on how I felt. Some days I was able to get to my little workstation, but on many other days, I couldn't touch it. It was too much to face, and I always found that I had more 'important' things to do. Some days, I could get a couple of hours done, while at other times, I only worked at it for 15 minutes or so, before I had to stop. Telling this story was hard for me most of the time, and some parts of my story brought up awful memories, and it was torture trying to get everything I wanted down on the page. It was painful and draining, and I have never had so many headaches in my Life. On the other hand, it did also bring back lots of happy memories that kept me going but made me miss many people I came across in my Life.

This is not one of those self-help books, and I don't feel that I am in any position to advise on any subject. Yet parts of my story might help someone else. I do hope so. That would make my efforts worthwhile. I have severe problems with my memory, but thankfully I kept a lot of notes, so I am sure that everything written here is the truth, as it happened. I am aware though that I might have some of the dates or even years, incorrect, but I am happy that all the detail is accurate. I have left out stuff that I was unsure about, and couldn't find notes to help me. I have not used many names of people either, because I cannot recall all their names, and felt silly trying to include some names and leave others out. I could say this is a result of my age, which probably is a factor, but my memory problems go as far back as I can remember. Yet, there are people who I have mentioned who are pivotal to my story and have had a significant influence on my Life. I have no problem, including their names. I am aware too that many of the tales I write about are based on my perceptions of the events and the way they affected me. Others might disagree, but I am confident that this book is a true reflection of my life story. I have tried to ensure that every detail is accurate because I want to tell the truth and nothing else. Some people will feel offended, but that is not my intention. I needed to include them to help make my story clear to everyone.

If you read this, you will see that I am quite naive for a 59-year-old, and it will be evident that I didn't learn my lesson on many occasions when I really should have. The older I get, the more fragile and vulnerable I seem to get, and I often long for those brilliant days I had growing up. I know that many people have lived a far worse life than I have, and while I feel deeply sorry for all those people, I feel grateful in some ways for the experience I have had.

As with all thrashy stories, mine contains sex, politics, and religion, but not the way you might think. Sex is a recurring theme throughout, but my book is not solely about sex. Religion and politics had their parts to play in my story, and with faith, I have left a lot out, because I am not sure where I stand in God's plan. There is not so much about politics because it is a subject, I don't have any time for, but it is an integral part of this book. It is a book about how I managed to get this far in life and the issues that tried to stop me. Parts of this book talk about the Gardai and the justice system, love and hate, loss and pain as well as work and sickness. It is also a book of secrets as I have never told anyone the whole story of my life. Mostly this is a series of intertwined stories, that together make up my Life and are what made me who I am.

This is my story, and no one can take it away from me, but I hope that it a small contribution to society.

Chapter 1

Growing up in a different world

I am sure that Wednesday the 5th of April 1961 was a special day for many people, especially my Mam and Dad. That was the fateful day I was born in the maternity ward of the Lady of Lourdes Hospital in Drogheda. I was the first-born child of Michael and Mary Moroney. I was christened Patrick Peter Moroney, but have been called Peter since my birth. What trouble and confusion that has caused me when dealing with official paperwork like driving licenses, passports, and the bank but this was not unique at the time. I learned as I grew up that it was common. I was born into this world on a Wednesday and who would have thought that the old Mother Goose Nursery rhyme was right. "Wednesday's child is full of woe".

I am the oldest of 8 children, six boys, and two girls. My Dad was a seedsman when I was born, and my Mam used to work in a local factory, but she quit to become a full-time mum. When I was born, we lived in my Granny's house at 2 St Jane's Terrace on Scarlet Street with my Granny and Grandad, who were my Mam's parents. It saddens me that I have no memory of my Grandad whatsoever, and can barely remember his funeral in the Cottage Hospital in Scarlet Street in 1966. I just remember being out the back of the hospital with crowds of people all milling around behind the hearse, waiting to walk behind it to the church. While I never remember my Grandad, I grew to have a wonderfully close relationship with my Granny, who was always there for me. We got on famously, and I did spend a lot of time with her. Many years later, one of my cousins told me that my Granny thought the sun shone out of my arse. I was her favourite which made me very proud and willing to do anything I could for her.

We did not spend much time with my Granny and Grandad on my father's side, but I remember my Grandad "Pops" being a funny man who was happy and delighted to see us. He wore a big smile on his face and always tried to cheer everyone else up. I was a bit afraid of that Granny (Mary)and found her to be a very serious, if not ferocious woman, who I was cautious around. I probably have that all wrong, just like I was always wary of men with beards. Maybe she was just the typical Irish Mammy type figure, laying down the law, and keeping everyone under control.

My Mam had two brothers, Ben and Oliver, and a sister Ann. Ann emigrated to Canada when I was young, and Oliver moved to England. Ben lived in Drogheda all his

Life, and I got on brilliantly with them all when we were together, especially Oliver, who I remember as being a bit 'crazy' hilariously. He always wanted to make us laugh, but unfortunately, he died before I ever got to know him as an adult. Dad had two brothers, Larry and Paddy and a sister, Catherina, who got me to become a Manchester Utd fan when I was very young by buying me Utd or Red Devil football gear, bags, etc. Larry was away working in England when I was young, and I don't recall seeing too much of him, but Paddy was always close, and I saw him a lot and his wife Theresa was my favourite Aunt.

I was baptised in St Peter's church on Sunday the 9th of April, which is when I received my own Holy Spirit. As far as I am concerned, we have had plenty of ups and downs, and I doubt I would be here now if He wasn't on my side and helping me through this challenging Life. My God-parents were my Aunty Ann and Uncle Paddy, and I believe that Paddy was the reason I was named Patrick but called Peter, at least that's what I was told. All considered I knew that I was born into a wonderful and loving family, and that was a blessing for me. I would like to think they all thought the same.

My earliest memory is of my Dad coming home from work one lovely day and putting me on the bar of his bike and bringing me for a spin up and down Scarlet Street - what joy that was, and still is. It is a very fond memory of mine and always brings a smile to my face. My Dad was working for Irish Cement then and would cycle to and from the factory on the Boyne road.

IN TWO MINDS:

We moved to a new corporation house in Ballsgrove in 1964, and I was immediately

impressed with an indoor toilet as my Gran just had an outside one, which was always full of spiders and creepy crawlies. It was a horrible place to go during the day, but a lot scarier during the night. As you can imagine, I didn't spend too long sitting on the 'throne' there. I couldn't wait to get out of there every time I went in.

I had a sister, Bernadette, born in 1963, and a brother John, born in 1964 and the new house seemed fantastic for all of us. It had a big back garden, a front garden, and across the road was "The Green', a huge play area that we used for all kinds of games and sports, even building grass forts after the grass was cut. It was a massive open place of freedom and joy for all the kids in Ballsgrove. We played football, tag, games, and anything else that would keep us occupied and happy. Fifty yards away was the local shops which carried most of what we ever needed, especially sweets and ice cream. In the new house, Mam and Dad had their bedroom, and the new-borns slept there for the first few months too. Bernadette had her own room and myself and John, and later all the other boys shared the big back bedroom. It was all so wonderful, new, and exciting. Daily necessities, like milk and bread, were delivered to the door every day, and though we were far from wealthy, we had all we needed and never went without food or a warm bed.

I started school in 1965 in the Daughters of Charity infants' school on Fair street and spent two years there. I only have very vague memories of being there, but I remember my teacher as being friendly and kind, and I got on well with everyone. Nothing untoward or exceptional sticks out from that time except that I got lost in Dublin when I was four years of age. Everyone in the country, well it seemed like that, would go to Dublin for Christmas shopping on the 8th of December, the day commemorating the Feast of the Immaculate Conception. We were in Roches Stores, a department store in the 'big city', and I separated myself from Mam and Dad and went to play in the window display. You have to imagine that the store was packed, like shops in Dublin used to be, and my parents were panicking searching for me. A shop assistant found me and reunited me with them. I thought they would murder me, but instead, I got a big telling off for running away on my own and not staying close to them, and then got smothered with hugs and kisses and lots of "Thanks be to God". I wonder whether I just wanted to play with the toys on display, or just escape the crush of adults shopping as if the shops were all about to close forever.

Dad got a car about this time, a black Morris Minor, with the registration number DIY 869. Isn't it funny how I can remember the 'important' things in my Life but not other things or occasions that I would love to be able to recall and live again? The car made a huge difference to us as a family, and especially the kids. Mam and Dad took us out every Sunday after dinner, and I do remember having a great time on the beach, playing on the pier and hill in Clogherhead, running around the woods in Townley Hall, but my favourite trip was up to the airport. We went into the airport for some days and on the road behind the airport on other days. In the airport, we would be checking everything out and looking out the windows at the planes outside. I still remember the old aeroplane that used to be hanging from the ceiling. When we were behind the airport, we would be amazed and excited when planes flew just overhead when they were taking off or landing. It was all so much fun, and our lives were packed with things to do and enjoy.

We got our first television in 1966 before the World Cup in England which meant we watched some of the football. Television was never that important to us then. We preferred to be out playing on the green or that game on the road where the way to score was to hit the kerb on the other side of the road and catch the ball when it came back. Television became an excuse when it was time for bed, pleading with Mam and Dad to let us stay up until the program was over. Mam was the boss in the house, doing all the work, minding the kids, and organising everything. Dad was the big boss, who provided for us all and was often used by Mam to threaten or scare us if we didn't behave. My Granny was with us every weekend and sometimes during the week, helping Mam and spoiling us every chance she got. I still remember the sneaky pennies I used to get for sweets in the shop across the road.

The World Cup in 1966 was important to the rest of the family and me, not for the football, but that is when I got my nickname - Mogs. It started as Morocco as the kids I grew up with, said I looked like a player from there, but it soon shortened to Mogs. I don't know how you get to Mogs from Morocco, but the name stuck and all my brothers and sisters and even my sons were called Mogs. It did feel good because it was original and unique, and I never met anyone else nicknamed Mogs. It did become funny at times when someone called Mogs and myself, and my brothers all turned round to answer the call.

It was a different world then compared to now. The key was put into the front door when we got up and the last one in at night took it out. My Mam would leave the money for the rent man, breadman, milkman, insurance man among others on the kitchen table, and they would just open the front door, call out their names and collect what was owed, with no issues, problems, or arguments. That was the same for everyone on our street, and we knew every household in the estate, and that was nearly 400 houses. Delivery drivers and others would often stop and ask where someone lived, and we were always able to point them in the right direction. It was friendly like someone imagined utopia should be like, and a real community spirit existed.

Friday was the day when we all got a comic to read. We got one each and then swapped and shared them until we had them all read. We got the 'Beezer, Dandy and Beano with annuals every Christmas. It was not all fun, though, we had our chores every day, like washing and drying the dishes, which was the single cause of most arguments in the Moroney household. On Saturday mornings, we had to clean the house from top to bottom, with the worse job being washing and then polishing the linoleum throughout the house. The only way to polish it was on your hands and knees doing a little bit at a time. The boys had to ensure that there was plenty of coal, wood, and turf in for the fire when the weather was cold. We had to keep the front and back gardens clean and tidy, as well as the shed and had to cut the grass with one of those old push lawnmowers and a pair of grass clippers. Saturday was bath night but also the night we got ice cream mixed with lemonade. What a treat. None of this was unusual, and every house had similar if not the same arrangements, and every neighbour, except one, was as pleasant to all the kids around and treated us with kindness and a kind of respect only kids get.

It was a super time to grow up. Everybody looked after everybody, and Mam, Dad, and Granny looked after us. We had breakfast, dinner, tea (really another dinner), and supper every day. I think Mam lived beside the cooker. Neighbours dropped in all the time, for a chat or to borrow something until they went to the market. Relatives were calling, and sometimes the house was as busy as the shops in Dublin on the 8th of December. It seemed as if someone was visiting all the time. I still remember Mam commenting that the house was like Euston station, and it was.

The market was a massive part of Life in Drogheda then. Everyone went there Saturday morning for the fruit, vegetables, potatoes, and eggs. It was always full of people. Everyone seemed to know everyone else, so spent more time chatting than shopping, which was no bad thing at all. At Christmas, turkeys were waiting to be bought, killed, and plucked before being cooked and eaten. The noise was deafening as they screamed as if they knew what was going to happen, yet no one seemed to give it a second thought.

We always went to Mass every Sunday. When I was younger, we went to the Franciscan Church on Laurence street with Granny. We wore our Sunday best and always sat in the same seat, like most of the people there. There were foul looks and moans when someone came in and 'their' seat was taken. The Masses then were much more formal, and nothing was left out or shortened, meaning Mass always lasted an hour or so. Some of it was in Latin, which just meant that we had no idea what was said. Sometimes it just seemed to go on forever. When I got a bit older, when I was allowed to go on my own, myself and some of the neighbouring lads used to go to the Dominican church, because we all had to go to Mass. We would sit at the back and listen carefully to the readings and The Gospel, and then sneak out the back door and go over to the park to pass the time until Mass was over. We had to wait and listen to the readings and Gospel because our parents often asked us what they were about, and Hell would have been a preferable place to be if you didn't know. But we got away with it, I think.

To me, I was having a great time, living the life in a small town that seemed a million miles away from Dublin, the 'big smoke'. Everything, except maybe for the chores and bath night, was fun. In 1967, I got a major shock to the system when I was 6. I started primary school and came across strict discipline for the first time. The days of having a friendly teacher mollycoddling us were over. In primary school, there were a lot more rules to be followed, and teachers wanted to teach us, and we had to learn, or else. I went to St Joseph's Christian Brothers School on Sunday's Gate in Drogheda, but I was lucky that most of the kids I was with, in infants' school had moved there too. I was lost for the first few weeks but not alone, and that helped me settle in.

I used to cycle across town every day to go to school, which was no big deal then, and go down to my Granny's for lunch. She always had a lovely dinner waiting for me on the table when I got there. On special occasions, some of us from school would go to the cattle market and get chips for lunch. They had the best chips in the world, as far as we were concerned, and we loved just hanging around the market. The market was just around the corner from the school on Magdalene street, and it was a common sight, and smell, to see cattle and sheep walked to and from the market. Some farmers were lucky enough to have cattle trucks, but most of them had to walk. When it rained, we got our chips and sat in the auction shed listening to the auctioneer, trying to figure out what he was saying. The hammer was crashed to the table frequently, indicating a sale. We didn't have a clue what was going on.

Looking back now, I did have a great time in that school, making great friends like Kevin Dawe (rest in peace) and many others who I remember but can't recall their names. That happens to me all the time. It was very strict, and I found that very hard to take, but we always got a big bun, like a hot cross bun, for morning break and played in the schoolyard like we were wild animals released from our cages. Of course, sports were necessary, and nothing more so than Gaelic football and that was the one game I was decent at. I was picked for the school teams through the age groups and even started playing for the Wolfe Tones outside of school hours. I played in a lot of positions, but mostly in midfield, and took all the free kicks. The school pitch was out on the Termonfeckin Road, and we often had to run down there to 'warm-up' for the game. That wasn't too bad, as we were young and fit, but trudging back after the game, tired and often sore, was not an enjoyable experience. Then having to cycle home took every last bit of energy I had. Changing rooms and showers were only something we could dream about, and the couple we did come across were filthy, smelly, and wet. Our changing rooms were in the ditch, or behind a wall, no matter what the weather. So we preferred to get geared up in the school or at home when I was playing for the Tones. Even worse for me, and everyone else at the time was that I had an old pair of heavy leather brown boots that were as heavy as lead. I had to clean them after every use unless I was playing again that evening. First, I would scrape off all the muck and dirt, and more often than not, leave them somewhere to dry. When they were dried, I had to clean and polish them with Dobbin; I think it was called. It was a horrible chore that took some of the fun out of Gaelic. The balls back then were made from the same leather, and seemed to get a lot heavier when they were wet and would sting my hands every time I caught the ball.

At home on the green, we played a lot of soccer or whatever game was the flavour of the month, like tennis when Wimbledon was on television, or cricket in the summer and rugby too. I was never as good at these games as I was at Gaelic, and although there were plenty of soccer clubs around, I never joined them as you could be barred from Gaelic if you were caught playing for a soccer team. The horrible 'foreign game' rule. Yet we still found lots to do and occupy our time when we were not at school. We were old enough now to begin exploring everything outside Ballsgrove. During the lovely days in the summer, we would walk out the fields, or up the ramparts beside the river Boyne, go down to the docks to see the boats and cranes, or go to the station to see the trains.

There were lots to do for us boys and we seldom just hung around Ballsgrove when the weather was kind. Nobody ever bothered us or told us to get off their land or property, but maybe that is because they did not know what we were doing some of the time.

One exciting but dangerous thing we used to do was up high on the Viaduct bridge over the River Boyne and the docks. We would wait until we saw a train coming, then hide in these little inspection holes under the tracks, until the train passed overhead. It was very noisy and smelly, and everything shook like it was an earthquake, but it was exhilarating. We would be delighted with ourselves climbing out of those holes after the train had thundered just over our heads. Talk about cheap thrills. That is precisely what that was. The viaduct was a great place to view Drogheda, the docks, ships, and cranes below as well as the river Boyne flowing beneath us. On a good day, we could see out as far as the sea and maybe even the ships coming in to dock.

There was nothing much to the west of Ballsgrove, except for Donore Village, Townley Hall, and a small wood in Oldbridge. And of course, a few apple orchards where we 'truffed' apples when they were ready to be picked. I am not sure which was better fun, getting the apples, or being chased by the farmer. We also searched for the biggest and best chestnuts from the chestnut trees. We used these to play the game 'conkers' where you put a hole through the centre of the nut and tied some sting on it and used this to try to smash the other person's chestnut. It was a craze, and everyone did it. It did cause arguments too, mostly when some people used dirty tricks like filling the chestnut with sand or baking it in the oven. It was also dangerous, and I don't know how many times I got my fingers smashed with a flying chestnut.

On good sunny days, we would cycle out to the Bettystown beach, play on the dunes and the beach until it was time to go home, and we always had to be home for mealtime. That was the main rule, unbreakable and unchangeable. I had to tell Mam where we were going, and she would remind me, again and again, to be home for the next meal, be it dinner or tea. I was always home on time because I was afraid someone else would eat my meal, and I would get in trouble with my Mam. But most days we just headed out the fields as far as Donore or Townley Hall and made our own fun. Once when we were going through the grounds beside Marley's lane, where the school is now, we found a bit of rope, and I decided to ride a cow. I tied the rope around the cow's neck, to give me something to hold onto, got on the cow, and he took off like a cheetah chasing its dinner. Of course, I fell off but got the rope twisted around my ankle, and the poor cow dragged me all around the field, and only stopped when it could run no more. I ended up in the hospital with a busted ankle, where the rope had tried to cut my leg off, but I was okay. I was fortunate as the lads later pointed out where my head had just missed a concrete block. I got away with that, but my promising career as a rodeo rider was over.

When we could, or rather when we got money, our allowance off Mam, we would go to the pictures (the cinema in today's language) for the Saturday matinee. There were two cinemas in town, but we always went to the Abbey Cinema, and I don't remember ever being at the Gate cinema. The Abbey was always packed with kids. The ushers, usually ladies, were always trying to keep us quiet until the short before the main movie started. That was nearly always a Batman cartoon, and we would all start roaring out the 'biffs' and 'Kerpows' as they came on screen. God bless those ushers; they had an impossible job. We would all be hyped, pretending to be Batman, Tarzan, or some other hero for the rest of the day. Different things thrill people in different ways, but a huge thrill and experience for me, was when my Dad brought me to the Abbey to see the film 'The Battle of the Bulge' one night in 1967. I loved the movie, but much more than that, I loved going to the pictures with my Dad. I do remember almost floating out of the cinema and home. Unfortunately, the Abbey burned down in 1969. Dad brought me down to the top of the Grove Hill, where we could watch the flames dance on the building against the dark skies above. It looked like the fire was trying to reach the sky. It was an amazing sight but a sad day for the town and the people.

I have never really had heroes or understood hero worship, but the closest person to a 'hero' for me those days was the Duke himself - John Wayne. I loved watching his movies. We only had three television stations back then, but I remember that RTE used to show a lot of John Wayne films after the 9.00 pm news on either a Friday or a Saturday night, and I was allowed to stay up to watch them. I remember the first time I saw him killed in a movie, and it completely shocked me, and I could not believe what I was seeing. To me, it was kind of real and not make-believe. The film was "The Sands of Iwo Jima" where he was shot at the end. I felt distraught that he was killed as I believed that he could never die. It took me a while to get over that. Other essential viewing at the time in the Moroney house was "Top of the Pops" on BBC and Opportunity Knocks with Hughie Green. Joey Maher and his family won the weekly show a few times and the whole town was so proud and talking about it nonstop. Tom and Jerry and all the other cartoons were also very popular, but I never bought into Doctor Who and the Daleks. I thought it was so stupid. My logic was that the Daleks were cumbersome and immobile and could be stopped by throwing something over them to cover them up, or just push them down the stairs. They were too easy to defeat, yet lots of people loved the show and were intimated by the Daleks. To me, they made no sense at all, and while I loved, and still do, watching someone else's vision for the future or different worlds, I couldn't watch the Daleks.

When Dad was home and not on shift work, he took control of the telly, and it was a battle trying to convince him to let us watch what we wanted. If he got up to go to the kitchen or toilet, we immediately changed the station, and he would roar at us when he came back. He always wanted to watch the news, even after just watching it on another channel. Sometimes he relented, just to get a bit of peace, and left the living room, probably to bang his head against the wall outside. Mam was far more relaxed about the television but always seemed to be elsewhere doing the housework or looking after babies.

The only thing I was terrified about at the time was quicksand. There were lots of scary stories at the time about banshees and the 'Red Hand' in the trees on Grove Hill, but they never bothered me. Lots of movies and tv shows of the time featured quicksand. I thought it was a terrifying way to die and thought that quicksand was everywhere and not just on TV. When out playing, I would be anxious if we came across a big puddle or damp patch of ground in case it was quicksand, but to this day, I have never come across any.

While all this growing up and living Life was going on, school became fun for me rather than education. I became a bit of a 'messer' in class, and that got me into a whole lot of trouble. I remember one occasion when I was still in the junior part of the school. I put the teacher's leather into the gutter on the roof. The leather was the punishment tool of choice. It was about a foot long and was close to an inch thick, shaped to fit comfortably into the punisher's hand. I was just able to contort myself out the top window and put it in the gutter. The Christian Brother had no idea where he put it or how he could have lost it. However, there was a huge shower later that day, and the leather was washed down to the playground and found. The teacher went mental on the class, and eventually, someone squealed, and I was caught. My punishment was immediate and very painful. I got six of the best on each hand from this wet chunk of leather, and the palms of my hands were red raw for hours. Yet, too stupid or boisterous to learn my lesson, I had many more interactions with the dreaded leather. Once I was kept back when school was finished, given a good lash with the leather, and then sent down to play Gaelic for the school. I don't remember what I did that day, but I was in agony and could not touch the ball with my hands. You can't play Gaelic football without good hands so I couldn't play properly. It wasn't long before I was taken off and called an idiot.

I know that many people might disagree with me, but I don't think the leather done my school friends or me any harm at all. It was apparent back then, and I suppose this has helped make me who I am. I see everything in black or white, so to speak. If you did wrong and were caught, you were punished. We all knew that. I accepted that as the punishment when I was caught doing something wrong. Years later, in the same school, I was caught doing something wrong by Mr Green, and as punishment, I had to wait after school until he was ready to go and carry his brown leather case to his car for him. To me, that was much worse as it was so embarrassing and humiliating, and I had to do that for a whole month. Everyone used to laugh at me and take the piss. Still, I got by, by doing what I had to.

Mrs Moroney didn't rear any stupid children but education, and homework, was something to be done, and everything in Life would be good. So, I never exactly excelled in school but was good enough to stay out of trouble, most of the time. I did learn something, though, and that was that I could not sing a note. All the students were assembled in the big yard to practice singing for some big event. We were all singing, and I was giving it socks when suddenly the teacher stopped us before having us sing in small sections. When it was our turn, the teacher looked at me and told me to shut up and stay quiet for the rest of the session because I was ruining it for everyone else. I have only tried to sing about five or six times since and I am still as bad.

Life was great at home, and two more boys joined the Moroney clan. Colm was born in 1967 and Noel was born in 1968. Now there were five kids in the household, and all the boys slept in the one bedroom. The only time I remember being unhappy back then was when I got yellow jaundice and had to stay home for a month or so. Initially, no school was brilliant, but I soon became bored silly, especially when everyone else was at school, and I had no one to play with. That was the first time I experienced loneliness, and I was not too fond of it. It was a strange new feeling that troubled me then and many times since. When I went back to school, I had to catch up very quickly, with double homework. I had no clue what the teacher was talking about most of the time and didn't want to be left behind, so I worked hard to catch up. I could do this when I wanted to. It's a shame I didn't like to learn more all the time. Now I love to learn something new every day.

I did drive my Mam and Gran crazy as I loved to untie their aprons when they were doing something, and I loved to steal a mouthful of gripe water that was for the baby. I loved the sweetness of it and got some whenever I could. No wonder I have diabetes now. The only time I ever got into big trouble at home was when I was ten years of age and had a big argument with my Mam. I believe it was over money. I had a little job, and the house rule was that half of it should go to Mam for the house, but I didn't want to share my money. I felt so bad later and thought my Mam did not love me anymore. (How many times have I believed this since.) So, I ran away. I got on my bike and went up to the train station, with the idea of getting on a freight train, and going wherever it took me. But the train station staff seemed to be all over the place that day and watching me closely. So, I gave up on that idea and started cycling towards the airport, where I was going to stow away on a plane. How I was going to get on a plane with my bicycle, I had no idea, but I was going anyway. I headed up the Dublin road full of energy and enthusiasm for my new Life, leaving all my troubles behind me. I cycled for hours until I got to Swords, about 25 miles from Drogheda. I was tired, hungry, and over the row with Mam. I dropped the idea of flying off to exotic locations. Loneliness and hunger were driving me now, but I had no idea what to do until I saw the Garda station.

I went in and told the Garda my story. He was brilliant. He phoned the station in Drogheda and asked them to let my parents know where I was, and that I would be on the next bus from Swords to Drogheda. He even bought me a coke and a cream bun to eat. Then he put me on the bus to Drogheda with my faithful steed, my bike, carefully placed in the luggage hold. The ride home on the bus was very uncomfortable for me, as all kinds of thoughts entered my head like I was going to be killed by my parents or placed in an orphanage or worse, just kicked out of the house. But I shouldn't have worried. The little bus station in Drogheda at the time was on the top of the Marsh Road, and Mam and Dad were there to greet me, and there was no eviction, fighting, or threats at all. They were just delighted that I was safe and home. We even laughed about the long cycle and presenting myself to the Garda station in Swords, but it was the first and last time I ran away from home.

In April of 1970, I was confirmed in St Peter's church in Drogheda, with the rest of my classmates. Yes, I did get the slap on the face, but I barely remember that or the ceremony itself. But it was a momentous occasion because I was now old and big enough to wear long trousers for the first time. No matter what the occasion before my confirmation, short trousers were all I had and was allowed to wear. They were ok in the summer but horrible in the cold of winter, and they looked so childish, especially as part of a suit. Those days were over me now, and I was delighted. I was a big boy now.

That same year another brother joined us, Brian. The house was filling up fast, and there always seemed to be a new baby in the house.

I started working at ten years of age, helping Ramie Smith, our breadman. I did it mostly for the big cream buns he would give me. But sometimes he would give me a few pennies as well, and that was a bonus. He delivered bread and cakes from Peter Lyons bread, and I often went with him into the big bakery on Stockwell street in the town. The size of the place and the vast ovens took my breath away. I still remember the rhyme we all used to say; -

Peter Lyons bread

It sticks to your belly like lead,

The more to eat

The more you want

Of Peter Lyons bread.

It was a wonderful new experience to have my own money, so for the summer of 1972, I got myself an unofficial job as a tea-boy when the new Holy Family Church in Ballsgrove was being built. I made the tea and kept busy running to the shop for the workers. They would all chip in to give me a few shillings every Friday, and almost every time I went to the shop, they gave me a few pennies. It was great working with men too and having a laugh, even if I was often the butt of their jokes, like going around the site asking for skyhooks. But it all came to an end too soon. I was in the part of the church where the sacristy is now, and there was a demonstration wall there. I didn't know that it was not cemented to the floor and leaned on it. It fell on my foot, and I had to hobble home. My Mam took off my shoes and sock, but when she got my sock off, the nail on my big toe came off too. So off to the hospital again. I was also barred from the site when the bosses heard about my accident. The money I made though, came in handy as the Moroneys went to Bettystown on holidays later that summer. We stayed in a building which was just across the road from the beach. We played on the sand, in the sea and on the dunes every day. We even played in the water and on the beach when it was lashing rain, because we were going to get wet anyway. One day we found, up near Mornington, what looked to us like a small shark washed up on the beach. It had so many sharp and dangerous-looking teeth. It was nearly 3 feet long, but it was dead.

Every time we went into the water after that, we were looking out for sharks and afraid we would get bitten, or we would try to scare everyone by screaming 'shark' and pointing close to them. On another day, my brothers and I were playing football on the beach when Johnny Giles came along and had a kick about with us. I had no idea who he was until the others told me, and then I felt privileged. We couldn't wait to tell everyone, but I don't think many believed us at all. Like most things, the beach was a very different experience back then. The place used to be full of cars and people on the weekends, especially on a Sunday. Families would park up in their vehicles or arrive in big groups when the bus arrived. Mams would get out to get the kids sorted and looked after. Dads would put the radio on to listen to the football or hurling. Kids would have a super time in the water, on the beach, or playing in the dunes. Holes were dug, sandcastles built and many people buried in the sand. Ah, the simple things in life are still the best. We went back there again there following year for our holidays and had just as much fun.

Following my accident in the new church and after the summer, I got myself a little job with a farmer selling potatoes in the market on Saturdays. He was a lovely gentleman, but I can't remember his name. The craic between him and the customers was excellent, and he could have thought many marketers a thing or two about customer service. He sold two types of potatoes - Kerr's Pinks and Records, and he sold them either loose or in 4 stone bags. My job was to carry the spuds to the customers' cars, mostly in 4 stone bags, and then help him deliver to people all over the town. It was good work, and I built up my strength a lot even though I was still as skinny as a rake. That went on into 1974 when another accident put an end to that. We happened to be delivering in Ballsgrove behind my uncle Paddy's house when I fell off the trailer as we were driving down the lane. I landed flat on my face, broke some teeth, cut my face, lips, and nose, and ended up in the hospital again. At least I know where my good looks went. That was the end of that job, but work was work and work was money, and if I ever needed anything for myself, I had to buy it myself. That was the way it was back then, not just for me, but for everyone I knew. So that year myself and John, Pat Devlin from next door, and a few others went to work on Berrill's farm on the Slane road, outside Drogheda on Saturdays. Peter Berrill would pick us up in an old pick up at 6.00 am or shortly after that, depending on when he got up. Even in the winter when it was freezing cold, we would travel on the back of the pickup and be delighted to get off the truck and start work, to keep moving and try to warm up. We picked carrots, or potatoes, thinned turnips, and on some occasions cut down and chopped trees on the land to sell as firewood. Most of the lads would finish and be home by tea time, but Pat Devlin and myself were often asked to stay to help wash and bag the vegetables so they would be ready for the market in Dublin on Monday morning. So, when Peter dropped the rest of the gang home, we went into the house, and his mother would pile the dinner into us. We ate like people who had never seen food before, as we were starving, having only had a sandwich at lunchtime. That would invigorate us for the work ahead. We washed the vegetables through a long rotating barrel that looked like a circular grater from the inside. Loading the veg at the top of this barrel was not too bad, but being at the bottom, collecting the produce in plastics and then tying them tightly, was a lot more difficult, especially when it was freezing. I had no idea what kept my fingers stuck to my hands or if they were still there at all. We had plenty of laughs and banter to help pass the night, and I even got to see a calf being born one night. It was amazing. But it was worth it, even after paying half to Mam, having my own money to do with as I pleased and I bought a new, proper pair of football boots and other football gear as soon as I could.

I did also have a brief but embarrassing flirt with acting in primary school. We were studying a play called 'The Smuggler's Den' about some boys who came across a den full of stuff before the smugglers arrived back. The play was to be part of the school's annual entertainment show. When all was ready, the show was performed to a big audience, including my parents, in the Parochial Centre in Drogheda. We were the bee's knees. We felt like stars, even though we were all very nervous. We had dressing rooms with seats and lockers. When the play started, everything was going ok until one of my significant parts.

The stage went into darkness, and I was supposed to light a candle. I could not get the matches to light for ages, and when I did, I could not find the candle. I was mortified and completely forgot what I was supposed to say next. Thankfully one of the other lads, I think it was Alan Milne, said my lines for me. One of the teachers, seeing the disaster unfold, turned the lights back on as if the candle lit up the 'cave' and I was not involved for a few minutes. I took the chance to put my heart back in its place, reboot my head, and finish the play sweating like a pig and overly conscious of making another mistake. Any chance of an acting career ended there and then. Around the same time, my Dad was involved in the musical 'Oklahoma' and had a big singing part. Of course, we all went to see him in the Parochial Centre and he, unlike me, handled himself brilliantly and sang ever so well. We were so proud that night and amazed at how well Dad performed. My Dad was a star, in my eyes, anyway.

The significant ground-breaking event in 1973 was that I finished primary school and started secondary school. Life was great, and I believed that this would last forever, living a carefree life and having lots of fun, but how wrong I was - Wednesday's child is full of woe.

1973 was like every previous year, as far as I can remember. It was great and lots of fun. I started secondary school, went on a fabulous family holiday, started a new part-time job, and welcomed another brother, Michael, into the gang. That was six boys and one girl in the family now if you were counting. The house was full, noisy, and always busy. All us boys shared three beds in the big back bedroom, while Bernadette had the small room all to herself. Meals were eaten in shifts, in the small kitchen. I had to be ready when called, or I might lose my place and my food. We ate like pigs in a trough, stuffing the food down us like we were never going to get any more. We were always hungry when mealtime came around, and I guess that was because we were all lively and active during the day. I was a picky eater and never ate fish. I remember the fishermen with their nets catching fish beside the ramparts on the River Boyne, and I often went there with Dad, and he would buy a fresh trout or salmon from them for Friday dinner. We were not allowed to eat meat on a Friday because we were Catholic. I have in my head that I got very sick when I was young after eating fish and could never touch them again. Even when the family was eating fish, I would have to take my dinner out of the kitchen because the smell made me nauseous. I still can't take the smell.

That summer the family went to a place called the High Chaparral in Castleisland, Co Kerry. The whole holiday was a wonderful experience for all of us. Apart from the odd trip to Dublin or the airport, we had stayed in and around Drogheda. The journey down the county was fantastic, even if the car overheated. That should not have surprised us too much as the car was full. There were Mam and Dad, with six boys and one girl. Plus, all our luggage, on a scorching day. It took us 7 hours to get there, but it was well worth it in every way. I was the navigator guiding us through all the towns and villages on the way, and the mountain ranges on the way looked terrific. Being the oldest and lanky, I was lucky to get the passenger seat at the front of the car to myself. The High Chaparral itself was about a mile outside Castleisland, and it was a holiday complex, made up of a lot of wooden chalets centred around a big house that served as the reception, dining room, and music venue at night, for the adults. At the front of all this was a big field and it was full of ponies. To us, they were horses, and we were riding them around every chance we got. The people who worked there, and one of them was only 11, were brilliant teaching us and helping us ride correctly. One day they asked us if we wanted to go up the mountains and help them ride back more of the ponies. Dad came with us, and it was a long trek. When he got back, his arse was sore, and he wasn't sure if he would ever sit again. How we all laughed that night. Most days though, after breakfast, and a few circuits of the field on the ponies, Dad would take us to see the sights of Kerry. Everywhere we went was so beautiful that you knew God did some of his best work there. We went on the Ring of Kerry, up the gap of Dungloe, onto Inch strand, into Killarney in the park and on the lakes. Every day was new and fascinating, and we loved every minute of it. Then once we were back in the High Chaparral, we were back on the ponies and had to be dragged off them at night. Some months later, Dad pointed out an article in the Sunday paper about that 11-year-old. I can't remember his name, but the piece was about him being the youngest horse dealer in the country. Amazing.

Shortly after we got home, I started secondary school in St Mary's Christian Brothers School on the Beamore Road in Drogheda. That was on my side of town and was nearer to me than St Joseph's. Drogheda was divided by the River Boyne (and still is). On the North of the river were County Louth and St Peter's Parish in the diocese of Armagh. South of the river was partly in County Louth and partly in County Meath but was in St Mary's Parish and the diocese of Meath. St Joseph's was in St Peter's parish and County Louth while St. Mary's was in St. Marys on the border of Counties Louth and Meath. I still remember walking into school that first day.

I was overawed and excited at the same time. Most of my classmates from St Joseph's went on to St. Joseph's Secondary school, but a few I knew moved to St Mary's, mainly because they were from St Mary's parish too. Many of the new students came from St Mary's Primary School in Congress Avenue. Still, a lot more came from villages and areas in County Meath such as Laytown, Bettystown, Duleek, Donore, and even as far as Ardcath and Kentstown. So, there was a great mix of boys from lots of different places. I settled in very quickly and was put into a class that studied Irish, English, Maths, History, Geography, Latin, French, and Science. From the outset, I did not want to be wasting my time with Latin. To me, it was a dead language that would be of no practical use to me then or at any time. So, I did absolutely nothing when it came to Latin. Neither did I see any value in studying ancient poems by Shakespeare, Milton, or others I never heard of before. I could not understand why we had to waste so much time and effort on this outdated stuff. It was of no practical use as far as I was concerned. I can see now how my brain was developing, and I was starting to evaluate what others thought was important. I was, rightly or wrongly, making decisions about what was important, useful, or of value to me, and what wasn't. Mam and Dad, and Granny too, brought us up properly. I knew right from wrong, and to respect everyone, even if I questioned myself about whether they deserved it or not. To my mind then and all since then, I felt that respect had to be earned. Sure, I had respect for almost everyone I had known in my young life, but I began to notice that not everyone was the same. I started to see and experience greed, selfishness, and dishonesty around me and I found that disturbing and wrong. I loved and still do, the truth, and hate lies and that started with me about this time. I am not proud that lying became such an integral part of my life years later. I developed a kind of personality, where I wanted to help others who required help, and an aversion to people who looked down on others. I did everything I could to avoid or walk away from such people. I still find it hard to deal with people I feel have hidden agendas, or who lie to achieve their own goals or aims. I can't stand liars or 'fake people' who don't care who they hurt or offend, once they get what they want. That was, I suppose when

I began to set my own core values, and while I would not change them for anything, they have caused me a whole lot of pain and grief since.

Just as in primary school, I did what I had to, to get by and stay under the radar. There were no leathers in St Mary's, but punishments like lines, double homework and even getting the wooden duster thrown at you were common-place. Sometimes the teachers prevented me from doing what I wanted to do, like sports or being on time for work after school, and that felt a whole lot worse.

Sport again was very important in St. Mary's as was PE, but basketball was a hugely popular game in school. It was all new to most of us, and many of us played any chance we got. I played for the school team in different age groups, but I was never really that good or confident. Yet it was fun and kind of like a new fad to me, and many of my friends in school played too. The School was blessed with some brilliant and talented basketball players and won a lot of competitions and trophies. Most of the training sessions took place in the school gym in the evenings, which give us something positive to do after school as well as some-where to go. But Gaelic football was still my game, and I continued to play for the Wolfe Tones and played for the school teams. The training in the school was horrendous. We had to run to the Gaelic fields in Bryanstown to warm up before practice, and the evil teachers often made us run down the Dale and up the 101 steps. Then we would start training proper—pure torture. Again, the school had some very talented Gaelic footballers, and I believe some of them went on to win all Ireland medals with Meath, and another played for County Louth but never had the same success with them. Yet I enjoyed playing Gaelic more than any other sport, perhaps because I felt more confident and thought I was better at it. I did not worry about whether I was doing the right things or what to do next. I just went with the flow and kind of felt in control of myself and how I played.

I got on well with everyone in the school, even Bridie the canteen lady who we used to help out, so we got free grub or sweets. She taught me how to make creamy coffee by first mixing the sugar and coffee, then add a teaspoon of water and mix to a paste before adding the hot water. I made coffee that way until I stopped using sugar. I made great close friends too. Alan Milne had also moved to St Mary's and lived close to me in Ballsgrove, and we became great friends with Ray Berrill and Don Carolan. Most days we walked to school together then home for lunch and back to school again. Notice the way that dinner had changed into lunch with the advent of secondary school. On break times boys would be playing basketball, soccer and any other game they had space for, but a few were sneaking around behind the school to smoke, and it was not too long before I was giving it a go. Stupid boy, but it was seen as cool back then. So, for once, I thought I was cool. I was not averse to a bit of 'mitching' either and took days or half days off school when I shouldn't. A popular place to go when mitching was to the Linen Hall pub where we were let play pool out the back. We knew we would not be spotted there, so it was safe that is where I learned to play pool. On lovely days, we would go up the ramparts or go on the railway tracks to the Platin cement factory. Bold boys!

I started a new job in SuperValu Drogheda. There was an old small supermarket in the town called Lipton's. That was taken over by SuperValu who opened the first big supermarket in Drogheda. I don't know whether they bought out Liptons for all the equipment, or to stop any local competition. The first job we had when I started was to move all of the stock, shelving, and equipment to the new purpose-built store in the Abbey Centre where the Abbey cinema used to be. Then the job entailed stocking up the shelves, keeping the store clean, or hauling the stock up the stairs from the storeroom when the lift broke down, which I swear happened every week. Still, it was great craic there, and I had money to keep me going through the week without asking Mam for some.

Another job I had was taking people's shopping to their cars and collecting empty trolleys. That was when I came across my only real bully. He was about a year older than me, from the 'faa side' (St Peters), and was always harassing and bullying me for my money. I never give him a penny, and sometimes it came to blows, but I wouldn't give in. I was never a fighter even though I had been in a couple of scraps, but I was not going to hand him over any of my hard-earned money, and open up myself to be intimidated by him all the time. He was a thug though, the first I came across. Years later, when I was living in London, a friend pointed out the headline in the Sunday Press, joking that it referred to a friend of mine from Drogheda. I took the paper from him and read the article, and it was my bully from all those years ago. He was jailed in England for killing his children with a hammer. How lucky was I???

As they say, time flies when you're having fun, and time did seem to pass very quickly for me back then. It was strange at times having one group of friends based around the school, another based around home, and even more based around the football team. Nothing wrong with that, but I realise now that was a time to be treasured. The following year we went back to the High Chaparral and had another brilliant time, but this time we went to visit even more places. I think the best view I've ever seen in my life is called the Nun's view just outside Killarney looking over the lakes and mountains. I have been back to see the beauties of Kerry a few times since and I still love the place. I even followed the Kerry Gaelic football team from then, and I thought they were the 'aristocrats' of the game. Louth never seemed to get to the televised stages of the all-Ireland.

The ponies were still there, and we rode them as often as we could. This year we were far more confidant riding the ponies and taking good care of them, which I loved doing.

It is a shame that The High Chaparral is no longer there. It was such a fun place for us kids, and I'm sure the adults too had a great base to explore Kerry. Back in Ballsgrove, there is a big old house at the top of the Grove hill owned by the Kanes. Mr Kane kept showjumpers (hunters) at the back of the house and had built a small showjumping arena there too. I used to sit on the wall and watch him putting the horses through their paces. After lots of begging, I eventually got him to agree to teach me how to ride a horse correctly and in exchange, and I would look after horses and clean out the stables. He taught me how to ride and jump and how to care for a horse. I loved it even though cleaning out the stables was tough and smelly. Sometimes he asked me to take one of the horses up to the end of the Ramparts and walk them in the River Boyne. That was to ease the cuts and scrapes on the horse's legs, and it was a massive thrill for me. The best being when I would gallop the horse through a field and then down the green on the way home. What beauty, power, and exhilaration. I was so lucky. I have loved horses ever since and I think they are such beautiful animals.

I think if I got green shield stamps every time I went to the hospital; I would have been a millionaire. I cannot remember how many times I went to casualty, but I was a regular. The green shield stamps were the huge marketing thing of the age where they were exchanged for goods free of charge in Dublin. It was all the rage. The stamps were looked after like they were gold dust until they were exchanged for household goods, gifts and a massive range of other equipment. They were rewards for purchases from lots of retailers, and it seemed like everyone collected the green shield stamps.

As you probably guessed, I was playing Gaelic football for the school and ended up back in the hospital. During the game, I blocked a shot, but as I diverted the ball, I was kicked on the hand and broke three fingers. So, I had to go to the hospital again and get my fingers strapped up, and everybody says that sport is good for you. It is really, but bad things happened to everybody, and it was no big deal. I had a great family, enjoyed lots about school, was working part-time, playing lots of sports, and still having time for friends. I wish I could do that now. Life was great for my family and me, and it was never going to change or was it?

Chapter 2

A defining Year

In February 1975 my little sister Valerie was born. Mum and Dad were delighted that, at last, they got a little sister for Bernadette. The family was complete. It was a huge change to have a little sister rather than another brother, but she added to the family. She was treated like a princess by everyone in the family, even the little dog, Oscar. There were our parents and eight children living in the house, and Mam often commented that it was a real madhouse, and she wasn't wrong. Even Dad got confused at times when calling one of us. He would call us, and when he went to him, he would say he meant to call another one of us. It was funny at times. Poor Dad, he must have said "I meant John, Colm, Noel, Brian or Michael" to me a billion times.

In April, I was playing Gaelic for the Wolfe Tones one evening up in Rathmullan Park, where St. Nicholas Gaelic

Club is now based. The game was nearly over, and it was a draw match. We won a free-kick, and I stepped up to take it. It was a long-distance out, so I had to put all my strength into it. I focused on the kick and slotted it right over the bar. It felt like my leg went after the ball and over the bar too. We had scored the point and won the game, but I had hurt my leg badly when taking the kick. It felt like I pulled something, so I just grabbed my gear from the ditch and hobbled home. I was often sore after football games, so I didn't pay too much attention to it that evening. However, when I got up the next morning, my leg was very sore right down to my foot, and Mam decided to take me to the hospital. I saw a doctor in casualty, and he said that I had pulled a muscle in my leg and I had to rest it, and I would be fine. He told me to come back in a week so they could monitor my progress. That was on the 22nd of April 1975, just a few weeks after my 14th birthday. I wasn't too upset at the time as I thought it was just another injury to add to my catalogue. I did try to rest it as much as I could, but I found it hard to sit in doing nothing, so I did go out to hang with the boys to pass the time, but I didn't do anything that would hurt my leg.

The following week on the 30th of April, I went back to the hospital to get my leg checked out. I went there on my own, partly because I was a 'big boy' now, and partly because I knew Mam already had her hands full at home. I didn't think it had got any better, but I wasn't a doctor and did not know how my body worked. I was sure the doctors would examine me properly and fix me up. I thought I was in good hands. In the Lourdes hospital at the time there were two surgeons, Mr Sheehan and Mr Shine, who seemed to run the hospital along with the Matron and Staff Sisters. Both these doctors were seen as almost God-like, and to be treated by either was a privilege. When I attended A&E the week before, I saw a doctor on Mr Sheehan's team, but this time in the weekly clinic, I saw Mr Shine himself. Mr Shine seemed friendly and professional. I sat in his big office while he examined my leg, asked me a few questions, and said that he was not happy and I would have to go for an x-ray. He called for a porter to bring me a wheelchair and wheel me to the x-ray department. I got my X-ray taken, I waited for the prints, and a porter brought me back to Mr Shine's office, straight past two huge queues waiting to see a doctor. Usually, I had to stay in the line after x rays, but this time I didn't. How privileged and special I felt.

As far as Shine was concerned, when he looked at the x-ray, I had torn a muscle in my right thigh. The previous week, the doctor said that I had pulled a muscle. Not exactly the same, but close. Mr Shine also told me that I would have to stay in hospital to give my leg a chance to heal. Because I was on my own, the hospital needed parental permission before I could be admitted. Mr Shine himself wheeled me up to the office, behind the hospital reception area, so that they could contact my parents. We had no phone at home at the time, so we tried to get my

Dad at work in Irish Cement. Eventually, the receptionist got him, and it wasn't long before he and Mam arrived in the hospital, and I was admitted to the third floor. I was put into one of those six-bed wards and confined to bed. I had to use a commode to go to the toilet but we some laughs. I even got into trouble there too. The chap in the bed next to me distracted the student nurse, and I shoved a few black grapes down the back of her uniform and pressed until they squashed and leaked all over her. The Ward Sister, the Matron, and Mr Shine came and told me off, and the poor nurse got a bollocking too. That was unfair because she was just the victim of our stupid prank.

The strange and unusual thing at the time was that Mr Shine would drop in to see me and see how I was, at night, without his entourage of junior doctors, sisters, and nurses. The other patients would wonder who I was, to be getting special attention from such an eminent doctor. Some were Shine's patients too, but he did not visit or check on them. After a week, I was allowed out of bed to practice on the crutches. It was not too bad, except the palm of my hands would sting. On the 10th of May, which is probably now the saddest and most painful days in the calendar year for me, I was discharged. My Dad picked me up and brought me home. I was supposed to rest, take it easy, and go back to the clinic the following week. In other words, no school for a while more yet.

I went back to the clinic the following week. In the Lourdes Hospital at that time, the main entrance was in the centre of the hospital, facing the graveyard, and the reception was just in that door. I presented at the reception and had to wait in the immediate vicinity. I stayed there, until the Ward Sister, Nurse Culligan called me. She was in charge of this part of the hospital and knew what everyone, especially the nurses, was doing every minute of the day. She seemed to be very good at her job and in total and absolute control of that area. It was always jampacked with lots of people either waiting to be called to A&E or the clinic. When I heard my name, I had to go down the corridor through A&E or casualty, to the clinic waiting room. This waiting room was small and kind of L-shaped and also bustling. Right across the entrance was the door to Mr Shine's huge office, probably more massive than the waiting room, where I had seen him before being admitted. To the left of his office, as you looked at it, were three little wooden partition cubicles, where the different doctors and nurses on duty attended to the patients. On our side of the room, on the other side of the entrance, was a little dressing station.

I thought that my luck was in that day, as I did not have to wait too long in the waiting area. One of the nurses called my name and escorted me to one of the cubicles and asked me to stay there until the doctor came. Inside the door, there was an examination bed on the left, and a sink on the right. On the west wall facing the door was a little window. Outside that window was a palm tree growing healthy and strong, despite our changeable weather, and I was curious about how it survived out there. I sat on the bed, taking all this in and waited for the doctor.

When the door opened, the first thing I noticed was that it was Doctor Shine himself and not one of his team. That was great, wasn't it? The second thing I noticed was that when the nurse tried to accompany Mr Shine into the cubicle, she was blocked off and not invited in. I don't know what he said or what went through her head, but at the time, it didn't seem abnormal or unusual to me. Mr Shine remembered me and was polite and soft-spoken and asked me how I was, how my leg was, and whether I was on my own or if my parents were with me. I told him that I was fine but was not sure which was the sorest, my leg, or the palms of my hands from the crutches. I also told him, I was on my own because I, nor my parents, expected that I would be admitted as an in-patient again.

He asked me to take my trousers down and lie on the bed. I did this and dropped my pants but did not take them off. They were scrunched up around my feet. I lay on the examination bed on my back and was looking straight at him. I didn't feel nervous or ashamed in any way. I was well used to being examined in the hospital. He began pressing and touching my thigh, asking if any touch or bit of pressure was sore. Sometimes I answered that there was no pain where he touched, but other times, I could feel the pain and let him know. He told me that I was "a fine healthy boy" and that my leg was getting better, but I

47

would have to stay on the crutches for a while, and not put too much pressure on my right leg.

Then he started examining my stomach just underneath the waistband of my underpants. There was nothing wrong with my gut. But he was the God-like doctor, and I was just a dumb kid from town, so I said nothing. As he continued pressing, he started going lower and lower, touching and feeling all the time, like he was looking for a lump. He kept going lower and lower, pressing and touching, until he reached my balls. He played with them in his hands, the way we used to play with marbles, and I just lay there. I could see nothing except his face, and I will never forget the sight of his tongue and the way he rolled it around his lips. It was like he was experiencing some pleasure or even a thrill. I was frigid. I did not move, so I had nothing else to look at. He then took my penis and masturbated me until I came in his hand. I did not move or say anything. I did not understand what he was doing to me. I didn't know it was a sexual act. I had my first ever ejaculation. I was excited and confused at the same time. I had no idea what had happened, but it felt kind of good to me. Shine washed his hands in the sink while I stared at the palm tree. When he had dried his hands, he turned his attention back to me. He repeated that I was a fine healthy boy and told me to go to make an appointment for the following week. I went to reception and booked myself in for the next week. I left the hospital, and on the way down Windmill Road, my feelings were all over the place. I was shocked, and I was excited, but I did know what to think. That was my very first sexual encounter. Nowadays, I'm sure kids know a lot more about sex before they are ten years of age than I did then. I never even thought about girls or girlfriends. Girls were more like enemies than friends and not part of my world just yet. Boys kept to themselves and girls did likewise, except maybe in the family home.

The same thing happened every time I went back to the hospital. I am not sure how many times I went back to that clinic, but I always had 4 or 5 times in my head. I was seen every time by Mr Shine and not one of his team, and he was always on his own, with no nurse present. It was not as if there were no other doctors on duty. I noticed them running around all the time, going from one cubicle to casualty and back again, with nurses never far behind. Shine always followed the same pattern, asking how I was, examining my leg, then stomach, and so on. He would have his pleasure with me, tell me I was a fine healthy boy, and ask me to come back in a week or two, whatever suited him. I got used to it, and never felt as excited or confused as the first time, and didn't think about it too much. I thought it was like any other procedure in the hospital. On the 14th of July, he told me I was doing very well, and I didn't need to come to the hospital anymore. He told me to go and see him in his private rooms on Fair Street instead. He gave me a date and time to remember. The following week I went to Fair St. I had no idea where his building was and had to walk the street looking at the plaques beside the doors before I found it. I knocked, and he answered the door himself. I didn't have to wait very long in the hallway before he called me into his examination room, which was at the back of the house. The place was different, but everything else was the same as in the hospital, and the same abuse happened every time. But only two or three times here as far as I can recall.

I never told my Mam or Dad or anyone else what was happening. I did not know what to think, and who was I to question things I knew nothing about. I thought it was a normal thing that every boy went through but never spoke of. I knew too that no-one ever talked about their 'privates' as it was a 'dirty' topic. My Dad was pleased that Mr Shine had taken such an interest in my well-being, and even went to offer payment to him, but he said there was no need. I was getting free treatment in a private clinic but was paying in other ways. I was still on crutches and due to come off them very soon. I had to go back to the hospital once more for the final check-up before giving up the crutches. I did not see Mr Shine that day. I was kind of disappointed because I did not get to see the 'boss' who I had got used to seeing. Another doctor examined me, and he told me that my leg was fine and I could leave the crutches there.

That same evening, I was messing about on the street with a basketball when I scraped my hand up one of the old wooden telegraph poles and got three splinters stuck between my finger and nail. So, I had to go back to the hospital again. The strange thing is that once I was taken to casualty and seen by a nurse, Shine appeared magically, like Mr Benn in the TV show, and treated me himself. I'm sure that many of those other patients waiting there on beds or chairs, wondered how I was treated so quickly. I had to get injections on both sides of my finger, to blow it up like a balloon, before he removed the splinters. Then he just left.

I was off the crutches, mobile, and able to start playing sport, which was good news. I never got to play Gaelic football again outside school. One of the managers of the Wolfe Tones heard about my recovery, which only lasted the whole summer. He called to my house, and Mam answered the door. She went mad when he told her he was looking for me to go back playing Gaelic with the Tones. She was furious because we got no word, card, or enquiry from them when I was in the hospital or since. She ran him from the door, making it very clear that I would never be going back there again. I have never seen her so angry, and as far as she was concerned, if they did not care about me, I was not to care about them, and that was that. I stuck then to Gaelic, basketball, and other sports around the school, and I got involved with Leinster Schools Basketball Association. I trained as a basketball referee and enjoyed that, and refereed lots of games in the North East of Ireland, mostly school games. It gave me something else to do with my time, as I had enough of doing nothing. I was not able to do anything when I was in the hospital and then on crutches. The other significant benefit to me was that I had a new responsibility, and I thrived on that. I always tried to do my very best, so I would not let myself or anyone else down.

The family did go on holidays that summer, but I did not go with them. I had to stay at home for my hospital appointments, and I thought that I was a 'big boy' now and too old for family vacations. So, they went off, and I stayed at home. They went to the Isle of Man on the ferry from Dublin. Meals were no problem, as Granny looked after all that for me. No parties either, that was not our thing back then. Anyway, the neighbours were so close and connected, that Mam and Dad would probably have found out immediately on the 'mother's secret information line', the forerunner to the internet. They always seemed to know what was going on, no matter where they were.

I don't believe that the abuse had an immediate negative effect on me in any way, well it didn't seem like it did. Some noticeable changes were maybe just a part of my growing up. I found that at times I just wanted to be on my own and did enjoy my own company, some of the time. I still hung around with my mates and had good times with them, but I was questioning friendships. Overthinking what people wanted from me, became more common. I was having trust issues and judging people, even though

I knew that was wrong. Who was I to judge? I was no better than anyone, but no one was better than me. I have always thought that we were all equal and should treat everyone the same. Lots of people were better than me at nearly everything in life, like basketball, football, singing, working, and they used their gifts, but as far as I could see, I had no unique talent. Yet I believed that as people on this planet, we were all equal. As we used to say back then, I was brought up, not dragged up, and I knew right from wrong, truth from everything else, and to be polite and understanding with others. I learned to treat people, in every situation, the way I would like to be treated and have tried to live by that rule all my life. If I was not able to do that for some reason, like I felt a person was a gobshite, then I just walked away. I learned to avoid and stay away from people I did not feel comfortable with, and I was probably far too quick to accept the way I felt and act accordingly. I know some people thought I was somehow aloof or even ignorant, but as far as I thought, I was just protecting myself and trying to live a life with no drama, not hurting or offending anyone.

Chapter 3

Young Man

Back to school that year, was both a buzz and a blur. We were to sit our Intermediate exams after that school term, and we had to be ready. Most of the work was supposed to be done before Christmas because, in the New Year, we would be getting ready for the mock exams and then the exams proper. The Intermediate exams, after the third year in secondary school, were important back then as they were supposed to decide your future. If you wanted to carry on in school and do the Leaving Certificate examinations, then you had to get a good enough result to move on. If you had an apprenticeship in mind, like becoming an apprentice electrician, carpenter, or whatever, then you had to try to get a result that was better than the boys who would be applying for the same apprenticeship. I was not very good with my hands, and an apprenticeship never appealed to me. But I was not allowed to leave school unless I went on one, so I had to get a good enough result in the 'Inters' to progress.

I still played football and basketball in the school and hung around there some nights. I was still working in Supervalu as well and putting some effort into schoolwork and studying. I was mostly happy and content with my life and what I had, and I always seemed to be busy, which made the days fly by.

1976 came in, and the pressure in school was ramped up to the max. Some teachers had almost finished the curriculum for the year, and some were miles off. So, we were learning new stuff and studying old material. We were also preparing for exams proper by doing the mock exams and all the time being pushed to do our best. It was a pressure I had never experienced before, and I wouldn't say I liked it. All we seemed to do, as the exams came closer, was to do revision, study, and still try to learn new topics. It seemed to take up every spare moment of the day, at the expense of enjoyable pursuits like sports, hanging out, going for a walk, or to the pictures. A number of us had lost our jobs in Supervalu that year as more companies started opening supermarkets in town and its business dropped and, so at least I did not have to work when getting ready for the exams.

The Intermediate exams came and went in a blur as if one exam melted into the next. For the exams, I worked on the subject that was due next, then went home, dumped all books and copies relating to that subject, and started on the next one due. The books were not discarded as

they had to be kept for John to use next, and then hopefully Colm, Noel, Brian, and Michael. I didn't even study
Latin at all. When that exam came round, I sat there for
thirty minutes, as was required, then got up and left. I did
write sone answers on the exam sheets while I was there.
I was absolutely but pleasantly shocked to have even got
an E result for that. It was a fail, but I was expecting much
worse. I passed on the other subjects I took, and Mam,
Dad, and I were happy with that. Job done!!

After the exams, I managed to get a full-time job working
in a diesel workshop for the summer. Most of the time, I
was cleaning out diesel injectors for trucks. It was a good
craic there with the lads from the other small workshops
surrounding the little yard down the quays. That helped
the days pass by very quickly. I was careful and vigilant
doing my job, but often got stuck when removing parts
from an engine. Mostly because I was afraid to do something wrong, or break something. The money was decent,
though, and more than I had ever earned before. That
helped tremendously. Even after I gave Mam her half, I
still felt like I was rich.

The Bay City Rollers were the big craze around this time,
and everyone was wearing tartan, - tartan scarves, shirts,
trousers, skirts, or even ordinary clothes with tartan edges
and trims. I am delighted to admit that I never wore tartan
to celebrate the Bay City Rollers, but I was stupid enough
that summer to buy a two-tone brown pair of platform
shoes when they were all the rage. I laugh now when I

think of them and remember walking down the Grove Hill, full of myself when I fell off them and nearly broke my ankle, - the sin of pride. I suppose the only redeeming features of the year was that I had passed my exams, had plenty of money for myself, and Queen released Bohemian Rhapsody, and everyone loved it. We even knew all the words.

The family went off again for their summer holidays, and I stayed at home. I bought myself some nice stuff, (except maybe the platforms) like wrangler jeans, cheesecloth shirts, and good trousers, but I saved most of my money and had that for the year ahead. After summer, it was back to school, where we had suddenly changed from 'big boys' to young men, and we had to behave as such. I skipped 4th year as I convinced myself that it was just a doss year and it would be better to get the Leaving cert done as quickly as I could. We had to take seven subjects for the Leaving Certificate exams, and I took Irish, English, Maths, History, Geography, Economics and Chemistry. I wish now I had put more effort into Sciences before the Inter exams, but I could just not get my head around Physics, and now I am fascinated by engineering and the science behind it all. I had no clue what I wanted to be or do after school, as regards a career, so I just went with the flow. I still played sports and got on well with everyone. I was like that.

I did behave in school all the time except for once in Geography class. I was sick of the teacher, as I thought he was useless. One day he was trying to explain something, and

I didn't know what he was saying. I put my hand up and asked him about it, and he started reading straight from the book. I said I could read that and asked him if he knew what it meant because I didn't. He raced down the class and slammed me against the back wall. He was a huge man, about 6' 4" and I certainly felt that. He then threw me out of the class and reported me to the Principal. I was never allowed back into his class again. I was fuming and felt humiliated by this idiot. From then on, I had to carry my school desk out into the corridor and work on my own, but I did, and eventually got my own back on him.

I worked away in school, doing what I had to and started to notice and get interested in girls, but I still had trust issues. I was fussy about what girls I hung around with, or went out with. I did date a few but was never interested enough to keep it going. When I finished the fifth year, I got a job working in Butlins Mosney looking after the snooker and pool tables, and I stayed around the holiday camp when I was off. I was meeting more people but spending a lot more time in my own company. The work was easy, but long and tedious. Having little to do did not suit me at all. But the benefit was that we could go anywhere in the camp and enjoy all the facilities. I took full advantage, and I did that as much as I could.

One day, after I was swimming in the indoor pool, I was drying myself when I noticed a young boy just sinking below the water close to the deep end. He seemed to be struggling to get himself back to the surface, but not rising at all. I looked around for the Lifeguard, but could not see him, and by the time I looked back at the little boy, he was at the bottom of the pool. So, I jumped in, dragged him to the surface, and hoisted him out of the pool. His mother had noticed something was going on and came to the boy when I got him out. To my absolute astonishment, she gave him a hefty wallop on the back of his head, and swore and scolded him like some sort of banshee. She was so engrossed in her tirade that she never turned and said thanks or anything like that. I was glad I helped but felt sorry for the poor lad who may have wished he stayed at the bottom of the pool. For the rest of the summer, I enjoyed being in the holiday camp and mostly had a great time. I even started drinking. I favoured Smithwicks and Guinness. Generally, I thought it was brilliant and very adult to be drinking. I even helped out in the big music lounge when it got hectic and got free pints for that. Mostly I got the bus to and from Drogheda, and sometimes I got a lift. On some occasions, I stayed in Mosney in someone else's chalet. There were plenty of girls there, and that made for an exciting summer. As usual, it was over too soon, as far as I was concerned. Then it was back to school for the Leaving Certificate.

I still enjoyed school, except for having to sit outside the geography class, and got on well with all the other teachers. Just as before the Intermediate cert, the pressure was now on to get the curriculum finished and get ready for the exams. I still had no idea what I wanted to do with

myself, but going to college or university was never considered because of the costs involved. We had an excellent career guidance teacher, but even with his help, I had
no idea what I wanted to do career-wise. I was sure that
something would come my way, and I let myself believe
that.

I started working in bars in the town, starting first in the
Laurence Inn and the Cellar Bar underneath it, and then
in the Star and Crescent recreational centre. I began to
go out to the trendy bars of the time, like Mc Phails, when
I was off over the weekend. Most of the time, I was with
Don Carolan. Don was a couple of months older than me
but looked about twelve. That was great for attracting the
ladies, but no help in getting past heavy-duty bouncers.
The pleading, begging, and stories we had to tell to get
them to let him in at first. But they soon got used to seeing
us, and we could get in anywhere.

The start of the Leaving Certificate came upon us very
quickly. I felt prepared enough and took the exams with
a kind of readiness. I had studied as hard as I could in the
months leading up to the exams. Like before, it seemed
like the exams melted into one another, and it was hard
to focus on one subject, without drifting into the one that
was coming next. I remember that the weather was beautiful for the duration of the exams and I studied in the sun
as much as I could. The geography class I was in, was for
the ordinary paper for the Leaving, not the Honours paper. However, I had made my mind up before, to take the

Honours paper, which I did. I probably did it to prove to that teacher that I was more than capable of doing well without his help. The exams finished just as quickly as they started. I was delighted they were over, and I was finished school, at last. I felt free as if I was released from some prison. I remember thinking though that I was a capable student and would have done much better if I had applied myself throughout the whole of secondary school. Hindsight is not always a great thing.

After the exams, seven of us went camping around Europe, and that was a brilliant experience and a chance to see parts of the world I had never seen before. The only time I was ever out of Ireland, was a short school trip to Edinburgh a couple of years earlier. I cannot remember that at all except that we were there. We had been planning this trip for almost a year and travelled in a minibus. We got the ferry to England from Dublin, drove to Dover, and got the ferry across to Calais where we camped for the first night. Then we travelled to the South East of France before going into Switzerland, where we stayed for five nights at a wonderful campsite up in the Alps in a place called Kandersteg. We got the chance to explore the Alps, and I will never forget how we walked on the snow, wearing only shorts and trainers. The snow on the ground was cold, but the sun was shining brightly and was quite warm, which made no sense at all to me. That was the day we went to visit the Blue Lake. Another day I went on a pony trek up some trails in the mountains that I would not even walk on now. The trails wound around the alps and were very high but awe-inspiring. The drop-down from the track on these cliffs was so deep. It was terrifying looking down, trying to see the bottom. Yet it was all so beautiful and a feast for the eyes. We spent every day exploring the Alps, and we played football with the locals after dinner. It was fantastic. Well, nearly all of it was. I was a huge cheese fan at the time, and when we went to a restaurant one night, I ordered a cheese fondue. I had never eaten it before, but I was sure I would love it. When I got the steaming pot of cheese, I got stuck in straight away, but as soon as I swallowed the first mouthful, I felt very sick and had to run outside to vomit it and everything else in my stomach up. Cheese fondue was not for me.

We spent a day in Berne on our way to Germany, and the city was so organised, clean and tidy, and everyone was so friendly. That was not the case when we crossed into Germany in the Black Forest. Because of the troubles in the North, which I tried to avoid altogether; we were stopped at the German border. The police were not buying our story of being a group of lads camping around Europe and were very suspicious of us. They were trying to ask us questions, but none of them could speak English, and we had no German. They watched us like hawks and kept us under guard, pointing their guns at us. They stripped the minibus and carefully searched all our bags and every panel on the bus. A helicopter arrived and hovered overhead while the guards continued their search. It was terrifying for us as we had no idea what would happen next. We were not allowed to move during all this. The longer we stood there, the more worried we became. The guards found nothing of interest to them, and after a bit of discussion allowed us to enter their country. We had to pick up all the gear they had put on the road and pack it all back onto the minibus. We were all very relieved that we were free to move on.

We drove for a while and stayed in a lovely campsite beside the Rhine. There was a small town nearby where we got some supplies and treats to have around a campfire that night. I had never seen a river as big or as wide as the Rhine in my life. I was surprised and fascinated by the number of ships and boats using the river. It was like a motorway for vessels of all types and sizes. I was seeing and experiencing places I might have seen on television, but being there was so much different and better in so many ways. I must have spent the whole holiday with pure amazement on my face.

The next day, we went to Luxembourg and had planned to spend a night in a lovely small town called Diekirch. When we got there, it was full of American military personnel, who were all gathered for a parade to commemorate their honoured General Patton. I think that was where he was buried. We found a spot on a campsite and erected the tents and got something to eat. That night we met and hung with a bunch of American marines, who told us stories from their experiences in the Army. We were immediately taken in with tales of their training in Alaska, the deserts of America and Africa, and their trips to Asia and Germany. They even went back to their base to get us beer, wine, and cigarettes as they only had to pay pennies for them. We had a great night, sitting on the banks of the river swapping stories, but mostly listening to theirs. They were not much older than us but had seen and experienced so much more in their young lives. The next day we went to the parade for General Patton which showed us the might of the American armed forces, with jets flying over the cavalcade. There were all sorts of mechanical weapons like tanks, jeeps, troop carriers, and even mobile bridges. The Americans were indeed wearing their best, and I saw silver helmets that were more reflective than any mirror I ever saw, and pleats that I could have used to shave. They certainly know how to turn out in memory of their own. It was a fantastic spectacle, and after the parade, we met with our new American mates and had another great night. We had stayed two nights instead of one so had to leave early the next morning and make up the time before we got to Holyhead in Wales for the ferry home. We did manage it by travelling all day and night, and when we got on the ferry, my name was called out over the intercom. I went to the restaurant, and one of the staff introduced himself to us. He was a friend of Dad's, and he had arranged dinner for us that night. That was just what we needed after the long journey, and we had a beautiful meal of steaks and all the trimmings. Fair play to Dad. The trip on the Irish Sea passed very quickly, and soon we were off the ship heading to Drogheda. Shortly after that, we were home to be greeted by family after our incredible adventure.

Then the time came for the exam results, and we all went up to the school to collect our results and certificates. Some of us went up with high hopes and anticipation, while others went up with despair. I was hopeful and expected to do quite well, for me anyway, and I was very interested and nervous to see how I did in Geography. I collected my results in the gym, ran out into the corridor, tore open the envelope, and pulled out my results. Amazingly I had done very well. I got Bs and Cs in everything except in Chemistry and Geography where I got a D. A D in honours geography with no teacher. I was over the moon with that, as well as my overall result. It was a good finish for my education, and now a new part of my life was about to start. That Sunday at Mass, my geography teacher came to my Dad and spoke about how it was a shame that I did not do well in Geography. My dad replied that I took the honours paper and got a D in that which I would never have got if I had stayed in his class. He stormed off bewildered and disgusted. Payback was not a bitch for me but maybe was for him.

At 17, while still in school, I convinced Dad to teach me how to drive whenever he could. I picked it up quickly enough as he often explained his driving to me when we were going on trips. I had also reversed the car out of the drive for him on many occasions. I got my driving licence when I was 18 and Dad put me on his insurance. That was very kind of him but also very smart too. It became my job to take the rest of the family out on Sunday after dinner. I didn't care once I had the car. I kept up the old traditions, taking them all out to the beach, Clogherhead, Townley Hall, and anywhere else I could, but not to the airport. There was no way I could, even with Bernadette's help, keep them all together and under control in such a busy environment. Sure, they would have ended up on different planes flying away from us forever. I wasn't risking that. So, I kept quiet and never mentioned the airport.

Chapter 4

Love and Work

The day or evening of my 18th birthday was a great day for me. We had dinner and cake at home and then I went into the sitting room. My Dad came in and asked me what I was doing that night, and I replied that I had nothing planned. Dad just told me to get my coat. We went to the Railway Bar, and he bought me a pint of Smithwicks. I was so proud of that. He, and Mam, knew I had been drinking but did not want to know until I was officially 18. I was now officially an adult, drinking in a real man's pub with my Dad, and I loved every second of it. I often went with him to that bar after that. That was the very day I thought I became an adult.

I was in the town one Saturday afternoon, with Don, standing beside the Tholsel, collecting for charity, when I met Valerie for the first time. She was with her younger sister Denise, and we chatted for a while. I liked her immediately. I cannot explain what exactly attracted her to me so much, but I felt something. After she was gone, I was still thinking about her. I decided to ask her out. I left Don and went across the town looking for her, but I could not see her anywhere. I knew her name, I knew she had recently moved to Drogheda from London, and that was about all. Drogheda was such a small town at the time, and I soon found out where she lived and where she worked. I had asked a few people, and they were able to tell me what I needed to know. A few days later, I went up to the factory where she worked and went in asked for her. I had to wait for a few minutes, and every one of the workers was staring at me as they passed. I suppose they were wondering what I was doing there. When she came out to the entrance, I was waiting, and I asked her out. She was so embarrassed, which made her look even more attractive to me, but she agreed to go out with me. She told me later that she was already going out with some-one, but she fancied me and broke it off with him. She was born in London and lived there all her life. Her Dad took her and her youngest sister home to Drogheda after her Mam had passed away. Her Dad, Paddy, was originally from Drogheda. Her two older sisters had started their own families and stayed on in London.

I think our first date was downstairs in the Central Bar in Drogheda and I got on very well with her. I was working as a barman in the Star and Crescent at the time, so I met her whenever I had a night off. We went to pubs, clubs, the cinema and I started taking her out with me when I took the kids out on Sundays. Dad had a Volkswagen Beetle at the time. How all of us, Me, Val, and my brothers and sisters, fitted in the car, I will never know, but we did and had lots of fun at the same time. I could also use the car for date nights when Dad was not using it. I felt that I could trust Valerie and thought that she was a genuine person who wanted to be with me. I liked that.

After a few months, we did break up, through no fault of Valerie's. It was the change from spending all my free time with her and not my mates. It was about growing up too fast and responsibilities to her that I never experienced before, and I wasn't sure I liked. I can't say if I felt in some way pressurised, but the feelings were too new, too different, and I guess I just needed time to sort it out in my head. I did, of course, miss her, but not at first. I believed that I was doing the right thing, but as time passed, I started doubting my decision. I kept myself busy, caught up with my life, and was playing lots of new sports like Badminton and Squash, snooker and still playing pool. I was not playing Gaelic anymore but had a brief stint as a goalkeeper for a soccer team. I did not like that role at all. I didn't like spending a lot of time with nothing to do, and then under pressure to stop the opposition from scoring. That was just like my personality. I had to keep busy all the time and didn't know how to handle much pressure.

After a few months, we got back together, and even though I tried to manage my time better, I still ended up spending most of my free time with her. That got me thinking about my career and future, and while working in the Star and Crescent was brilliant fun, the hours were long and late into the early morning. Doing that for the rest of my life did not appeal to me. I started looking for and applying for a new job. I still had no clue what I wanted to spend my life working at, so I looked for anything, and everything and maybe something I liked would fall my way. I had applied to join the Air Corp and got through to the final interview stage, but the information pack they sent me included the stipulation that if I signed up, I would have to stay for 12 years. That seemed like far too long to me, like going back to primary and secondary school again, so I declined. What an idiot! I would love to be a pilot, flying high in the sky to different places. It was a job I would have loved.

One Saturday, Valerie and I decided to go to Dundalk for a few hours. I had the beetle, and we gave a chap a lift. We were driving on the main road from Drogheda to Dundalk. As we approached the bridge beside the church in Kilsarin, a car just pulled out right in front of me from a road on the left. I was going to hit him and thought about overtaking, but a white lorry was coming on the street from the other direction. I pulled the car onto the hard shoulder and stood on the brakes. The hard shoulder was just loose gravel, and we slid on it like it was ice. We slammed into the edge of the wall over the little river or stream beneath.

Valerie and I both shattered the windscreen with our faces, not that either of us recalls that exact moment. I was knocked out as the next thing I remember, is waking up, lying on the ground. I didn't know where Valerie was. I could not see anything because I could not open my eyes. They were hurting like hell but felt like they were glued shut. My whole face was wet with blood and burning with incredible pain. Lying there, blinded, and not knowing what was happening, I was asking for Valerie. I heard a priest (I assumed) giving someone the last rights. I was screaming, demanding to know what was happening and whether those prayers of death were for Valerie or me. Someone told me they were for her and not me, but I was not relieved at all. I felt worse for Valerie, and I thought I had lost her forever. I had no clue what was going around me or what happened to Dad's car. Anyone kind enough to be there to help, just said the ambulance was on its way and we would be fine. I wasn't so sure about that and hearing Valerie get the last rights had me imagining the worse. I felt that she must have been in an awful condition, or even dying, and I thought that I would never see her again. I was calling out for her, but I didn't get a reply, and I got scared.

After what seemed like ages, two ambulances arrived, and they each took one of us to the hospital in Dundalk. I don't remember that at all. I must have blacked out which was not surprising considering how sore I felt. I woke in the hospital. I was on my own in casualty, and I was desperate to find out how Valerie was. I didn't know if she was dead or alive, or even in Dundalk hospital. In their unique

way, the nurses answered kindly without telling me anything. I was in agony but overwhelmed by all the crazy
thoughts I was having about Valerie. After a while, they
said to me that Valerie was ok but needed a lot of stitches
in her face, but she was alive and would survive this. That
eased my anxiety, and I was able to worry about myself.
I still could not see because the glass had penetrated my
eyelids and cut off some of the layers of skin in my eyes.
I had a gouge under my chin bone from ear to ear and a
long gash down the right side of my face. I needed more
than 100 stitches, even on both eyelids, and would need to
get a skin graft in the future. I had broken a little bone on
my hip when I crashed against the steering wheel. I was in
bits, but I would recover, and so would Valerie. That was
all that mattered.

Mam and Dad had arrived when I was getting all the glass
removed from my face. When the nurses felt that they had
moved all the shrapnel, I went for an x-ray to see if there
was any glass left in my face. That was when I felt the most
pain, or so I thought. There was glass left in my chin, but I
did not know until they placed my chin on the x-ray table.
My face exploded in pain. I cried like a baby. Then I had
to go back to casualty to get the remaining glass out of my
face and get stitched. They got me all patched up, but I
had to stay in the hospital for a week. Valerie had to stay
in as well. I was so thrilled to see her when I went to the
ward and so relieved. She looked a right state, but I didn't
care. She was alive.

I was thankful that Dad was not angry or upset about the car. He and Mam were just concerned about us and hoped we would get through this. He told me that the car was smashed beyond repair, and joked that it was time to get a new one anyway. I found out later when I went to see it that I had bent the steel steering wheel when I crashed, and that was how I broke that small bone on my hip.

When I was in the hospital, the Gardai called to see me. There were two of them. They told me the crash was my fault, and I was going to be charged with dangerous driving. They said I was driving too fast and was a danger on the road. I could not believe what they were saying to me. I tried to explain how I was motoring along in a long stream of traffic doing the same sedate speed as everyone else. I told them how I moved to avoid hitting the car that pulled out onto the road in front of me, and that I was sure it was this driver who caused the crash. I explained and explained, but I don't think that they were accepting anything I said. They spoke with Valerie, and she gave the same account of the crash, but she didn't think they were even listening to her. I started to have my doubts and imagined the worse like I would be going to jail.

Fair play to my Dad. He asked me what happened, then asked Valerie and believed our version of events. There was a pub on the road just about 50 to 100 yards from where the accident occurred. Having no car, Dad had to get a lift to the hospital from Michael Govers. He and Dad went into this pub every day, making enquiries about the crash and looking for witnesses. Thanks to their persistence, they found two men who were not willing to make a statement to the Gardai, but would to a solicitor. My Dad got a solicitor, and he spoke with both witnesses who told the same version of events as I did. You see, it was the local priest who was driving the car that pulled out in front of me. I could understand why these two men, and probably many others, were reluctant to come forward. Priests were revered and treated with massive respect back then, and if being the local priest was not a big enough deal, his family owned the two big hotels in Dundalk - the Imperial and the Ballymascanlon. The statements from the two witnesses got me cleared of any charges. Yet it was almost a year later, when the priest eventually admitted that he was coming from a funeral, had drink taken, and was thinking about that when he pulled out onto the main road without thinking or stopping. Priests are supposed to lead us in truth and honesty, and not let others suffer for their mistakes, but maybe the priest missed this class in the seminary. This whole shocking episode only added to my growing lack of trust in those that I was supposed to respect and believe in.

Valerie spent a couple of days in the hospital and discharged, I was allowed to move around the ward on my own, and I was happy with that. During my stay in the hospital, there was a soccer match in Dundalk between Dundalk and Linfield. There was a massive fight between the two sets of supporters. The ambulances were coming to the hospital, dropping the injured off, and going back into the town to collect more. I was nosey and went down to casualty to see what was happening there. It looked like a hospital during a war. There were people with all kinds of cuts and injuries lying everywhere, even on the floor. It was impossible to walk through them. People were waiting to be seen in the hallways and corridors with more trying to get into the hospital. It was chaos, and I have never seen anything like it. I went back to the ward and told everyone what I had seen.

Then on Friday, I was allowed to leave. No matter how bad the accident was, I was delighted to be getting out of there. On Saturday, Valerie was up in our house in Ballsgrove, and I suggested that we go down the town. I felt much better after all the treatment I received, and Valerie was mobile and feeling much better too. She did not want to go, as we still had stitches and plasters all over our faces. We would have looked brilliant at Halloween. However, I insisted because I just wanted to get out into the air and because I knew what the people in the town were like. There were already all kinds of rumours about us and what physical damage we suffered. I knew if we went downtown and everyone saw us, all those rumours would soon stop. She came with me, reluctantly, and everyone stared, shocked at our appearance at first, but that soon passed and we were able to move about as if nothing had happened. We were no longer the talk of the town.

A few weeks later Pope John Paul came to visit Ireland and a vast field this side of Kilineer outside Drogheda, was set up for his visit to our part of the world. I went because I wanted to see the Pope and felt that it was too good an opportunity to miss. I knew that I was not fully recovered from the accident, but I took the chance that I would be fine. I think that everyone in Drogheda went as well as thousands from all over the North East and Northern Ireland. We all had to walk all the way there and were then were shuffled into these big cattle-like pens in the field. The stage looked amazing, the music was super, and I had never seen so many people in the one place in my life. The song "The Lonesome Boatman" sounded just divine like it was the angels themselves singing it. The atmosphere was friendly and expectant, and the build-up to the Pope's arrival only increased the anticipation. When the Pope arrived, the crowd went wild with excitement. I don't recall much after that as I collapsed and moved to one of the First Aid tents. I was treated and given some oxygen and had to wait there until it was all over, so they could drive me home. I was still too weak after the accident, and the long walk and standing among crowds of people just became too much for me. I did manage to get a quick glimpse of the Pope as he passed by in the popemobile and I have no regrets about going there, to be part of such an incredible happy crowd, and get to see the Pope.

Later that year (1979), Valerie and I went to visit Valerie's family in London. It was great meeting her sisters and families, and we got on well. Coming from a small town in Ireland, it was challenging to accept and appreciate the size of London. It was a whole new learning experience for me. It seemed never-ending but hugely impressive at the same time. Greenwich, where Valerie was from, was probably bigger than Drogheda itself. We packed as much as we could into the weekend and had a great time. Valerie was delighted to spend time with her sisters, Anne and Patricia, and their families. They too were glad to see that Valerie was okay after the accident, and I suppose, happy to meet me and see who I was. I was glad I met them and was now able to visualise who she was talking about. They were very friendly and welcoming to me, and we all got on brilliantly, except maybe for George, Valerie's brother-in-law, offering me a minced meat sandwich for breakfast. That looked disgusting to me, and I refused.

I was getting serious with Valerie, and I no longer felt pressurised or uncomfortable about our relationship in any way. I was far more relaxed about it, and Valerie was becoming a very important person to me. I had no trust issues with her or ever thought that she wanted anything from me, except me. It was simple and straightforward, and I liked that. I remember the night, or early morning to be precise that I knew I was in love for the very first time. Valerie was living in Maple Drive with her Dad and sister. That was right across the town from Ballsgrove. I had walked her home after a night out. That was common then as taxis were hard to find. Once I got her home, I walked home to Ballsgrove.

The journey seemed to fly by, even if it took an hour or so. On the way, my stomach was tingling; my heart was dancing in my chest. My head was full of feelings and emotions that were more than agreeable. I had never experienced anything like that before. Walking across Drogheda from Maple Drive was a lot easier for me that night, as I seem to have floated home on hovercraft shoes fuelled by love. It really was love, and the first time I had ever felt anything so beautiful and so powerful. I knew what it was and was thrilled for myself. My love for Valerie did grow after that, but I have never felt like that ever since, maybe because it was the first time I had ever felt such powerful emotions and realisation. It's nice to remember that night, and how happy I was with the first real pangs of love.

I joined Kenny's garage as a trainee car salesman shortly after the Pope's visit, but I did not like that at all, even though I got on well with everyone there. I didn't know enough about cars to have the confidence required to chat honestly to customers, and I found that there was too much time with nothing to do. I did love driving all the cars around, but that was the only part of the job I enjoyed. Luckily though, I got another job offer as a trainee supermarket manager with Quinnsworth and started in their store in Dundalk. At first, I travelled up and down on the bus, but then I got a bedsit in a lovely old lady's house in Dundalk, close to the store. She treated me like my Granny did, and I liked to help her out whenever I could. I would buy the groceries she needed and pack them away when I could. The hours we worked were horrendous, often about sixteen hours a day, and even more when we were doing a refit or reorganising the layout of the store. That was just the way it was those days. We were on salaries and expected to do what was required. Whereas hourly paid staff did not have to do such hours because they would have to be paid overtime rates. One Sunday evening, my Dad was driving me back to Dundalk when we were in another crash. Just south of Dunleer, on the main Drogheda to Dundalk road, we went over a very steep hill, and just on the other side of the peak, a car had pulled up and stopped on the road. We did not see it until it was too late. Dad tried to drive around the stopped vehicle, but just clipped the end of it, which put us into a spin. When we eventually came to a stop, I was able to get out of the car quickly enough and moved away as soon as possible. I thought Dad was doing the same, but when I looked back, he was still in his seat. I could see flames starting to lick around the car from under the engine. I ran back to help, and when I got there, another driver was already trying to help Dad get out. His seatbelt was stuck, and I could feel the heat from the flames climbing quickly up the sides of the car.

At last, somehow, Dad got the seatbelt off and was able to exit the vehicle safely. We moved well back from the car, and after a few minutes, the petrol tank exploded, and it was thrown about five or six feet into the air, before smashing down in an almighty crash of metal and glass. We were, thankfully, unhurt, but were in shock for a while. The fire brigade and cops arrived to put the fire out. The car was completely destroyed, but no one was hurt. After it was all over, I got a lift to Dundalk, and the cops took Dad home. Just a simple accident that I was able to survive.

In Dundalk, I tried my best and worked hard, but that was not the problem. I was not working as a manager-to-be, taking ownership and responsibility for the work and tasks I had. I was not making a difference as I should, and I was seen as a shop assistant in a suit. That was not what the trainee managership scheme was about. At one of my regular performance reviews, the area manager told me that they were moving me to Lifestyle Sports in Mary St. Dublin. He explained how this was a second chance for me, and maybe my last. He thought that working in a sports shop would be good for me. That was in 1980 and when I started to come into my own and wanted to be successful.

Lifestyle Sports had just been rebranded from Johnny Giles sports and was owned by Quinnsworth, which was part of the Primark group at the time which was Penneys in Ireland. Lifestyle was towards the bottom of Mary Street just across from Penneys. Most of the year it was a sports shop, selling all kinds of sports goods, sportswear and fads of the time, like roller skates. However, for the Christmas season, half the store was converted into a toy shop. During the summer the craze was always for

Gaelic and Hurling gear, tents and camping equipment as well as summer sports like tennis, or football kits when the Euros or World Cup was on. It wasn't a big store like Quinnsworth Dundalk, but it was always hectic, especially on a Saturday. The best part for me was that it closed every day at 5.30 pm so I could run and get the 6.00 pm train home to Drogheda. I had all evenings off, and that was brilliant. Fred Tate was the manager at the time, and he took me under his wing. I was interested in every aspect of the business, and I made every effort to do well. He was easy to like and was a good teacher. I got along with all the members of staff and that paid off for me. As I learned from Fred, I passed it onto the team and shared responsibility with them. It worked a treat. I started to feel that I was achieving something, and I was enjoying work much more than ever before. I was behaving more like a trainee manager.

The big problem at the time was shoplifting, and although we had an excellent permanent security guard, and different store detectives every day, this stealing was going on all the time. Every day we caught people shoplifting and had to wait until the Gardai would take them away and prosecute them, or just let them off with a warning. I must have caught hundreds myself, as it was not very subtle most of the time. It was just a craze. They probably knew they might get caught, get a caution, and be let home. I did learn one very valuable lesson at the time. I noticed a young woman stealing sportswear and putting it in her bag. Then like a startled bird, she just bolted out the front door and was in Penneys before I could catch her. I alerted the security staff there, and they watched her put some clothes into her bag. They stopped her as she left the store and brought her into the security office where I was waiting. While we were there, waiting for the Gardai, she started explaining that her shoplifting was to pay for her drugs. She related how she began on cannabis but did not heed the warnings about how she was heading down a dangerous path to more potent drugs. She started using more and more Cannabis until it was no longer enough, and before she knew it, she was using the more dangerous stuff. She showed me the holes in her upper arms where she injected herself. The only way I can describe them is that they were like nostrils in her arms. I could see her muscles quivering at the end of these three nostrils. Her muscle was greyish with slight tinges of red. I have never forgotten that sight, and even though I had never touched any drug before that, I knew then I never would. They were just too dangerous and too easy to get hooked on.

Christmas in Lifestyle Mary St. was a whole different story. With the toys, snooker tables, football kits for kids, and everything else on offer, the store was crazy busy, and we often had to stop people coming in until some customers went out. The checkouts worked non-stop from opening time at 9.00 am until closing. We could not even take deliveries during the day except it was an emergency item like the roller skates that were the craze. We took the deliveries at night. The store resembled a bomb site every night at closing, but we would take the deliveries in from 5.30 pm when the road opened to traffic and lay the boxes out for the night shift to pack away. We had no storeroom for overstock. There were no 5.30 pm finishes for most of November and December. There was a night shift for the Christmas season, and they started at 10.00 pm, and by the time we came back in at 7.00 am, the store would be full again and looked very presentable. My job was to work with the staff and make up some kind of a list of toys we needed. Then I would ring round all the Quinnsworth stores in the country and just take the toys we wanted and organise transport for delivery that night. Then we would go through the sports section and do the orders for the suppliers to deliver that night too. It was a fantastic experience, and though the hours were super long, the satisfaction of seeing a plan come together, and everything working as it should be, was gratifying. I just loved it.

My Granny moved to a kind of sheltered housing estate for the elderly called John Paul Court about this time. She was relocated there because her house in Scarlet St was to be demolished. It was a lovely little house in a beautiful estate, and she loved it there. I was thrilled for her. The other, more mobile neighbours, looked after her too. They would visit a few times a day, just to check that Granny was ok, or see if she needed anything. She enjoyed that because she could chat away to her heart's content. I loved to drop up and help out when I could, whether it was cutting the grass, cleaning, or whatever. She always seemed to have jobs for me to do, but I suspected it was so that she could give me a few quid. I didn't want the money; I just wanted to do whatever I could to help her.

In 1980, I went into the Lourdes Hospital to get the skin grafting done to fix up my face. I only found out after I checked in and was put on a ward, that it was to be Mr Shine who would be operating on me. I was not perturbed at all because my abuse never entered my head. He was polite and helpful when he examined my face before the procedure. He dealt with me professionally, but it seemed he didn't remember me. He carried out the operation the next day and even removed a verruca from my foot at the same time. Before I knew it, I was back on the ward. I was very keen to see what difference the operation did to my face, but I could not touch or remove the bandages until the doctor had a look. One was just under my chin, and the big scar from ear to ear was gone. The wound under my right eye was reduced in size and covered by another small bandage. There was a tiny one where the verruca used to be. The next day Mr Shine visited and checked his work. He was pleased, and I got to see for myself. I was delighted with the results. I looked kind of normal again. That warranted a few days off, and a chance to rest.

I was beautiful again(stop laughing), and life was good. I was enjoying my work and having evenings off. I was getting on brilliant with Valerie we were grown ever closer all the time. She was still very quiet, especially with people she did not know well. I loved that and everything about her. I was still able to use Dad's car whenever he wasn't using it, and I was saving now for a car of my own and the insurance.

We went back to London for another visit that summer, and after that, I bought my first little car. A friend of my Aunty Ann had a garage in Clogherhead, and he got me a little mini. It was tiny, some shade of yellow, but it was mine, and I was able to use it whenever I wanted. I used it to drive to work and managed to get my own parking space behind the big Penney's store. I knew all the management and security personnel there, and they found a slot for me. That was very handy until some little feckers in Drogheda stole my car and smashed it up. I had no car for a while until the insurance was sorted out, so it was back to other means of transport to and from Dublin. Luckily a man who lived behind us, went to the fruit market every morning and I was able to get a lift from him. I was always very early for work, but it meant I got a lot done in the hours before opening time, and I didn't have to walk to the train station every morning. If Jim was off or not available, my next-door neighbour, Patsy, who was a lorry driver with Irish Cement, offered me a lift and always went out of his way to get me as close to Dublin City centre as possible. Both Jim and Patsy were very kind and helpful, and without them, I would have struggled. The trains were always stuffed with people every day, and it was a long walk to the station. The buses were ok for getting home, but in the morning, they were unreliable and took almost an hour and a half to get to Dublin. But as soon as I received the insurance money, I got another car, and for the life of me, I cannot remember much about it, except that it was a little blue Fiat. But I was back on the road and not relying on others, which I always found uncomfortable for some reason.

In 1981, Valerie and I received some compensation from the car crash, and I started wondering what I should do with mine. I was thinking that it was like a windfall and a sign that I should be thinking about marriage. I felt that we should use it to get married and put a deposit on a house. I was sure I was doing the right thing and made my mind up reasonably quickly. Once I had that settled in my mind, I just had to find the right time. Soon after, Valerie was in our house in Ballsgrove as she often was. I saw my chance and took it. I was desperate to ask her to marry me as soon as I could. I brought her up to my Sister's room, and I just suggested we get engaged and then married. I proposed to Valerie in the most romantic way - not. She didn't say yes, she wanted a proper proposal. Instead, she told me to go down on one knee and ask her to marry me. I did as I was told, and she said yes, without hesitation. I think that last bit is the most romantic I have ever been in my life, but at least she got the proposal she always wanted after she told me how. She was happy and agreed that it was a great opportunity. We didn't set a date but were keen to get engaged as soon as possible. We had no date for the wedding because we wanted to wait to organise the church, the priest, and the reception first. When I told Fred at work, he gave me the Saturday off work, which was rare, and organised a visit to his wife, who worked in a jewellery supplier in Dublin. So off we went to the big smoke.

We called in to see Fred and everyone at work first, as they had never met Valerie. That was nice for her and them. After that, we walked across the Liffey and then went and got the ring. Valerie picked one almost immediately, which astounded me. She was delighted with the ring she chose. That's all that mattered. She was thrilled showing it off to everyone, and for a while, kept checking her finger to make sure it was still there and not lost. I was delighted with myself for thinking about marrying her, and because she consented. I was so happy, and Valerie was too.

1982 did start a bit rough for us with the heavy snow in Ireland that January. I was at work as usual when the snow started. When I finished for the day, I could not get the car out of the car park with all the snow. I went to see if I could get a train or a bus, but none were operating. I tried to get a hotel, but they were all full. The paths and roads were treacherous with ice underneath the snow, and nowhere in the city was open. I slipped on the snow and hurt my thumb, and then decided that the only place I could go, was back to work and stay there for the night. It was safe enough because there was a big shutter on the front entrance. I got back there, opened the shop for myself and then made sure it was securely locked for the night. I didn't want anyone getting in. I tried to make myself comfortable in the office, but I just could not get warm. I didn't get any sleep, and the night seemed to drag on forever. In the morning, the radio told me that the snow had brought the country to a standstill and everywhere was closed. When I went out to Mary St., I noticed that the little bakery across the road was opened, so I managed to get something to eat for breakfast. When I went back to the office, the phone started ringing, and Lifestyle Mary Street became the head office and information point for the whole of Quinnsworth. A couple of directors and senior managers even dropped in to see what was happening in the company. They each went across the road, and I got more hot food, which was helping warm me up. I stayed there on the phone all morning, answering the questions as much as I could. Some people even rang in to complain that Quinnsworth was not open that day. I have no idea how they even managed to get the phone number, and I felt annoyed that some people wanted to complain under such circumstances. In the afternoon, I locked up the shop and went to see if I could retrieve the car. I moved as much snow as I could with my hands and a sheet of cardboard. I got the car out on the road and headed for home. I usually took the back road to Ashbourne in and out of Dublin, but I was not sure if that road would be open, so I went for the main Dublin-Drogheda Road past the airport. It was very slow progress, but eventually, I got close to the airport, and then the traffic did not move. The snowdrifts on that road were more than six ft high, and we were going nowhere. I got out and saw that a section of the road that was cleared earlier had fallen in and blocked the road again. I was going nowhere. A JCB came and cleared a path through the snow, and I was able to continue my journey. It took me eight hours to get home that day, but once I was home, I was delighted and relieved that I managed to make it. I was exhausted from the journey and because I got no sleep the night before. The next day, I went to the hospital again because my thumb was throbbing with pain and I guessed it was broken. It turns out I was right, and it had to be strapped up for a while. The hospital was jammed with hundreds of people suffering from breaks, strains, and bruising from falls in the ice and snow, and I spent most of the day there. I was fed up waiting but was glad when I had the x-ray and treated.

Valerie and I decided that we wanted to get married in the Holy Family Church in Ballsgrove. I still went to Mass there, and any time Valerie went to Mass, it was there too. However, she now lived in Moneymore, which was in St Peter's Parish, and according to the rules, she had to get married in St Peter's. We went to see the parish priest in St Peter's, and he got the bishop to give her special dispensation to marry in the Groom's parish. Once that was sorted Fr Farrelly was happy to marry us in the Holy Family. Then we looked at hotels and decided to have the reception in the Village Hotel in Bettystown and picked a day which we knew was available in both venues. We had to do a pre-marriage course in the community centre on Fair street, which we both hated, and even sneaked out of once when another couple asked us to do a runner and go for a drink.

I don't know about you, but I found that the pre-marriage course and organising important things like dresses, suits, photographers, music, transport, food, and everything else took a lot of the fun out of the build-up to the wedding. It was chaos at times, being organised one day, and then someone letting us down, and having to reorganise again. It wasn't like it was to be a big lavish swanky affair, just a good wedding that we would both enjoy and remember for the rest of our lives. Valerie was working in Dunnes Stores in Drogheda, and I was still in Mary Street, and everything seemed right to me. We were perhaps a bit young to be married, but we had the finances in place, were indeed in love, and the world seemed to be on our side.

The date we picked or ended up with, I'm not sure which, was the 3rd April 1982 two days before my 21st. It flew in, even with Lifestyle sports being even busier than the previous year. The big day drew closer, and we had our respective stag and hen nights in March. For my stag, we started in the Star and Crescent, went to a couple of other pubs before finishing off the night in the El Molino night club in Julianstown. On the way home the lads stopped the minibus on the Dublin road, took me out, and stripped me, before they all jumped back onto the bus, leaving me in all my glory and only a small jacket. I had to dart home between cars, walls, and bushes to protect whatever dignity I had left. When I got home, they were all in my house waiting for me, laughing their heads off. Luckily, we are not allowed guns in this country. Valerie enjoyed her hen night but did not have to face any of the humiliation I had to endure.

The big day came, and as was usual back then, it was on a Saturday. My best men were my brother John, Alan Milne with Don Carolan. Valerie had an army of bridesmaids and flower girls. There were her sisters Denise and Patricia, my sisters' Bernadette and Valerie, and her niece Mary. There was a lovely crowd of family, relatives, friends from both sides invited, and now it was time to get married to each other. I did not see her the night before, as per tradition, and on the morning of the wedding, myself and the best men went down to get our hair cut. Obviously, we went into the pub, but only had 2 pints each, which gave us plenty of time to get home, washed, and dressed up for the big occasion. I don't remember how, but the best men and I ended up wearing a wine-coloured jacket over a dress shirt, a wine dickie bow, and black trousers. It might have looked okay then, but it did not age too well and looks hideous now, to me anyway.

When we were all ready, just a few minutes before 1 pm, we walked over to the church, which was only 100 yards from the house. Valerie and her entourage were fashionably late, but thankfully only by a couple of minutes, because I was standing waiting for her, and I was so nervous. I was sweating like a racehorse and hoping it would not start dripping from my hair to my face. I think my legs just wanted to leave me altogether, and they would not stop shaking. I was sorry I had taken those two pints, which I expected to come back up at any moment. Then I heard gasps and some claps from behind me, and I took a quick peek and saw Valerie walking towards me. When Valerie arrived at my side, I calmed down and just got carried away with the whole occasion. She looked gorgeous, and that helped put me at ease. We got through the entire ceremony without any problems, and although I was embarrassed when we had to kiss, it was like the first time I ever kissed her. It was the kiss that sealed our love, our marriage, and our future. No wonder it felt so good.

After all the well-wishing, chatting, and photographs, we headed off in convoy to the Village Hotel. It was beautifully set up; the band was already there, and the meal would be on time. But the photographer took ages with the photos, and we had to delay the mealtime. Plus, it was the English Grand National Day. So, while all the ladies were sitting waiting and chatting at their designated places in the dining room, all the males were in the bar drinking pints and watching the Grand National. I even joined them to watch the race. There was no way we could serve the food until that was over. I even had a couple of bets on the race because it was my lucky day, but didn't win a penny. But everything came back together after that, and we all had a great time. It was the kind of reception we wished for. We had a room booked for the night, where we would stay and keep all our clothes and presents, but there was a tradition that you left the hotel before all the guests so that they had the chance to give us a big send-off. So, we changed out of the wedding suit and dress for our evening clothes and went back to the wedding reception to leave officially. It was such a great send-off with jokes, laughs, best wishes, and love filling the air. The best men and Andrew Towell had decided that we should all go to a nightclub in Navan, but when we got there, the bouncers would not let us in. The best men and bridesmaids were still wearing their wedding finery, and the bouncers thought it was some kind of joke, but eventually relented and let us all in. The funny thing is that once we got in, got a table and chairs together, Valerie and I fell asleep and had to be woken when it was time to go. They got us back to the Village, and we slept as happy as we have ever been.

The next day was fantastic because we were starting on our own as a married couple. The fact that we were Mr and Mrs was sinking in. We had a lovely breakfast, cleared out the room, and I went to pay the bill for the wedding, and I got a lovely pleasant surprise. The hotel had made a mistake when quoting us for the wedding, and it was a couple of hundred pounds cheaper than we expected. That gave us that little bit extra for the honeymoon. We moved all the presents to Ballsgrove and said our goodbyes. We got a lift to the airport and checked in to the airport hotel for the night. The flight was not until early the next morning.

When we checked in and got everything into our room, we went to the lounge, and there waiting, were the best men, the bridesmaids and lots of others, and we had a bit of a session. We didn't stay too late as we had to be up early, and we were still tired after the wedding.

We went to Toronto for our honeymoon and stayed with my Aunty Ann and her family. We got there in time to celebrate my 21st birthday. My granny was on the ball again. She sent my card and present over to Ann so it would be there when I arrived. My Aunty Ann, her husband Liam and children Paul and June took care of us and showed us around the city. They took us up the CN tower, to the zoo, along Young street which, they told us, was the longest street in the world, and to different places every day. My cousin, Vivienne, took us to Niagara Falls, which was a fantastic trip that we loved. We loved every bit of the honeymoon., It was a super holiday for both of us, and it was great to see my Aunty again.

We had bought a new house before we got married, but it was not ready for us. When we got home, we got the keys and moved into our new home in Rosevale, and life seemed to be set up nicely for us. It was all working out so well, and we were very happy. We enjoyed having people call to visit us in our own house, and we settled into the Mr and Mrs roles quickly. It was lucky that we got married in April. Valerie was a few months pregnant, and she started to 'show' soon after we got home. We both knew but decided to keep it to ourselves until after the wedding. Now we had something else to look forward to, and it would be the start of our own family.

That year Quinnsworth opened a brand-new flagship store in Artane and Fred was transferred there to look after all the non-food departments, like sports, toys, and homewares. Flagship stores were where the company showed off its excellence, so everything had to be perfect, or as near as possible. It was like a promotion and a reward at the same time for Fred, so he transferred there. I was promoted to manager of Lifestyle Sports in Mary Street. I was delighted with that, and I knew I would do well, because of the staff, and the way we worked. It, like everything in my life, just seemed to click together.

About that time, I got involved in basketball again. Some of the lads who had played basketball in school were very keen to get back into it. I joined up in an administrator role, forming a committee and looking after venues, bookings, transport, etc. We started a new club and called ourselves the Panthers. We managed to get the team into the Dublin District Basketball League even if it was just in the 4th division. The lads were just too good for that level and won the league. We did not celebrate too much because the win was expected, but it did set the standard for the future. I went to the games in Dublin whenever I could and took part in some training sessions just to keep up my fitness. The team grew year by year and got better week by week, and in the next few years, they won winners' trophies in the League, the Cup, and the top 4 competitions.

I loved the way they played together, and the camaraderie of everyone involved. It was good for me, gave me something to do, got me out of the house, and kept me in touch with the lads.

In October that year, our first child was born in the same hospital I was born in. It was a difficult birth for Valerie as she was overdue and had to be induced after she had been in labour for 18 hours. Then forceps had to be used, so I had to leave the room. I did not get to see the baby being born and just waited outside like most expectant parents - panicking, pacing up and down, and incredibly anxious. But all was well. Valerie gifted me a beautiful son, and we called him Wayne. We had the names picked after months of searching when Valerie was pregnant. I have to say that it started as a bit of a joke when I suggested we name him after John Wayne, but the name Wayne for a boy grew on us, and it wasn't in any way popular at the time. We did not know the gender of the baby before birth because it did not matter to us, whether it was a girl or a boy. The most important thing to us was that he or she was born healthy and had all their bits in the right place. He was perfect, and he turned out to be a wonderful baby and a reason for happiness. I was ecstatic. I had played a small part in creating another human being. He was a part of me. I wanted the very best for him and us as a family together. Valerie was delighted too and was a very proud new mother. Everything was brilliant, and I had the world at my feet. I had a good job, a loving wife and now a beautiful son living in a new house.

Chapter 5

My world starts to change

In Lifestyle Sports, I got a new assistant manager, and he was useless from the very first day. He was the son of one of the directors of Quinnsworth, and he acted like he was the director. He made no effort to be helpful or to do his job, and he looked down on the rest of the staff and me. I hated that, and I still hate it now. However, I always tried to teach him to get him involved and to be part of the team, with little success. When we started planning for the Christmas period, and all the hours and the work we would be doing, he got a huge shock, and he resigned. I was happy with that, but there was no suitable assistant manager available anywhere to replace him. Still, I felt that was no big deal. We had a great team, and they always stepped up to the plate when asked or when they thought it was necessary. Christmas was coming in very fast, and we were as busy as ever. I knew what to do and how to manage the shop, and I had a great team. In other words, I felt that I was in control of myself and Lifestyle Mary St. A new shopping centre, the Ilac, opened close by that year and one of the big shops in it was the Hamleys Toy Store. For Christmas, they decided to open on Sunday afternoons and drew big crowds of customers, so I got the idea in my head to work to open Lifestyle on Sunday afternoon. No Quinnsworth or Penneys had ever opened on a Sunday before. The first people I had to speak to were the most important and most affected by this idea, the staff. I put it to them at one of our weekly staff meetings. I planned to open for the four Sundays before Christmas from 2 pm to 5:30 pm. As I waited to see what their response would be, Jackie, the supervisor in the sports department, came to me and told me that everyone would work whenever required except if they had something else planned. I was so delighted with them. They were a dedicated team and even after their union got involved and demanded they don't work on a Sunday, they worked. Then I had to present the plan to my area manager who was a bit sceptical at first but thought it best to run the idea by the directors. They were intrigued by this, and one of them even rang me to see if it was a joke. I told him that the city centre was incredibly busy on a Sunday and it was a massive opportunity for us. They agreed, and it turned out to be an enormous decision for Lifestyle, Quinnsworth, and the retail sector in general because as each year passed more and more stores started opening on a Sunday for Christmas. The first Sunday we opened we were so busy that we emptied the shop and almost burned the registers with all the sales. Directors and senior management called in to see what was happening, and I had them serving customers or packing bags at the Checkout. The staff loved that and chatted away with the bosses as if they were mates. We had planned well and had plenty of deliveries coming at night and the night shift due in at 10 pm. Two directors who were still there at 5 pm thought we would never get the shop fixed up in time to open in the morning. But we did, just as we did every day. My only problem was, having almost half the staff there on a Sunday was just not enough.

I went back to the team, and they all agreed to work every Sunday until Christmas except if they had something else planned for that day. I organised a Christmas party for the lot of us and secured a significant enough contribution from Quinnsworth. The next three Sundays up to Christmas, we were just crazy busy and the sales compared to the year before were outstanding. As much as I loved being in the middle of things, and part of something I thought was exceptional, I was glad when Christmas came along, and we got a few days off. In the New Year. I gave all the staff a couple of extra days off with pay for being so brilliant and helpful, but we kept that to ourselves and told no one else, especially management. It was the right thing to do. I am not suggesting for one second that I was the best manager in the world, or even in Quinnsworth. Even though I tried to be fair and a good manager, I was also very demanding and expected that everyone worked hard and did their fair share of the work involved. It was the staff who made the shop work all year round, and I was privileged to be a part of that success.

Shoplifting was still a considerable problem in Lifestyle Sports, but it got worse, for me anyway. One day I noticed a man putting a box of three golf balls into his trouser pocket. To me, he looked like a farmer. As was the procedure, I kept my eye on him until he left the store. Once he was outside, I approached him and let him know that I believed he had taken a packet of golf balls from the store without paying for them. He just said "it's alright I know, I know" and allowed me to escort him back to the office in the shop. Once in the office, he immediately told me that he was a Garda sergeant based in a station in Dublin. I did not know what to do so I contacted the security chief in Quinnsworth, and he told me I would have to get the Gardai involved to protect myself and the company. The reason was that if we just let him go, he could have gone to a solicitor and complained about false accusations. I called the Gardai but did not say anything about him being a Garda sergeant until they got to the office. It ended up going to court, but a deal was done behind the scenes, and he was not prosecuted. It did mean that the Gardai, our local station was in Store St. did not respond to us when we had apprehended shoplifters or if they did respond, it took them hours to get to us. That was their way of getting back at us, and this went on for about a year until everyone forgot the issue.

At that time, too, I was doing some work for Lifestyle sports throughout the country. I was looking after another store they had opened on Grafton St for Christmas selling toys mostly. That was handy enough as it was not nearly as busy as Mary St. and I only had to spend about an hour or so there every day. There were twenty-something Lifestyle Sports shops up and down the country. I sometimes covered for the buyer when he was out of the country or not available, placing orders for lifestyle sports and helping, advising, and guiding the other managers. I enjoyed that because it was brilliant to be able to help others and the company at the same time.

Later on, in 1983, I was promoted again to the area supervisor for Lifestyle Sports. They gave me a new company car, a Ford Escort estate, and I worked from the office and warehouse facility in Cherry Orchard, Dublin. I was responsible for all the Lifestyle Sports shops and had to visit them all regularly. I did not know what I let myself in for. I was driving around two thousand miles a week outside working hours to get to all the shops. I loved visiting them but trying to do all my work in a short visit was not possible. I loved it when I had something tangible to do like new planograms, or a new layout, but I hated visiting any store and nothing constructive happening. I could discuss things with the manager and staff but was never sure if anything would be done, or whether I was being listened to or just ignored. I did feel I was talking to myself on many occasions.

I wanted to do my job well and help grow Lifestyle sports and all involved. I started to doubt myself and wished I had not left Mary Street. Apart from playing sports, but not Gaelic, that is the first time I remember questioning myself, doubting my abilities, or doubting my work. Another part of my new position was to organise and carry out the refits in all non-food stores. I enjoyed that aspect of the job, even though it generally meant weekends and long days, working on getting the store reopened on time. The reward was getting it all done correctly and on time, and everyone could see the results. I was always delighted with the work we did and seeing the shop look all clean and new.

It was not all bad as when Christmas came along, I did not have to work the crazy hours in Lifestyle Mary Street, and had my first normal Christmas for a long time which meant a lot more time with Valerie and Wayne. There were no re-fits in the build-up to Christmas, which was the busiest time of the year. I loved spending more time with the little Mogs even though Christmas meant nothing to him. He was too young. I also got to spend some time up in Ballsgrove with the family, and as usual, it was a madhouse that was full of joy and excitement and lots of visitors.

I learned how to plan and manage my time better by always arranging to visit the stores that were furthest away, like Cork or Waterford, in the early part of the week, which meant I would be home most of the time for the whole weekend and not staying away. It did mean that I was away for three or four days at a time from Monday on, but knowing that I would be home for the weekend, except when there were re-fits, kept me going.

In July that year, one Thursday at 8:30 pm I was in Clonmel Lifestyle shop when I got a phone call to tell me that the big re-fit in Dundrum, Dublin was brought forward and was going to start at 7 am the next morning. I had all the plans and drawings for that re-fit, but they were at home, so I had to drive home a couple of hundred miles, find the plans and drawings, get some sleep and get to Dundrum in Dublin for 7 in the morning. I was raging all the way home and wondering what idiot had decided to have the re-fit that weekend, and give very little notice. I got home, found the plans then got some sleep. Valerie got me up the next morning and had breakfast ready, which was lovely. I said goodbye to Valerie and Wayne especially, because I was not sure when I would be able to play with him again. When I got to Dundrum, I had to ring around the other Quinnsworth stores and get trainee and assist-ant managers to come and help with the re-fit. We got a good team together and worked long hours into the night. When finished, I would drive some of the workers home before driving home myself. We had the move finished on Tuesday and had the shop looking like a shiny new store should look. Everything in its place and no gaps or spaces anywhere. On Tuesday afternoon, I was happy that all the work was finished. I said thanks and goodbye to everyone and drove home.

However, I never made it. Just the Drogheda side of the Platin cement factory, I fell asleep. I was less than 5 minutes from home. I woke up lying in a field beside the car, which was upside down and smashed to pieces. I was a long distance away from the road. I could see that I had driven over a ditch. I was going relatively fast and had hit the bank of the trench and careered through the top half of the hedge. There was just a big hole in it. I tried to focus and clear my head, and I noticed shreds of my coat, suit jacket, and shirt scattered around the field with the rest just hanging off me. I could see that my ankle was covered in blood, and my shoe was nowhere near me. I was thrown out of the car. I saw that there was a house nearby, and I made my way there. I don't even recall getting to the building and the next thing I remember I was in the Lourdes Hospital again. I had ripped the skin off my back, and my foot was severely cut and full of glass. The pain in my foot did not seem so bad, but that was probably because my back was in agony. I was treated in the hospital for a few days and let home, but I had to make my way to the hospital every Tuesday and Thursday to get my wounds cleaned and redressed. The pain I felt when they were cleaning my back was excruciating.

I have to admit in hindsight that the physical damage I suffered was not the most damaging to me. I was off for a long time and very quickly got bored and started overthinking because I wasn't able to do anything. I thought maybe that the crash was for the best, that I had risen too far, too quickly to a position that I wasn't good enough for. Thoughts became beliefs, and I found ways to blame myself for the situation I was in. I doubted myself more than ever, and I had no way to release all the negative thoughts building up in my mind. I started to believe that I was a fraud who had conned my way through Lifestyle and was only good because of the great staff in Mary St. Sometimes the pain in my back was unbearable, even with all the medication I was on. I struggled to cope with the agony and all the issues building up in my head. One day, after I visited the hospital, I tried drinking it away. That didn't work either, as neither the pain in my back nor my head was eased in any way. Deep down, I knew something was wrong with me, but I had no clue what it was and tried to carry on as if it would all just go away.

The pressure was building up in my head from all angles. Work wanted me back before I could go back, and I was in an argument with them about maybe splitting the country into two areas and having two supervisors. I suggested this so that I did not have to drive so much every week. Financial pressures during this period began to challenge me. We were never what anyone would call well-off, but after the crash, I was on sick pay only. The only answer I could come up with was to go back to work, but I wasn't able to. The mortgage on the house seemed to be increasing every month. When I was working, I used to get paid monthly, and I remember doing the shopping after I got my salary, then paying the bills, and then had nothing left for the rest of the month. Now that I was off, it became impossible to pay all the bills. I did not like that at all. That was not what I believed life was all about and I'm sure my feelings of worry and pressure cascaded down to Valerie and Wayne.

When I was fit enough to go back to work, I refused to go back as Area Supervisor, due to the long hours driving required and secretly because I did not think I was up to the job. As the discussions between Quinnsworth and myself dragged on, and my financial problems worsened, my Dad got me a job up in Platin loading the cement trains for Irish Rail. I enjoyed that and should have stayed there. I even thought about applying to learn to be a train driver. I would have enjoyed that, and it might have secured our future, but I never appreciated what I had until I lost it. There was no pressure involved in my job on the railway, and I liked that too. The only part I didn't like was when there was little or nothing to do. I kept myself going by greasing the points on the railway any time I felt bored or started overthinking, but overall, I enjoyed myself there and got on well with everyone. I really should have stayed with Irish Rail, but I had too much downtime with nothing to do, and that just had me overthinking.

Eventually, everything got sorted with Quinnsworth, and they invited me back. I was stupid enough to agree, and Dad was not pleased. I was adamant that I was not going to go back as an area supervisor, driving such long distances, and still doing the hours required in the stores.

They agreed and had another role in mind for me. They took me back, and they had me going into stores troubleshooting and fixing up stores that were not performing to budget. I went to Artane first to help Fred out and get the sports department up to scratch, and then I went to Navan. I thought that they were both easy enough to fix up even if they took a long time. I don't believe my heart was entirely in the job anymore, but I still tried to do my very best. I was always like that. I did what I could, but I was not enjoying it at all. I don't think I was enjoying anything anymore.

Life drifted on and week drifted slowly into week, month into month, and maybe basketball was the only thing keeping me going, but I was not as committed as I had been. I felt the need to cancel and stay at home whenever I could. I could not stand to let anyone down, but there were times when I just couldn't go. I preferred being home, playing with Wayne and having Valerie look after me. To me, helping others, and not letting them down is what I was born for. Anytime I do anything for someone else, it helps me feel better about myself.

When I was working on the railway, and in financial trouble, I gave the house back to the bank. I got sick of the pressure, and I could not cope anymore. It was driving me crazy, and our debts grew every week. I gave up the house before it was taken off us. Valerie was not too happy, but she understood that we had no choice and accepted our fate. Thankfully Wayne was too young to understand. We went to live with Valerie's Dad, and it was a big change for Paddy and us. We all got on well enough but living in our own home had kind of spoiled us. The good thing was that we had stopped ourselves falling into more debt and had a lot more disposable income. We were not living with Paddy too long before getting a house from the Corporation in Rathmullan Park. Once again, we had a home of our own, but it badly needed to be decorated. The neighbours were friendly, and we had a big back garden. It wasn't Rosevale, but it would do.

Concerning myself, nothing much changed. I got a bit of a boost when we moved into Rathmullan, but that did not last long. I was withdrawn, moody, and unable to find a way out of this malaise. Valerie got pregnant in 1986, and the hope was that this was the new start I needed. My head was still a mess, and I didn't know what I was doing half the time, and then in August 1986, my beloved granny died. I was so devastated that I don't remember anything from the funeral or burial or even what happened later.

She was my favourite, and her passing hurt me in ways I did not understand. I was so sorry and upset that I had lost her forever. I did not know how to cope except by working. That has always been and still is my way. Burying myself in work to distract me from the demons in my head, I kept on going through the motions, but still kind of involved in the basketball.

Simon was born in the Lourdes Hospital on Tuesday the 10th of February 1987. He did bring great joy to the family and me. I hoped that it was a sign that the future was bright for all of us. He was a great baby, but there was a cheek with him from the very first day. He did prove to be the tonic I hoped for, but on Saturday when he was coming home from the hospital, I wanted to go to the big basketball cup final in Dublin. I collected Valerie and Simon from the hospital that morning, and she was happy to let me go, once I came straight home when it was over. The Panthers won the game, and we got back to Drogheda. It was tough trying to get home to my family as everybody wanted to celebrate the cup win and wet the baby's head. I couldn't leave, but I couldn't stay, so I organised that we have a couple of drinks in the bar, then all go home to see the baby. Valerie got the shock of her life when we all knocked on the front door, but I think she was delighted too. Everyone got to hold and play with Simon, and it was a fantastic end to a beautiful day.

The next day, I was still feeling good when I was cleaning up the house, throwing out all the empty beer cans and bottles, when I started thinking. It was then I decided that we should never have alcohol in the house unless it was for an extraordinary event or occasion. I did not want my children growing up looking at their Dad sitting in front of the television with a beer in his hand. Neither did I want them getting up in the morning and seeing bottles and cans everywhere. So that was it. I never have alcohol in the house unless something special is going on. The rejuvenation I felt when Simon was born and came home did not last. The country at the time was in a mess, money was tight, the future looked bleak and even the rumours I heard about education scared and worried me. I was wondering and imagining all sorts of a horrendous outlook for our little family, and I believed that Ireland was going to go back to pre-1960 days. I wanted to give the boys the best chance in life and for the future, but the news and stories of the day suggested that might not happen at all. I was still devastated by the loss of my Granny. So, all this pressure and my inability to cope made me feel worse. Everything got me down, and I got the crazy idea that if we upped sticks and moved to London, everything would be better. I truly believed that. What an idiot. I even had my first and only big argument with my Dad. He did not want us to go. I cannot remember anyone who thought it was a good idea, except Valerie, who was going home to the place of her birth and would be closer to her sisters. Her Dad was living in Drogheda, but she was still keen on the move. My family was affected, too and not happy with me. But I was thick and stubborn and had made my mind up to go, and that was that. Even some of the lads in the Panthers asked me not to go, and unfortunately, they folded soon after.

Chapter 6

London

So, in 1987, the Moroney family moved to London, or more honestly, scuttled away from Ireland with hopes of a brighter and better future. We stayed with Valerie's sister for a while before we got emergency accommodation in a place called Plumstead. There was a DIY chain, Great Mills, I think, that was opening a new superstore close by, and I got a job there as assistant manager. The work was second nature to me, even if it was a completely different range of products, and I was soon organising and getting everything done the way we used to do it in Ireland. I found this easy as it was like the re-fits I used to do back home. We were on schedule for the opening all the time, even when contractors were behind schedule. We would layout the stock on shelves as per the plans in any space we could get and move the whole structure into position when the contractor had finished. It worked a treat. I did find it strange that I had far more retail knowledge and experience than anyone else who worked there, even management from other stores that were helping out. I threw myself into the work, and I settled down fairly quickly.

Valerie was pregnant again, and we were happy. Valerie more so because she was close to her sisters and because I was not a moody fecker anymore. The move to London only registered in my thick head a few days after we had moved. It was like I woke up from a dream, but we had moved, and we couldn't just go back. So, I tried to make the most of it, and my mood improved, and all seemed good. I was still working in Great Mills when Lee was born. He was due in March, and I had stayed in with Valerie when I was not at work. One night, the 31st of March 1988 to be exact, she suggested I go for a couple of pints because she thought nothing was going to happen. Nothing did happen till I got home, and I only got to bed when she screamed out. It was time to go. Lee was born on the 1st of April in the Greenwich District Hospital, which was a Friday, and was a big bouncy baby from the start. We had three boys now and no girls but we kind of decided to leave it at that. Enough was enough, and while Lee was another blessing to us, he was also so demanding from day one, and I'm not sure how much sleep if any, we got in the first year of his life. Yet he had this chubby, smiley face that would make you laugh every time we looked at him.

Soon after that, we moved into a council-run three-bedroom apartment in Charlton, which was much closer to

Valerie's three sisters. We got Simon and Lee one of those double buggies. There were only 14 months between them, so they were very close then, and thankfully stayed the best of friends. Wayne was five years older and was already in school. He had done a year and a bit in school in Drogheda and found school easy. He made friends quickly but did not tolerate any assholes (A bit of his Dad in him), and he loved meeting all his cousins in London. He went to primary in East Greenwich, which was a decent school, and it was much easier to get to, either by foot or bus from the new flat in Charlton. Things were looking up for the Moroneys in London, and I started to believe that all our problems, well mine really, were behind us.

I got promoted to manager of the Great Mills store in Luton. It was a real shit hole but was very busy. Having visited it a couple of times, I knew I could get it sorted out, but it needed a lot of work. More products were missing from displays that were on the shelves and more gaps than actual products. Everything was a mess, but I reckoned it just needed a lot of hard work and organisation. It was a bit difficult staying in Luton some nights and travelling the other nights, but Valerie and I were sure it was a brilliant opportunity, and we had a chance to make a better future for us all. I had a deputy manager, two assistant managers, some 50 staff, and not one of them was interested in putting the effort in that was required. The deputy manager and assistant managers did not want to work for this stupid Paddy and were not afraid to say that in front of the staff. The deputy assumed the promotion would be hers and was not happy when she was overlooked. She was not going to help this new manager who took 'her' job. In the few months, I was there; I found out that they had three managers in less than a year before me, and I could see why. I still kept trying, working on trying to get a team together, but even when some members of staff showed enthusiasm, or agreed with what I wanted to do, they were picked on and bullied by the management team. I even had the idea of restarting over by getting rid of or transferring the management team and talking with the staff to see who I should keep and who needed replacing. That was blocked by the Head Office, with no explanation of why. It was an awful experience for me and hurt me terribly, and as far as I am concerned, just emphasized my lack of coping skills and the weakness of my sensitivity. My area manager, who I only met twice, did not give a damn. He was in a well-paid job, living the good life and he was not going to let me ruin it for him. It was not long before the end came. I was accused of taking money from the petty cash box. I assume it was the deputy who reported me. I was suspended and investigated. A few days later, I was interviewed in the lobby of the Greenwich District Hospital by the investigator. It was the only place I could think of that was safe, and there were plenty of places where we could talk. I was innocent and told him so, and I was able to prove it. I had set up a system that two managers had to sign every time anyone opened the cash box. I suggested to the investigator that he look for this sign-in book and he would see that the last time I was near it was a few weeks earlier. I had checked the money and receipts. I found that it was a few pence short. I recorded it, and the deputy manager signed off on it. I had not been near the cash office or petty cash box since. Thankfully Valerie was with me to help keep me calm and composed. Later he found all this to be accurate and told me so, but I had no intention of going back to work there. I am pretty sure that I would have fixed up that store in time if I was able to follow through on my idea, but I knew the trouble and hassle that would take and I was just too fragile for that.

Soon after that, I got a job as the assistant manager in the Co-op Supermarket in East Greenwich. That was a nice little store with a lovely manageress who I got on excellent with. The store itself needed something done. The stockroom room was full while the shelves were empty, most of the time. I thought that a proper count and ordering system would make everything right. I took responsibility for that, and it did not take very long until the warehouse was empty and there were minimal stock-outs or gaps on the shelves. It also made the daily tasks more manageable as the stock did not have to be continuously moved up and down the stairs to the warehouse. All the items that were delivered went straight on the shelves, and there were enough deliveries in a week to ensure that we did not need the warehouse. There was a bonus that the shop was close to where we lived, and there were no long journeys for me anymore.

On the face of it, all seem to be going well for my family and me. But this could not be further from the truth. I was struggling big time, mostly because I did not know what was going on in my head. I was only at peace when I focused on work. I did not understand why I was feeling this way. I did not know why I was sad all the time, and apart from work, I did not know what I was doing. I could not understand how I could manage work with no problems, but could not control myself, my life, or my family. I was blessed with a beautiful family, yet they were cursed to have me as a husband and father.

This Co-op supermarket was close to a pub I used to frequent call "The Old Friends". It was a lovely friendly pub that I visited soon after I arrived in London and found it to be very welcoming. I made some good friends there, especially Spud. We used to meet up, have a chat and play some pool. He was very easy to get on with and good company for me. After a few months of working in the Co-op, something snapped in my head, and I started drinking every day and night after work. As soon as I finished my shift, I was in the pub, and I stayed there until closing time and then went home. I don't recall any arguments with Valerie about this, but she did plead with me to tell her what was wrong. How could I tell her, I had no idea myself, but I've since come to realise that I was self-medicating, trying to ease my pain and the torture in my soul. Of course, it did not work, it never does, but I still know that far too many of us self-medicate every day looking for the same relief. I often wonder how many addicts, either alcohol or drugs, became addicted, trying to ease their pain and cope with life.

After about three months on the beer, I went to work one day as usual, and I remember being up in the warehouse and I just burst out crying. It just dawned on me what I was doing and how I was hurting my family. It was like an epiphany. Sure, I was looking for a way to ease my pain, but the way I was doing it was hurting Valerie, Wayne, Simon, and Lee and I never realised that. It is the one thing I never wanted to do. You might think that this sounds stupid and it probably is, but I was so wrapped up in my problems, that I could not see what was right in front of me, - the family I loved so much. I became so involved in my own shit that everything outside my head; even my family, did not matter anymore. I dried my eyes the best I could, but my face was all red and splotchy. I went to the manager and told her I had to go home. She did not question me or anything and just said sure, probably because of the way I looked. I went straight home to Valerie, sat down, and talked to her. I apologised to her and begged for her forgiveness, and I asked for help. Valerie was willing to help in any way she could, but that was not so easy. I had no idea what was going on in my head. I knew I needed help but with what? So, I said all I could say at that time, even though I thought it was a lie. I told her that I was an alcoholic and needed help. Valerie did not seem to be convinced, but I think she was happy that I had opened up to her, and she did want to help me in any way she could. She made enquiries and found out that there was an AA meeting nearby. I agreed to go, and Valerie came with me as support. Wayne was at school, and Valerie got a friend to look after Simon and Lee.

There was a big crowd at the meeting, and the stories I heard shook and scared me. Yet, I felt that I was not as bad as everyone there, and I could sort myself out. I stopped drinking immediately and did not drink for months until I went to a Christmas party and had a drink to see if I had a problem the next day. I enjoyed the few drinks I had and went home happy with no ill effects the next day. That was great, but I still had not even identified what was wrong with me and how I could fix it. I had no interest in going to the doctors at all. I was a man and needed to take care of myself. Macho bullshit you might think, and be right.

That same year I got promoted to store manager to a small shop not far from where we lived. It was a simple enough project to bring the shop up to the standard required. There were only a few staff in the shop in total, but all they needed was a bit of direction and encouragement. My training and experiences in Quinnsworth helped me tremendously, and the store was easy to sort out. Soon after that, I was promoted again and moved to the Co-op Supermarket on Brixton Hill, South London. What a disaster! The shelves and fittings were that old that I had never even seen them before. I thought they were from the Second World War.

The staff though were lovely, and I sat down with each of them to outline my plans for the store. I asked each of them if they were happy to help me. They did because many of them had been there for years and just loved their little shop and enjoyed working there. They were part of the furniture and willing to get the shop looking as best as we could. They wanted something to be proud of, and I explained that I would do all I could to secure new shelving units, fixtures, and fittings. The initial improvement was easy because the shop had been poorly managed, but after that, it took time to get everything the way we wanted. I gave the staff responsibilities for all sections, and they took ownership and were happy to do so. There was a small deli counter that had huge queues on Saturdays, and I think most of the customers wanted to buy the sliced crumbed ham. It was so tasty. The Butcher worked at the back and pre-packed all the meat for sale in the meat fridge. It was good, it was a challenge, and we had a good team, but if I thought the shoplifting problem was bad in Mary Street, here it was an awful lot worse and a lot more violent.

I was only there a couple of days when the windows and the steel bars surrounding them were cut out and a load of cigarettes stolen. That was okay though because there was no staff there through the night, so no one got hurt. During the day though and the early evening when the shop was opened, shoplifters had no problem lashing out, hitting and kicking anyone in their way, or using anything as weapons. We got a big huge security guard, but it was too much for him, and he left after a couple of days. We got another guard in, not as big but very effective, and not afraid to keep all the known shoplifters out altogether. Security was an area we ramped up immediately, with new security boxes for the cash received and all valuable stock, like cigarettes. We put in a new steel secure room at the back and had all the doors and windows strengthened and blocked off where possible. We made new rules about staff being on the shop floor alone, to guard against intimidation or violence, and we updated all the locks and cash handling procedures. It seemed to work, and we all felt safer. We started enjoying our job, and the amount of stock taken away in robberies was well down, but shoplifting was still a big problem. I must have been doing something right as I was only there for three months when I got a significant pay rise.

All seemed good at home except that I was still dedicating too much time to my work and not enough time for my family. We were doing well but missed home. Even Valerie had the idea of going back to Ireland as soon as we could. We agreed that we would save up hard and build up a deposit for a house and go home. I was feeling better, maybe due to the fact I was putting so much effort into my work and didn't have much time to myself. Anytime I was off I tried to spend as much of it as possible with the boys, whether that was playing in the house, going down the park, or for a spin. Simon and Lee loved to play fight with me and were not afraid to get stuck in. Simon even gave me a black eye once. Lesson #123456, never let the boys play fight with shoes on. Another game myself and Valerie used to love, though probably not politically correct now, was dead soldiers.

We used to get them to lie down and pretend they were dead soldiers for all long as they could. Sometimes we got 10 minutes of peace and quiet from this, or maybe longer if we bribed them with chocolate or sweets. Wayne was too old for this, and he was a very quiet boy, more interested in studying or reading, looking up dinosaurs, or maybe ancient Egypt. There was a rugby and cricket club beside where we lived, and that is where I fell in love with rugby. It was the Blackheath Rugby and Cricket Club, one of the oldest in England, and when I got a chance, I brought the boys to see them play. They seemed to enjoy that, but even when they got a bit fed up, they could play by themselves, and I just had to keep watch, in case they ran onto the pitch. I brought them to the cricket once, but they did not enjoy that, and we left within the hour.

I brought them down the Valley once to watch Charlton play, but I never took them again, even though I went a few times myself. The language and racism made me feel very uncomfortable with the boys there, and of course, Simon picked up on it and learned new swear words, which he would say whenever he wanted to test us. He knew how to 'push our buttons'. I went to the Valley, and the Crystal Palace ground when they were redeveloping the Valley.

Overall though the boys were brilliant and never gave us any real problems. I was seen as strict by Valerie's family, but I just wanted the boys to grow up knowing right from wrong and having respect for others, and I could not have wished for three better children, even though Simon was a cheeky brat, and Lee could make a mess out of thin air.

We tried to get the boys interested in every club in South East London, from soccer to karate and everything in between, but they would only stay for a few weeks before declaring they did not like it and did not want to go again. We ended up with lots of sport's gear that was never used again. It was clear though from early on that Simon felt he was Lee's protector and mentor and always watched out for him.

Almost directly across the road was Our Lady of Grace church and primary school, and both Simon and Lee went there, which made it a lot easier for Valerie. We all went to Mass across the road, and I got involved in church life, becoming a regular reader and helping out around the church whenever I could. We were going to Mass there for about a year before I found out that the building between the church and school was a catholic club, and it was where a lot of parishioners, and Irish people, met for a chat after Mass. We all made some friends there, and we felt we were part of the community. I learned how to play the card game Kalooki there and passed it on to Valerie and Wayne, and it became our favourite game to play in the flat. It is similar in every way to rummy, but each player starts with 14 cards. Many a dull night was spent playing this at home.

Once, when cleaning outside the church, I came across the entrance to the crypt, which was under the church. I had to check it out as I had never seen one before. It was old, filthy and creepy but I soon came up with the idea of cleaning it out, painting and fixing it up, and opening a youth club there. I admit that I was thinking of Wayne as he had no friends of his age around when he was not in school. As you can imagine, the crypt was like something out of a horror movie, and it even had a giant wasp's nest. Other people got involved, but as is usual, only a couple of people who would actually do some work. We got the crypt cleaned up and decorated. We found games and activity sets, like a pool and table tennis tables, from the many donations we received, and felt ready to open. We announced the opening in the church bulletins and when we opened there was a big queue waiting to sign in and join up. It made all our efforts worthwhile, and I even made new friends. It went very well for the first year or so, and Wayne made new friends who lived locally. I would help out as much as I could, and I enjoyed being part of the club.

Chapter 7

The Road to Hell

It seems to me that any time I ever got on the right track, and things were going well for me, life took a turn for the worst. Like that Stain'd song, "It's been a while... since I fucked up again".

The Co-op on Brixton Hill was getting busier day by day. The good atmosphere in the store grew, and the staff were pleased, but good things never last. It started one day when I was covering the door when the security guard took his break. One of the regular shoplifters tried to enter the store. I saw him and got to the door before him. I slammed the door closed, and it smacked him right in the face. I was not sorry, but I became a marked man after that. Soon the cops came and said a complaint of assault made against me, and I had to go to the police station with them. At the station, I was met by a sergeant who explained that he was following procedure and he knew the shoplifter I described. He helped me with my statement and then organised a lift to bring me back to the Co-op.

Not long after that, I was in a car crash on the way home, my fault entirely, but thankfully I escaped with just a sore head from the bang with the side of the roof. I was stopped at a junction, waiting to turn right onto a busier road. It was lashing rain, and I could see a car's headlights coming from my right. I thought I had plenty of time to make the turn, but I was wrong. I had completely misjudged the distance, and it smashed into me. My car was wrecked, and the other one was destroyed. I had no car while the insurance was sorted. I had to travel by bus, sometimes taking three buses to get to work and home. I felt that hanging around bus shelters and stops left me vulnerable, and I was right. I was attacked four times in a few months at bus stops and once actually on the bus. I generally fought my way out of it and got home safely. It didn't seem to affect me too much at the time. One evening, I was in Brixton Village waiting at the bus stop, when I saw two men throw another man under a double-decker bus. I could not wait to get out of there, and jumped on the next bus that came along, even though it was not going my way. The next day I read that it was a local detective that I saw, and the bus had run over both his legs. I felt terrible for him and berated myself for not intervening, but at the same time, a sensible part of my brain was telling me I did the right thing by staying out of it and jumping on the first bus that came along.

Then one day in the Co-op, there were only four or five of us on the shop floor, and a gang of five or six lads and with heavy metal chains came in to rob the store. They went straight for the kiosk, and just lashed the girl behind the counter over the face with one of the chains. I heard a commotion and went to see what it was all about. When I got to the front of the shop, I was confronted by three or four lads, and they immediately attacked me. I lashed out as much as I could and connected with one of the assailants right on the face, but in doing that, I slipped and fell on the floor. They whipped and battered the crap out of me before running off. All that, and all they got was five pounds, due to all the security measures we had put in place. We called the cops and the Co-op Security Department, and soon the shop was full of police and senior co-op management. I got one of the staff to take the very sore staff member to the hospital. So many people interviewed me that it was like the crime of the century. I just wanted to get out of there. I was aching all over, and even standing hurt me. I was advised to go to the local hospital, but I suggested that I go to Greenwich District Hospital, because it was near my family. They agreed, and I rang Valerie, told her I was going to the casualty dept in Greenwich and left.

I was in an awful state when I was seen by the doctor in A&E. The longer time passed the more pain I felt. I had a broken hand from connecting with that lad and had lots of cuts and bruises, but thankfully nothing else was broken, except perhaps my spirit. Valerie and the two youngest boys were in casualty when I arrived, and though Valerie was delighted to see me, she was shocked at how I looked. She left after a while to feed the boys and get them to bed. The doctor wanted me to stay in the hospital, but I was not keen and made a deal with him that I would be back there at 8 in the morning to finish the tests. When I got home that night, I tried to reassure Valerie and the boys that I was going to be okay. I kept my word and was back in the hospital the next morning and had to undergo a barrage of tests, and then needed all my cuts and some bruises to be covered with plasters and bandages. The doctor was happy to let me go home once I promised him that I would rest and look after myself.

When I got home, Valerie was very anxious because the Co-op head office had phoned, wanting to know why I was not at work. I was livid, called them on the phone, and had a big row with the regional manager's secretary. She just insisted that it was the policy that you should ring in if you weren't going to be at work. I tried to explain that I went to the hospital after being attacked, but that didn't matter to her. The doctor had given me a certificate and suggested I take at least a week off work, and I was to go back and see him in two days. I told her this and told her to pass it on to the regional manager, and if he had a problem, he could ring me. I thought that it was a fucking joke, but it wasn't, and it hurt me more than the beating I just received. As usual, I had put my heart and soul into that job in Brixton Hill, and fought off many attacks, and this is the way they were treating me. I was furious, disappointed, felt let down, and began questioning my own value again.

I did go back to work there but not for too much longer. I want to think it was because management knew I took too much punishment, but I know it was to replace a manager in a busier store. The best thing about this is that this store was in Charlton where I lived. The previous manager was very good at his job. The supermarket did not need any big fixes or changes. I was happy to be working so close to home, barely five minutes' walk away, and did not have to drive or get buses to Brixton anymore.

Despite having escaped from Brixton, and working in a lovely store, very close to home, my mood dramatically sank, and it all happened very quickly. I had no clue what was going on with me. I lost interest in work, life, and everything in general. I was sad all the time and often cried like a baby, even at work, but I was careful that no one saw me. I became very irritable and frustrated because I knew something was wrong with me, but I did not know what. Work was no longer the distraction from the problems in my head. Instead, it grew to be another problem. I felt I was sinking down a well, and couldn't stop myself from falling further. I had felt like this before but never this bad. Things went from bad to worse day by day, and soon the thoughts of even walking the five minutes to work, made me feel very vulnerable, uncomfortable, and sometimes afraid. As a manager, I always preferred to spend as much time as possible on the sales floor. But now I hid away doing "very important jobs" in the office or the storeroom or anywhere away from people. It came to the stage that I could not cope with anything in my life. I was a disaster.

Valerie was concerned because my behaviour at home was nothing to be proud of. I did not want to engage with the boys in any way because I felt that I was a failure and that they would be better off without me. That went on for a few months, and I was hospitalized twice with chest pains. They were eventually diagnosed as stress-related. I hated being in the hospital, and the diagnosis of stress-related illness did not sit well with me. I kept going to work, even though it felt like torture to me. I was so close to the edge; it was frightening. I thought that any little thing could break me and it did.

I had a Saturday booked off for Wayne's First Holy Communion, but the week before the big day, my area manager came in asking me politely if I could change my day off from a Saturday as the store needed me. I explained to him that it was a significant day for Wayne and our family and that I had booked the day off months earlier. I told him that I was not able to work that day. When he left, I felt that I got my message about the importance of Wayne's first Holy Communion across to him. I was sure that I still had the day off for it. Then on the week of the Communion, the regional manager, who I had never met, came in and we ended up having a row. The outcome was that I had to go to work at 7.00 am and take a couple of hours off for Wayne's Communion then be back to work straight afterwards. I was letting Wayne and my family down again, and that just broke me or pushed me right over that edge. It may sound trivial and even stupid, but that is how I felt, and I just could not cope with anything life threw at me anymore. I can't even recall a single thing about Wayne's communion, but I knew I had let him down, and to me, that was like the end of days. I became more withdrawn and felt like I was useless at everything in life, especially being a Dad.

Soon I literally could not get up out of bed. Not because of physical reasons, but because my head would not let me. All these thoughts swirling around my head like a devilish sand storm, forced me to believe that if I got up, Valerie and the boys would see right through me. They would know that I was a complete failure for them, and I was going to make things worse. I was not worthy of them or anyone, and seeing them, talking to them, or just being with them, made me feel more guilty for being such a fraud and failure. So, I did all I could; I avoided them. I waited until they were out of the house before I got up and went to work. I hated going because people needed to talk to me or ask me questions, and I felt that I could not help them at all. I thought I would only cause some kind of unforeseen disaster in the shop and would be labelled a useless idiot for life. I was a con man who had been lucky, pretending to be a good husband, father, person, and manager and was about to be caught out in my lie. I was a liability and was about to fall to the bottom of the well and take those I loved most, with me. I hated myself and everything about my life. I had chosen or accepted the jobs I took. I had spent three months drinking every day, and my only regret then was that I stopped. I had no confidence or self-esteem because I didn't deserve any.

Even when I was in the hospital with chest pains, I did not speak about how I was feeling, but just about the chest pains. Once out of the hospital, I always went straight back to work. Soon after Wayne's communion, in 1991, I went to see my doctor, Dr Challacombe. After a long chat with her, she suggested that I had depression, anxiety and was experiencing a mental breakdown. I remember that I got up, told her she was wrong, and I stormed out of her office. I was a man, with macho feelings and ideas, and too big and thick to be suffering from depression. I could not accept the idea that there was something mentally wrong with me.

I heard all the stories of 'mental cases', lunatics, and crazy people and I did not want to be one of them. I could not be. So, I left her office in a huff and went home to share the news with Valerie. I told her as if I was speaking about somebody else. It wasn't me; it couldn't be me; the doc was wrong. So, I stewed away, but what the doctor had said would not leave my mind. I could not stop thinking about it, and I was still getting worse day by day. The worse I got, the worse was the atmosphere in the home. By this stage, I could not, in any way, go and do my job, so I was off sick. I could not cope or face up to anything I imagined I would come across. It was like I was some sort of fortune-teller, I could see the future, and every single part of it was bad news or a failure. I just stopped talking to anyone. Valerie and the boys had to suffer through this, and they had no idea what I was going through.

My sleep became so erratic that for a couple of weeks I would get no sleep at all, and then my body would almost shut down, and I would sleep most of the day for weeks on end. The good thing I remember from that time, was in the middle of the night when I was pacing the rooms, I used to go into the boy's rooms when they were fast asleep. I sobbed my heart out to them while trying to apologise for my behaviour. It was the only time I could talk to them because I knew they were asleep and could not hear me, but maybe my words would register somewhere in their conscience. I cried and tried to explain what was going on with me and beg for their forgiveness. I told them they were the best thing that ever happened in my life, and I was so sorry for hurting them. That was the last thing I wanted, but in the cold harshness of reality the next day, I was not able to bring myself to be the daddy they deserved. I just could not do it. It is not that I did not love them; it was that I hated myself and could not feel for anyone or anything. I was a real-life walking zombie, and my head was a mess.

The benefit of my long confessions to the boys at night was that I was saying out loud what I was feeling and experiencing. It was the very first time I was honest with myself, as well as the boys. I heard myself explaining things, and they became more real for me. It wasn't just in my head anymore; it was on my tongue and out in the open. My words were like a waterfall with the words spewing out of my mouth, but what I had to say was not so beautiful. I think there was some relief in getting things off my chest, or more accurately out of my stupid brain and into reality. I wondered plenty of times since if the boys ever heard me or were pretending to sleep when I was talking to them. I don't think I wanted them to get to know my demons, and I didn't want to pass them on.

After a while, with Valerie's non-stop encouragement, I went back to see Dr Challacombe. I apologised as soon as I met her, and we went on to have a long conversation about me and my mental health. I was prescribed antidepressants, sleeping tablets, and tablets to try to calm me down. I was starting to accept that I had depression; indeed, that it was quite severe, but it was still a massive shock to the system. It went against everything I thought I was. I felt that I had somehow allowed it to happen to me. I didn't think of it like the flu that anyone can catch, but more like something I had given myself. Yet, even when I learned what I was suffering from, I got no immediate relief. Anytime I went to a doctor before and was told what was making me ill, I was always glad to know what it was. This time, I felt no different.

I was stupid or naive enough to think that with the meds I would be fine. I wish that were the case. Even with the tablets, my first suicide attempt was not far away. I was at the very bottom of that well now. I could see the light at the top, but every time I started climbing, I fell back to the bottom. Each time I tried to get back up to that opening, I used up more and more of the energy in my mind and body, until I had nothing left. My tank was empty, but there was an escape door marked "Way Out". It did not say 'Suicide' or 'Death', but it was telling me how I could escape this shit I found myself in. I felt useless, a failure, and I knew Valerie and the boys would be better off without me. I was causing all the problems in our house and with them. I believed this and started to think that once I was gone, their lives would immediately be much better, and they would be much happier. There were no thoughts about funerals, burials, devastated families, or friends. Everything in my life would disappear, and we would all be better off.

The mind is a marvellous thing, but not when it is infected by depression and stops you from thinking clearly or rationally. As the thoughts and feelings, which are a part of my depression, took more control of my mind, the ideas of suicide grew from nothing to everything. What had started as mere second long thoughts, strengthened and developed into urges that would not leave me alone, until I believed that the only option for myself and Valerie, Wayne, Simon, and Lee was to take my own life and free theirs. It was not death to me. It was an end to my pain, as well as the grief and hurt I was destroying my family with. It was the ultimate pain killer. Every time I slept, I had visions of a lovely decorated dagger, with an ornate red handle sticking out of the centre of my chest with blood, the same colour as the handle, pouring slowing and calmly out of my chest and down my body. Thoughts turned into powerful urges, which turned into plans, and then an acceptance that I was doing the right thing. One Sunday, we all went to Mass as usual, and I prayed to God, telling Him of my plans and asking Him if I was doing the right thing. I was looking for answers or a sign, but I found nothing. That is not to say that God had let me down, but I believed in some warped way, that he was okay with my plans. I had a few drinks in the club, Dutch courage you could say, went home and took all my tablets. Valerie heard something, came to investigate and found me and my empty tablet bottles. After a row, some roaring and shouting, and using the boys to bribe me, Valerie got me an ambulance, and they took me to the hospital. I wanted the tablets to take me and my pain away. Once in the hospital and assessed, my stomach was pumped out using some form of charcoal. I conked out when this was happening, and I woke up on one of the wards.

I was disappointed I had failed to end my pain and misery. What a useless idiot I was. I would have to start the whole process again, and while the suicide was easy for me, the planning was much harder. I had a little 'spark' in the brain, always making me ask if I was doing the right thing. Not just for me, but Valerie and the boys. It wanted me to live. Lies then became a regular part of my life. I was displeased that Valerie brought the boys to the hospital to see me, and I lied barefaced to them when they asked me questions, like how I was, and if I would be okay. I lied to Valerie saying that I would never do that again, even though I knew I would. I hated lying and still do, but it didn't bother me then. I could see the pain and concern in the boys' faces, and I told them everything they wanted to hear, and Valerie too. I am deeply sorry to say that Mam and Dad or my brothers and sisters never came into my consideration at all, except that they were far away, and I could not hurt them.

The next day, while still in the hospital, I received a visit from a psychiatrist. My problems did not go away with my attempt at death, and talking to him was not much help. I told him what he wanted to hear and that I had no plans or intention of trying to suicide again. When he seemed to accept that, I told him I was physically abusing the boys at home. I don't know why I said that, but it could only have been to get the boys away from me. The reality was that my head was so confused that I could barely add one and one. I never physically hurt the boys. I could not think clearly at all. That same day a social worker visited Valerie and the boys. The boys were out playing, and even after Valerie insisted that I had been lying, she had to call the boys in so the social worker could see them and ask any question she wanted. The boys were put on the "At-Risk" register, but the social worker could see that I never harmed them and they were removed from that register after that. Once that was cleared up, I was allowed to go home.

Because of my naivety, I started to believe everything I was told. I would get better soon; I would get help soon, all this will pass quickly! I had to have hope! I didn't get the help I was promised and didn't start to feel any better. I just felt worse, though how I thought that was possible, I didn't know. Dr Clallacombe was all I had. That is why I don't like the idea of hope replacing suicidal thoughts. Hope is not under my control and can be just another thing to let me down. Hope always brings disappointment, which impacts negatively on all my feelings and thoughts. Hope just lets me down and pushes me further down that well to Hell. I tried to do what I was told and have hope, but every time I did, I took it too literally and hung on to that bit of hope like someone hanging off the top of the well by their fingertips, hoping the rocks would hold. I felt so let down when no one came, and the stones crumbled away. Hope, when I lost it, was just another way of hurting me.

It was this that convinced me that I was right to want to take my escape route at the bottom of my well. The promises and well-meaning comments everyone said to me, actually made me worse. I believed what everyone said to me, but when I did not feel any better, I slipped further. I had for a short while, let myself hope that I would get better soon, but that was a lie and let me down. I still felt all alone, and to be honest, a whole lot of crazy. I was lying a lot. Anytime anyone asked me why I was not at work, or what I was doing, I told them I was off with chest pains. Even that simple lie, dragged me further down into Hell, and I could not cope with that either. Every time I told a lie, I felt even more guilty and ashamed of myself. I knew I was hurting myself and them by lying, but I could not tell anyone the truth. I could not admit I had severe mental health problems. I wanted to have something physically wrong with me, rather than depression, and I didn't care how serious it was. I used to pray to God to take away my depression and suggested that he could break both my legs and arms instead. Anything would surely be better and easier to handle, and I would not have to lie all the time, and I would not be hurting those around me. I thought too that it would not hurt as much.

Instead of feeling better, I began to believe that there was a lot more mentally wrong with me, and I could not cope with that. Added to that, we were now experiencing severe financial difficulties because we were only getting £51 a week due to the employment systems of the day. Technically I was still employed, and I could not terminate my contract because I was under a medical certificate. I could not get full social welfare because I was still employed. Everything I touched turned to shit, and I could see no way out of the financial hole I had put us in.

This time, there would be no failure. I would escape my torture once and for all. I would do it in a way that left no time to be resuscitated or helped. The planning was easier this time, and I kept things very simple. The hardest part was trying not to give any indication that I had a plan, but lying and acting were also becoming easier for me. I was sure that no one had any idea what I had in mind. I waited until Valerie, and the boys were out and would not be back any time soon. I smashed the window in the bedroom and cut my wrists. I waited for death to take me and my pain away. Two cops were passing close by and heard the glass breaking. They investigated and saw that I had broken the window. They called out, but I ignored them. They came to the front door, but I pretended no one was home. They knew someone was in and threatened to kick the door down if I did not open it. I did not want to leave Valerie with that problem, so I had to let them in. I tried to cover my wrists with towels, but the blood seeped through them. They knew what I did, and wanted to get me to the hospital, but I pleaded with them to leave me to die in peace. I explained how I could not go on in this life and would be better off dead. They listened and sympathised, but insisted on taking me to the hospital. Once there, I was cleaned and stitched up and sent home without any visit or talk with the psych team. It was a quick in and out job that just emphasised to me that even to them, I wasn't worth their effort.

I was as useless at suicide as I was at everything else. I had failed again, but strangely this put me off taking my life for a while. I thought that I wasn't able to do that properly and was just hurting myself more, physically now as well as mentally. In my mind, I would only fail again if I tried.

IN TWO MINDS:

Dr Challacombe got in touch with me. I think Valerie was in contact with her, and she arranged to meet with me. I was pleased that someone was taking an interest in me. I met with her, and she convinced me to go to the Psychiatric Day Hospital, which was just next door, underneath Greenwich District Hospital. She made an appointment for the next day, and I promised her I would be there and on time.

With Valerie still behind me all the way, I went there the next day. Valerie walked me to the front door, and then she brought the boys home. I went in and was welcomed by a nurse. She told me that I was expected and said that the doctor would be with me soon. The place seemed to be busy with lots of patients or clients moving around, and some of them said hi when they caught my eye. I thought that was nice and it helped me feel a bit more at ease. After a few minutes, I met Dr Birchnall, the psychiatrist, and we had a good long talk together. He prescribed new antidepressants and introduced me to the rest of the team and showed me around. More people smiled and said hello, and I appreciated that, but I wasn't able to smile back. I just muttered hello to them. I didn't believe that anyone could help me, but I went to appease Valerie, and in the nicest possible way, keep her off my back. I had promised the doctor that I would go, and I kept my promise. They encouraged me to attend every day, and without thinking about Valerie, I agreed.

I started having regular sessions with Br Birchnall and attending group therapy daily. Poor Valerie had to load Simon and Lee into the buggy, and escort me to the front door of the day ward and then get the boys home. Then she came back down again to collect me when it was time to go home. It wasn't too far away, less than half an hour walk, but a tough ask when pushing a double buggy.

All the staff seemed very interested in me and helpful. All the other patients using the service were friendly, and more importantly, not judgemental. After all, we all had the same or similar problems. In group therapy, I sat there for 6 to 8 weeks and did not open my mouth. I was listening to other people's stories, but I had absolutely no feelings at all, and I was utterly indifferent to even the most horrific stories of abuse. It wasn't me; it wasn't in my life; it didn't affect me, so I didn't give a damn. I had my own problems and did not want to be listening to other people's evil tales. I couldn't cope with my demons, let alone theirs. But still, I sat there every day waiting for the session to end, so I could get a coffee and biscuits, and try to chat with the others about anything except mental health. I didn't mind that, and it helped me settle into the group. They were always encouraging me to talk about myself, but they were never forceful about it. They just thought it would help me. I wasn't so sure and felt that they would laugh and ridicule me and my problems, and see that I was just a fraud. I thought that they had more severe problems and that mine were insignificant in comparison. So, I just kept my mouth shut.

Eventually, I felt kind of outside the group because I wasn't contributing like everyone else. With gentle persuasion, I talked just a little at first. I spoke about myself and my family. After some more sessions, I talked about what I thought was wrong with me. I described the physical attacks culminating in the one in Co-op Brixton in detail, but it was as if I was talking about something that happened to someone else. I went through this for a few sessions but was still indifferent about the whole thing, and more importantly, came to the conclusion that these assaults were not to blame for my mental health difficulties. The psychiatrist and the nurses were also convinced that this was not the cause of my depression. Now I was even more confused, and my brain started thinking that there was no real cause, it was just me, and if there was no cause, I could not be 'fixed' or made better. Just brilliant, I was doomed. The only good thing I got from talking was that everyone else in the group congratulated me for sharing with them, and no one laughed at my issues or judged me.

Chapter 8

Revelations

Thankfully that year, I was assigned a counsellor, Leslie Marshall, who visited me at home twice a week. I liked her, the way she spoke with me, and the way she always tried her best to explain to Valerie what was going on and give her ways to cope too. I liked that because I definitely could not help her, because I could not help myself, and I really could not explain what I was going through. Any time I tried to be honest with her, I got frustrated with myself, imagined that the truth would only hurt her, and even sillier, pass my illness onto her. Some kind of depression contagion, and so Valerie had no idea what was going on.

Though I got on well with Leslie and started to trust her quickly, I still found it very hard to open up, but at least she did not push me too hard. I was way too fragile for that. We eventually discussed and dissected the assaults, but still, I felt nothing and found little relief. We kept talking about my depression and what I was going through. I did not think that I was getting much better, but at least I had Leslie and the psych team there, and more importantly, listening to me and trying to help. I felt that I was getting professional support and that, on its own, relieved some of my pain and anguish. Leslie helped clear my brain a bit so I could think a bit more rationally. It's kind of true what they say, a problem shared is a problem halved. I reckon that the talking I did with Leslie, was a bit like letting some of the shit in my head flow out of my mouth. I heard myself say stuff that had only previously existed in my head and saying it did bring some relief. It was just like the times I spoke to the boys when they were asleep. I didn't have hope for the future, I was too far down for that, but I could feel that something positive was happening. Until then, I had not met anyone who I could talk to like this, not even Valerie, but that only made me feel more guilty, and I wanted to find a cause so that I could get better and talk to her and the boys properly.

Leslie had been visiting me for about six months when she suggested that the next time we meet, it should be in her office in the hospital on Shooters Hill. That was not far for me, but the thoughts of going up there on my own terrified me. Valerie was still escorting me to the psychiatric day hospital, with Simon and Lee in the big double buggy; otherwise, I might not have gone. Leslie had asked me to go on my own, and I did that. She suggested that we were very close, to what I did not know. I trusted her, so

I made my way up there the following week. I took the 5-minute bus journey and was very alert, looking around all the time, making sure I met no one who knew me. I did not want to see or talk to anyone I knew. I arrived on time, and Leslie met me straight away. I liked that. I hated waiting for ages. I would start to overthink and panic and be such a disaster when I met someone, that my brain would not be able to tell my mouth what to say. I have to say that unfortunate distress has not left me yet.

I met Lesley in a lovely brown wood-panelled room, and we started chatting about everyday things and about how I was feeling, which was fine. I was anxious, and a bit scared, because she had changed the venue, and had asked me to come on my own. Something was going on, but I didn't know what. Then she said she wanted to explore my past further. We had already spoken a few times about growing up in Drogheda, so I was comfortable with that. We had talked a lot about family life at home, and even about me falling out of touch because I did not want them to know how I was struggling. I am not exactly sure what happened next. All I can remember is that I started to get vivid images of my sexual abuse by Mr Shine, in my head as if they had happened the day before. I could see his tongue rolling around his mouth very clearly as if he was standing over me again. It is not that I spoke to her that day. Instead, the words flowed out of my mouth as if I had no control over them. I told Leslie about my visits to the clinic in the Lourdes in 1975 and his surgery on Fair St., and I described what happened to me. Apart from being embarrassed telling a lady about my abuse, I kept going until I finished the whole story. I am not sure if I even took a breath. It was flowing out of me, and I could not stop it if I wanted to. When I was finished, I was shaking like a leaf, but I immediately felt some relief. For the first time, I began to think we had found what had caused me so much pain.

Leslie was in no doubt, even that day, that it was a significant factor in my depression, and I was so delighted to hear that from her. I found some cause, but more importantly, a belief that I would, at last, start to feel better and I would "be cured" of depression forever. That day, I got something far more valuable and helpful than hope. I think it was much more useful, for me anyway, to start to believe that I would get better. When I began to believe, I started to feel better, and my recovery and return to 'normal' now depended on me, with help and support.

The images of my abuse played over and over again in my head like an endless DVD, and I had no off button. I started overthinking about the whole abuse and, naturally for me, looked for all the ways I was at fault. I went to the hospital on my own. I told no one what was happening. I didn't cause a scene when he masturbated me. I let him do it, so it was, of course, all my fault. All these feelings and thoughts nullified the relief I had felt with Leslie, but we had a cause, so surely the cure would follow. I went back the following week to see Lesley in the hospital, and went through the whole of my abuse again, and got more relief and more belief that I was on the right track. Leslie tried to convince me that none of it was my fault, but even though I heard her, my brain would not accept that. After that Leslie came to see me in our flat and I was at last, able to go through everything with Valerie. She was sickened by what Shine did to me. She was, after the shock, delighted that I told her and at last, she knew what had happened to me and why I was so depressed, isolated, and narky. I was delighted that at last, I could explain to her what I was going through. That in itself was a massive weight off my shoulders. Sharing the story of my abuse with Leslie, and then Valerie did give me a boost and eased my depression.

There is one thing that still causes me regret and pain now, and that is the fact that since my depression took hold of me, I have never bathed the boys. The newspapers those days were full of stories of people who were abused becoming abusers themselves. That terrified me because I believed what I read. When Valerie was washing Simon and Lee in the bath, I never even entered the bathroom. I was terrified of what would happen. Of course, since then, we have learned that the stories of the day were full of bullshit, and people who were abused did not automatically become an abuser or paedophile. That's way too late for me now. I still miss that to this day and believe that I missed a huge opportunity to bond with the boys. I had, of course, washed Wayne when he was younger, but it hurts me to think that I bathed him, but not Simon and Lee. It's as if I neglected them big time. It's just a small incidental thing, but it hurts me so much.

During the worse part of this depressive episode, I took long walks, down by the River Thames, and over as far as Canary Wharf, which was mostly under construction at the time. Valerie was so concerned for my safety, especially near the river, that she followed me at a distance to keep an eye on me, and I never found out until years later. These walks did not make me feel any better but did not make me feel worse either, which happened all the time I did nothing and stayed in the flat. I would be alone with my thoughts, and every thought turned into a negative or a problem that I had no chance of dealing with. So, I would just sink further down that well and get more depressed. As my depression started to ease off, I began to enjoy the walks a bit more and took an interest in the progress of all the new buildings in Canary Wharf. One day I even took Wayne, and when we were walking past some studio there, Donny Osmond came rushing out and knocked Wayne to the ground. I was furious with him, but he just looked at Wayne, then me, and jumped into his car. It was someone else who made the apologies on his behalf. I used to like him when he was younger and, on the TV, but was not impressed with him that day.

The rules back then, were that the maximum time a counsellor stayed with a client was twelve months, and Leslie had to stop seeing me as a client or patient. However, we

discussed what I was going to do in the future. After thinking long and hard about this, and with her approval, I decided that I was going to go home to Drogheda and report
Mr Shine for what he did to me. I had three great reasons
for doing this. 1. I wanted to stop him from doing this to
anyone else. I could not believe that I was a once-off and
that he did not abuse anyone else. I was sure that I was
one of many and that he was probably still at it whenever
he came across a 'fine healthy boy'. 2. I wanted justice for
my family and me, and 3. I wanted closure. I was doing
well, feeling much better in myself, far more able to cope
with life, but I needed to finish this for good. I believed
that reporting him to the Gardai in Ireland would be the
final step in my recovery.

When I was finished with Leslie, I was feeling better in myself, but I didn't feel ready or strong enough to make my
complaint. I was still attending Dr Birchnall and group
therapy. After I had opened up to Leslie and Valerie, I
felt comfortable enough to tell the doctors, nurses, and
members of the group. That helped too. It seemed that
every time I spoke about what happened, that tap in my
head opened up and let a bit more of the pressure and
depression out. Thankfully, everyone was so supportive,
and I did not feel as embarrassed as when I told Leslie.
I finished in the Psychiatric Day centre in the summer
of 1993 and was still determined to report Shine, but I
had to try to sort out my life and finances first. Before I
finished in the psychiatric day hospital, all the talks we

had, were about me going back to Ireland to report Shine, and get this sorry business finished. I believed that doing this would complete my recovery, and I would have that fresh start, be finished with depression forever, and have a happy life with Valerie and the boys. Everyone was very encouraging, saying that it would indeed help me beat depression once and for all, and I believed them. Their encouragement and best wishes further convinced me that I was doing the right thing.

We invited Mam and Dad to London for a visit and to give them and the boys some time together, and secretly, to tell them about my abuse. They were delighted that I contacted them and looked forward to seeing the boys. It was not too long before I collected them from the airport and took them home. It was just lovely seeing them playing with the boys, and the boys were so happy and excited. Even though the scene of joy before me was brilliant, the talk I had to have with Mam and Dad was burning a hole in my chest. I knew it was going to be very difficult for me, but far more so for them, so I was eager to get it out and over with as soon as possible. Valerie eventually managed to get the boys away from their grandparents and sent them out to play. She went out to the balcony, to watch over them and give me time and space to talk to Mam and Dad. They had no idea what was coming. I sat them down on the sofa directly in front of me, and I could see that they recognised that this was to be a serious conversation. I started talking about my depression and apologising for not keeping in touch, as I should have. It did not take me too long to tell them about my abuse. I felt that it could wait any longer, and it poured out of me like when I told Leslie for the first time. I did not go into much detail with them. I just gave them the basic facts that I was abused, about when and where. It seemed like it was over in a flash, even though it wasn't. I watched them as they just froze in time, for how long, I have no idea. They just sat there like statues, looking at me, but not seeing me or anything else for that matter. I was delighted I told them but immensely saddened at what they must have been thinking right then. I could not imagine what they thought, but I guessed it was a lot to do with how they let me down and what they had 'allowed' happen to me.

After what seemed like ages, I could see the statues come alive and be overcome by complete and absolute shock. Their mouths could not have hung any nearer the floor, and their eyes suggested they could not tell if this was reality or a dream. The faces of my Mam and Dad contorted in pain, disbelief, and confusion and when they spoke to ask me questions, just gibberish came out. I tried as hard as I could to hold myself together, but seeing what they were suffering through, broke my heart, and I cried my eyes out. I babbled on trying to get to the end so it would be all over. Valerie was watching and came in then to get us tea and coffee, and I think that was what brought them back to reality. It was easy to see that it was unbelievably painful for them, and I was so sorry I had to do that, but it was something I was sure I had to do. With the tea and coffee in hand, they tried to ask some of the million questions that were in their heads, and I answered them as best as I could. I had said what I had to, put them through such pain, and now wanted this to be over. They slowly eased off as I tried to reassure them that it was all over now. I explained how I was in a much better place and was planning to make a complaint to the Gardai when I was ready. They seemed to settle down, and soon they stopped asking me questions about the abuse.

We started talking about everyday things, but Dad needed to get out, to move, to suck in air to clear his mind of such disgusting thoughts. He brought the boys over to the shop to get ice cream. We didn't tell him that we were teaching Simon about road safety and letting him walk across the small roads by himself, once he walked with us. When Dad tried to hold his hand crossing the street, Simon was not too happy and refused, and we had a good laugh about that when they got back. Poor Dad. It was wonderful having my parents over, and we travelled around and took in the sights, and had a lot of fun with the boys. I just wished I had been as good a parent to Wayne, Simon, and Lee as my Mam and Dad were to the eight of us back in Drogheda.

When I was depressed, I never got in touch with anyone, not even Mam and Dad, and I was glad to reconnect again. I had lots of reasons for this, some rational or reasonable, and many irrational. While I didn't want to hurt anyone,

I didn't want them to 'catch it' from me. I did not want anyone to feel sorry for me or to see I was just a failure. I could not deal with that at all. I didn't want anyone to see how I had let them down and that I had grown into such a disaster. I could feel other people's emotions, and I sucked them into my own being like a powerful vacuum sucking in filth from the air. I felt their hurt and pain, and that just made me feel more guilty.

We gave Mum and Dad our bed, and we slept with the boys. One night I got up to go to the toilet, then went back into my bed, beside Mam and Dad. What a fright we got when Mam woke up and I was climbing into bed beside them. It did give us plenty to laugh about, and I was cautious any time I went to the toilet at night time after that.

Chapter 9

Complaint

In 1993, I got a job as an assistant manager at Superdrug. There was no way I wanted to go back to the Co-op, and a fresh start was what I needed. I was sent to Superdrug in Woolwich to train and learn how they operated. That was very close to me, but there was nowhere to park. Luckily it was just a short bus ride away. I got used to their policies and procedures, as well the way they operated quickly. I was promoted to manager of a Superdrug store in Thamesmead. That meant a pay increase. The salary increase was brilliant because we were in so much debt. It was easy to get to Thamesmead by car, and there were plenty of parking spaces. It wasn't a terrible shop, but it needed a lot of work because some of the staff just did not care and did not help out at all.

I spoke with them on a one-to-one basis, and it was clear that a few were not pulling their weight, which affected how the others worked. I found out that a few of the staff were brilliant and wanted the shop to do well. Some of the team left straight away because they guessed what was coming. I told them how I operated, and that was enough for some of them. Others had to be pushed out when the opportunity arose. That didn't take too long, and then we had a decent team. I hated having to do that to people, to take away their livelihood, but I did not think there was any other way. It worked so well for us that a director of Superdrug called in one Saturday to see for himself how this store could take such a massive jump in sales in just a few months. He asked us all lots of questions and seemed to be very pleasantly surprised by the answers he got, and he was very complimentary to all the staff present that day.

I was still feeling better with every day that passed, but the idea and the thoughts about going to make a report to the Gardai about Mr Shine would not leave me. We had an excellent Christmas in the Moroney household that year, with the only little hiccup for me being when Valerie tried to remind me of the great Christmas, we had the year before. I did not have or have ever had a single memory of that Christmas, or the one previous. My mind was blank. Valerie tried to tell me about events and good times that happened to help me remember, but I just could not recall anything. That was another symptom of my depression, my memory was just awful, and I could only remember fragments of certain things as if I had, some form of selective memory. Apart from that though, things were much better at home, and once Christmas was out of the way, I made plans to go to Drogheda as soon as I could, with Valerie's blessings of course.

It all happened on the 1st of March 1994. I flew home from London to Dublin and got to Drogheda in the afternoon. I was staying in Mam's house and went up there first to drop my bags off. I had no idea what I was doing or how to go about it, but there was a solicitor in town who I was in primary school with. So, I went down to his office, and without telling his secretary anything, asked to see him urgently. I wanted to ask him how to report Shine. He was busy, but when he heard who I was and that I was over from London on a critical matter, he agreed to see me when he was free. By the time he came out of his meeting, the secretary was gone home, and it was just the two of us in his office. I told him what I wanted to do and why and he just sat down what his mouth wide open, staring somewhere far away for the longest time before he snapped back into the present and told me I should go to the Gardai and make a statement. He even rang the Superintendent who arranged for a Garda Sergeant to be there and available when I reached the Garda station. The Garda station was at the end of narrow West Street and is now called Barlow House.

I went over there straight away and went in. The sergeant was there, and he guided me through to the back room on the same level as the front door. We had the usual small talk, and then he described the process. He told me that

I should talk about what happened and he would write it all down. I sat across from him at a table and made my statement. I described exactly what happened to me. The memories and images of the abuse were still vivid in my mind. They had never really left my mind since that day in Shooter's Hill. Making the statement was a lot easier than I had feared. I had told the story so often, and once I started, it flowed out like every time before. As I was talking through the abuse at the hands of Shine, he asked to stop for a few minutes and left the room. I thought I heard him getting sick in the toilets or heaving at least. When he came back, we chatted for a while before I continued giving my statement. The sergeant may not have been too happy with what he had to listen to and what he had to write down, but I was delighted and relieved that I had done it at last. I had made my complaint against Shine after all this time and felt a lot closer to my three goals of justice, closure, and stopping Shine from abusing others. I was genuinely pleased with myself for telling my story of the abuse exactly how it had all happened, and I didn't stutter or get lost at all. When I was finished, I signed the pages of the statement, and the Garda told me that they would send me a copy. He told me that the Gardai would handle everything, and he emphasised how I was not to tell anyone else about Shine or the abuse. Now, according to my naive brain, the Gardai would investigate and arrest Shine. I really believed that.

It was, as I expected, a massive weight off my mind. I stayed for a few days in Drogheda, catching up with a few people and family before I went back home to London. Mam and Dad were delighted that I had made the complaint, and like me, thought my life would be far better. It was wonderful seeing everyone, but I was keen to get home and tell Valerie what happened because I knew she was just as anxious about it as I was. When I got back to London, everyone was happy, cheerful, and I was convinced then that I did the right thing.

I got Valerie to write her own statement for the Gardai, and we posted that to the Superintendent about two weeks after I went home. When she wrote it, she let me read it, and I was shocked to read about how close my marriage came to ending and what a real prick I had been to her and the boys. And the worst part was that a lot of what she wrote, and we discussed then was entirely new for me. I had no memory of it at all.

I suppose that the director's visit to Superdrug in Thamesmead helped me and my new career, and in 1994, I was promoted and transferred to the newish store in Surrey Quays shopping centre. This centre was not too far away, but a lot harder to reach. It was on one of the main routes into the city, which was always full of cars. The traffic there and back moved at a snail's pace. That meant getting up earlier and getting home later. Yet I felt things were going well for us, and the future looked bright. The shop looked well with new fittings and check-out units, but that was the end of the good news. The shelves were full of gaps, and the stockroom was so full that I could not get into it. It was full of ridiculous items of stock, like nearly 2000 of one type of slow-selling razors. That was more than a year's sales and the costs involved in them alone were outrageous. It was clear that there was a big job to do, and I would need everyone doing their bit. The staff too were a bit hit and miss in regards to their commitment to the job but my biggest problem was the area manager Linda Allen.

It took a few weeks to list everything that was in the warehouse and update and correct the stock and ordering system. Then we returned what we could and sent lists of the over socks to all the Superdrug stores in South London and encouraged them to order stock off us if they needed to. It worked, but it took a long time. Most of the staff bought into my new plan for the shop, but some did not want to know. Again, I am sorry to say that I could not make these members of staff be part of the team and I had to get them out one way or the other, which I did. I was doing well, making a good impact, and the team was warming to me, but not my area manager. She would not even call me Peter, though she knew full well, that was my name. Instead, she kept referring to me as Paddy the Irishman, Irish Paddy, or just Paddy. That went on for a while until I could take it no more. We were in the staff canteen when she called me Paddy for the last time. I roared at her that my name was not fucking Paddy, that it was Peter, and she should call me that and nothing else. I snapped and was very angry. I stormed out of the canteen and went to find something to do and calm down. I think her problem was that she was responsible for Superdrug Surrey Quays before I got there. So, she was responsible for the staff and the mess with the ordering system and the warehouse. My arrival had just highlighted the problems to the whole of Superdrug, and I'm sure that's why she was so off with me and even racist. I was certainly not going to be a victim of racism anymore. I have seen and experienced plenty of racism, and it annoys the hell out of me.

Shops did not open on a Sunday at the time, but I often brought Valerie and the boys into the store to help me finish a job or perhaps carry out a planogram change. I think the boys liked the work and would help me finish so we could go to get something to eat. Valerie was not left out either, and she had plenty to do to help, and I was very quick pointing out that the more help I got, the faster we would be done. Oh, I'm a horrible husband and father, but our relationship was on the up. Simon has started school the year earlier, and Lee began that year. Wayne had moved into Secondary school, but the school he chose was miles away, close to Croydon. It was an excellent catholic school, but it meant him having to leave around 6.30 am and getting three buses there with the same journey home after school. But he was a great boy and never complained at all. A few times when I was off, I would drive him to and from school, if he wasn't doing something with his new mates, and that would take me an hour each way.

Again, I put far more than 100% into my job in Super-drug, as that is the person I am. I knew perfection was impossible, but still, I tried for it whenever I had any responsibility. I tried my very best not to let anyone down, especially myself, and the people I felt responsible for, the staff. After all, I did not have a great history and had already let many people and myself down. We made every effort to get the shop running as well as possible, with the promise of it being a lot easier when we got everything running as it should. In September at the manager's meeting, Linda announced that everyone would have to work all night Christmas Eve and then St Stephen's day to get to store prepared for the New Year sales. Not because I didn't like Linda, but because I did not like this plan, and thought it stupid and unfair, I stood up and said that would not be happening in Surrey Quays. I explained how the staff had worked so hard over the last year, and that Christmas was above all a family time. I explained how I would be home with my family after we closed on Christmas Eve, and I was sure that all the staff would have something planned for their Christmas and did not want to be in Superdrug in the early hours of Christmas morning. That Christmas, sales were up more than 400% on the year before, and it was Christmas Eve before we knew it. The shop closed at 4:30 p.m. on Christmas Eve, we tidied up, made sure everything was secure, and I thanked everyone and sent them home. My assistant manager at the time, was ok but terrified of Linda, so after I had locked up, she returned to the store and started getting ready for the New Year sales. My best friend Linda turned up a couple of hours later to see if I was there and found out I wasn't. We were off Christmas Day and St Stephen's day and when I went into work the next morning at 7 a.m. Linda was waiting for me. When we got into the office, she gave me an envelope. I opened it, and it was a written warning. I took that written warning, crumpled it up, and said I was not accepting that. I threw it back towards her, but if ever there was a time when the phrase "shove it up your arse" was relevant, this was that time, but I said no more and walked off. Despite Linda, I still enjoyed working there, especially when it was busy. I loved the buzz and the atmosphere and felt it was like a reward for all the hard work we had put in. Yet my lack of strong coping skills meant that the written warning, even though I did not accept it, and heard no more about it, hurt me and affected my confidence and self-esteem. I was questioning whether I did the right thing at Christmas by letting everyone enjoy their few days off and whether I did the right thing when given the written warning. I couldn't answer myself.

We continued improving the relations in the Moroney household, and I honestly felt that I had put all the horrors of the previous few years behind me. I guessed that I would have to go to court to testify against Mr Shine, and stupidly believed that it would be sooner rather than later. I was happy to be working away, and once again, I was on the up.

I found out later that year that Supt O' Boyle, who was in charge of the case, had received my medical records from the hospital and I was able to point out to him when the abuse occurred in 1975

In early 1995, I received a letter from Superintendent O'Boyle asking if he could come over to London to have a chat with us about the case. I immediately started thinking that they had finished their investigations, and it would soon be over. I thought he was coming over with some good news about the case and the upcoming trial. I would get my justice, closure, and Shine would not be able to abuse anyone anymore. How wrong I was. We arranged his visit to coincide with my day off so that I could give him all the time and attention he needed. He arrived on the 4th of May, and I met him in the flat. Valerie was not there as she was at work, and the boys were at school. I had managed to get Valerie a part-time job in Superdrug in Woolwich, which she enjoyed and it gave her something to do outside the home.

O'Boyle was very pleased with himself because he had never been out of Ireland before on official Garda duty. He was polite, asking me how things were, what was going on in my life, and we talked about where Valerie and the boys were. I thought he came to deliver good news to me because of his demeanour and how relaxed he seemed. But he was just softening me up and trying to put me at ease before he revealed, in questions, the real reason for his visit. To say I was stunned would have been the understatement of the year. I was blown away to a place in the darkest recesses of my mind. A second person had made a complaint about Shine, and he was over to accuse me of collusion. He said that he could not believe that there were two separate complaints about such a brilliant and well-liked doctor. He suggested that the only way this could happen was if I conspired with another person. He was adamant that I, very cleverly, made up my whole story about this abuse. He wasn't thinking about how it was ruining my life, but he seemed to be very sure that I had recruited someone else to corroborate my made-up story. I was never that clever. He took another statement, which was my answers to all his questions, including everybody I had told about my abuse. He was very keen to know who I had spoken to. He wanted me to tell him I said it to someone in Ireland so that he could prove collusion and not have to investigate Shine anymore. I told him the truth about who I had spoken, and the fact that I was not making this complaint up, and that I was not conspiring with anyone. I got overwhelmed, very defensive, and my stupid mind went into overdrive, and I imagined the worse. I was being accused of something serious and didn't think O'Boyle believed me. I could not believe what he was saying to me, but still, I knew his theory about collusion had no basis. Later, when I had calmed down and let my brain process the news, I was delighted that someone else had made a complaint. To me, it made my case stronger. I did not know if the Gardai saw it the same way.

O'Boyle would not give me any details about the other complainant, or his complaint, but I imagined that Shine had found him to be a 'fine healthy boy' and that his abuse would have been similar to mine. I did not handle myself well this time. I just couldn't control my thoughts and was very angry, upset, and hurt by his accusations.

He left me and made a quick visit to Valerie at Superdrug, and though she didn't make a statement that day, he was asking her about who we had told. She wasn't very impressed, but she answered any question he had as best as she could. O'Boyle didn't mention collusion to her, but she knew that this visit was not the good news we expected. When she got home, we discussed his visit, and I tried to put a positive spin on it all, but deep down, I was incredibly disappointed in him and the Gardai. It hurt me much more than I was willing to let on, but I hoped I could get over it. I was just about able to handle myself and keep myself from letting despair, worry, and maybe depression take over my life again, but I fought like I was fighting for my life, which I actually was. The more I thought about it, the more I believed the case was over before it had begun.

A month later, my Mam rang in a great deal of distress. The local newspaper, the Drogheda Independent, had published an article about the abuse in the hospital and mentioned that one complaint had been made. The details in the piece made clear to my Mam that it was not me they referred to. When she read the article to me, I did not know what to think. I was panicking like crazy but did not know what to do. I decided to go home and try to find out what was happening. I took emergency time off work to go home to Drogheda. I got the first flight I could, out of Heathrow. Once there, before I even went home to my Mothers, I went to the offices of the Drogheda Independent demanding to speak to Paul Murphy, the editor, and author of the piece.

I was not calm or collected. I was furious, and I was not moving until I got the chance to speak to him. I was causing a bit of a commotion, so he came down to the front desk and invited me back to his office. We walked to the back of the building, and many of the staff looked at me as if I was a deranged killer. Once in his office, he tried to calm me down and talk to me. He had no clue who I was, or why I was so annoyed over that article. When I told him who I was and why I was so mad with him, he said to me that the piece was about the man who made the second complaint and although there were rumours, my complaint didn't officially exist. What was happening?? I was lost, confused, and getting angrier by every detail he told me about what he knew. I wanted to know a whole lot more, but he couldn't continue the meeting there and then but suggested that I return at 7 p.m. that evening, and if it was ok with me, he would invite somebody else along too. I did not know whether he was lying to me, trying to get me out of his office as fast as he could, or being genuine. I accepted his offer because I just had to get out of there and get some air and try to clear some of the crazy thoughts buzzing and stinging my brain like a nest of wasps. I needed a bit of time to let my mind process what was going on and to try and stop my whole world from imploding.

I went up to Ballsgrove to say hello and get something to eat before I went back down for 7 p.m. There was no way I could be cheerful or have any proper conversation, and only Mam knew why I was home. She shielded me from everyone and made sure I had plenty to eat. I guess she could see the pain in my eyes. I was so confused and could not understand what Paul was talking about or what he meant when he suggested my complaint didn't exist. I gave my statement in the Garda station and the second one in London, so what was Paul talking about? Surely, he had it all wrong. Well, I found out very soon after 7 p.m. I got to the office of the Drogheda Independent just before seven, and Paul quickly answered when I knocked on the door. I was glad that he was there and wasn't lying to me earlier. The other person invited was Dr Fenton Howell, who was a big shot in the North Eastern Health Board. He told me that my complaint was never forwarded to anyone by Superintendent O' Boyle or the Gardai. It was not given to the hospital, so they knew nothing about it. It was not sent to the North Eastern Health Board, so they knew nothing about it, nor was it sent to the Irish Medical Council. All I could manage to think was 'What the hell is going on'.

I had no idea why the Gardai did not give my statement to the hospital or the North Eastern Health Board, and when

Fenton asked me about this, I stated that the Gardai told me that they would look after everything. I explained how the sergeant specified that I was not to tell anyone about the abuse or my complaint against Shine. I did what I was told, and expected the Gardai to do their job. I was never told or advised to report it to the hospital, the NEHB, and the Medical Council. All this just blew my head away to the next universe, and I was not sure how to cope or what to do. Luckily, I had a copy of my Garda statements with me, and Paul photocopied them for Fenton. He assured me that he was not going to let me down and was going to mind them carefully until he delivered them to the hospital and North Eastern Health Board the next day. I took convincing, but Paul reminded me that he was there, and he would ensure that Fenton would do as he promised. I felt it was all a lot of 'cloak and dagger' stuff, but my head had left me, and I was confused. What was I to think?

I thought that Superintendent O'Boyle and the Gardai were making a fool of me, not taking my complaint seriously, and maybe protecting Shine. It seemed plausible to me that they were all part of some local 'Old Boys Network' and were doing everything to block his prosecution. I could not see, in my own little world, any other reason why the Gardai did not forward my complaint to the Lourdes Hospital and other relevant agencies. I could not understand how O'Boyle managed to get bits of my medical records for the mid-70s, without telling the hospital why the police wanted them. I was so confused and hurt and felt betrayed by the Gardai. I questioned why this was happening at all, and why was it happening me. I was lost again; in a world, I couldn't understand. I felt that I was let down again by those I should have been able to trust.

Fenton did keep his word, and he handed copies of my statements, as well as Valerie's to the senior management of the hospital and NEHB. The whole episode, the actions and behaviour of the Gardai, and my perceived failure in making my complaint correctly, truly broke my heart as well as my brain. It pains me to say that I allowed my depression to retake hold of me. I opened the cover of the well, and let it flow back into my mind like fog on the water.

I have absolutely no recollection of anything that happened after that until I got back to London. My head was in bits, overthinking everything about the case, and my depression gaining an ever-increasing influence on my thoughts. I started blaming myself again. I had done everything wrong, was one thick stupid git, and was daft to think that making the complaint was the right thing to do. Once back in London, I did not know what to do, but I was angry, frustrated, and sinking lower into that well of sadness and melancholy. I had to do something to try to fight my negative thoughts, so I reached out to a Government Minister, who had made some decent sound bites in the news about the case. I generally could not stand politicians. They remind me of the Philistines from the bible. But Liz O'Donnell seemed different and genuinely interested in the case against Shine. I wrote and asked for her help, advice, and anything else she could help me or my complaint with. I explained as much as I could in a letter and hoped she was on my side because I thought the Gardai were definitely not. In the Dail, she asked the then Minister of Justice, Nora Owen, about the allegations of collusion, the rights of the alleged abuser, and who had decided not to forward the complaints against Shine to the Director of Public Prosecutions for prosecution. I read that in the newspaper. As if I didn't need another kick in the teeth. I found out through the media that someone had decided not to prosecute Shine. My blood was boiling with rage, and I felt like the world was against me. I thought I had made a huge mistake in making the complaint, but I was too thick-headed to stop now. It was like my depression was controlling me, and everything connected with my life. It was working to control me entirely sooner rather than later. It was winning the battle in my head, and I was living in London. I was far from the 'action' so to speak, and away from the case, or lack of one. I decided that I had to do something—one last stand against the Gardai, the so-called justice system, and my depression.

As soon as I could, I came home intending to find out what was going on with my complaint. I made numerous attempts to see O'Boyle, but he was always 'out', 'unavailable', or 'busy'. The Gardai on the desk in the Garda station must have told me to come back about 50 times, and I always did, but he would not see me. I even tried to make an appointment, to no avail. Mary Robinson was the President of Ireland at the time, and she was opening the new youth centre on narrow West St. right across the road from the Garda station, and I went along. I knew that O'Boyle would have to be there. I noticed him immediately. He was dressed up in his finest uniform and looked very proud meeting and assisting the President in front of a large crowd. As soon as she finished saying her few words, I approached O' Boyle and demanded to speak to him there and then. He did not want to talk to me, but I insisted and caused a bit of commotion. He agreed to meet me when the President was gone, but I didn't trust him. When Mary Robinson did leave, he went around behind the Garda station to get his car. I was watching and caught him inside the gates. I stood in front of his car and would not move. Other Gardai started to take notice, and I was sure I was going to be arrested and locked up. But at this stage, and the way I was feeling, I didn't care. He had to meet me then; he had no choice. In his office, I demanded to know who had made the decision not to forward the files to the DPP, and it became clear to me that it was his decision, but he never actually admitted it. I implored and begged him to send a file straight away to the Director of Public Prosecutions and wondered aloud if he and Shine were part of some old boys' network. I argued, pleaded, and tried everything I could to convince him that my complaint was genuine. I reminded him that the Director of Public Prosecutions should decide if the case warranted further investigation and a trial. After a lot of arguing, I had nothing else to say, and I left his office and the Garda station feeling drained but pleased that I got my arguments across. I had no idea if I had achieved anything to benefit the case. I was spent, but I got a lot off my chest. The initial contentedness I felt, faded away to the dark depths of my brain where my depression turned it all into another waste of time.

I cannot say what happened after that, in Drogheda or how I got back to London. I just can't remember anything. When I went back to work, the area manager and a regional manager were waiting for me. That was all I needed. My head was in a mess, and I knew that this couldn't be good news. I had never met the regional manager before. Immediately Linda laid into me about the state of the store. In truth, it did look a mess, but I just told them that the shop looked fine when I left a few days before. I had booked a few days off, and she knew that. I got the assistant manager and asked her why the shop was looking so untidy and dirty. She was making excuses, and was saying something else and just stopped after saying "Linda said". I noticed this blunder and so did the regional manager because after that he asked me to walk around the store and the office and have a chat. It was friendly about work, about the staff and Ireland. I didn't mention my real reason for going home. What delighted me the most was, that a year or two earlier, that might have broken me, but now I had stayed calm, collected, and handled myself very well. I was delighted with that. For me, that was a hugely positive step.

I found out later that year that the Gardai submitted the files to the Director of Public Prosecutions, but this was nearly two years after I had made my first complaint. I did not care that it was probably the question to Nora Owen in the Dail that pre-empted the submission, and not my meeting with O'Boyle, once the DPP had them now, and surely it would just be a matter of time until the case against Shine proceeded in the public courts.

By November, my depression was gaining more control of me and everything I did. That annoyed and disappointed me. I had convinced myself that I had already beaten my depression, learned from it, and was a lot stronger mentally from the experience. I truly believed that I would never reach as low again and that I had the skills to stay mentally healthy, even if the case would get me down from time to time. But I didn't win at all. I had just covered it up with a lid, and now I had opened that lid and allowed depression to do what it wanted. It was slowly but surely taking over my mind, my thoughts, and my feelings again. I still managed to keep working in Superdrug, but that was relatively easy for me. The shop was set up as we wanted, and the staff had responsibilities for their sections in the store and done all the work and orders that were necessary. Honestly, I did not have too much to do;

just be there to help whenever I could and keep everyone focused on the best customer service possible. I was
slipping down that well again, and I was a lot weaker and
more vulnerable than I thought. I allowed the actions, or
the inactions, of Superintendent O'Boyle and the Gardai
to hurt me and let my depression to find a way back into
my mind. I was a failure again and becoming more and
more useless as each day passed. I knew what was coming, even if I tried to distract myself from the obvious, but
surely it would not be as bad this time around. I had developed ways to combat my depression or distract myself
from it as often as I could. Getting stuck into work helped,
as did playing with the boys or going somewhere together.
Surely, I was a good person, and soon God would see that
and intervene before everything fell apart again.

That November, Our Lady of Lourdes Hospital in Drogheda
got in touch, and their CEO wanted to meet me. My stupid
little brain couldn't figure out why they wanted to meet
me, except that they wanted to try to make the whole case
disappear. We made the arrangements, and I met with
Basil Cronin, the CEO, and Anne Lennon, the head social
worker in the hospital, in a hotel in Kensington in London. We discussed the case, as far as I could, as well as my
family. I was wary about discussing too much with them,
in case they reported me to the Gardai for discussing the
abuse and Shine. I did not trust them. Despite it all being
friendly, I wanted to get out of there as fast as I could. I
did not feel comfortable, and I could not work out why

we were meeting at all. Even when it was over, I was as puzzled as I was before. They were kind enough to offer to pay for a counsellor for me in London, but I did not want counselling at the time, because I felt that I had been through all that before. Even though I was getting worse, I was afraid to open up the Pandora box of pain and misery in my head.

I was trying my best to deal with my depression by avoiding my thoughts and feelings and distracting myself as much as I could. I suppose I was hoping that it would just go away. The only way counselling works is by talking openly and honestly, and at the time, I didn't think I could do that. I did still feel macho about it, and I was afraid to accept that I was going to fail again and let everyone down, especially Valerie, Wayne, Simon, and Lee. In hindsight, I was stupid, and maybe should have accepted counselling, but I was not sure if this would be something that would damage my case against the hospital. I wasn't going to take that risk, and I even thought that their counsellor would see that I was just a fraud and fooling everyone, including myself.

After the meeting, I went back to work, but I wasn't able to keep my mind on the job. The shop was busy, and I stood at the check-outs saying hello to all the customers, and trying to cheer myself up. Basil Cronin seemed to me, after a lot of thought, to be a typical CEO or maybe even a seedy salesman, telling me what I wanted to hear. I had my doubts about him and didn't think I could trust him.

175

I wondered if he was a part of the 'old boys' network' too and wanted me just to disappear. Anne seemed genuine and turned out to be a point of comfort and help over the next year or so for me and what a year it turned out to be. I felt that I could trust her and that she would have loved to help if her boss didn't overshadow her. I wasn't happy, but just more confused. My thoughts drifted to all the things I did not say, and all the questions I did not ask, and I made myself feel stupid and useless. I am good at that.

All that time, I was writing and pestering anyone who I thought was involved or connected to the case in any way. I was trying to encourage or force any progress at all. It was all I could do at the time to keep some sort of control of my thoughts and feelings. It was just a silly way to pretend to myself that I was, in some way, involved in my own case. I was possessed and was afraid that my complaint, and the other one, would be ignored and forgotten about and Shine would be free to carry on abusing boys. I wrote to the Superintendent, to the Irish Medical Council, and the new review group set up. Their mandate was to examine how the hospital procedures, related to the case against Shine, were handled, and to see what policies and procedures should be in place. Later that year, Shine was stopped from working as a doctor, by whom I do not know. At least that was some good news at last for me, but I didn't know how long would that last without some kind of prosecution. It did give me a lift for a while, but that did not last long.

In early 1996 I went home to Ireland to meet with the Irish Medical Council. The registrar interviewed me, and they decided that there was a prima facie case for an enquiry into Shine. The DPP eventually chose to prosecute, so the Medical Council enquiry was postponed indefinitely. At last, I thought, a decision had been made, and the case would proceed quickly now. I also met with the Independent Review Group, and I believe that one of the significant decisions of this group under the leadership of Mary Hederman O'Brien, was that no doctor or medical professional should see a minor without the presence of a parent, guardian or approved individual. That was good too because it stopped Shine, and would protect children from being abused, at least in the hospital. The not so good part was that the review group found that the hospital acted with the utmost integrity. I disagreed with that, but then again, I was completely biased.

Thankfully, despite all this, things were not too bad at home. Wayne was 13, attending secondary school and doing quite well there. He never had any problems other than the long bus journey to and from school, and maybe when the teacher, talking about the Battle of the Boyne, was corrected by Wayne when she mispronounced Drogheda. She was not pleased and wanted to know how he thought it should be pronounced. He just replied that's where he was born, and that's where he used to live—end of discussion. Simon was nine, and Lee was eight, and both were doing well in school. The boys never came home with a bad report.   Simon was still the cheeky one, and Lee was as crazy as the Mad Hatter when at home, but very quiet when outside. They had good friends around and in school, and Wayne was attending the youth club under the church. He was also serving as an altar boy in Our Lady of Grace and then training other boys and girls to be altar servers too. In St. Joseph's Church in Greenwich, they had a big 250th-anniversary event planned, and they asked Wayne to be the altar server and look after the 20 plus Bishops who would be attending. Wayne did it and handled himself and the whole ceremony perfectly. I was very proud of him that night and was always proud of them, but I had let them down so much in the past, I was trying my level best to make sure that did not happen anymore. We were working on clearing all our debts, and then we could think of going home. I could, and maybe should, have left London then, and Valerie would have been happy to leave too, but I could not go home yet. I had nothing to show for all my years in London. That was my thinking anyway, or maybe it was my depression talking.

Chapter 10

Blood clots

One Saturday night in May 1996, I decided to go out for a pint, as I usually did because I had no work on a Sunday. I went down the road to the nearest pub. I went in, got a pint, and got chatting to a couple I knew. I just didn't feel right and decided to go home. Once home, I told Valerie how I felt, and I went to bed. I was not long in bed when I got a massive pain in my chest, and my first thoughts were that it was stress-related like before, but it felt a lot more painful. I knew something was wrong, and I got up and moved around to see if I could stretch it out. That didn't help at all. The pain got worse, and every time I tried to breathe, my chest stung in agony. I decided then to get dressed to go to the hospital. In hindsight, I wonder why I did not do that whenever I felt something was wrong with my mental health. I drove to the hospital, got examined, was given a couple of tablets, and sent home. The doctor said that there was a virus in my chest, but I would be better soon enough. I went home and went back to bed. The tablets did not work, and the pain in my chest became unbearable, and I just could not breathe. I didn't want to go back to the hospital because I thought I had been appropriately diagnosed and would be just wasting my time.

Valerie eventually got me to go back to the hospital at 6 a.m. When I got there, I was seen by a different doctor who called for the medical team on duty. They examined me, sent me for tests, and when the results came back, they told me I had a pulmonary embolism. They had given me morphine for the pain, and it was working, and I thought I was cured and wanted to go home. I did not know what pulmonary embolism was, but they explained that it was blood clots in my lungs, and I would have to stay in the hospital for a while. They put me in a ward on the top floor, and the window beside me was facing the North. I could see Canary Wharf.

When the consultant came to see me the next day, he had no idea how I had managed to get blood clots in my lungs. He explained how it usually came from thrombosis, or blood clots in the leg, which move up to the arteries between the heart and the lungs. It was common for people who got little or no exercise and were sitting most of the time, but I was still as skinny as a rake and spent most of my days on my feet. He put me on a blood-thinning infusion along with pain killers. I was told to stay in bed, and I was not allowed out to use the toilet or get out to wash. When I learned that I would be staying in the hospital, I asked a nurse to ring Valerie and get her up to date. Valerie arrived early that morning, and while she was very sympathetic, I felt that she was fed up coming to see me in the hospital. I was in an awful lot of pain but was glad that I went to the hospital when I did. A nurse told me that I would have died if I did not get to the hospital that morning. I did not tell Valerie that.

The doctor who had seen me first on Saturday night was sent to apologise to me. She was friendly, and she told me that she had started her shift the day before she saw me and had been working since. No wonder hospitals made mistakes, but I was alive and for once, thankful I was. I was on the top floor of the hospital when the IRA bomb in South Quays, beside Canary Wharf, exploded, and I could see the plumes of smoke and dirt through the binoculars, my brother-in-law Doug, had loaned me.

They sent me for more tests to check if the clots were from my leg and then to ensure the clots in my lung were dissolving. The tests were carried out in the Queen Elizabeth hospital in Woolwich, and I travelled there and back with a nurse. They put something, barium, I think, into the veins in my leg to look for blockages or damage. The pain of that was as bad as the blood clots, and it seemed like they had pumped heavy iron into my veins, and after all that, they found nothing to indicate Thrombosis.

I got Valerie to keep in touch with Superdrug and let them know what was happening. Some of the managers came to visit me in the hospital, which I appreciated. Linda visited too, but I got the feeling that she was more interested in finding out how long I would be out sick.

I had kept my depression at bay by working hard, or in other words, distracting myself from my problems. It was working, but now I could do nothing except thinking, and for me, that just leads to trouble. My depression had an open mind to corrupt and a massive opportunity to establish itself in my head again, and that's precisely what happened.

I started feeling and believing that I was a real idiot, because I had let myself think that I had beaten my depression, when in fact I was just fooling myself, Valerie, and the boys. I had lied to myself and them, and this just proved to me, how weak I was. I was a fraud, fooling everyone into thinking I was mentally sound, and all these thoughts just pushed me further down the well. Then I received a letter telling me that I would have to leave the job or get sacked. I didn't want to get sacked, so I resigned. Linda got the last laugh, and I'm sure she was thrilled with herself. I didn't appeal or anything like that. I was just not interested at the time, and not able to do anything about it from the hospital. Losing my job just added to my feelings of uselessness. I could not understand why this was happening to me. I did beat my depression for a while, then had it under some kind of control, even if it was ever-present. Then a physical illness had attacked me out of the blue and pushed me further down my depression well. I had tried so hard all my life, and kept climbing out of that well, only to fall back in. I was sick of fighting all those little battles in the war against depression.

I wondered why was I being punished so much, and why was my family being hurt so badly too. Was God punishing us because of something I did, and if so, what was it? Why was He punishing my family as well as me? I thought about a whole melting pot of questions I had no answers to, and I needed something to help me stay sane. I was dragged down by the so-called case and was writing letters and complaints to everyone I could think of, including the Taoiseach, the Garda Complaints Board (about Supt O'Boyle), the Minister for Justice, and Liz O'Donnell TD. Yet I never received one reply that was satisfactory or helpful.

We had found the main factor of my depression and had dealt with that as planned and advised. I was guided through that terrible episode of depression and despair, yet despite all the great support, I was depressed again and being pushed down that well as fast as ever. I did not have the energy to fight anymore, and I didn't think it was worth it. I hated myself, I hated my life, and I was a massive burden on my family, and I did not want to put them through the torture they faced when I was depressed last. All the negative feelings were amplified by my inability to even walk around the hospital ward. I wasn't able to move. I had not been in touch with my Mam and Dad, and my thoughts had me believe that no one, not even

Valerie, Wayne, Simon, or Lee, loved me at all. Evil, or my depression, was winning, taking over my thoughts and feelings. Thoughts of my suicide, the plans, the happy ending for everyone, took up every waking minute of my day, yet I said nothing.

I did not learn my lesson from the previous episode of depression and told no one, and did not seek help because I was this stupid thick Irishman, who was too proud and macho, to reach out for the support that would have saved my life. I also had this idea that going for help would do me no good, because all the support I got the last time, did not stop me from becoming depressed again. They were just more people I felt I had let down. I was not going to go back, just so I could let them down again, and I did not want them to see how I had failed them and all their excellent work.

As for my faith, I still thought of myself as a good Catholic, going to Mass regularly, when I was not in the hospital. I suppose that I just took it that I believed in God without really thinking about it too much. I did not blame God for my troubles but blamed myself. I felt that I must have been a horrible person in a past life, like Hitler or someone just as bad. I have never prayed too much for myself, as I always believed that to be selfish. Still, I always prayed for Valerie, the boys, my family, and anyone else I could pray for, especially those who just died and their families. However, when I did ask God for something, it was always about healing me from my awful depression. My irrational thinking even had me believe that God was happy for me to take my own life and end my misery. Maybe my depression was a fair punishment for trying to kill myself.

Shine had been out of work in the Lourdes, whether he was suspended or what, I don't know. But he returned to continue as a surgeon there in August. That for me was the final nail in the coffin. It was inevitable that I was going to take myself away from this cruel world as soon as I got the chance. I did not belong here and could not cope at all. I was out of my league. Some people may think that I was selfish, but the truth is, I was not thinking rationally at all. When I did think of Valerie and the boys, and my whole family, I just felt more guilty for letting them all down. I had a kind of tunnel vision towards my suicide and the end of all my pain and misery. For me, it was easy to see that taking my life was the only way I could do it. I did have lots of stupid ideas about running away, maybe joining an outfit like the French Foreign Legion, but I could not do that. Firstly, because I could not make a decision to save my life, and secondly, wherever I went, my head would have to go too, and I would be bringing my depression with me. I was 100% certain that my life was never going to get better, and despite all the chances I had in life, I had failed myself and my family.

I spent five weeks in hospital and was then allowed out for a weekend before I had to go back in again. When I was eventually discharged from the hospital, I knew I would take the first opportunity to take my life. I was horrible to the family when I got home. The more I argued with Valerie, the more I hurt her. I knew what I was doing to her, but it just made me think suicide was my best option. Then Valerie was talking about leaving me and taking the boys. Who could blame her, after all, I was putting her through? That further convinced me that suicide was best for me.

I made my plans, and one day, Valerie and the boys went out to the shop, and I tried to gas myself in the oven. I wasn't as smart as I thought I was. Valerie was suspicious and thought something was wrong. She came back into the flat and caught me, and somehow, I ended up in the hospital. I don't know where Valerie was, probably waiting for somebody to come and mind the children, but I found myself sitting alone in one of the hospital corridors. I don't know how I got there, or even if anyone had talked to me. There were no staff around or watching over me, so I just got up and walked out. I was in a daze and had no idea what I was doing or where I was going. I didn't have any thoughts or plans for suicide then, so I just walked. I was a zombie again, and my mind had just completely shut down. I don't know what happened in the hospital after I left, but a police car stopped me in Greenwich, close to the Cutty Sark, checked my name, and brought me back to the hospital. All I remember after that is that I was put into the psychiatric ward, attached to the psychiatric clinic I used to visit. I had to go voluntarily or be sectioned.

Only from what I heard later and what I discussed with Valerie; can I say that I was in an awful state in hospital. I was almost completely catatonic, and nothing anyone could do would bring me round. They tried bringing the boys down to talk to me, and even my friend Spud, but it did not work. Even in such a safe and secure environment, I tried to kill myself, but they were stupid little attempts that had no chance of success, but I had no idea what I was doing. I even ended up in one of those padded cells, which I thought were only in the movies, but were real and used. My psychiatrist, Dr Craig, thought that electric compulsive therapy, ECT, would work for me, and apparently, I agreed and gave my permission for him to proceed. Again, I don't remember anything about this, but find it hard to believe any doctor would take or accept my word in my state. When Valerie heard about this, she tried to stop it, but couldn't because I had given my permission. So, she got in touch with my Mam and Dad, and together with my brother Noel, they came to London to save me. That's precisely what they did.

The first thing I remember from that stay in the psychiatric hospital was that I was in the padded room on my own when one of the nurses opened the door. I saw my brother Noel standing there. That registered something with me and kind of woke me up for the first time in ages. I had been in the psychiatric ward for five weeks. I don't know whether it was the shock of seeing him standing there or the recognition of a face from my past life, that kick-started my brain again. They brought me to a room where Mam and Dad were with Valerie. I think I just cried my eyes out. I am still not too sure whether it was with shame for being caught like that by my parents and brother, or if it was because of my happiness to see them. Their visit though, did take me out of my catatonic state and woke me to reality too. I had no idea that I had agreed to undergo ECT, but I was pleased that I now had the sense to refuse. Together they all spoke to Dr Craig on my be-half and told him that I did not want the ECT to go ahead. They told him they were taking me home to Ireland, and that I would be under the care of Anne Lennon and the doctors in the Lourdes Hospital, Drogheda. The plans were already made, and our seats on the flight booked. I was okay with that, but the thoughts of going to the Lour-des hospital again terrified me. I imagined all sorts of things, like Shine, would be there waiting for me, or they would not look after me properly after all the trouble I had caused and other stupid things like that. It was very fright-ening, but my family was around and doing everything to support me and even doing my thinking and making my decisions for me. I was not able to do anything at all, and I was happy to be told what to do.

Chapter 11

Depression

I suffer from clinical depression and as far as I can work out, have done since 1991, when I was first diagnosed. I might have been depressed before that, but didn't know. Depression is classed as an illness because that is precisely what it is. It is an illness that primarily attacks the brain, but can lead to secondary physical problems for the sufferer. It is different from other diseases in many ways. It cannot be transmitted from one person to another, and there is still a terrible stigma associated with it. Therefore, it is a more personal illness that we are reluctant to talk about or seek help for. It is never the same for every sufferer because we are all different. It cannot be seen on any scan or x-ray, and it has often been referred to as 'the hidden disease' because many of us hide it so well. Not being able to see depression, sometimes has us believe it is not there, as in the early stages of my own depression. Having depression is very hard to accept, which makes talking about it, and getting help, that much harder.

I still find it very hard to tell anyone how I feel. I will lie and say that I am fine. At first, I didn't accept that I was depressed, stressed, or suffering from any mental illness because I could not see it, as I can see broken bones on an X-ray. I thought the doctor was wrong and maybe even stupid for suggesting such a thing. Someday someone might find a way to map depression in the brain, and that will help. Perhaps I would have accepted that I had depression much earlier if I was able to see it on a scan. Sadly, I have learned that it is not only me that is affected. When I am at my worse, it impacts on my family, even Mam and Dad. So, depression affects a lot more people than the person suffering.

There are different levels of depression, from mild to moderate to severe clinical depression. The American Psychiatric Association defines depression as – "Depression (major depressive disorder) is a common and serious medical illness that negatively affects how you feel, the way you think, and how you act. Fortunately, it is also treatable. Depression causes feelings of sadness and a loss of interest in activities once enjoyed. It can lead to a variety of emotional and physical problems and can decrease a person's ability to function at work and home".

In the last 30 years or so, I have lived with all the various levels of depression, from mild to severe. I feel I am in a mild stage at the moment, and I am happy that I am not severely depressed. All the psychiatric professionals I have discussed this with, agree that a significant factor in my depression was the sexual assaults at the hands (literally) of Shine. There are other factors associated with that abuse like it was my first sexual experience, that helps my depression, and not me. Making my complaint official and the ensuing court case has no doubt strengthened my depression, and, at the same time, weakened my ability to fight back. I do accept that these reasons enabled my depression, but I knew that there had to be different elements contributing. I did not understand why I was affected so severely and painfully. After all, many other people have suffered sexual abuse as I did, or worse, or other childhood traumas, yet were able to manage their lives much better than I did.

I have learned that two main parts of my psyche contribute to my depression, and they are my core values and my poor coping skills. My core values are the beliefs that I hold deeply in my heart and soul and are what I feel are crucial for my life. They are what I base everything in life on and what guides me every day. They define me, and how I behave and when I can, they drive my decision-making. My core values are based on honesty and truth, helpfulness and generosity of spirit, loyalty, respect, and compassion. I also believe in doing my best at all times and never hurting or letting anyone down. I developed these from an early age, and I think they are set so I can live the way Jesus wanted me to live.

These core values have contributed to much of the pain in my life. I have them fixed so strong, like concrete pillars holding up my personality, that when they are broken or questioned, I am deeply hurt. I find it hard to accept that my core values are very different from other people. Yet, to me anyway, most other people seem to live life the way they want, when I can't. I can't seem to be able to change or adapt these values, but I wish I could. I wish that they were not as strong so that so many external factors didn't hurt my mind. I can't stop these negative thoughts and actions from influencing my feelings and allowing my depression to grow. It is like whatever happens to me, hurts me, especially when my depression has more control. It doesn't matter how small it is. If it challenges my core values, it makes me feel worse, and I start questioning myself and then doubting and down the well I go.

It seems that I have little or no capacity to deal appropriately with external factors that affect me. I struggle to cope when I think that someone has let me down. They don't even have to do anything because I just perceive that they have. I feel hurt, betrayed, let down, and even angry. These feelings and thoughts easily find their way into the darkest recesses of my brain and just grow in influence on me. They stay there as they hurt me, and grow in strength every time they do. They influence me to think badly about myself like I am a useless failure and a fraud. It is a truly awful way to feel, especially when I don't think I can do anything to help myself, or don't have the energy to fight back.

We all should have strong coping skills, but mine are not what they should be. Coping skills are the methods a person uses to deal with stressful situations. These should help me face any issue in life, be able to comprehend the problem and work through it. Then I should be able to decide on the right course of action that will solve the puzzle, and then take that action. Coping skills allow us to solve problems and issues like this whenever they occur. None of this seems to work for me. I am a coward when it comes to coping, and the more depressed I get, the less I can even understand the problem, let alone do something to solve it. If the issue is simple, then most of the time, I cannot make my mind up what to do. When I struggle so much, I keep trying to train myself to let it filter right through my brain, no matter how long that takes. I often sleep on my problems and then see if I can understand it and work out a solution that I can manage. When I can't decide what to do or make my mind up, I get annoyed and frustrated with myself, which just allows my depression to gain a stronger hold.

I also know that I am overly sensitive, and this has been another cause of pain and misery for me. Many little things that others can deal with easily, seem to hurt or sadden me. I don't watch nature programs because I feel despondent when the predator catches and eats the prey. I feel sorry for the little animal and think about its family as if I was grieving for them. I don't read too much about tragedies. I feel awful when I read about them, so try to avoid them as much as I can. I can't read any reports of rape or sexual abuse, because that just makes me feel sorry for the victims and their families too. I just can't cope with that grief, and I fear that it will bring my own abuse sharply into focus. I am too soft to handle much of what daily life throws at me. I try to avoid any chance that I may be affected in this way, which helps make my isolation seem to be the best option I have.

I still believe in, and live by my own core values, even though it can seem like a magnet attracting all sorts of problems. I don't think my coping skills have strengthened at all, which is just another excuse to stay isolated, and away from and issues that I would have trouble dealing with. Yet I am coping reasonably well and trying my very best at the moment. Distractions and avoidance seem to be the best strategies I have, and they are doing what I expect them to.

I used to believe that no one was afflicted the same way I was. Therefore no one could understand me and no one could help me. I have learned that there is some truth to this because we are all truly unique, and that, without depression, is a wonderful thing. I now know that I am just one of many people who suffer from depression. While we are all different, our depression can vary from one person to the next. However, it is always similar and has the same overall effect – a feeling of sadness, uselessness, and hopelessness that you can truly only understand if you ever suffered from clinical depression.

The sadness can get so bad that it weighs me down like a ton of bricks. Eventually, it reaches a point where I feel so low that sadness or misery does not describe it any more. As it weighs down the mind, I get headaches and neck pains as if I was physically holding up those bricks. It is an almost unimaginable feeling that is so dark and deep, that it buries any chance of joy or happiness deep within the blackness. It is so bad that I feel that the darkness has enveloped my brain, blocking out any possibility of light, or anything that might cheer me up.

I honestly do hate the hopelessness associated with depression. It means that I believe that as the depression escalates, nothing in my life is going to improve, and neither is my depression. The whole future is bleak and nothing at all to look forward to, even if there is a lot of 'good' things on the horizon. I have often thought that I could predict the future, and it will be just as bad as it is now, or even worse. Nothing will change for the better. Of course, I cannot predict the future, or even what will happen in the next ten minutes, but my depression tries to convince me that its predictions are accurate and nothing positive will happen. It is what I believe no matter how many times I have lived with these same thoughts and recovered. I try my hardest to believe that that there is some happiness still to come, but sometimes it does not seem to be able to get through the darkness.

The hopelessness also contributes to my self-isolation. I might be open to doing something which involves leaving the house, but I then start to think of all the ways I could mess it up, and I convince myself I am better off staying in. It takes massive effort just to go shopping, but I make it that bit easier by going very early in the morning before I have the time to start thinking about it. If I do start thinking about it, I end up finding reasons not to go. Reasons that seem perfectly valid to me, but would seem silly to others. My mind, or depression, continually reminds me that I cannot be hurt when I am at home, so I am better off not going out at all. It does not always win but is always there nagging at me, trying to have me all to itself.

I can go days without talking to another person, even on the phone, but although I spend most of my time alone, I seldom feel lonely. I seem to manage this part of my life well enough, probably because I am so used to it now and because it is much easier than going out meeting people.

Then there is the acting and the lying. The intensity of the pretending required depends on the level of depression, and I always have to appear to be in good form when I meet anyone, even at family events. The more acting and lying I do, the more hurt I feel. On many occasions, I lie about how I feel, and that hurts me from my head to my heart. I start to feel guilty and ashamed of myself, but I keep up the acting and lying until I get home. Then I get reminded of what a disgraceful person I have become. When I get home to my 'safe place', the adrenalin rushes out of me, and I feel so physically and emotionally drained, that it hurts. I always feel awful about lying and guilty for telling lies. Yet, I cannot stop myself. I lie to ensure the conversation stays well away from my mental health. I am sometimes surprised at how that little phrase "I'm fine" can hurt me so much. Just a small lie, but a lie all the same and it leads to me questioning myself about why I could not be honest and tell the truth. I find the best way to stop this is to stay at home, which tries to block any motivation I have for going out.

I have often felt useless, no matter the situation, and only felt useful when I could see the results in my hand, like financial results in retail. I feel worthless when I don't do the things I wanted to do, or if I find mistakes in something I did. If anyone mentions anything about a job I am doing, I feel useless. It doesn't need to be criticism; it could just be a question or comment, and I feel worthless. Yet I needed constant reassurance and to be told that I did a good 'job' just to start to believe I am not useless. Sometimes it felt good achieving something, no matter how small, and I use that to help me fight my thoughts of uselessness.

I find that the more depressed I become, the less I enjoy anything. I always try to keep myself busy, to distract myself, but I am always searching for a little bit of enjoyment. I need that to prove to myself that I am alive, mentally and physically. Every time I watch a game or put on the tv, I am looking, or even hoping for something I can enjoy. The relief, or little boost, I get if I do like something, is like being lifted up on the wings of an angel. It is a very welcome feeling and one I need to keep going.

I have learned that the more depressed I was, the more irrational or illogical my thinking became. My upside-down logic would find ways to convince me that everything was my fault. Everything I do is wrong and a waste of my time. No matter what it is, it is wrong or my fault. It is like my depression controls my mind, my behaviour and my actions. The more control it has, the more irrational my thinking becomes. My depression wants full control of my mind. When it gets this, it tries to get me to take my life, and it makes suicide seem reasonable and logical. The thoughts were terrifying, but so real.

I have always lived with doubt and low self-esteem, but have learned to cover it up on most occasions. I was able to have some control over my emotions when I was working, or more accurately distracting myself from my problems, by burying myself in work. It did not matter what I was working on, once I was able to focus on that instead of myself. I always felt that my role in retail was just holding all the pieces and people together. I needed them more than they needed me. I am sure of that because I know that with my lack of self-esteem and confidence, I would not have tried to carry out the plans in my head. My doubt, lack of self-esteem, and self-belief worked to counteract any motivation I might have, by telling me that I can't do the task, or it too will be useless.

Even now I still struggle, because I have little respect or love for myself and as my depression worsens, I hate myself and everything I am or have been. Even the thought of being blessed with three wonderful and awesome sons turns into a fluke and reminds me of what a terrible Dad I have been. When severely depressed, I can't love them, or anyone. My depression takes this ability and locks it away in the darkness, where I cannot reach it. I believe that neither the boys nor even Mam and Dad have any love for me at all. After all, who would even like such a miserable failure and person? These horrible thoughts then have me thinking, that no one I ever met in my life likes me. As well as encouraging my isolation and deepening my depression, this does something else that I am terribly guilty and very sorry about. Like the Johnny Cash song "Hurt", all my friends have gone away, in a sense. It is more accurate to say that I have pushed them from me by not keeping in touch or staying in contact. When I do feel better, I still don't contact them because my guilt and depression convince me not to bother. I believe that because I have not kept in touch, they don't want to know me, and the feeling of me interrupting or interfering in their lives stops me from making any contact. There are also the thoughts that I don't want them to see what a failure and useless person I am. I make myself believe that they are truly better off without me in their lives at all.

Today, when not severely depressed, I still have limited confidence in my abilities, which tries to stop me from doing what I want to do. I am either going to make a mess of it or not finish it at all. That happens to me for even the simplest tasks and happens every day. I know that I have to keep going somehow, and it would be far worse and damaging to my mental health if I were to sit around doing nothing. That just lets my depression influence my thinking even more. That's what depression wants me to do, do nothing to occupy my thoughts, so that it can take more control of me.

I feel that I have been tired for 30 or maybe even 300 years, and it is not just the tiredness, but a weariness and a lack of energy, like the batteries are dead. I almost always get plenty of sleep, mostly 7-8 hours, and on the odd occasion even 10, but I never wake up feeling refreshed, or think that I had a good night's sleep. I wake up tired. It is a tiredness that I feel from my head to my toes and often leads to more headaches. I have no problem getting to sleep because I am so tired, but I still always use a trick I learned. I try to focus on something I saw on tv, like a movie, rugby or football match, or maybe something I read. I focus on analysing that, not my problems, and it works for me. I have become fascinated with space travel and often go to sleep imagining that I am piloting a spacecraft. This getting-to-sleep aid did take getting used to, but it works for me and helps me get my rest. As far as I am concerned, it helps turn my brain off for a while.

My major problem is that when I wake up, at maybe 3, 4, or 5 in the morning, I can't get back to sleep no matter how many movies, tv shows, or books I try to analyse.

My eyes feel so heavy and tired, but I cannot get back to sleep. Yet I can't get up out of the bed because I haven't enough energy and my depression want to 'have a word' first. It seems that the depressive part of my brain wakes up with a vigour and enthusiasm that I would love to have. It wastes no time in stressing me out and making me anxious about what lies ahead for me. Then after a while, I feel that I can get up. I have set myself a morning routine that I follow every morning. It is what I do to stop thinking. Thinking stops me from doing anything. Once I have had my breakfast, I have to start doing something before my brain stops me, and I keep going like that all day until around lunchtime. From then on, the tiredness becomes so bad that I can't do any more little jobs, and I have to rest. I get through the day by avoiding thinking as much as I can, thus limiting the influence of my depression.

The jobs or list of tasks in my head every morning, have to be done, or else I feel useless and a failure again. My brain bangs around in my head, telling me what I have to do. It becomes an urge as if it was a matter of life and death to me. I don't often get my list finished before I get too tired, and I have to try to convince myself that there is always tomorrow. I put so much pressure on myself and always have done. Even at work, the most pressure I felt, came from my mind, and not any bosses. The pressure I put myself under just leads to more stress, and that only feeds my depression.

My favourite sport to follow is rugby, particularly Leinster and Ireland, but as the depression takes hold, I don't get much joy from watching them on TV. Not even brilliant scores or tackles can pique my interest. It is like I am indifferent or have no feelings whatsoever for the game at all. It becomes like other sports that I don't like. I watch every game I can so that I might get some enjoyment. Sometimes I just turn it off, because I get frustrated with myself when I cannot generate any real interest. I know I do enjoy the games when I am in good form and get excited many times with the action playing out on TV. There is not much that cheers me up more than Leinster or Ireland scoring a try. I find that no other game has the same interest, intensity, and excitement for me. I also enjoy the hurling, especially the Munster championship and the All-Irelands. While the game is so fast and physical, I admire the skill levels of all the players at the top level. They score points from miles out and crazy angles, and I imagine them as snipers shooting from a long-range rifle. The game is very physical too, and the tackling is ferocious but fantastic to watch. It can be very entertaining and enjoyable to watch when I am in the right 'mood'. I do watch some of the Premier League soccer games on TV, but the difference is noticeable when I watch one after the rugby or hurling.

It is hard for me to have an interest in anything, not only sport. I used to love all the little jobs I had to do around the house, especially in the garden. I found it enjoyable and relaxing when the sun was shining. Now it has become more of a chore, and I find it difficult to enjoy myself like I once did. I find it hard to focus and concentrate on what

I am doing and cannot generate any interest. It is always hard for me to motivate myself to do anything at all, especially if I have given myself time to think. My motivation comes from the hope that I might enjoy it, and the knowledge of what I will feel like if I don't do it. Many times, I have to bribe myself into doing anything. I often promise myself a coffee, maybe with a biscuit or a bun, if I get a particular job finished. Other times, I promise myself a movie. It does work to get me started on something, and once I do begin, I like to get finished. Depression takes the joy out of everything I do, and that is why I feel it is not interesting.

I have been and still am affected by weak memory, and that too can be very frustrating. I have found that my memory tends to be quite useless when I am severely depressed. There are times when I struggle to remember things that should be safely tucked away in my short-term memory banks. For example, when watching rugby, the commentator often comments on the last match. I know I watched it, yet I can't remember anything about it. I get frustrated and annoyed with myself, and on and on it goes. It seems that the slightest thing can upset me or deepen my depression. My long-term memory is just as bad, and I often find I cannot remember specific events. That annoys me when people talk about them, and I have no idea what they are talking about, even if I was there.

I find it hard to concentrate on books. I often find that I am reading something that has no context for me, and I can't remember what was leading up to this part of the story. Generally, my mind is trying hard to interrupt me and get me to focus on my problems or my failings. I prefer to read shorter articles where I can concentrate until the end. Even watching a movie can cause me the same issues, and I have to focus hard and try not to think of myself. Strangely enough, I have no problem reading books when I go on holiday and can follow the story easily enough. I believe that it is because I can relax, and can therefore concentrate properly.

I cannot relax at all because my brain won't stop, except when I go away to Caleta De Fuste in Fuerteventura. I have been going there for several years now, and it is like an escape for me or a release from my personal prison. There I can enjoy the hot sun, the lovely walk along the Atlantic Ocean, and it is the only place I can read books and enjoy them. My mind gives up telling me all the things I have to do because I simply cannot do them over there. I can't do the garden or painting or anything like that, so there is nothing I can do but relax. I can't do that at home, even on the sunniest of days. I have to be doing something or worrying about what I have to do and what I am not doing. So, I just love to get away to relax, get some sun, and enjoy the lovely walks in the much cleaner air in Fuerteventura. It is such a fantastic feeling when I can kind of shut my brain down for a while and not be stressed, anxious, or sad. I love it so much that I try to get away at least twice a year. It blows the cobwebs from the darkness in my brain, and I always feel a lot better for it.

As my depression worsens, the only thing that feels real to me is that I am dead inside. Valerie always used to say that she could see my depression taking over when she noticed my eyes. She described them as dark and lifeless. The saying 'the eyes are the window to the soul' is right, and what she could see was the darkness inside me. Many times, when driving, I drove like a lunatic. I went at very high speeds on small country roads and flew like a rocket on motorways. I was driving well above any speed limit in force. I wasn't doing it to get anywhere at a particular time; I was doing it to try to feel alive. I would have to concentrate as hard as I could and focus on my driving and the road. The adrenalin would kick in and give me a boost, and I would get excited. I would turn the radio up high to blare the music and force me alive inside, and I did feel something awake in me. It was like self-harm or self-medicating and just as risky, but it was giving me some relief, so I kept doing it. But like everything else, when I got back into traffic, I had to slow down. I felt as bad as ever, so maybe it was not worth the risk, but I could not see that at the time.

Worry is something I cannot remember living without, and it is with me always. Even during the mild stages, I worry about everything, even about worry itself. I worry about the boys all the time, but I am sure every parent does that. I worry about Valerie all the time, as well as my parents and extended family, I worry about all the tasks I have in mind and whether I will get them done correctly or at all. I worry about every single thing in my life, and the only way I can control this is by distracting myself and trying to focus on something else or give myself something to look forward to.

Going hand in hand with the constant worrying about every little thing is my anxiety. I get anxious about everything, like going to the shops and even family events. They fill me with dread and fear. I get so nervous and apprehensive that it is as if I was about to get executed. They help me isolate myself away from the world that has me so anxious. It is a daily battle, trying to overcome my anxieties. I do try to live with them, but I feel that I have to build up my confidence and self-esteem first. Then I might be able to go out, meet people, and nullify some of my anxieties. Like everything else about me, it depends on how I feel.

These are not the only symptoms that feed into my ever-decreasing circle. I can get annoyed and irritable very quickly, and I have become ultra-aware of myself. I try to keep calm and explain to myself that getting annoyed or irritated is no good for me. Sometimes it works, but other times I have to find something to do, to distract myself so that I can calm down. It is far too easy to let my annoyance or frustration worsen the way I feel, so I try to stay in control and not let anything upset my balance.

That is what depression does to me. All these things are the symptoms of my illness. Together, they make up my depression. One symptom feeds and strengthens another, and it feeds or enables another, and on and on it goes. Each symptom, pushes down the next, on the ever-decreasing circle down the well into Hell. The lower down this well I go, the worse I feel all over, and the closer I get to that exit at the bottom. Suicide is not my Hell. Being severely depressed is. Sometimes, I think that I am not afraid of Hell, because I have lived there for so long.

I refer to depression as "it" simply because I can't call it him or her. It is not a person. It is something intangible that I can never see but feel inside my brain and my soul. It is not my friend in any way. A friend would not hurt me so much. Neither is it, my enemy, because it is not a person. It is an illness, just like many other illnesses we encounter, except that I think it causes much more pain and misery. It is an illness that seems to be able to influence me by exerting some kind of control over my thinking. It is a combination of all my 'bad' feelings that sometimes have, unlimited power over me. Its goal is to control the way I feel, behave and act completely. It is a sad, miserable 'it'. It is real, as real as the wind we cannot see, and I genuinely wish I never had it

When we are depressed, we are advised to talk to someone, and I agree with that, especially if anyone is experiencing thoughts of suicide. I don't believe that anyone can manage and treat their depression on their own, yet we all try to. I know I can't. How could it work when I think irrationally and believe what my depressed and illogical mind tries to tell me? I often think about the days and weeks before I was diagnosed, and I am sorry that I did not go and get help there and then. Maybe it would have led me to a happier and better life.

Talking does help because sometimes we don't understand or believe what we are experiencing until we say it out loud, and hear the words for ourselves. That on its own can bring some relief. It might also help us understand what we are going through and what can be done to help. Not only is talking helpful, but it is also necessary if you want to let someone know what is bothering you, and absolutely crucial if you want to get professional help and support.

Research shows that a combination of anti-depressant medication and psychotherapy is the quickest and most effective treatment for depression. However, it is essential to understand that anti-depressants are not a cure for depression. They are more of a stabilizer, working on trying to normalize the chemical imbalance in the brain associated with depression. When depressed, we have a low output or level of vital chemicals, like serotonin, and the anti-depressants try to bring these levels back to normal. The anti-depressants, therefore, help ease our depression and allow us to feel better. They can help us think more clearly and rationally, and this makes therapy easier because we can better describe what we are experiencing. I am on the highest doses of anti-depressants allowed, and it is hard to see if they are working. But I am still here and functioning, and I'm sure my chemical imbalance would be totally out of whack without them, and I would feel far more depressed.

It does not matter if you prefer to talk to someone you trust and feel comfortable with first, rather than a medical professional, because you will get it off your chest and relieve some of the tremendous pressure in your head. Then hopefully, they will help you get to a doctor or psychiatric professional. Going to someone to talk about your deepest feelings can be daunting, but it is the only way to battle depression and get rid of suicidal thoughts. Talking to a medical or psychiatric professional is also the only way to access anti-depressants and therapy. It is always much easier if you have someone with you. It is like having crutches to help you walk. They guide and support you and do the rational thinking that you can't seem to do. It makes this frightening first step a lot more manageable, but you have to talk first and ask for their help. Otherwise, no one will know what you are struggling with.

The best, and unfortunately, sometimes the only option, is to go to see your GP and at least you can talk openly, and maybe get started on anti-depressants. It may not be the cure you need, but it is far better than nothing, or the other alternative -suicide. It is a start to your healing process and often works for many people, especially when depression is treated early.

As for myself, I feel a fraud right now. I would like to think that I am encouraging people to talk and seek help when they first start thinking they have depression, or when they start having thoughts of suicide. Yet I don't speak to anyone except my psychiatrist and doctor. I am ok talking to the psychiatrists because that is what they are there for. However, with Doctor Neary, I am reluctant to speak to him about my depression or how I feel, especially when I slip into the moderate or severe level. I don't want him to think or feel he has failed me. I just feel like more of a failure. I have to be pretty desperate before I am candid with him. I do think that I have let him down.

I don't talk to the boys, my Mam and Dad, or my family about my depression because I don't want to hurt them anymore or have them worry about me. I do enough of that for all of us. I have put them all, especially the boys, through so much pain that there is no way I am going to add to that. I have been like this for so long, that I am now used to bottling things up in my head, even though I know it will explode back at me, whenever my depression worsens, just like all the distractions I use to get me through the day. I know it won't help cure my depression, but it keeps it at bay for a while, and I'm happy about that. I am learning, though. I ring the psychiatric clinic if ever I feel I am slipping and ask them to help me. It works for me.

Chapter 12

Home

The Sunday morning, in September, after Mam, Dad and Noel arrived in London, they, along with Valerie and the boys, came to the psychiatric ward of the Greenwich District Hospital and collected me. They had lifts arranged from Valerie's family, and we drove under the River Thames to the City Airport. Before I knew it, we were all on a plane flying home to Ireland. It all seemed to happen so fast, maybe because I was still in a daze. I was returning home a failure. I had let everyone in my life down. Now my Mam, Dad and Noel had been dragged into the trouble of my own making. I wouldn't say I liked that, and I did not know what to expect, or what would happen when I got home.

Once home, everybody was tremendously helpful, and I got to laugh for the first time in ages. We were in Noel's house, and I was just sitting there in a world of my own, not involved in the conversation or anything. Noel just put my new niece, Lilly, on my lap. I had a tiny baby in my arms, that could not look after herself, so I had to look after her. She was smiling at me, so I smiled back and then started playing with her. Yes, it was a distraction, a big positive one. We played, she laughed, and I laughed. Not a false or forced laugh, but a laugh. A laugh that I missed. A laugh that I did not remember having for ages. A laugh that brightened my mood. A miracle laugh!

I don't remember where we stayed at first, but I think it was in Ballsgrove. Anne Lennon got me registered with a local doctor, who has been fantastic to me ever since, a psychiatrist who was older than Methuselah, who was no help to me at all, and Alan, a tremendously helpful therapist. When I met Anne in the hospital, I was very anxious and as nervous as I had been at my wedding, but she was able to calm me down. Somehow, we ended having a walk down to casualty and where the clinic was, but it had all changed. Shine's room, the cubicles, the palm tree, and even the little entrance that was outside the clinic area, were all knocked down and replaced. It was all new to me, and the main thought in my head then was that I could not prove where my abuse had happened. Just like my Granny's house was gone, the place of my abuse was gone, and I felt I needed that to prove my case against Shine.

I could not work out if the fact that everybody was doing everything for me like I was a little child was the best for me at the time. It was another thing I spent too much time overthinking and getting nowhere. I could not even decide or make my own decision on that. They were right, of course, I was too fragile, confused, and depressed to do anything myself, and I was so lucky to have them on my side. I was home though, and that helped, but not being able to walk very far or do much for myself was a problem for me. The blood clots on my lungs had affected me physically, and I struggled to walk any distance at all. I needed a little motivation to try to get back to the Peter I liked and had loved sometimes. I needed something to help me tackle one of my biggest enemies and threats to my mental health, - my overthinking when I have nothing to distract me. When that happens, life looks far bleaker than it actually is, the future looks terrifying, and the day to day pain continues non-stop. As far as I could see, nothing was happening with the case. When I reached out looking for answers or progress, I got nothing back. I even wrote a letter of complaint to the Garda complaints board about Superintendent O'Boyle and his accusations of collusion, and him deciding not to send the files of complaints to the DPP. For once somebody wrote back to me within a reasonable time, but it was not with good news. My complaint was deemed as inadmissible because it was not within a six months' time limit and the fact that Superintendent O'Boyle had retired.

We rented a private house on Trinity Street in Drogheda, which was very close to the town centre, and I had started visiting with Alan once a week. My new Doctor, Paul

Neary, had me visit him regularly, so he could monitor my progress following the blood clots, and get to know me a bit more. I went to see the psychiatrist a few times since I got home, but if you add it all up, it was less than 10 minutes in total. He just asked what medication I was on and then said make an appointment for next week. Dr Neary though was much more interested in me, and because of my poor physical condition after the blood clots, suggested that I try a Back to School program. Wow I thought, I had never considered that, and when I left the doctor's that day, I went straight over to St Peter's Parochial Centre where he told me the back-to-school programme was based. I qualified due to long-term sickness. I was accepted and started a week or so later, and it turned out to be a huge blessing for me and a great help in fighting my depression. Maybe again, it was the distraction that I needed. I always knew that overthinking was no good for me, yet I still did it. I couldn't help myself unless I was distracted like when playing with Lily or concentrating on my studies. Every time I tried to analyse a problem, I ended up with two, then four, then more, and so on— each one causing more pain and anguish on top of the last. I was aware that it was almost impossible to reach a happy or satisfying conclusion when analysing your own problems when depressed. It never ends well and, in my case, deepens my depression, or forces me further down that well.

Yet the Shine case was never far from my mind. It seemed to me that nothing was happening, and all I could do was write letters to try to get something moving. Nowadays, there is a lot of talk of cover-ups in public scandals, but back then, I was very concerned about cover-ups regarding the investigation against Shine. I had heard a rumour that there were two complaints of sexual assaults against Shine in the 1970s. I thought this was crucial evidence in the case, and I thought that maybe the hospital or even the Gardai were trying to cover it up. I wrote to the Gardai with this information, and with a suggestion of someone else they should talk to about Shine. The ward sister at the time, Sister Culligan was brilliant at her job. She was the one who admitted patients from the general waiting area to the clinic waiting room, and she knew exactly what was going on everywhere during every moment of her shift. In the clinic waiting room one day, we even giggled when she caught two student nurses laughing. She knew something was going on from 50 yards away. My thinking was that Nurse Culligan knew that Shine was excluding the nurses when he met some patients, especially the minors. I was also sure that she knew something about what was going on in those cubicles. She was in absolute control of Casualty and the clinic, and even if she did not know exactly what was going on, she surely must have questioned this in her mind. I don't know whether I was completely naive, or stupid, or just clutching at straws, but to this day, as far as I know anyway, these issues were ever raised or investigated.

I also thought about the nurse that Shine prevented from entering the cubicle that first time. I wondered what she thought at the time, and whether she and the other nurses knew, or maybe speculated or gossiped, about what was going on in the cubicles when Shine was alone with a young boy. I had also passed comment on this to the Independent Review Group, and to this day, I cannot understand why no one ever came forward, and I guess the Gardai never interviewed any of them.

The Gardai never replied to my letter. The only good news I got regarding the case that year was that Shine had to take an immediate leave of absence when he returned to work in August and then retired in October. At last, one of my goals had been reached. I am not sure if this good bit of news would have stopped my suicide attempt in August, but I think that it may have made me think again.

I believe that Valerie and the boys were delighted to be home, even if Simon was too young to remember living here, and Lee had never lived in Ireland. During my good times, when my depression left me alone for a while, we had come back to Drogheda for a holiday and to meet everyone. Most of the time I had been home, I was dealing with some crap from the Shine case. Once home now for good, we managed to get Wayne into St Mary's, my old secondary school, and he settled in there very well. It was much easier and quicker for him to get to school and back, except that he had to walk all the way. But that didn't seem to bother him at all. He also had the bonus of being excluded from learning Irish, which delighted him. We knew that Wayne was intelligent from an early age, and his school reports backed this up. I think that made it easier for him to adapt to his new school and living back in Ireland. He quickly made good friends and settled into living in Drogheda again.

Simon and Lee were accepted into the primary school in Congress Avenue, and did very well there, except maybe in the first week when a few boys were slagging off and picking on Lee over his English accent. That ended very quickly when Simon stepped in, and there was never a hint of trouble anymore. That was Simon, Lee's protector. I was called up to the school, and even though the Principal said that Lee was harassed, they thought Simon's response was over the top. I replied that he was just defending his brother, and if anyone should be punished, it should be the bullies. Simon was not punished, and we never heard about it again. Any school report we got for the three boys were excellent, and it was clear that they loved being back 'home.'

The only other little bit of trouble Simon and Lee got into was one day they were playing football out the back of the house, and they kicked the ball into the neighbour's garden. The woman of the house took the ball and told these little boys to go back to England where they came from. Simon cheeky and quick as ever, said that they were home and this is where they were from. I was actually at the back door and witnessed this and told her to mind her own business. I have never liked racism, and I have never taken kindly to anyone interfering with my children in any way. Unfortunately, there were a few cases of this in London, where the boys had harassed. I was never afraid to go to the parents or even chase older lads when they picked on the boys. Mostly they played in peace, but much of that had to do with neighbours of ours. They caught a lad who was trying to set up a drug-dealing area for himself in the children's playground. They put him standing on the roof of a car and put a noose around his neck, and threw the other end over the lamp post. I heard all the commotion and went to investigate and got a huge shock when I turned the corner and seen this guy hanging from the lamp post. He was screaming and crying, but nobody was trying to save him. They revved the car and inched it forward so that only the tips of his trainers were touching the car and the noose stifled his cries. Eventually, they cut him loose and told him what would happen if he or any of his mates ever came near this part of the estate again. I think he got the message. I thought Drogheda was different and did not expect that my boys would be subject to racism or abuse like this, but it seems like I was just naive.

Valerie seemed very happy too, taking up little part-time jobs, and we were a family again. The strange thing is, the more my mental health improved, the more my guilt increased. As the depression eased, I could think clearly. I felt very guilty for what I had put Valerie and the boys through, over the past number of years, and guilty for letting them see me in such a condition. I didn't look after them the way I promised or gave them the life they deserved. I could never be sure the boys even loved me and always thought they deserved better.

Early in 1997, I got the good news that the Director of Public Prosecutions had decided to prosecute Shine for indecent assault. I wasn't sure what indecent assault meant in legal terms, but I didn't care once he was going on trial. A few other people had made complaints against Shine following articles in the local paper. It had taken almost three years since I made the complaint, but at last, something was happening, and I started to dream that it would be all over soon. That was great news as far as I was concerned. The case was set for the local District Court, and I made every effort to attend in the Old Hill Hall, whenever I could. It was early that year that the case was first mentioned in the court.

Shine was there, and it was the first time I had seen him since 1980. It was tough, but I did manage a good look. He looked older and frailer and to me. He still had a smug look on his face, even though he mostly kept his head bowed down. I could not imagine why he looked so arrogant as if he knew something I didn't. He just sat there as if he was waiting for some appointment, and that unnerved me. As soon as it was called, the solicitors had their say, and the case was adjourned. It was all over in a flash, and the complaints weren't mentioned. That was a bit of a shock to me. Throughout the year it was adjourned more times than I can remember, before it was suspended again, to allow Shine's request a judicial review of the case in the High Court. I didn't know anything about the legal system, and I could not understand how the case was mentioned, and then adjourned all the time. It seemed to me like everyone was treating it like some trivial matter and not the serious charge I thought it was.

That only had me questioning the Gardai and the judicial system even more. I could not directly fault any of the Gardai involved in the case, except O'Boyle. He had accused me of collaboration with another witness, and then, as far as I knew, decided there was no case to answer, and did not bother to forward the case to the DPP. On top of that, he did not deliver the complaint to the hospital or the North Eastern Health Board. I thought at that time that none of the Gardai involved had any real experience in dealing with cases of sexual assault. Maybe I was wrong, but I had the feeling that they were learning as they went along. I am a massive fan of 'learning by doing', but I don't believe that the senior Gardai on the case should have been in charge if they had no similar experience. I also felt that the Gardai involved in the case were useless at keeping their word and terrible at keeping the victims, up to date with the progress of the case from day one. That was an awful aspect of the whole case, and in my vulnerable mental state, I kept thinking the worse, like the case did not involve me anymore, or that no one believed my story. It just caused me a lot more pain and meant that I was always mentally vulnerable to any negative influences on my brain. I did notice though, on a couple of occasions, that it was the Ward Sister Culligan, who collected Shine from the court. That just made me think even more, and I was sure that she knew precisely what Shine was doing to young boys. The state solicitor prosecuting the case at the time seemed useless to me, and one day was not even there when the case was called, so it was just adjourned. I went to see him in his office one day to complain, and when I walked in the front door, I could hear him on the phone in his office as his door was open. He was ranting and raving at someone on the phone. I know it's rude and not very honest of me, but I strained to listen and hear. I got the feeling it was somebody who had been abused by Shine, Then I heard him tell the person on the phone to fuck off, and he hung up. I did not stay after that as I knew I was wasting my time. I didn't leave it at that though. I wrote a letter of complaint about him to the Director of Public Prosecutions, but no one there even bothered to reply.

Victim support got involved and always let me know what happened in the case with Shine when I was not able to make it myself, but it was the same news every time- adjourned, adjourned, adjourned. In reality, the only thing that happened in the whole year concerning the case was that all complainants were to be examined by a court-appointed psychologist. Later that year, I met with Alex Carroll, the appointed psychologist, and had a long full session with him. I always tried my hardest to keep the abuse out of my head, because it caused me nothing but pain and misery. Still, when I was talking to the psychologist, the images and memory flooded my head like it happened the day before, just like the first time I told Leslie. Again, once I started, it just flowed out, an unstoppable flow of words that would not stop until I finished everything I had to say. I had made my complaint again, to someone different, yet with all the same details. I felt good after that. I thought I had proved myself, and my complaint would be believed now. I was sure that this was beneficial to the case, and it would all be over soon. How many times have I felt that?

Another major thing happened that year. Detective Pat O'Donnell, who had taken over the case after Superintendent O'Boyle, retired and the case passed to Detective Pat O'Neill. The new Superintendent Doggett was taking a very keen interest. O'Neill was the third different lead Garda in charge and someone else to try to 'rely on' to push the case forward. Maybe it was a time for hope, but again, this relied on others and not myself, and carried the same danger of failing me.

As the weeks passed, I was feeling a lot better. I was still visiting Dr Neary regularly and had weekly counselling sessions with Alan. It helped too that I thought the case might be moving at last. Studying was helping me also, and I was starting to feel kind of normal again. We got our own house, rented from a housing authority, in Rowan Heights, Drogheda, and that set us up brilliantly. It was a new house, well built, with a front garden and a decent sized back garden and plenty of room, much more than the house on Trinity Street. Things were going so well for us, that I had the idea once again, that all my mental health problems were a thing of the past. The boys loved the new house, the space, and their new rooms. Wayne got a small room of his own. Simon and Lee shared their bedroom and had lots of room for everything they had. The estate itself was lovely and clean, with no through road, which meant little or no traffic and plenty of peace and quiet. The boys could play out the front on the green like I did when I was young, and they had a real sense of freedom in and out of the house. I think the most common phrase for me became 'shut the front door', but it was brilliant, a new start for all of us, and hopefully, I would never 'fuck it up again'. We knew most of the new neighbours because we had to attend a course before receiving the keys. Wayne made an immediate impact because he became the babysitter of choice, and was always in demand at the weekends, which gave him plenty of cash for himself. We had a home now, and one we were delighted with. We were delighted to get visitors to a home with space and comfort, but most of all, the boys were thrilled and even closer to their schools.

Going back to education was a real boost for me and my mental health. I made new friends very quickly and even met some I had known before. I went to classes five mornings a week and quickly settled in. The course was a year-long certificate in social studies, and I studied information technology, economics, psychology, politics, sociology, and maths. I was a much better student than I was back in secondary school, and every week I found it easier to walk the distance to the course without a break. My physical strength was improving, which was a big plus for my mental health too. I found the subjects quite interesting, except for politics, and found that I was able to manage them easily enough. What was even more important to me, was that I was able to help others that were struggling especially with maths, psychology, and economics. It was the first time in ages I felt that I was of some value to somebody else, and it thrilled me. I do not doubt that going back to education helped my family and me. We were getting on well. Everyone loved Drogheda compared to London, and maybe, just maybe, I might have a decent future after all. I had no plans for the future or what I wanted to do with myself, and just wanted to do the course as best I could, and then see what happened. Just like back at secondary school, except I was putting the effort in, but wary of making any mistake this time, or taking any job I could not handle.

As part of information technology and communications, I had to apply to colleges and universities. I had no plans to go to college, but I put maximum effort into this project, not to get a place in college, but because that is the way I am. I also wanted to keep up the good results I was getting on the course. I applied to various universities and colleges and gave them all to the teacher. I thought no more about them, just like all the other assignments I had completed. Then early in 1998, I received a letter from Trinity College in Dublin inviting me for an interview and an aptitude test. Me going to university seemed about as far removed as me becoming an astronaut. Still, I discussed it with Valerie and the boys, and I decided to go for the interview and the aptitude test and see what happened. I took the aptitude test one Saturday morning, and though I found it very difficult, I felt that I did ok. I did get most of the questions answered.

A short time after that, I had to attend Trinity for the interview. Luckily enough, it was the same day as a trip booked to visit Leinster House. I was able to travel with them on the bus to Dublin. I had no interest in visiting Leinster House. At the interview, the Dean of the Economics Department, I can't remember her name, was asking the questions. The first thing she asked me was why I had picked Bess (Business Economics and Social Studies) and not psychology, and I replied that I did not see myself having a career in psychology. I was happy with the interview and thought that I handled myself quite well, which was unusual for me. I guess it was because I did not believe that I was going to go to Trinity, so I had nothing to lose. I was able to answer all the questions and not freeze and come up with the correct response hours later. That is something I am good at, even in everyday conversations with people I meet. I get my head in such a tizzy and blurt out things before my brain wakes up, and then I regret what I said, and that only leads to more annoyance and frustration on my part.

In May, the social studies course was nearly over, and I was feeling physically ready to look for a new job. I just had the end of year exams to do, and then I would be finished. I had no idea what I was going to do or what kind of career I wanted. I received another letter from Trinity College, informing me that I was accepted as a mature student on their Business and Economics course. I had almost forgotten about Trinity. I was not expecting this at all. I began to think hard, and I discussed it with Valerie and the boys. Valerie was very supportive, and I think the boys were even impressed. No one in my family had ever been to university, and while it would be a financial struggle, it was a massive opportunity. I concluded that if I did not accept the place, I would regret it for the rest of my life, and I had enough regrets already. Valerie agreed, and the boys thought it was cool. I wrote back, accepting the place, and the new exciting challenge education would bring. I finished my exams in social studies and got marvellous results in everything, even politics, and I set myself up getting ready for college.

That summer, I took on a couple of summer jobs to build up some cash for going to university. I sat down with the boys and explained that going to college would be difficult for all of us. I told them that I had no idea how much work I would have to do at home, but I guessed a lot, and that money was going to continue to be tight for the years ahead. I explained how that would mean that I would have less time to spend with them, but that I would do whatever I could to be with them. They were just delighted for me and wanted to support me in any way they could. We started to go and play snooker, once a week if the boys were free, and it became our own special few hours. The way each of the boys approached the game was an accurate description of their approach to life.

Wayne was careful, considerate, and examined all his options before taking the shot. Everything was deliberate and precise, and he knew what he wanted and was delighted when shots worked out for him. Simon was a different kettle of fish. He would mess about trying to distract his opponent from taking a shot, no matter if it was me, Wayne, or Lee. But when Simon was taking a shot, none of us was allowed to move or take a breath. Then he was very serious and put in so much effort to get what he wanted. He had to succeed. He did make us laugh, and I think he enjoyed that just as much as the snooker. Lee thought it was brilliant being out with his older brothers, especially Wayne, and playing the game with us all. I don't think it mattered that it was snooker once we were all out together having a laugh. Lee always seemed to change personalities when he left the house. At home, he was quite noisy, but when he left the house, he was quiet within himself and a bit reserved—a bit like changing from an extrovert to an introvert. While Simon would be annoyed and disappointed if he missed a decent chance, Lee didn't care as he would get an opportunity again. Simon so wanted to impress, and Lee was just happy to be there and involved.

Chapter 13

College Life

In 1998 the Shine case almost ground to a halt. I got a reply from the letter I wrote to the DPP from the Chief State Solicitor. He told me that the state solicitor knew Mr Shine and he was recusing himself from the case. Sometimes my intuition amazed me, but it was still a shock to learn that my thoughts on the old boy's network were not a complete fabrication. Yet I wondered why it had taken him a year to admit this. A lot of time was wasted by Shine's legal team in the High Court, and even when I thought that we would be moving on soon, they threw another spanner in the works. This time, even though we had met with a court-appointed psychologist, they insisted that we were assessed by their consultant psychiatrist Dr McCarthy. So, I just saw that as more delays, and it felt like it would never start properly let alone end.

I found TCD to be a fantastic new experience from the moment I got there. I turned up as requested for Fresher's

Week, the week before classes started, to register. I immediately met with lots of other mature students. The mature
student society had some drink and food organised, and
we got to chat, and I was able to find out who would be
studying the same course as myself. It turned out to be a
fair few, and many of them became great friends throughout the following years. I met Joe, who was working as a
bouncer in Dublin city to help pay his way through college, and he turned out to be my best friend in college,
and outside too. We did a lot of studying together, and
he was the positive influence that helped me keep my
negative thoughts and feelings at bay. He was great craic
too, always cheerful, but determined to take the fantastic
opportunity to study at a world-renowned university and
get a good degree. He was just what I needed. I also met
Mary, who was a year ahead of me in college but came
along to meet the new batch of mature students. That
was her – kind to a fault and willing to help anyone she
could. She became our guide through college and lectures, as she had been there for a year already. I could
always go to her or Joe and ask them anything, especially
when the work piled up, and I was not sure that I would
ever get it done. There were plenty more I met that night
that became good friends and someone I could rely on
to help me through this exciting but nerve-racking new
challenge. I felt fortunate to have them and privileged to
have the chance to study at Trinity.

College itself started with a bit of a bang, as anyone who
did not take on honour's maths for the leaving certificate,

basically had two weeks to catch up. Making so many friends so early helped me really settle in quickly, and as a group, we got on brilliantly with the other students who had just sat their leaving certificates that year. The first four weeks flew past and then we were off for a week, for reading week. The day we finished, I was talking to Joe and Mary and the others, commenting on how far behind I was already, but they told me that everyone was behind. It's just the way it was, but I had a reading week to try to catch up. They were a great bunch of friends, and I love the way they supported each other and then organised a get together for Christmas or when the summer exams were over. I loved those nights out, drank too much, and had a great time. I used to get the late bus home but missed it most nights, and Joe took me to stay in his house. I am sure that he made me miss the bus on purpose, but I enjoyed going out with all of them. When we got back to Joe's at 2 or 3 in the morning, his mother would get up and make us a fry. My Mother never did that. Yet, I still had issues with my self-esteem and my confidence in my own abilities. I wanted to do well. I was never going to be top of the class, but I had this opportunity and did not want to waste it. I wasn't exactly sure how to study correctly, but I knew by looking at my notes when I got home, that I would not be able to read or remember them in a few weeks or months. So, the way I studied was, I rewrote my notes clearly every single night and then made a go at my homework, and then assignment work. It helped me feel confident that I had the right information, and that I knew what the subject was about. If I wasn't sure when I was rewriting my notes, I would spend time working on it until I knew. That was quite common with the technical parts of maths and economics, but I worked hard at it. I continued to do a little bit of work on the weekends, delivering Chinese food and working in the Whitworth Hall Amusement Centre and tried hard to keep up my snooker dates with the boys.

In Rowan Heights, Wayne continued his cushy little number babysitting for the neighbours. There were a few locally, who found Wayne to be excellent with their children and very reliable. He enjoyed it too because it got him out of the house and put some money in his pocket. When he felt he got too old to babysit, instead of going out with his mates, Simon stepped into the breach and became the babysitter of choice for many of our neighbours. It turned out that he was excellent with young children and was very popular with them. He was delighted to spend time with the kids and earn some money of his own for the first time. Some other evenings he would come with me when I was doing the deliveries for the Chinese, and he always got far more tips than I did. He loved to remind me of that. He was about 12 years of age when he started babysitting and one night when I was in the house, and Valerie was working, five different neighbours came to the door one after the other looking for Simon. When I told them that he was already babysitting, they were all disappointed and told me how brilliant he was with the children. I was chuffed to hear that, and as Simon got older, I could see that he had a very special place in his heart for all those younger than him, especially Lee and those he used to look after.

Some of these kids often came knocking on the door to see if Simon would go out and play with them. If he was there, he did, and the little kids loved that, and I think they loved Simon too. Joe gave him some weights that he didn't want anymore, and at last, Simon found a form of exercise that he loved. Simon and Lee took part in sports at school, but not much outside it, while Wayne was far more academic than sporty. Simon put the weights in his bedroom and used them regularly. He was always fit-looking, but he developed a very strong athletic build that suited him. Lee would play with the weights an odd time but did not become as dedicated as Simon.

For all my subjects in the first year of college, I had exams before Christmas, then before Easter, and then the final year exams in May. I enjoyed all my subjects except maybe sociology. I could not accept that shopping centres, cathedrals and churches somehow represented sex, so I skipped a lot of these classes. Thankfully I kept up with the notes, which I used to get off other mature students. Nevertheless, I was enjoying this whole new experience, even if I had to work very hard to keep up, and I had made a lot of new friends and was meeting new people every day. The other great thing about Trinity was that no one, from the professors to the students, and everyone in between, ever tried to look down or belittle me. While we were all from different backgrounds and different places, we were all in the same boat now, so to speak, and I really felt that.

Early the following year, Mr Justice Geoghegan in the High Court, refused Shines application for a judicial review. I had managed to get to the High Court for the judge's decision, and I was delighted with the outcome at first, and everyone in the court was cheering and clapping until the judge told us to behave and be quiet. The joy did not last though, as Mr Shine's solicitors served notice of appeal to the Supreme Court, which was in effect another delay allowable by law. I was sure he had his legal team instructed to keep the case away from an actual criminal trial. Especially as the Director of Public Prosecutions had just decided that they wanted Shine prosecuted in the Circuit Court and not the local District Court. All I could think about was how long was this thing going to go on. It was almost five years since the date of my first statement, to the judge's decision in the High Court, and we were no closer to a trial. Victim Support was still involved and observing procedures, as well as trying to help us, but on some occasions like this one, I just couldn't be helped. I was angry, very angry with this legal process, and it was still tough to get any information from anyone. I am sorry to say that sometimes I took my anger out on those from victim support, but they never deserved that. They were there to help in any way they could, and support the victims of Shine. I always apologized with a note or something, and they were always very kind about it. However,

I still believed the system did not work for victims, and while it was difficult to buy your way to freedom, having money allows your team to dictate everything regarding the case.

That first year in college, my Junior Freshman year seemed to fly by, and I am not sure how I got there in the end. I remember that Christmas sitting down after Christmas dinner to work on some project that was due on the first day back in the New Year. Still, no one in the family was bothered at all. That Christmas morning was brilliant, with the big breakfast, presents being opened, going to Mass, going to Granny's to meet the Uncles, Aunties, and Cousins then home for dinner. It was great fun and a lovely time to be together, and I was able to work on my projects because the boys wanted to play with their presents. It worked out for everyone. I enjoyed Christmas, especially seeing the boys so joyful as well as my nephews and nieces. That made me as happy as giving out my presents had been.

Soon the annual examinations came, and I was very nervous, and I had another huge problem to overcome - worrying. I have always been a terrible worrier since depression first got hold of me. I worried about the exams, but most of all, I worried about letting myself, my new friends, and Trinity College down. As is always the case with me, the exams were not as bad as I thought they would be. I had put the work in, and having so many friends around before going into the exam hall, helped me tremendously.

Everyone was very encouraging and assisting other students too, which to me anyway, was very supportive. I shouldn't have been worried though because I got good results in all subjects, even sociology, and I was delighted with that.

I worked again during the summer but tried my very best to find ways to relax. I am not very good at that; my head does not let me relax unless I have something to do that keeps my mind occupied at the same time. I always need to be focused on something I enjoy, to distract me from all the negative and depressive thoughts that constantly flow through my brain. Painting and decorating around the house or working in the garden was a chore but became a hobby that I enjoyed. Sometimes I feel there is nothing more enjoyable than pottering around my garden in the sunshine, listening to my own choice of music, and able to stop and sit down for water or a coffee anytime I want. It is more than just a distraction from my depression or mental health problems; it is an enjoyable way to boost the way I feel, physically and mentally.

My depression is why I always felt that I needed to be doing things, especially if it was for someone else, which made me happy. I am, by no means, a great gardener or even a good one, and it seems that my speciality is growing weeds, but I loved doing the work. I love to see plants grow, and that cheers me up. My favourite plant is the rose, and I have plenty of them growing in the front and back gardens. It's the little things in life that make the most significant difference, but to me, they are my lifebelts, my distractions from depression, and short periods of contentment.

Life was good in the Moroney household, and I returned to college that year with great enthusiasm, and I wasn't as nervous as I was when I started the year before. I got my results from year one and was very happy. They equalled or exceeded my expectations, especially in Maths, which I worked extremely hard at. I was very keen to catch up with my mates and get on with my studies. It was great seeing them all again and getting back together. As with the previous year, the time seemed to fly, and it was not long until we were sitting our Christmas exams, which for some subjects, were worth 20% of the year's total. I was confident enough until I sat the accountancy paper. I had forgotten to bring my calculator, and while I was able to do some of the work, I was unable to finish any question. I knew that this result would not be good. The rest of the exams went well for me, and I was happy with myself. I had only one project to do over the Christmas break. That gave me a bit of free time with the boys.

After the first accountancy lecture in the New Year, the lecturer approached me and asked me how I had done so badly in the Christmas exam. I explained how I left my calculator at home. Without a second thought, he just said that whatever result I got at Easter, he would give me for the Christmas exam too. I thought that was very generous and understanding and I told him so and thanked him. I was getting on very well with all my lecturers and tutors, and I think they knew I was doing my best. I was never a genius or anything like that, and it sometimes frightened me to see some of the younger students pick up on everything immediately and have absolutely no concerns about assignments, homework, or exams. Some people were born with brains to burn.

I had finished counselling and had weaned myself off all my anti-depressants and other medication with my doctor's help. I did feel good initially and mentally healthy and again believed that I had beaten depression, and this time for good. Life was playing its part too. The only dark cloud on the horizon was the court case, but that seemed to be going nowhere at all, but I believed that I was strong enough to deal with anything the case threw at me.

All the talk in the second year, or Senior Freshman year, was about the Foundation Scholarship (schols) exams before Easter. The idea was that you studied all the topics for the rest of the year and then sat these special exams at Easter. The Schols had an honourable place in Trinity for hundreds of years. Anyone awarded a first got an exemption for the rest of the year, and free accommodation on campus until the end of 4th year. If someone got a 2.1, they were exempt for the rest of the year, and that result stood for the year. I was doing well enough at this stage and liked all the subjects I had taken for the second year, and decided to give these schols a try. I am not sure why I took the chance, but I reckon it was to distract myself by being too busy to think and being off from Easter was very appealing.

Things were changing at home. My depression was growing in strength again. It started gaining influence in the summer because I had little to do, and the criminal case against Shine was in my thoughts more frequently. Something was amiss between Valerie and myself, but I did not know what. I felt that we were just drifting apart. Well, that's the way I thought anyway. I suppose I saw the massive effort required to do the schols as a way to focus my brain even more, and I didn't want to be at home at all. I was avoiding my problems at home. It meant staying back every night in college to take the extra lectures and tutorials that were due. Getting a first for me would have been a dream, but I knew I was not that clever. Still, I liked the challenge, so I was aiming for the 2.1 and finishing the school year at Easter. I don't think I've ever worked so hard in my life. I was at it day and night, on the train, in college, at home, and probably even on the toilet.

The time flew by for me, and the exams came up far more quickly than usual. For some of the exams, I stayed in a local hostel so that I could stay studying in the libraries until they threw me out. Staying in Dublin meant that I did not have to be rushing and putting pressure on myself travelling from Drogheda before the exams. It wasn't too bad because I ate in college while studying there, and all I needed was somewhere to sleep. When I was invested in something, like work or my studies, I put everything I had into it.

That year I also got involved in the Students Economic Review. I was honoured to be working with some gifted students and staff from the economics department. We did what we could when studies allowed, but I found it enjoyable. It was a great bunch, and they put together a tremendous Annual Economic Review, and I learned a lot from it. My contribution was limited, but I was happy to be a small part of the project.

I sat the exams before Easter, and it was a bit posh and old-fashioned, maybe a throwback to hundreds of years before, and we had to sign a big ancient book before sitting the exams. The exams flew by, and I was hopefully finished for that year but was not too sure or confident. For the week after Easter, I took Valerie and the boys to Killarney for a week. It was a perfect opportunity to try to reconnect with Valerie, and give the boys a little holiday away from home. I did not bring my car because I was not sure if it was up for the journey, so we took the train. The only holiday we had previous to that was when I took the family home from London, and that was usually by car to Holyhead in Wales and then the ferry home. One of those trips home did give me my favourite word. We were travelling up the motorway in England, the boys were asleep in the backseat, when Simon suddenly woke up, looked out the window, and said "Ow look - Speeps". It still sounds so much better than sheep, and we had a great laugh in the car.

We stayed in a holiday home in Killarney and explored everywhere we could, and the boys had a super time. One day we started walking and kept going until we reached the gap of Dungloe, a distance of about 13 km. It took us hours, but we were determined to get there. There wasn't a bother on the boys when they got to the gap, as they ran around climbing and playing as if they just got up from a rest, but Valerie and I were wrecked. We stayed there for an hour or so, the boys exploring everywhere and it was a beautiful place to be. We had dinner in the restaurant, but the meals Valerie, Wayne, and I were awful. I would have needed a chainsaw to cut the meat. The boy's dinner was much better. We were starving as we were afraid to try anything else, even though the waitress offered. There was no way we were able to walk home, and we had to get a taxi. Despite the terrible food, we had a super day but spent the rest of it lounging around the holiday home and trying to relax.

Simon and Lee were getting lots of interest from the girls staying in neighbouring holiday homes. Maybe Lee not so much, but Simon loved the attention and I realised he was a bit of a lady's man, even at 13 years of age. Other than that, we kept busy all the time, visiting new places that I barely remembered from when I was young. We had lovely weather which allowed us to go out and explore and enjoy the sights.

While in Killarney, Joe phoned me and told me that the schols results were posted in the economics department. He asked if I wanted to know how I got on. Of course, I did, but then I didn't. I did not know what to do. Anyway, after the mother of all arguments in my head, I wanted to know how I did and asked him to read the results for me. He read them out to me, and I had received my 2.1, and I was delighted, as was Joe. I was on the street in Killarney with Valerie and the boys at the time, and they were as excited as I was to learn my result. I told them, give Valerie a big kiss, and hopped and danced around with the boys. We were all delirious with joy, and went and got something to eat and then stuffed our faces with cakes and buns. I got what I wanted, and we had a great holiday with the boys. Brilliant!

The long trip home on the train was even brilliant. We were playing that game of cards called kalooki, and we were teaching others how to play it. We even got involved in singing songs (I pretended) and telling jokes on the way home. What a way to end the little holiday. Why could I not have been that parent all the time for the boys?

Despite the fantastic holiday and my brilliant exam results, my depression seemed to be waiting for me when I got home. At least, it had just simmered away in the background when I was studying and taking the exams.

Thankfully too, it didn't come to Killarney with me. There did not seem to be any one trigger this time, except maybe the case against Shine, but my depression snook up on me and was exerting its influence, and I sank quicker than a stone in a pond. My depression quickly infected my mind and started to retake control of my life. I thought that I had this damn thing beaten, but once again, I had fooled myself and everyone around me. Once again, these thoughts of failure began to dominate every waking moment.

Wayne was in his last year in Secondary school, and Simon started there too. The Leaving Certificate exams were coming up for Wayne, but we had absolutely no worries and knew that they would not be a problem for him. Simon was thrilled to be going to the big school, and many of his classmates from primary school went there too. So, he settled in very easily. Lee went to school without his big brother, but he was okay with that. They still went most of the way together.

I went back to college but was struggling. So, I made the very disappointing decision to go back to Dr Neary for help - again, which meant back on the anti-depressants. He contacted the service I was with before and asked for counselling for me as soon as possible. That, to me, was just another sign of my weakness as a human being. I was not able to cope on my own. I couldn't function without medication and therapy. I was not very happy about this, but what else could I do.

I was in college for all my lectures and tutorials, but I might as well have been on Mars. I wrote my notes and then rewrote them, but I was losing touch and not able to concentrate. I was only able to talk to a couple of friends like Joe and Mary and started spending most of my time on my own. I had all the old feelings or reasons for keeping to myself but tried so hard to distract myself by studying. It was hard trying to keep some control over my depression, but it was problematic for the Moroneys and me. All I did was college work, upstairs in my bedroom, and again pushed my family away. I did not let them get too close in case they realised how bad I felt, and still did not talk about my depression at home. I had already hurt them enough and had just let them down all their lives. I even made excuses so that I did not have to take them to play snooker. They didn't deserve a father like me, and I didn't deserve to call them my family. I even did a 'Britney' long before she did. I shaved my head completely. I don't know why I did that, but soon after, I found myself just balling and crying in Trinity in front of everyone. I might as well have been on my own.

I was just in the moment and broke down. Soon after that, I went to see my college tutor, Michael Harrison and requested permission to take the year out. I did not tell him the truth. I just said I had family problems. He was very helpful and suggested I see him before returning the following September. I was back telling lies, anything except the truth that I had depression, and it owned me. In hindsight, I should have stayed in college because all the free time I had from then on, just led to me over analysing my problems and digging myself deeper down the well.

Simon settled well into secondary school and enjoyed the opportunity to participate in more sports, especially cross country. He was well-liked in the school and seen as a good pupil, but he was still the cheeky one. Wayne was getting ready for his leaving cert, but it did not seem to faze him in the slightest. Lee was still in primary school, and he was still a happy boy, and doing very well. Valerie was working in a Chinese takeaway a few nights a week, and I was like a dead man walking, with no feelings, interest, or engagement in Life. During the previous years in college, I had been able to help others, especially with Maths, but now I could not help myself. I had to wait until the following May until I got back into counselling. I was not able to get the same counsellor as before but got another nice chap who I got on well with.

In May 2001, more than seven years after I made my first statement to the Gardai, the book of evidence was finally served on Shine, and the case promptly adjourned. The book of evidence was the evidence against Shine for the trial. The case was adjourned three of four more times that year, and each time, I fell further down that well. The detective in charge retired that year, and even he was ashamed of the so-called justice system that had so far failed us miserably. More complainants had come forward over the years which, to me, made our case more vital and all the more urgent. I was aware that I had no idea how many boys Shine had abused.

I was helped as I got accepted back into counselling in Rian around that time. I was thinking more about the case and the impact it was having and had in my life. I thought that I would be better off if I had nothing to do with it, but I still wanted something to show for my efforts. I decided that I would withdraw my complaint, and then see if I could get the newspapers to do an article on Shine and publish the two statements, I made to the Gardai. I still wasn't sure, so I wrote to the Taoiseach, the Attorney General, the Gardai, the DPP, Victim Support, Irish Survivors of Child Abuse, Minister for Justice, and Liz O'Donnell making them aware of my plans and asking for advice and guidance. I received plenty of replies, but mostly they were just acknowledgements of the receipt of my letter. They were no help to me at all.

I was no use to Wayne when he got expelled from school not long before his leaving exams. One of his teachers involved him in a head shave for charity. After he got his head shaved, the headmaster noticed him and said it violated school policy and just expelled Wayne. He didn't mind, as he was able to study at home and would be allowed to sit the exams in St Marys. I am sure that Wayne had a few choice words to say to the principal when he was expelled, but it was not the last time he caused us trouble.

I went back to college that year (2001) and did miss my old classmates who were now a year ahead of me. Joe was still around, but Mary was finished. Joe was in his final year, and I was starting 3rd year again. I was a bit more alert than the last year because I was back in counselling and back on the anti-depressants. I was willing myself to do well and get a good honours degree. I had no career plans because I had no idea what I wanted to do after college. I just wanted to give my final years my full attention, and not be distracted by the future. The case against Shine was called again in the Circuit Court and adjourned. I had decided against withdrawing my complaint following conversations with the Gardai and victim support. I was promised that it would be all over soon, and as always, I believed what I was told. I studied very hard and enjoyed it much more than the previous year. I was chatting more and getting involved with my classmates in college and reaping the benefit by learning a lot from the students around me. I even fully embraced group projects, instead of finding ways to do my portion of the work on my own, away from everyone else. Thank God I was living my life somewhat normally as whatever mental strength I had, was going to be tested further than ever before.

Chapter 14

Simon

That October Simon got suspended by the same Principal. Valerie and I met with him in the school to find out why and he told us that he might be expelled, for taking drugs in the school. We knew Simon never touched drugs. He was smoking cigarettes, and I'm sure that he had taken alcohol, but not drugs. I had drilled that into the boys since they could walk, and they knew how I detested them. We chased down the Gardai drugs liaison officer, who told us that he had never heard of or come across Simon. We took Simon to Dr Neary so that he could check for drugs and give us a note for the school saying Simon did not touch drugs. The doctor asked to see Simon on his own. Simon went to him for a few weeks before the doctor called us in and told us that drugs were not the problem. Dr Neary was convinced that Simon had a mental breakdown in school that day. My head exploded with stupid thoughts about how Simon had contracted his mental health problems from me, and it was another thing to add to my book of faults, but the news to come was far worse than any thoughts I could muster. I also thought of that idiot in school jumping to the most outrageous conclusions about Simon without the slightest effort to talk to him and find out what was happening with this student, that had never been in trouble before.

The doctor told us the basics of the story because Simon couldn't bring himself to say it to us. Weeks later, he told us himself in more detail, as far as he was able to. Simon was still babysitting whenever he could and would help out all of our neighbours when asked. Sometimes Simon did not get paid on the night, but always got it later. He had grown into a powerful young man from using the weights and often used his strength to protect others. Simon would stand up to anyone, even if they were a few years older, and had the boyish good looks that made him popular with the girls. He could lift the bar full of weights, and when he gave to bar to me, I could barely move it. It took all my strength to stop it from falling to the floor. He was proud of that and always took pride in his appearance, always doing his best to look very presentable when he left the house.

One day, that September, when Simon was outside playing with the little kids, our next-door neighbour called Simon into her house to give him the money she owed him for babysitting. She sent her little children out to play. Once the kids were out, she closed and locked the front door. Then, before Simon knew what was happening, she pinned him to the wall in the hallway while sticking some-thing sharp into his side. Simon could never be sure what she was holding, but he thought it was scissors. She raped him up against the wall, as a birthday present to herself. Then as soon as it started, it was over. She paid him his money and told him not to tell anyone - ever. She said to him that if he did tell anyone, she would lose her kids. She was still pressing that sharp object into him. Then, as casually as anything, she unlocked the front door and let him leave. The bright, bubbly Simon, with the big smile, died that day.

The news broke us, just like my story of abuse had broken my Mam and Dad years before. I felt so sorry for Simon, having to endure and now remember such a wicked dirty act. We couldn't even hug him for a while. He didn't want anyone touching him. He was pale and looked about half his usual size. He was truly broken. This lively, happy, powerful boy with the big smile had turned into some-thing that could not carry the weight of pain and sadness on his shoulders. The doctor put him on anti-depressants and was going to push the Child and Adolescent Mental Health services for an early appointment.

Despite all our years of experience with depression, we did not know how to help Simon. Despite the worry I had for him, I could not lie and tell him he would be better soon. I didn't want to give him something to cling on only to have it let him down later. He had lived his entire life with a depressed person, and I doubted that he would not believe or accept anything I said to him. He started isolating himself in his room, but not doing anything. He picked up the weights a few times, but his heart was not in it like it usually was. All joy in his life was gone. So, we treated him as best as we knew how. We made sure that he had the basics - food, drinks, and clothes available whenever he wanted them. We let him have his space but always invited him to join us. Sometimes he did, and sometimes he didn't want to. Now two depressed people were living in the same house. I cannot say if Simon had the same feelings or thoughts as I had, but it was heart-breaking seeing him suffer. I could not make him feel any better but wanted to avoid making him feel any worse. I tried my distraction ideas with him, and sometimes they worked, and other times he didn't care or have the heart or motivation to even try.

I hated seeing Simon struggling, and I could see the change in him. Our neighbour next door got a new live-in boyfriend, and he tried to wind Simon up every chance he got. He was a little rat of a man, who made himself feel better by trying to make Simon feel worse. But it did work. He did make Simon feel worse, if that was possible, about the way he thought about himself. Simon could have ripped him apart if he wanted to, but it never came to that. Simon had no interest in defending himself or anything else for that matter. I did wonder if the verbal abuse affected Simon, but he just said that it didn't. I guessed that he was lying to me, but I did not want to push him or upset him anymore.

So, I left it at that. That Christmas was a shitty time in the house, and it was even hard trying to get Wayne and Lee to enjoy it, let alone Simon. Thankfully they had plenty of friends outside the house and were able to enjoy some good times with them.

In 2002, we eventually got Simon to make a statement of complaint against our neighbour to the Gardai, just as I had eight years before, even though it was very hard for him, and he was never sure if he was doing the right thing. He even went to the Gardai himself a couple of times to try to retract the statement and make this whole thing go away and who could blame him. He was well aware of my case and probably thought his complaint would last as long and cause the same pain and suffering. We went back to the school with all this new information, fully expecting that they would apologise to Simon. We all wanted him to go back to school, which he had missed. However, when we explained what had happened to Simon, the Principal said that he did not accuse Simon of taking drugs but selling them. Some boy, he would not say who, or let us talk to, had reported seeing Simon with a bag of drugs for sale in the playground. The other people present, like the deputy principal, were as surprised and shocked as we were. We could not understand what was going on. We all knew he was lying, the others said it to us after he left, but he was the boss, and his word stood. I don't know what he had against Simon, or Wayne the year before, but I thought that he had some kind of inferiority complex and felt the need to prove himself, and show that he was the boss, even if he was wrong. The news did not help Simon. He had been lied about and betrayed, and he was adamant that he would never go back to school there.

When the Gardai interviewed her, the neighbour denied every single bit of Simon's complaint. It turned into one of those 'he says, she says' cases. I knew her ex-boyfriend knew the truth and would be able to help Simon's case, but he did not want to get involved and would not talk to the Gardai. He had told me before that he thought the world of Simon but didn't prove it when he had the chance. He was just a big coward. I had only been to the District Court in Dundalk to hear that the case against Shine was adjourned again. I was in the horrors. I couldn't take anymore, and I flipped. I went out one night and drank a lot of whiskeys trying to figure out what I was going to do. I never drink whiskey.

I do like the taste, but I don't drink it as I don't think I can handle it properly. With lots of whiskeys onboard, I made my mind up. When I came home, I picked up a hammer and screwdriver and went next door. My stupid plan was to beat the crap out of him for picking on Simon and make her confess to raping him. I would use the screwdriver the way she used the scissors on Simon, but I would push a lot harder if I needed to. I knocked on the front door, but they would not answer. So, I used the screwdriver and hammer to try to force my way into the house. I could hear them behind the door shouting abuse at me and calling the cops. Yet I kept trying to get in their door. I smashed one of their windows when the screwdriver slipped, but I still could not get to them. The cops arrived before I could get into the house, and arrested me. I was charged with attempted burglary and had to pay to get the window fixed. I had achieved nothing except a criminal record. As bad as that episode was, it was not my most shameful act of that year.

I was also very annoyed with the case against Shine. I thought that once we got into the Circuit Court, the judge would set a date for the trial. Then, and at last, Shine would be prosecuted. I was so disappointed and angry that I stood up in the court and challenged the judge. I told him that I made my complaint in 1994 and that it was now 2002 and questioned why he adjourned again and set no trial date. He didn't have me arrested but tried to explain how the justice system worked. I was not listening because it was not what I wanted to hear. This case was never going to go to trial, and if it did, Shine would probably have died first.

One day, I received a phone call from one of the neighbours saying that Simon was lying in a heap at the bottom of the stairs inside the front door. I asked her to call an ambulance, and she rang me back later to tell me the ambulance was there. I asked her about any cuts or marks, or even blood, thinking that the neighbours might have attacked him. I was happy when she told me there was nothing like that, but Simon was out cold. Instead of heading home, I went straight to the hospital and had to wait nearly a half an hour for Simon to come in the ambulance. As usual, I thought the worst, but thankfully it was just because of the terrible traffic in town on a Friday. Simon was examined and admitted to the wards, and thank God, and he got an excellent, caring consultant. He tested Simon for everything to determine what had caused the blackout. Simon was just going out the door of our house, and the next thing he remembered was waking up and the paramedics with him. The doctor told Valerie and me that the blackout was more than likely stress-related, and there was no other indication of physical illness. We explained how Simon was on the waiting list to see Child and Adolescent Mental Health Services, and he was annoyed that they had not engaged with Simon yet. So, he got in touch with them directly, and soon afterwards, Simon got to see a child psychiatrist. She just kept insisting that Simon went back to school. She didn't listen to what Simon had to say, and it seemed that she thought going back to school would solve all Simon's problems. I spoke to her, but it appeared that any help they could give to Simon was conditional on him going back to school. I thought that she was of no help at all.

Simon was in no fit state to go back to school, and his GP advised against it. He felt that he could not return after the Principal accused him of being on drugs, and then for selling drugs. He hated the Principal for doing this to him, and he felt that everyone in school would have believed the lies, and he could not face them.

The psychiatrist did do something, though. She arranged an appointment for Simon to see a psychologist. Simon got on well with this man, and for a while, we could see a bit of an improvement. Simon was diagnosed with bipolar depression, and I still think that is the worst form of depression, because it makes you believe you have recovered, and then drops you back to a worse position than before. It fools the mind every time, making you think that you are better for good, and then it comes back with a vengeance. Everyone feels even lower each time because they thought they were foolish enough to believe that it was gone for good.

When Simon was in the hospital, he went out for a smoke one day and met a lovely man called Pat Clarke from Cavan. Pat had just been diagnosed with MS and was feeling very sorry for himself and not sure what the future held for him. Somehow, they got chatting, and Simon cheered Pat up and helped him through those difficult moments. Simon was like that, very easy to talk to, and far wiser than he let on. The two of them became great friends, and Pat always met up with Simon when he came to Drogheda. One day Simon accompanied Pat when he went to see his doctor. The doctor thought that Simon was Pat's son. We knew every time Pat was due in Drogheda because Simon would fuss about how he looked and would always be well dressed, clean, and ready when Pat called. We found out later that they had some helpful conversations and Pat was able to reach places in Simon's mind that we couldn't. Simon felt comfortable and safe talking to Pat, which was brilliant for him and I'm sure it did Pat some good too. I will never have the words or vocabulary to thank Pat for all the good he did for Simon, and I will always be delighted that they were such great friends. It was especially important for Simon because, after a while, his psychologist was moved to a different area. Simon had no professional psychiatric support for almost a year. He did not go to any more appointments with his psychiatrist because all she mentioned was him going back to school, even in letters she wrote home to us about his non-attendance. She just didn't seem to understand or want to know why he did not want to go back there.

Like the old saying, when Simon was good, he was very good, and when he was bad, he was very bad. The mood swings associated with his bipolar disorder were frightening to witness and horrible for Simon. When he was good, he was as high as a kite, trying to pack as much as possible into every minute of his day. He was always on the move, going out with friends, going to do a bit of work, or meeting up with Pat. He was a joy to have around the house, bright and bubbly and making us laugh, especially with his silly 'whatever' replies, with a big grin on his face. It was years later that I found out that he used to steal my car after I went to bed. Not often but a couple of times. I did almost catch him because one day I went in the car with Lee and noticed that the gears were in the wrong position, but Lee covered up for Simon, saying that I must be imagining things, and asking who possibly would be touching my car. He was just as guilty because he was with Simon when he took my car, the little brats. I didn't even know he could drive, but he had been driving the van around when helping deliver the bread for one of the neighbours. He never told me that. We loved having Simon around when he was 'up', but it was a completely different story when he sank back into the mental quicksand of depression. It was like having two different sons who spent a few weeks with us and was then replaced by the other. When like this, it took something massive, to connect with Simon. He would only come out at night after the rest of us had gone to bed, so he could watch and make sure his Mam got home from work. It was even a considerable effort to get him to eat, and all we could do was keep encouraging him and telling him we were there for him. That's all we could do, and we always questioned whether we were doing the right thing or not. He was dead inside, something I was very familiar with, so I tried to think of what I wanted when I was in the depths of depression, and all I could think about was knowing someone was around even when I didn't want them to be. So, we tried to be around for Simon and made sure there was plenty of food around, and always clothes ready in case he wanted to go out.

I would like to think that my concern for Simon, kept a bit of a lid on my own mental issues and kept me distracted from myself. Without college, and seeing Simon struggle so much, my mind was able to think, and that was just bad news. My depression took more control of my thinking, and I became an angry, frustrated, and very moody person. I was living an existence that didn't matter to me, and I could not make any sense of it. I wondered did God allow Simon to be raped, to punish him and me. Then again, I asked how Simon could have done anything wrong in his young life. He was a good kid who loved to help others, who didn't deserve that. I was used to God punishing me even though I couldn't figure out why. I could not work out any answers to all the questions that were pounding against my skull every day. I lost any ability to cope I had and was just a sad, miserable man with no future.

Arguments with Valerie became more common until one day we had a huge row. She said something, and I lashed out and hit her on the head. What she said does not matter, but what I did does. It was the most shameful thing I have ever done in my life. It was a horrible, stupid thing to do and I should never have done it, no matter what the reason. Nothing justifies hitting a wife, a partner, or a woman, and it made me feel less of a man, less of a person, and not worthy of my place in my family. Valerie was so upset and hurt that she rightly called the Gardai and soon obtained a barring order, keeping me out of the house. I had to go and live in my Mams. I was ashamed and embarrassed. I am sure that I was not the only one to flip that day. I think the frustration, worry, and the years she experienced living with one depressed person in the house was an awful way to live. Then to have a wounded, hurt, and depressed son, who we couldn't help, pushed her close to the edge, and I just came and pushed her off it. I wasn't angry with her but felt I was rightfully punished for hitting her.

It was very hard living without seeing the boys every day. Wayne did not seem to be badly affected, and I couldn't tell what Lee thought. Simon was the worst affected and would not talk to me for a few weeks, because I had hit his Mam. He could not understand how or why I could do such a shameful thing, and he was right. Instead of helping Simon with his depression, I had made things worse for him, and I felt very guilty about that and being a dangerous husband. In time Valerie and I got talking to each other again, and I was able to return to our home. The strange thing for me about this assault is that it forced me into some kind of rational thinking. The shame and disgust I felt for hitting Valerie, somehow kicked my mind into some sense of reality, and I started thinking about how important the boys were in my life and that I had been wallowing in my sense of self for far too long and letting it control my life. I simply snapped out of it.

Simon was doing okay but was getting fed up with nothing to do. He was still helping with the bread run, but that was becoming a bit boring. After months of encouragement and the promise that things would soon be back to normal, we convinced him to go back to school for the start of the 2002-2003 year. We all hoped that it would give him something to focus on and help him deal with his depression. He had plenty of friends there, and that would be good for him. It turned out to be another disaster. We had been in contact with the Deputy Principal and kept her up to date about Simon's condition, and she was happy to see him back at school. She explained Simon's situation to the Principal, and he let him return. His first day at the start of the school year went fine for Simon, and he had a good day. On the second day back, Valerie met Simon at the gates during the morning break to give him his lunch. The Principal was in the front yard when he noticed Simon and approached him. The head was angry and fuming at Simon for wearing trainers instead of shoes. He made Simon feel smaller than the brain inside the Principal's skull. Simon lost any control or restraint and told him "Get out of my face, or I will hit you with this bottle". He had a plastic bottle of coke that Valerie had just given him for his lunch. We could never condone what Simon said, but we understood it completely. The Principal just roared at Valerie "you, take him home". Simon had stood up for himself, and after that, it would have taken a miracle from God to get him near that school again. More than that, it sank Simon deeper into depression faster than any of his previous bipolar transformations. It had taken him months to build up the courage and strength to go back to school and face everybody, just for it to be snatched away from him in minutes. His case against the neighbour seemed to be going nowhere. He went down to the Gardai to withdraw his complaint, but the inspector dealing with him called us.

We convinced him not to let his complaint stand, but to think carefully about it and talk to us, or even Pat, before making his mind up.

Lee had started in the same secondary school, even though we were concerned and talked to him about going to St Joseph's instead. He wanted to go with his classmates, and I think he knew before we did, that Simon was going to go back. I think that made it easier for Simon too. Following the latest incident, we got anxious that Lee was sure to be targeted by the Principal sooner rather than later. We went up to the school and spoke with the deputy. She liked Simon and promised us that she would look after Lee. She took him under her protective wing and made sure he was able to feel safe and comfortable in school. He did well and grew out of himself a lot more, maybe because his protector, was not around him all the time, or perhaps because he was just a lovely kid who got on well with everyone.

I started back in Trinity too. I had done as well in my third-year exams as I had in the previous years, and I was pleased with that. Now all I needed was one last big push, and I would have a degree of some kind. I picked my subjects for the year carefully. We had the option of doing a thesis or taking a general paper exam along with the other final exams at the end of the year. I was not confident that I could work on a thesis and keep up with my studies in my subjects, so I chose to take the general paper exam. I studied and worked really hard, and was happy that my mental state was much better than it had been the year before. I was able to think and concentrate, which was a bonus for me.

Simon started engaging in deliberate self-harm. One day he went missing with one of our sharp kitchen knives. We all went searching for him, but it was Lee who found him. Simon and Lee were best friends, the best of brothers, which meant that he was able to guess where Simon went. He did not want to tell us until he got to Simon. Somehow, Lee got him home, and he was covered with cuts and bleeding all over his chest, torso, and arms. He had cut himself wherever he could reach. I was shocked when they came into the kitchen that day. All I could see was blood and a blank expression on Simon's face. Once I gathered my breath, I could see that the cuts weren't deep, which was a blessing. They were bleeding profusely, and I couldn't stop it. I wanted him to go to the hospital, but he refused. I kept trying to stop the bleeding with anything I could find in the kitchen, and towels Lee brought to us. I looked at Lee to help me convince Simon to let me take him to the hospital, but Lee took Simon's side. After what seemed like ages, we got the bleeding stopped. I tried to clean them up as best as I could, and I asked Simon if he was sore. He told me he could not feel any pain from the cuts, but he felt better in his head.

I never engaged in deliberate self-harm, but I understood what he was saying. The wounds were like taps releasing the incredible pressure he felt in his mind. The cuts themselves were just incidental. He had to cut to relieve the stress and ease the pain in his head. It just goes to show the psychological distress he was carrying around with him. I asked him not to do that again, and he said that he wouldn't. He did do it a couple more times, but thankfully never as bad, and even went to the hospital once, using his mate's name. He could never get the same relief from cutting as he did the first time. He learned it was just a waste of time because the real pain always came back. It was a huge warning sign for us and though we were worried for Simon, we never actually thought seriously about Simon taking his own life, that was not him. Yes, it turned out that he was a very sensitive soul, who suffered severely from bipolar disorder, but that would never happen with Simon. The cuts and the bleeding were something he used to relieve his pain, not an attempt to take his life. That is what we thought anyway.

That Christmas was a wonderful one for us. Wayne was studying computer hardware and had a part-time job to give him whatever cash he needed. Valerie was still working in the Chinese takeaway, and Lee was doing well in school and got the odd shift in Mc Phails pub doing the 'bottling', dividing, and crating all the used bottles. He enjoyed that and having his own money helped too. I was feeling good but was putting every effort into my studies to get a decent result in my exams. I was looking forward to Christmas for the first time in a long time and planned to take a few days to relax and spend time with the boys.

Simon was still helping out on the bread runs, and instead of getting paid when it was due, he asked the bread man to hold the money for him until Christmas.

When he got paid, he went out and spent it all on presents for us. He had nothing left when he came home and had to 'borrow money' off me for a packet of cigarettes. He was just delighted with the Christmas presents he had bought for everyone, and he genuinely looked happy and pleased with himself. I had to close my eyes as he transported everything he had upstairs. It was great seeing him like that. I was delighted for him but wished that he could have been that happy all the time. On Christmas morning, he handed out his presents first with that big smile beaming across his face. We could see how glad he was, bringing joy into the house, and it helped us all have a great Christmas. He bought me a lovely watch and some clothes which I was delighted to receive, maybe just as much as he was presenting them. I thought that he felt that it was some kind of payback for us having to live with his depression, but I didn't care much about that once Simon seemed so happy.

Simon was still living through the ups and downs of his bipolar disorder, but at least he was able to enjoy life when he was on the high part of his cycle of depression. He was still the lady's man and popular with the girls, and one in particular who he got on brilliantly with. He even made a good impression on her mother. One night there was a gang of them up in Mandy's house when one of the lads stepped out of line. Simon did not like what he heard, and he made him apologise and then told him to go home, which he did. He loved going out and having fun with his mates when he was on the 'up' part of his cycle. It was great to see him able to go out and have some fun, but we always knew that he would sink again and become this different tortured soul.

Of course, it happened again. On St Patrick's morning 2003, Simon got a knife and tried to climb up on the roof of the house. I don't think he knew what he was doing, whether he was going to cut himself, or jump off the roof or maybe both. He would not let us near him at all. Not even Lee was allowed into the room. He couldn't get onto the roof, but we were panicking and had no idea what to do, so we called the Gardai. At the same time, that fecker next door was encouraging Simon to jump, saying "why don't you jump and do us all a favour". How and why I did not just go and kill him, I don't know. I wish I did. I was so consumed with Simon and wanted him safe. The Gardai came, and after asking what was going on, one went up the room to Simon. He convinced him to put the knife down and tell him what was going on. Simon ranted and raved for a while, but the cop was patient and listened to him.

We could hear all this from downstairs. The Garda didn't threaten him for having the knife or judge him in any way. He just listened to Simon and let him spill his guts and relieve some of the pressure that was exploding inside his brain. He then invited Simon down to the Garda station to continue their chat and to try to work out some way to help him. Simon went off with the guards, and we waited for word back from them. I just thought of how difficult it must have been for Simon to talk to us, but we were glad he was talking to someone, and we hoped it would help him. The cop managed to get a big breakfast for Simon and then arranged for Simon to go to the adult psychiatric ward in St. Brigid's hospital in Ardee and he agreed.

Because he was 16 years of age, he was too old for the children's mental health services and too young for the adult mental health services which started from 18 years of age. Somehow, the Garda had convinced the hospital to take him in and at least give him a proper psychiatric assessment. I collected him in the Garda station and drove him to the hospital, and he was calm and relaxed about it. I think he believed that they would identify what he was going through, and maybe suggest a cure or something that would stop him feeling so bad. He was hopeful. He spent three days there, was monitored and assessed by that psychiatrist I had when I came home from London, and a female just as old. We visited him every day, and he seemed to be doing well, and we all thought that this was what Simon needed and was the start of his recovery.

After three days, Valerie and I were in the hospital when we were invited to have a chat with the doctors. They just said that they were letting him go home because there was nothing psychologically wrong with him. Simon was devastated when we spoke to him. He felt that they had let him down, and he had wasted his time there. They gave no cures, treatments, or suggestions that helped Simon, except that they would work to arrange counselling for him as soon as possible. That drive home in the car was just horrible. Simon did not understand what was going on in his head but had raised his hopes when he thought he was going to be properly assessed, and maybe get some real help. He was so disappointed that he cried all the way home. He even mentioned the thought that he was crazy and not even the doctors knew what was wrong. He felt that no one could help him. It was heart-breaking to see him in such a state, let down again by the doctors, with nothing positive to grab on to. I think another part of him just died that day.

In April, we got the good news that an appointment was available for Simon to see a new counsellor. He seemed to be pleased that his stay in the hospital had achieved something, and I think that he was somewhat keen to start, to see if this new counsellor could help him. When he did meet her, he seemed to bond with her very quickly. Maybe, at last, he was getting the help and support he needed, and as the counsellor lived locally and worked outside the hospital, there was no chance of her moving to a different area. We all had a bit of hope for him.

The final year exams in Trinity were looming large and getting ever closer. I was studying hard but knew that I had to keep working to achieve my goals. All classes were finished, and I was studying at home all day, every day. I studied a subject for about an hour, then took a short break, and started a different topic. I tried this to stop my brain from becoming stale from studying the same subject. I felt that it was going well. The second week in May started with a bank holiday, and because I was so wrapped up in my studies, I forgot to remind Simon of his counselling appointment on Wednesday. We both completely forgot about it until Thursday morning when Simon asked me about taking him to counselling. Only then did we realise our error. The bank holiday Monday, and my studies, had thrown our days out of synch completely. He was disappointed, but we contacted the counsellor, explained what happened, and he got an appointment for the following week. He seemed to be okay with that, so I presumed that he was.

That Friday night, there was only him and me in the house. Valerie was at work, and the boys were out. I was upstairs studying, though I felt like Homer Simpson because it seemed like my studying was just pushing old knowledge out of my head. Shortly after 8 pm, I went downstairs to check on Simon. He was sitting on the couch, watching 'The Bill' on television. He liked that programme, and he looked like he was content and maybe on the way up out of the deepest hole of his depression. He was like that, and we could always tell when he was on his transformation from low to high. He wasn't there yet, but still, as far as I was concerned, the signs were good.

I went back to try to study some more, but my brain was full, and I could not force any more into it. So, I packed up all my stuff and lay on the bed, just to relax. As I was laying there, Simon came up to me and came into the room. He asked me if he could have a cigarette and I gladly give him one. I asked him if we were talking now and he just replied "not yet", and he went back down to watch television. He still used to stay up waiting until everyone, especially his Mam, got home before going to bed himself. I was delighted with the "not yet" because I believed that Simon was aware that he was on the way up again, and that we would soon be chatting as if life was perfect. I took it as a good sign and decided that he would be okay on his own and I went to bed. It did not take too much for me to fall asleep.

The next thing I remember is that I was viciously awoken from my sleep by the most horrible scream I have ever heard in my life. It could have been banshees. It took me a moment or two to register that it was Valerie, but I had no idea why she was screaming like that. I jumped up, ran out of the bedroom, and saw Valerie screaming and crying at the bottom of the stairs. As I went downstairs, I was begging to know what was going on, but she could not respond to my pleas. She could not talk properly with all the crying, but I could make out that she said Simon, and then she was pointing into the sitting room. I ran to the bottom of the stairs and could see that Simon was lying face down on the sitting room floor. He was not moving. I ran to him and turned him round to see his face, to try to see what had happened. He was not breathing or moving, and the skin surrounding his lips had a blueish tone to them, but there were no signs of physical damage anywhere. There was no blood. I had no idea what happened to him. I tried what I thought was CPR, but I am not sure if I did it correctly. I pushed at his chest a few times with a lot of force, then blew into his mouth but still, nothing happened. I kept trying, but there was no response, except Simon staring up at me. He was looking at me like he was back playing that 'dead soldiers' game again. Valerie's screams had woken the boys, but they did not leave their rooms. I suppose they were scared of what was happening, but I don't believe they imagined their brother lying dead on the sitting room floor. All my efforts made absolutely no difference to Simon, and I called 999 and explained to them that I thought Simon was dead. I tried CPR again, and I tried shaking him and slapping him on the face, in the hope he would wake up, but I was starting to see that he was gone.

I put my hand on his forehead and begged God to give me some kind of miraculous power to revive Simon and wake him up. I wished for some magic sensation that would flow from my body, through the palm of my hand and into his forehead, and bring him back to life. I was screaming at God to listen to me and help Simon. But nothing happened, so I begged God to take my life and bring Simon back, but He didn't. He didn't do anything to help. Nothing worked, and there was nothing else I could try. I hoped that the paramedics could revive Simon when they got to him. I closed his eyes and left him to rest. I went up to the boys, Wayne first, and told them, rather brutally in hindsight, that their brother was dead. I did not know how else to say it and get the message across. I did not want to pussyfoot around and make the boys confused. I got dressed and went back down to Simon and waited until the ambulance came. Valerie was still on the stairs sobbing her heart out, and it was like she was glued to the stairs. She could not move. The boys came as far as the bottom of the stairs to look at Simon and went back upstairs just as quickly. They loved their brother, and I don't suppose that they wanted to see him dead.

The ambulance arrived, and the paramedics attached Simon to different machines, but it was not long until they confirmed that there was no pulse and that Simon was dead. I begged them to try again, to try anything at all to revive Simon, but they said they were very sorry, but there was nothing they could do. Their attention turned to Valerie and me, but there was little they could do to help us. We just wanted Simon back. It was now early on Saturday the 10th of May. We had to wait then until a doctor arrived to pronounce Simon dead and the Gardai to come, and I suppose, investigate Simon's death. While waiting, I rang my family, and Valerie phoned hers. After that, I got talking to Valerie and asked her what happened. She explained how she was walking down the driveway beside my car when she got this horrible feeling that something was wrong. She looked in the window and saw Simon lying there. She ran into the sitting room, and she knew immediately that he was dead. Valerie didn't touch him or move him to check. She just knew and just started screaming the house down and crying like never before. Talking to the boys, I learned that Lee had come home first, and then Wayne. Simon seemed to be ok, but there was not much conversation between them. Nothing new in that. We all let Simon be when he was struggling because we did not want to put more pressure on him and always knew he would come out of it sometime.

The Gardai arrived and asked questions of the paramedics and us, trying to figure out what had happened. We didn't know, but the idea that Simon had taken his own life was staring us right in the face, and hammering its way into our consciousness, but we could not see any evidence. The doctor came and pronounced Simon dead. That was it. It was so simple. She talked to the paramedics, checked Simon for any signs of life, and pronounced him dead. It only took a few minutes to confirm that Simon was no longer with us in this world. Simon was dead and needed to be taken away in the ambulance. His soul was gone, and now they wanted to take his body too. I think that is when the shock took over my brain.

During all this, my family arrived and asked us what happened. We couldn't tell them because we didn't know and we couldn't speak properly. I had to shift my car out of the driveway, to allow the ambulance to get closer to the house, and nearly smashed into Noel's car outside. I could not see anything except Simon staring up at me. The ambulance crew gave us plenty of time to say goodbye to Simon, but it was not really goodbye because it was just a dream. It didn't really happen, and our minds would not let us accept it. I would wake up later, and Simon would not be gone at all.

Once we had all talked to Simon, we had to wait outside the room when the paramedics got him ready to take away. I went into the front garden. It was a beautiful summer morning when they took Simon out of the house and into the ambulance. We did not see him because he was covered and wrapped up. We pleaded with the paramedics to 'look after' him, and they promised to do so. There was nothing else I or anyone else could do. They took him away in the ambulance, and we were standing around the house and garden trying to make sense of what had happened. I felt it was like they were wheeling the body of Simon away, sealed up in a black bag, when he was not dead at all. I simply cannot explain what I was feeling at that time, except very confused and I remember wondering and asking what I was supposed to do now. Once again, there were no answers to my questions. I was sitting out the front of the house, eating not smoking, cigarettes, and trying to get my head into one piece. The next thing, one of my brothers, I don't know which one, alerted me to Wayne. He walked out the driveway going to work. I had to run after him to tell him to stay at home, but he was as bad as I was, totally out of it with shock and unable to think for himself. He was following his regular Saturday routine. I got him home, and he went up to change out of his work uniform. After that, we just tried to get some sleep, but that was impossible as our minds started to accept that Simon really was gone, or was he? We were lost. Our son and brother was supposedly dead, but my mind did not accept that at all. I knew he was deceased but didn't at the same time. I guessed that we would never see him alive again, but I wasn't sure. Nothing made any sense at all because my brain refused to work properly. It let the fact that Simon was dead touch my mind, but did not let it in, so I could process it rationally. It was a bizarre way to feel. When everyone else went home to get some rest, we were just on her own trying to figure out how we could fix what happened. But there was no fixing this, not ever.

The next few days passed in a haze somewhere between consciousness and unconscious. Simon had to have an autopsy because it was a sudden death, and we wanted that over as quickly as possible so that we could get Simon home to the house before his burial. We did not go near the hospital, because we could not take seeing him in a cold, lifeless hospital room. We kept in touch with them, even asking if he was ok as if he was in for an operation. Father David from our church, the Holy Family in Ballsgrove, and Paddy and Patricia Townley from the funeral directors called to help us make the necessary arrangements. The four of us, me, Valerie, Wayne, and Lee, not five of us anymore, made the decisions together, and we all had a say in the funeral arrangements. We were glad for the help, support and guidance because we had no clue what we were doing and could not think for ourselves.

The funeral directors brought Simon home, and we placed him in the sitting room. He looked so different, like a perfect waxwork model of himself. He felt cold, but it looked like he was at peace at last. Many people came to visit, to pay their last respects, and to commiserate with us. We were very grateful for all the support which helped carry us through the next few days. The busyness of the house and all the people who visited helped keep us distracted from our pain and suffering. I, like an idiot, kept going back to check on him to see if he was ok. But he wasn't. It was of great comfort to see so many of his friends, and classmates, call up to say goodbye to him and talk about him as if he never had depression in his life. We needed that, to try to block out the visions of him lying dead in the sitting room. Some of the kids that Simon looked after, called, and they were crying their eyes out. He had made a big impression on them, and they were distraught at his passing. Simon was the big guy that looked after them, but now he was gone. That was true of Simon in every sense; he could look after himself and everyone else, in a physical sense because he was so strong and brave. He loved doing favours or helping others any way he could and was very popular. Yet he could not look after his mental self and must have thought, that he would never win his battle with depression.

When the day of the funeral came, we all sat with Simon for a while and said our goodbyes. Notes, messages, and even his phone were pushed into every corner and crevice in the casket, to give him something to take with him. When it was my turn, I sat holding his hand, trying so hard to talk so that he could hear me, and I apologised for letting him down. I noticed the muscles on his arms and asked him why he had so much strength on the outside and just not enough in his head. I wasn't crying because I had no tears left. I had used up that particular well over the last few days. It was helpful that we all got a bit of time with Simon on our own, as it was a chance to say goodbye properly, and without anyone else listening. Then we all had to leave the room to let the funeral directors close the casket and make everything ready for his journey. When we came out of the house, I noticed that there were hundreds of people gathered around to give him the send-off he deserved. I felt that he would have loved that. It took a while to get moving because there were so many people who wanted to offer their condolences. Once everyone was ready, we walked behind the hearse to the Holy Family church. We stopped outside Simon's grandparent's house for a moment. When we got to the church hundreds of people were waiting for the funeral. The hearse parked near the back door of the church, and we carried Simon up to the altar.

The funeral Mass was lovely. Father David spoke wonderfully, I believe, and Eimear Carroll sang some beautiful hymns, but I missed most of it because I was in a trance just staring at the coffin. One song did wake me up though, and it was 'Sleeping with the Angels'. I liked that. He would fit in well in Heaven and would be looking after those there that were younger than him. It did help me that so many people turned up to give Simon a proper send-off and wish him well on his trip to Heaven. It was only when the Mass was over, and we were taking Simon to his final resting place, that I noticed how many people had turned out for Simon, including his classmates from St Mary's and even students from other schools all in their school uniforms. We were outside the church for ages, talking to people who were all trying their best to commiserate with us and help us through the day. Way too quickly though, we had to get moving and take Simon to Calvary graveyard. The weather looked dodgy, and it was a bit too far to walk, so we all clambered into cars, and there was plenty for everyone. Even taxi drivers were there with the taxi signs off, ready to help move the crowd to the graveyard. On the way to the cemetery, the rain came down as if we were under a waterfall. Thankfully though we were safe and dry in the cars, and when we got to the graveyard, the rain stopped, and the sun came out and shined down on Simon as if the gates of Heaven just opened for him. We laid him to rest in Calvary Cemetery, and it was very hard to leave him there on his own as if he was just asleep and not dead. I was sure though that it was only his body that was laid in the grave as the angels had come to take Simon up to Heaven and peace at last. We even let some doves (well white pigeons really) fly off to help Simon's soul on his way. Strange as it may seem I was pleased with the send-off he got. It was all lovely, very well organised, and comforting, and I thought that Simon would be delighted with how it all went.

We had the wake after we left the cemetery, but I don't remember much about that. All my friends from college were there, and I didn't even know they were at the funeral. There was a big crowd, and we got the chance to talk to lots of different people who all had lovely stories about Simon, and that was all so wonderful on such a day. I learned so much more about Simon and the things he did when not at home, and many of the tales just reminded me of how cheeky he could be, but then sadly, what he was like before the rape. Pat Clarke was with us all the way, and I was happy with that, not only for Simon but for Pat too. As the night wore on, I got the silly idea in my head that Simon had no cigarettes for his journey, so I had to get somebody to take me back to the graveyard so that I could leave a packet of cigarettes there for him. It was official now; Simon was dead and gone forever, but that still was not processed in my mind.

The next few days were busy with people calling up to see how we were and say hello. Some brought food or snacks, which we were delighted to get because no one could face dinner. When that stopped, or when the house quietened down, we found ourselves lost again. We didn't know what to do, and the question was "what happens now".

We found ourselves on our own for the first time since Simon died, and it was the first chance reality had to reveal itself. I am only speaking for myself here, but the pain I felt that day was the worst I had felt since Simon died. It was like God shoved his hand in my chest and tore out a chunk of my heart, the part that belonged to Simon.

One day we were cleaning up around Simon's bed, and we found a lot of empty tablet foils, and I thought we had found how he had died. They were under his mattress. The tablet foils were from Champix, a tablet prescribed to Valerie when she tried to stop smoking. We thought these were not potent enough to help Simon kill himself. We passed them on to Sergeant McGivern, who was in charge of the case looking after Simon and tried to put them out of our minds. We all took something that was Simons, to keep for ourselves, which I hoped, would help comfort us. I got a couple of his favourite tee shirts and a jumper.

Chapter 15

Suicide

The real danger with depression, in many cases, is that it wants us to become severely depressed and suffer so much, that we look for any way to escape our painful and miserable life. That escape is, far too often, suicide. The definition of suicide is "The act of deliberately killing oneself, most often as a result of depression or other mental illness". Yet this definition does not describe what suicide is or means to those that die or attempt suicide. Death is not thought about, except that it is a consequence of suicide. Instead, it is the end of the horrible pain we live with every day. The ultimate pain killer. That is what suicide is. It seldom happens at the outset of difficulties. There is a tremendous amount of pain and misery between the start and finish line. For me, it always starts with a thought but grows in length and frequency, the more depressed I get. The 'suicide' escape route at the bottom of the well becomes easier to reach, much simpler than trying to climb up again. Then finally, when I am struggling to survive, some little thing smashes down any coping skills I have left, and suicide appears to be my only viable option. A big problem I had with suicide was that I never realised or understood that if my suicide attempt was successful, that was it for me. The end of my life and any chance I had of having a future. A permanent solution to a temporary problem. I was never able to get that, or maybe my depression did not want me to see it.

I don't like the term 'deliberately' in the definition, because I feel that it implies some rational thinking. I admit that I am not logical or sensible when I make my suicide plans. My thoughts are turned upside down, and I can turn off the instinct of survival, we are all born with as if it was just a switch. If I were rational and still had that instinct, I would not be able to hurt myself in any way. My survival instincts would kick in and do everything it could to stop me from getting hurt. Turning off that switch, disconnecting it in my mind, means that it cannot stop me even if that is where my 'spark of life' comes from. So, I don't think that I deliberately tried to kill myself. I could not think straight, and while I intended to suicide, I was not in any state of mind to act consciously.

When I attempted suicide, I believed that I was doing the right thing for my family and me. I would no longer be a burden on them, and they would have a beautiful happy life once I was gone. I never thought beyond the act of suicide, and I am not sure if I was able to. I assumed, or maybe my depression insisted, that everyone would be great as soon as I passed. That was always good enough for me. Even after previous attempts, I did not, or could not, see the devastation and pain my suicide would leave on my family. Thoughts about this were blocked by my irrational thinking and became disconnected from the usual channels in my mind. It was always compelling for me, and I felt that I was doing my family some good, after so much misery. That in itself was a compelling 'reason to die'.

I knew I was a failure because I could not go about my day-to-day activities properly, or like a 'normal' person. When I looked at the past, all the jobs I had were failures because I never finished any one of them. I felt like a fraud for lying and fooling people into believing that I was any good. I had failed the boys all their lives. That is what I believed, no matter what anyone else tried to tell me. That was my upside-down logic that influenced my decisions. I believe too that Simon's thinking was probably much the same. I think his depression had him focused entirely on himself, and the exit route at the bottom of his well as well as his thoughts on being a burden.

There was always one thing that snapped the only bit of coping ability I had left. It was never the sole cause of my suicide attempt. Maybe it was the straw that broke the camel's back. I was depressed and could not see any improvement in my future. I was fed up with the pain and misery, and I could not take it anymore. I wanted my family to have a happy life for once. I was a useless failure who did not deserve a place with my family or in this cruel world. I don't think that my actual sexual abuse ever entered my mind, but the whole case and everything about it was always another reason I could not continue in this life. In other words, the list of reasons I had to suicide, grew all the time, while I could not come up with any reason to live. Not even the boys. As far as I was concerned, I was doing it for them too. This collection of factors, or reasons to die, is unbearable to live with until one more reason, or painful experience, is the 'straw'. During this stage, I simply could not find or accept any reason I had to live. It felt like I was at the bottom of that well, the water was filling up, and I could never get out, except by suicide.

The power and influence of these suicidal thoughts made them too hard to ignore. They were constant, taking every waking second, and waking me up when I fell asleep. I know I had that spark of life, but it was over-powered by the negative thoughts, and every time I thought of something I could live for, it was crushed by the darkness. These positive thoughts easily lost the battle because I simply did not believe them anymore. I didn't trust the spark because it had always tried to convince me that I would be fine, that things would be ok and so on. Now I felt it had just lied to me. I wasn't going to listen to it anymore.

However, I am useless at suicide, so I am still alive to tell the tale. At the moment, I am glad I survived, but I don't always feel that way. Not much has changed regarding my depression, but I feel happy enough to be in the mild stage. I have a little bit of control over myself and can get a little bit of enjoyment and happiness. All the symptoms are still there, along with the odd thought of suicide, but I can dismiss that, just like anyone else. The only regrets I have about my suicide attempts is that I failed to end the pain. I would have been happy to have departed this world and left my depression behind. I regret the pain I caused my boys and my family, even Valerie too. I never intended to hurt them any more than I already did, and I do feel guilty about that all the time.

I understand that suicide can affect anyone, meaning that anyone can have thoughts of suicide like mine. Anyone from any background, culture, country, society or group can have thoughts of suicide. As far as I can see, the problem is that we let these thoughts grow and fester in our minds until they become too powerful to stop. I believe that suicide is preventable if we get the help and support, we need. I may have attempted suicide a few times, but I have had thoughts and urges on many occasions, and it was the professional support I had that got them out of my head.

Yet I have learned that the time when someone believes their negative thoughts and decides that suicide is their only option, is relatively short. I should have known that with my history, but then again, I did not have any clue that Simon was contemplating suicide, or had a plan.

Maybe with all my suicide experience, I should have seen the 'warning signs', but perhaps I am too stupid to have noticed. If I could ever travel back in time, I would go to the 9th of May 2003 and tell Simon that the thoughts and feelings he had for suicide would pass quicker than his funeral. I would let him know of the devastation his death would leave behind. I could never see this when I made my suicide plans, and I think it might have stopped me, or make me think twice at least. The depressed mind seems to be able to block these thoughts out entirely, and it focuses on the plan and the suicide. It is like a kind of tunnel vision when everything is about the upcoming act of suicide, and everything else is blocked from view. I am positive that Simon would have thought again because he did not want to hurt anyone, and he might have listened if we talked to him about waiting a few days, at least until he met his counsellor on Wednesday. However, that is just wishful thinking now.

Anyone thinking seriously about suicide gives out 'warning signs', without knowing it. These are actions, behaviours and things we say, that indicates that the suicidal person intends to suicide. Maybe they are tying up loose ends or talking about a future they will not be part of. It can be anything like giving away prized possessions, saying goodbye to people or behaving in a way that points to them, thinking they will have time alone with no one interrupting them. I am sure that these are what made Valerie alert to the fact that something was wrong and I needed to be watched. You could say that the warning signs I gave off, saved my life.

There is always that little part of the brain that stays rational. That is my spark of life. It is hidden somewhere in my mind and always tries to be positive and keep me alive when every other part of my being is focused on suicide. It is the only bit of light in the darkness. I think that everyone has this spark, not just me. It is the nagging doubt that tries to convince me that suicide is not my best or only choice. It is what others can reach and expand when trying to keep me alive. It may not be as powerful as the rest of my feelings, but it is always there, working for me, and trying to beat any thoughts of suicide I might have. I am happy to say that it works most of the time for me and I can't blame it for the times I didn't heed what it was trying to tell me. I am glad and lucky to have it.

Chapter 16

God

While I was trying to deal with Simon's suicide and funeral, the final year exams at Trinity College were getting
ever closer, though they were far from my mind. The rule
was that you either sat these exams in May or you did not
sit them at all. I was in favour of missing them because
my head was not in the right place, and they did not matter to me anymore. But the boys insisted I went and did
what I could. I relented and agreed to do them. Simon
died on the 10th, was buried a few days later and I started
my exams on the 20th of May. I travelled by train as usual
but didn't study or read anything. My body was there, but
I wasn't. The only thing I can remember from the exams
is the chaplain of the college meeting me at the gates on
Tara St. the morning of every exam. He walked me to the
exam hall and took me to my seat. The Chaplain was kind
enough to make sure I got to and from my exams, and I
needed his help to get to the correct exam hall. I had no

idea where I was supposed to be. It was like I was never in Trinity before. I didn't study anymore after Simon died, but I doubt it would have made any difference. I don't remember doing the exams at all. I don't recall meeting or talking to anyone except Richard, the chaplain. I sat and wrote for the full 3 hours, but even later that day, I could not remember anything I wrote. I got through them all, which was a feat in itself. When they were all over, there was none of the usual joy and delight. There was nothing, no feelings. I had a task to do, and I did it.

After the wake, I did not touch a drop of alcohol for months. I knew that if I did, I might not have stopped. I could have easily kept drinking all the time, to try to make my pain go away. I was so afraid of this that it scared me, and I was very conscious that I had to look after the boys. They were struggling too, and again I did not know how to help them through this.

The neighbour who had raped Simon, still lived next door with her boyfriend. Thankfully they did not show their faces after Simon died. I, for one, did not want to see them because I might have done something and made a fool of myself. I was wound up so tight; the slightest thing could have set me off. I wanted Simon to leave us with as much dignity as possible, and I did not want to be arrested for something stupid. I had already complained to Respond, the housing association, about them, but had received no reply. Two days after Simon's burial, I wrote to them again, asking them to move the neighbours as far away from us as possible. We did not want to see them from day to day, which would have forced to us relive Simon's rape and the way that changed him.

I was still in counselling with Patrick, but it had changed to bereavement counselling, and I was struggling to come to terms with what happened to Simon. Not only his suicide, but his rape, and the pain and misery of depression he lived with every day for a year and a half. I felt so sorry for him that my heart cried all the time. There were thoughts of joining Simon, just to look after him. I wished that I was able to look after him now, and the questions rattling around in my mind needed answering. In the state I was in, I did not come to realise the solution; instead, it crept into my brain like water leaking into cracks in a wall. The only way to look after Simon and get the answers I was searching for was suicide. These thoughts were completely different from the ideas of suicide I had at other times. These were about looking after Simon and getting answers, not about me and my pain. Thankfully the thoughts did not become urges. It was the thoughts of Wayne and Lee that kept me going. I also had the memory of the awful pain Simon left behind. I did not want to hurt Wayne and Lee anymore. They had enough trauma in their lives, and I was not going to add to it. I had Patrick too who helped me focus on the boys and life itself, rather than joining Simon. I somehow managed to stay alive and keep my suicidal thoughts at bay.

I have no idea how long the shock of Simon's death lasted for Valerie, Wayne, and Lee, but I do remember when it wore off for me. I was trying my old depression tactic of doing jobs around the house to distract me, and I was painting the front door. An Aerosmith song that Simon liked came on the radio, and I just burst into tears. I thought I had no tears left, but I was so wrong. I just sat on the doorstep crying. I felt the shock flow out with the tears and reality taking its place in my mind. I had this realisation that everything that had happened over the last few weeks was not a dream. It was genuine and real, and the pain was real too. It was like Simon had just died that day. It was a new, different pain that ached in my heart and my head. I cried more than I cried when he died. I wept because there was no more doubting or denying that Simon was gone from this Earth. So, I cried like a baby until I knocked over the tin of varnish I was using. Then I just got mad. Mad at the can of varnish, livid at my awkwardness, and angry at myself. Raging really, that such a thing had happened and it was my fault.

I had let Simon down in the worse possible way. Why didn't I notice that he only asked for one cigarette that night, when he knew he would be up for a few hours waiting for his mother to come home? Did he have his 'plan' ready and why didn't I notice the signs? Why did I believe that his "not yet" was a sign that he was on his way back up? Why did I not go and sit with him instead of lying on the bed, trying to rest? Did Simon consider that he didn't want a life of pain and misery? Was he afraid of hurting us and everyone he loved? I don't think Simon could ever live knowing he hurt someone he loved or liked. These questions and many more bounced around my brain, and I had no answer for them. I then remembered a little note Simon gave us a few weeks before he died. In it, he said he was sorry for what he had become and sorry for hurting us so much. We were pleased when we got the note, but didn't want or need his apologies. We just loved him and wanted him to be better. Now I realised what it was – Simon's suicide note. Why didn't I see that at the time? I did not know where the letter was, but never thought to look for it and pass it on to Sergeant McGivern.

Out of pure anger, and a desire to look after Lee, I wrote to Father Nulty in St. Mary's Parish who was Chairman of the Board of Directors of St Mary's secondary school. I explained how their Principal was partly responsible for Simon's death. I also included the fact that we were very concerned about Lee in the same school and whether he would be picked on next. Lee was starting the third year and would have his Intermediate Certificate exams that school year. I explained how we were genuinely concerned that the Principal would target Lee next. We met with the Board of Directors and did not get the apology we wanted. It was the same old story in these situations. They did try to offer some comfort but said nothing else that was helpful or admitted that the Principal, and therefore the school, were to blame in part in Simon's death. Miss Clark, the deputy in the school, was at the meeting and offered her assurances that Lee would be looked after. She had been our point of contact in the school since

Simon was suspended, and she was always helpful and truthful. At least we thought Lee would be ok. Apart from that, it was just a waste of time and a big let-down. We had hoped for something, maybe an investigation or inquiry but got nothing that satisfied us. The school did arrange to plant a memorial tree for Simon on the school grounds later that year, which was a lovely gesture, but the Principal was not involved and moved elsewhere about that time. All Simon's classmates and teachers, as well as everyone else in the school, turned out to pay their respects to Simon and it was a lovely ceremony. I'm sure that Simon appreciated it too.

One big mistake I made after Simon died, was that I forced my grief down into some locked box in my head so that I could look after the boys, even though I had no idea how. I have no idea how I managed to do that, but I did, but it was not much help to me.

Simon's criminal case against the neighbour was dropped because Simon was no longer available to take part in any trial. That was a kick in the teeth, and yet again, life was beating up the Moroneys. It was hard to accept, but on the other hand, having Simon involved in a dirty criminal case after he was gone was not really what we wanted. We wanted to remember the happy, funny, cheeky, and loving boy we all loved, not the one raped and then plagued by depression.

Luckily enough, those neighbours moved out of the house next door shortly after Simon died. We didn't even know they were gone, until after they were gone. We didn't give a damn about where they were gone, or whether they were somehow 'pushed out'. We were just relieved they were nowhere near us anymore. The Housing Agency even offered to move us to a new home, but once those neighbours were gone, I didn't want to leave the last place I had seen Simon alive, even if this was where he died. There were rumours about how the neighbours from Hell had been threatened and told to leave town after Simon died. We knew nothing about any of the threats until later, and will never know whether they were genuine or not. I had to settle for the fact that she would have to live with the memory of what she did all her life. She got off lightly. That's what I thought anyway.

We were all in shock. A normal day to day life was pretty impossible even though life still had to be lived. Thankfully it was near the end of the school year for Lee, and taking time off did not affect his schooling too much. We didn't put any pressure on him to go back, instead let him decide on his own. He did not go back before the summer holidays, and we were okay with that. Dr Neary tried to get bereavement counselling for Valerie and Lee, but despite his efforts, no counselling was ever offered. I even brought Lee to group therapy in Drogheda once. It turned out to be useless and more harm than good because one person was allowed to dominate the session, and his problems seemed insignificant to us. We did not go back.

The other thing I had a real problem with after Simon died, was my Catholic faith and God himself. I believe in God, whether He believes in me is the question. Why had He gifted us with such loving, caring sons and then hurt Simon and his brothers before taking him away from us? I wondered if He took him to end his pain. If so, why did He let him be hurt in the first place? I was very angry with God for taking Simon away from us and not giving him a fair chance at life. I was mad at Him because He ignored my pleas for help when Simon died. I was not even able to pray because I could not forgive those who trespassed against Simon, as was part of the Lord's prayer. According to my faith, I was just supposed to turn the other cheek and forgive those that had hurt Simon and made him take his own life. I did try but could not excuse them. I tried to stop thinking about them, and leave them to God to judge, but that did not work either and just made me angrier. I am the kind of person who needs to understand things so that I can process them. If I can't understand, I just cannot work them through my mind. I couldn't figure out anything, let alone God's part in Simon's death. I called him names and asked him all these questions and more. It was the only time I was ever disrespectful to God, but I felt he deserved it. I wanted and needed some answers. I didn't care for the idea that he called Simon to Heaven for some particular reason, because I thought he was cruel to let him suffer and then take him away like that. I had let my family down so much, had suffered myself, but had never questioned God. I just thought I did not understand Him or His ways. Now I had failed Simon and my family, but God has failed us.

I even grew anxious about the Catholic church's stance
on suicide, where the victims were seen as having died
in Mortal sin and therefore not accepted into Heaven. I
even wrote to Fr David about this, and he told me that all
that changed, in Ireland anyway, in 1993, and he assured
me that Simon was safe in Heaven. This colossal disappointment with God himself was taking more and more of
my time and thoughts, but I wasn't getting any answers.
I didn't go to Mass for a while because of this, and I did
not want where Simon's funeral was. I was afraid that I
would have to live through the funeral again, except that
this time my mind would not be clouded by shock. I was
scared to go in case the torture in my soul got worse. I was
questioning my faith and belief in God. I just took Him for
granted. I was thinking about God and his existence and
his relationship with me. It didn't take my stupid brain
long to conclude that God did not love me, despite all the
times I spent at Mass, hearing that He did. I did not know
what God felt for me but thought that he had no time for
me, and I had no idea why. Instead of finding answers, I
found confusion, and the only thing that made sense was
that I had also failed God somehow.

After a while, I thought that there was only one place I
might get some answers, so I started going back to Mass
on Sundays. I was looking for something, anything at all.
I needed to understand what happened to Simon and why
God had put so much pain into our lives. I didn't accept
that God was testing me, because he had hurt the whole

family for years, not just me. I could not remember any extended period the boys lived without this pain. I also wanted to go back to Mass because I believed that Simon was in Heaven, and the only way I was going to see him again, was to make sure I lived a good life on Earth, as Jesus wanted, and earn my place in Heaven when the time came.

I went to Mass but found it very hard to concentrate and listen. I found my thoughts drifting away from the church to my own issues. The last thing I needed was having my demons trying to take over my mind in church, of all places. Then one Sunday, God spoke to me. I did not hear God's voice, and I did not recognise that he was talking to me at first. I was in Mass, sitting there on my own, listening to, but not hearing, Father David deliver his sermon. Something Father David said, got through to me and made me sit up and take notice. I don't recall precisely what he said, but it was like he was talking directly to me about my struggles with God. Everything Fr David said was an accurate description of my feelings and thoughts. He spoke about God and the ways He knew of my struggles, and how He would help me.

I looked at the people around me to see if I was just dreaming. I wasn't dreaming. God was reassuring me through Father David, but it was like He was speaking directly to me. At first, I was willing to accept, with complete astonishment, that God had spoken to me, but as the days passed, I started to believe that I was stupid and I had imagined the whole thing. A few weeks later, the same thing happened, and I began to believe again. I thought that it was my stupid brain, and the way I think, that was causing me so much pain and anguish. I thought that maybe God even hated me, but here He was talking to me, and I had the idea that perhaps he had been talking to me all through my life, but I was too dumb to notice. I didn't get any answers to my questions about Simon, but I started to believe that maybe I was wrong about my relationship with God. I was not sorry that I had shouted and argued with God because I knew I needed to get it off my chest, and there was no one else I could yell at. I felt that God was talking to me a few more times in Mass, and I stopped blaming him for taking Simon away. Instead, I asked Him to please look after and care for Simon up in Heaven. It wasn't only God I prayed to, to look after Simon. I prayed especially to Mary and Joseph because they were parents and had lost Jesus and could under-stand how we felt. I was searching for some comfort and looking for some reassurance that Simon was safe and well in Heaven. Probably a bit too much to ask for, and expect some kind of reply, but I was desperate.

I spent far too much time visiting Simon in the graveyard and looking after his grave. I had the idea and still do that Simon always liked to look presentable, leaving the house, so I should make sure that his Grave always looked clean and tidy. I wished that he was at peace forever and would become our very own Guardian Angel. I asked for his help for us all, especially Lee. I reminded him of how he was always Lee's protector, and I asked him to keep protecting Lee and Wayne. Some days I got some comfort from visiting Simon in the graveyard, even though I was well aware that it was only his body interred there, and that his soul was gone to Heaven. On other days I just felt too sad to stay there. I think the grave is his special spot in the world and deserves to be looked after.

Months after Simon died, I found something that cheered me up, and I immediately felt guilty, for enjoying something in life. It was a weird feeling to be happy and then guilty, but it was the start of good days slowly but surely replacing bad days. That was when all the sayings about Simon not wanting us to be in pain but to live our lives, started to make some sense. I was able to think about Simon and Heaven and what he wanted for us. I was also able to picture Simon when he was alive for the first time since he died. The images of him lying dead still clouded my mind, but being able to imagine him alive, gave me some good memories and helped me cope. That for me, was when I could think about the future and started to believe that we would find this new normal and learn to live without Simon while never forgetting him.

Lee went back to school when classes resumed in September. Miss Clarke, his protector in the school, made sure he was made to feel welcome and offered all the support they could provide. Wayne stayed at home for a while, stuck to his computer, playing games, before he decided it was time to go back to work. Unfortunately, he did not go back on his course, because he missed the end of year exams. Somewhere in the midst of all this Wayne and Lee swapped bedrooms and Wayne got the big room, and Lee the small one, but they were both happy with that.

We managed to have some kind of a decent Christmas that year but. I think everyone was trying extra hard to make the rest of us happy; after all we went through. I know that is what I was trying to do. It was the first Christmas day I went to the graveyard, and I tried to talk to Simon, and ask him to be with us for the day. I hoped that he could, and enjoy himself watching us all enjoy our presents and stuff our faces with Christmas dinner. After the cemetery, I went to Mass and then we all went to Ballsgrove for fun with the extended family. When that was over, we went home for the Christmas dinner. Once Christmas dinner was over, and the boys went off to do their own thing, I sat in the living room and tried to talk to Simon hoping that he had a good Christmas too.

In March 2004, 10 months after Simon died, his inquest was held in the old Community Centre building on Fair Street. The building was ancient, and it was a horrible place to go for the inquest. Myself, Valerie, Wayne, and Lee went there together, and we were nervous and apprehensive, not knowing what to expect because we have never been to an inquest before. When we got there, there were lots of other people there for inquests into the death of their loved ones. That made us feel a lot more awkward and uncomfortable. Thankfully we did not have to sit there and wait. Sergeant McGivern told us to go away for the morning and come back in the afternoon because Simon's case would not be called until then. He said that there was a good chance that there would be no one else around. I thought that was a good call because I don't think I could have sat with lots of other families there for their inquests. It was just too sad and morbid. When we got back in the afternoon, there was no one else there except for the coroner and the Gardai. The coroner told us that Simon had died from bupropion toxicity and that his death would have been relatively quick. I asked him to explain precisely to us what bupropion toxicity was, and he told us it was the Champix tablets and that they were very toxic. We were shocked at this because we had no idea that they were so lethal. At last, we knew what Simon died from, but it was of little comfort. It wasn't going to bring him back.

When Simon died, a drug counsellor called to the house to offer his help and support. I was annoyed at this because I knew that Simon's death was not drug-related, but the thought had never left my mind. I asked the coroner was there anything else in Simon's system when he died. I was also thinking of the Principal throwing Simon out of school for being on drugs. He told us there was nothing at all except Simon had been smoking cigarettes. That was a little bit of comfort for me. I knew he did not take drugs, and this confirmed it. I was happy for Simon because his name would not be tarnished by talk of drug-taking.

The coroner ruled that Simon's cause of death was an 'OPEN VERDICT' with depression listed as a secondary factor. At the inquest, the coroner has to believe that the suicide was 'planned and intended' beyond all reasonable doubt, to be able to rule it as a suicide. Just like the criminal cases, beyond all reasonable doubt. He did not believe that Simon's suicide was planned and intended because there was no proof. We had forgotten all about the note we received before he died, so the coroner had no idea about it. So, all he could list on the death certificate was an open verdict.

The inquest into Simon's death was over very quickly, but while we got some answers, I did not get the answers I was looking for. I know it sounds silly now, but I was hoping for some sort of clue about what was in Simon's mind when he decided to take his life. I also wanted to know when Simon had made his plan and hoped for answers to the many questions I had in my head since he died. It was years later when I realised that it would have been impossible for the coroner or anyone else to answer these questions. No one could ever answer me, except Simon himself. That was when I started accepting that there was nothing, I could do to help Simon now, except maybe to pray for him and look after his grave.

Chapter 17

Trial

As if things were not bad enough after Simon died, I received notification that summer, that the case against Shine was going to proceed in Dundalk Circuit Court that October. The prosecution involved six victims, who had accused Shine of indecent assault, and I was one of the six. Talk about bad timing. I had waited so long for this, but for it to come up now was unexpected and not very welcome. As if there was not enough crap bouncing around in my head trying to break me. All the thoughts of my visits to the hospital and Fair St came flooding back to me. There was so much over-analysing going on, that my brain could have been the size of Mount Everest. It was the last thing I needed that year, but thankfully I was still in counselling. Patrick, my counsellor, spent weeks trying to get me ready for what we expected would be a traumatic experience. Without him, I don't know what would have happened to me, or if I would have gone to court at all.

I did get some good news that gave me a boost like I got my batteries charged. I got a 2.1 result in my final year exams in Trinity. Hard as it was to believe, I had earned an honours degree from Trinity College. I was delighted with that as was Valerie, and the boys thought it was just fantastic. I thought Simon would have been delighted too and happy to share in the celebrations. I convinced myself that I got the 2.1 because of my previous grades. I knew I could not have done well in my finals. My papers probably looked like gibberish to the examiners. Maybe Simon was doing his work as our new Guardian Angel. I also received a lovely letter from my tutor Michael Harrison, congratulating me and wishing me well for the future. I was so happy to receive that even before I opened the envelope because it was addressed to Mr Patrick Peter Moroney B. A. I had letters after my name. Wow, that was great.

Wayne's 21st birthday was on the 7th of October that year, and because of all that happened with Simon's passing, we made a massive effort and had a big party in the rugby club. Lots of people turned up, and we had a great time and must have had nearly 20 people staying in our house for the weekend, with lots of Valerie's family over to help Wayne celebrate. I was thrilled that all went so well, and was delighted to see that so many of Wayne and Lee's friends were there to give them something to be cheerful about. Even some of Simon's friends were invited and turned up, including Pat, who I was thrilled to see again. As was always the case, seeing Wayne, Lee, my whole family, and everyone else happy was all I needed to be satisfied. I think that Wayne enjoyed his party and I was delighted that he was able to celebrate properly and have some fun.

The court case against Shine started on the 7th October 2003, the actual day of Wayne's 21st, nine and a half years after I made my complaint. There were six complainants, each one claiming that Shine had sexually assaulted him. I had never been to the Circuit Court in Dundalk before. When I found out which courtroom the case would be in, I went in to have a look and found it to be very old fashioned, the seats very uncomfortable and it all felt very claustrophobic. I was lucky that I always had someone from my family with me, especially Mam and Dad, who watched over me and kept me sane and somewhat composed.

No one from the Gardai or prosecution team got in touch with me before the case. I thought they would, to explain what was going to happen, or to put me at ease in any way. I felt scared, worried, nervous, and confused. I wanted it started and then to be over as quickly as possible. I tried my best to put my 'good face' on as much as I could. If ever my 'acting' skills and experience came into play, then this was the time. I was as composed as I could be. People were speculating and thinking aloud all sorts of things, and I did not want to get them in my head. I would have started overthinking, and I could not handle that. Thankfully Patrick had arranged to meet me during the trial to help me through it all. So, I had him and my family looking after me, and I knew I could tell them if I was struggling. That helped me keep my focus, and helped keep me kind of calm. That was as good as I could have hoped for.

Then all of a sudden, it was time to start. When the judge entered and took his seat, we learned that the case involving one of the complainants was withdrawn. We never found out why, even though the judge said that he would explain why at the end of the trial. I did not know that victim, but I felt so sorry for him. I don't know what would have happened to me if it was my complaint that was dropped at the very last minute. I didn't want to think about that. Then the jury selection began, and I don't recall a single thing about it. I couldn't tell you if I was even in the courtroom or not. Once that was over, the preliminaries began. I found out that I was patient A, and the others were B, C, D, E. The judge was Michael O'Shea, and the defence barrister was Felix McEnroy. The prosecuting barrister was John O'Kelly, who we learned had just two weeks to prepare his case. I don't know whether that was true or not. I hoped it wasn't.

Once the preliminaries were over, the trial itself began. I don't remember whether it was on the first day of the court case or not. I was just focused on me and my complaint and tried to shut everything else out. I was the first witness to be called for the prosecution. I sat terrified and nervous in the witness box, staring all the time at a screw in the wood directly in front of me. And that was before anyone asked me a question. I was trying so hard to concentrate and keep my emotions in check. I wanted to answer all the questions clearly and honestly. I did not want to do what I always do. I did not want to listen to the questions and answer before my brain gave me the correct reply. I was sworn in as a witness, and I felt that I was mumbling when I read out my bit. I did not want to do that, but my stomach was in my throat, making it hard for me to speak. I wished I had some water with me. I wanted to lubricate my throat so that I could reply to all questions clearly and be heard.

Senior Counsel O'Kelly asked his questions, which encouraged me to describe the abuse at the hands of Shine. I told the story just as I had done many times before, and generally, I was satisfied with the answers I gave. I had related everything about my visits to Mr Shine's clinic and his private rooms on Fair St. I was sure that I had included all the details and left nothing out. I wasn't happy but felt somewhat satisfied. I thought that everyone could hear me. O'Kelly was brief and to the point, and it did not take too long for him to finish his questions and pass me on to the defence barrister.

I was not sure how McEnroy was going to question me, but I did not think it would be easy. What happened, as far as I was concerned, was a day and a half of slander on my character and wild accusations that certainly hurt me. I was expecting tough questions, but not the ones he asked. He barely mentioned the sexual assaults, but very cleverly, kept them out of the jurors' minds. Shine's barrister was making lengthy statements about me, before tagging on a question. He brought up the collusion again with patient B and a suggestion that we did it together so we would get compensation from a civil case. I tried to explain that there was no contact between me and B until years later. I agreed that there was a civil case, but added that would never go ahead until the criminal case was over. I tried to stress that it lagged a long way in importance compared to this criminal case. I told the defence counsel that I was there for justice and not for money, but he just sneered and changed the subject. When I felt I might be getting my point across, he interrupted and changed the subject. I was getting mad and nearly burned the screw, by staring at it so hard. I was battling like crazy to stay calm. I was afraid to take my eyes off the screw and look at Mc Enroy in case I lost it altogether.

He asked me about my car crashes, and I got confused. When I was answering his questions about my road traffic accident, I was talking about my car accident in 1979, and I responded accordingly. When he accused me of crashing after drinking several pints, 5 or 6 he said, I could not figure out what he was talking about. I denied that I had any drink that day and suggested that my hospital records would show that. Yet, he persisted, and I started thinking that he had made a colossal mistake. I tried to answer his questions about the crash as best as I could, but I couldn't understand what he was talking about at times. He got me flustered and confused. I answered yes to a question when I should have answered no, and when I tried to come back and correct myself, he moved on to something different. I felt slighted and was getting angrier.

Then he referred to the assaults I suffered in Brixton, especially the last one and stated that these were the cause of all my issues and that I needed someone to blame and had picked Shine. Again, he tagged a question onto the end of his lengthy statement, and I tried to answer but got nowhere. I tried to explain how I was suffering from depression a long time before these attacks. As soon as I mentioned my depression, he was shouting over me asking an entirely different question. Mc Enroy was enjoying himself and beating the crap out of me. He then accused me of being a violent person and referred to me being charged with possession of an article contrary to the larceny act, referring to the time I tried to break in next door. Now I was on trial, not Shine, and it genuinely felt like that. I was hurting so much my head was in agony, I couldn't breathe properly, and I thought I was going to die right there on the witness stand. Somehow, I kept going, concentrating on what he was saying and on the screw at the same time. I was thinking, even hoping that O'Kelly or even the judge might jump in and stop this torture, but neither said a word to help me. I was on my own, but despite the rage, I was determined to see this through.

Mc Enroy managed to break my life up into three phases, living in Ireland, then in London and living back in Ire-

land. He stated that I had a persistent problem with alcohol. I argued that I did have a problem with alcohol
once in London, but other than that had no problem. I
told him I was a social drinker, who never took a drink at
home, but I don't think the jury heard a word, except what
I said about my alcohol problem in London. Mc Enroy
heard what he wanted the jury to listen to and then spoke
over me, so no one could make out what I was trying to
say. Every time I thought I was getting my point across; he
changed the subject to something different, and I was getting more and more frustrated. I raised my voice, just to
be heard or to try to finish an answer to the question I was
asked. That didn't work for me either. I was sure that no
one was going to believe a word coming out of my mouth
because they only heard what McEnroy wanted them to
hear. My quest for justice was fading fast, and I would
probably be locked up in jail for lying and causing all this
trouble.

Mc Enroy was trying to find out why I never played Gaelic
again for the Wolfe Tones, but he never directly asked me,
so I didn't tell him. He kept coming back to this as if not
playing anymore was a crime in itself. However, I did
point out to him and everyone in the court that he desperately wanted to know. I said it in such a way that the
court burst out laughing. That was the first and only bit
of support or encouragement I got while on the witness
stand, and the only time I got the jump on Mc Enroy. I was
still struggling, and silently begging for support or intervention from anyone, to no avail. I had to deal with all the

questions, accusations, and insults on my own. I felt that he was destroying my reputation, yet my depression was only briefly mentioned. Years of depression dismissed as if it was just an incidental tiny thing. I was hurt, fuming and I was confused when he raised the issue of me being admitted to hospital in 1975.

He said I was admitted for a hip fracture, and later Shine said the same thing. I tried to explain when answering both O'Kelly and McEnroy, that I injured my thigh. I spoke about the pain and where it hurt and being on crutches. It didn't seem to matter to anyone, except me, that they were trying to cover up my torn muscle with an injury that happened in an accident years later. I talked about Shine examining my thigh before he went on to assault me sexually. I never mentioned my hip or talked about Shine examining my hip. I knew that my statements were clear on that. I even thought they might be mixing up the complainants. I was confused and unsure of what was going on. Mc Enroy kept trying to emphasise that I was admitted into the hospital in 1975 with a broken hip. None of it made any sense to me at all. Sometime during all this, we finished for the day, but I don't remember a single thing about going home except that I drove Mam and Dad home and went home myself. I knew I was not finished in the witness box and could not relax at all, or stop thinking about all the questions I faced. I was getting more and more anxious and terrified about what I had to face the next day, and I did not know what to do about the significant discrepancy regarding the injury I suffered in 1975. I could not talk to anyone about this because the judge told me not to discuss the case with anyone.

The next day, it was much of the same. McEnroy was putting me on trial, not Shine. I kept my focus on the screw and tried to concentrate as hard as I could on what I was asked. I was resigned to the fact that no-one was going to interrupt on my behalf. I just wished that this was all over, but I tried to answer as best as I could. Mc Enroy was still playing with me and the court, making lengthy statements about how awful a person I was, before tacking on a question at the end, and then interrupting before I could finish my answer. It seemed that he loved every minute, while I hated the whole experience. When I finished giving my evidence and the cross-examination, everyone said I had done well, but I didn't feel that I did. I knew I had been forced or coerced into making mistakes, and I never got the chance to rectify them, but the Gardai were happy that I did very well. I was relieved that it was all over, even though the judge said he might call me back. I knew that I didn't have a broken hip in 1975, but thought that my actual illness was not as crucial as I imagined. Because no matter why I attended the Lourdes in 1975, masturbation was not part of prescribed treatment. But it still bugged me that they had it all wrong and because I had not noticed this before. I couldn't understand how the Gardai had got this all wrong, or why they never asked me about whether I had a torn muscle or broken hip in 1975.

When I came off the witness stand, I went outside, and I sucked the air into my lungs in huge breaths, trying to air out my brain and force it out of the focused state it was in for a day and a half. Once I was finished as a witness, I was able to stay in court and watch proceedings. I sat in most of the time, but sometimes I could not listen anymore and had to leave. I listened to the other complainants describe their abuse, and it was all so similar to mine. It was the first time I had heard the evidence of other boy's abuse. I thought it made for a strong case, but I think that prosecuting counsel believed so too, and relied on this too much. He spent a short amount of time questioning each of the complainants, inviting them to describe their abuse. Then McEnroy would take far longer cross-examining each one, while still throwing all kinds of accusations. Well, at least they did not have to stay in the witness box for a day and a half. Overall, I thought the first week of the trial went well for the prosecution and thought we had Shine over a barrel. I was amazed that I had made it through the questioning and cross-examination while keeping some semblance of composure. I felt like my head was held together with duct tape, and it helped that I had someone with me every day.

The second week soon got rid of the confidence I had in the trial, and the way it was proceeding. Shine was called to the witness box to defend himself and answer questions from the barristers. He denied all charges against him and said that he did not remember any of the complainants except one, patient D. He did not remember me, and using notes, questioned why I had returned to him in 1980, (to get the skin grafting done) if he had abused me as I had accused. He suggested that the complaints only existed because of the Press and their reports on him and the case. He suggested that there was only a case because of the "malignancy of compensation". McEnroy painted Shine as a world-class surgeon and an expert in genital matters and Shine loved that. I remember thinking that he probably was 'an expert', but not the way Mc Enroy was referring to. Shine stated that no child was ever seen in the hospital without a parent present. He also said that he had never seen a minor without a parent or guardian present. During a limited and disappointing cross-examination by the prosecuting counsel, Shine continued to deny any abuse occurred. Still, when O' Kelly pressurised him, he became flustered and was about to crack, and maybe reveal the truth. McEnroy interrupted and said he had a witness that he needed to present immediately to the court because he had travelled a great distance to get there that day. He saved Shine, saved his case, and we all knew it. The judge granted the defence barristers request without a peep of objection from the prosecuting counsel. I thought he would object and ask to be allowed to continue questioning Shine, or at least get Shine to finish answering that question. He let Shine slip through his fingers, and would not catch him out again. Surely, I thought, the judge and jury would have noticed this, just like everyone else in the court did. It seemed so obvious to me and everyone I spoke to thought the same.

I also expected the prosecution to call witnesses from the hospital or elsewhere to disprove Shine regarding his statements about only treating minors in the presence of a parent or guardian. I was surprised when O'Kelly called no one to prove Shine was a liar. I could not figure out why this was. The prosecution called one medical expert, who found that there was no need for genital examinations in each of our cases, and though questioned intensely by McEnroy, made a good case that genital examinations were not necessary or warranted in each case. Shine's team did call a load of witnesses, mostly doctors, who were nothing more than character witnesses. They eloquently told the court about how Shine was a brilliant doctor, and how respected he was. None of them was asked anything about Shine dealing with minors. Neither were they asked about rumours in the hospital about Shine abusing young patients, or anything related to the abuse. Again, I could not figure out why, or what O'Kelly's strategy was. O'Kelly just let them all ramble on and divert the jury from thinking about the abuse to thinking what a great doctor Shine was. No one ever said he was a bad doctor, but Mc Enroy wasted a lot of the court's time with these character references. By now, I was not sure whether we would get a conviction or not, and my confidence in O'Kelly and the case he presented was diminishing every day.

It was clear that Mc Enroy was dominating O'Kelly, and the judge was allowing his every request. I even got in trouble. I went to lunch one day with my Mam and Dad in the Imperial Hotel, and before going back to the Courthouse, I went to the toilets. Unfortunately, when I opened the door to the bathrooms, I saw one of the jury members there. I did not go in, and I went and found the Garda that was looking after the jury. I told him of our brief encounter in the toilet and left it at that. When the court restarted, McEnroy was quick to bring it up before the judge and accuse me of trying to interfere with the jury. He said he was outraged at such behaviour and he was really trying to twist the knife in. He loved the chance to make me seem more like a major criminal rather than just a witness. The Judge spoke to the Garda in charge and asked him about the incident, and then asked me about it. Our versions of the events were the same. It was a simple error on my part. The judge then told me I had acted impeccably, but he barred me from the Imperial Hotel for the duration of the trial. He told McEnroy to sit down. That was the first and only time the judge did not side with McEnroy. The case drifted on without anything exceptional happening, with McEnroy boring the hell out of the jury, trying I'm sure, to somehow distract them from our testimonies at the start of the trial. One strange thing happened when a jury member felt sick and Shine offered her a medical opinion. I have no idea how this was allowed to happen, but I'm sure the jury member was grateful.

At the end of the trial, O'Kelly's summation was brief, and he concentrated on the direct evidence given by each of

the complainants, and the fact that any genital examination or manipulation was not warranted. McEnroy took
far longer reminding the jury of what awful people the
complainants were and asked how Shine, such a world-
renowned surgeon, could be guilty of such an accusation.
He even blamed us for the delay in bringing the case,
while it was his team that used every trick in the book to
keep Shine away from a criminal trial. I thought that he
was trying to get the jury to ignore the direct evidence
and judge the complainants instead. Yet I felt that everyone, especially the jury, would see through this because
it all seemed so staged. The judge then charged the jury
and told them that if they had any doubt whatsoever, they
must acquit. Any doubt is not the same as reasonable
doubt. The judge did not mention or explain reasonable
doubt o the jury. I thought that anyone could have doubts
about anything and that the jury would have some doubts.
Reasonable doubt allowed for a bit of doubt, and the jury
could convict if they thought he was guilty, even if they
had a doubt or two. When the judge finished and sent
the jury to deliberate, I was not confident at all. I had
'reasonable doubts' about the way the judge charged the
jury. Later it seemed that it was only me who was having
these thoughts, so I thought that maybe I was just stupid,
and everyone else was right to be confident of the correct
outcome.

During deliberations, the jury requested to see the judge,
and they asked about the construction of the cubicles in

the Lourdes Hospital, where most of the abuse occurred. They were incorrectly told that curtains surrounded them. They were, in fact, solid wood structures. None of the complainants knew about this until later when it was too late. I can't remember how long the jury deliberated, but when they were ready, we were all called back into court. To my horror, one by one Shine was acquitted of all the charges against him, starting with mine. I was devastated, and I really could not believe what I was hearing. I thought that maybe I was dreaming or back in one of those zombie-like stages that flooded my brain with all kinds of crap. I was gutted, as was everyone else in the courtroom that day except Shine and his legal team. I had spent almost ten years on a journey to nowhere. For me, the result was that I did not get justice, nor did I get closure, and surely Shine could go back to being a danger to minors everywhere. The result grabbed hold of my brain and kneaded it like pastry. I had wasted the best part of my life, almost all the boy's lives and I had nothing to show for it. The shock in the court was unbelievable. Everyone was the same, and I just wanted or had to, get out of there as fast as possible. I couldn't listen to the disbelief in the comments anymore. We had failed. The Judge, the jury, and prosecuting counsel had let us down, but the defence counsel performed brilliantly for his client.

I left and disappeared from the court and went home, dreading the conversation I was going to have with Valerie and the boys, explaining how we had lost the case, and how Shine was still a free man. They had lost so much because I wanted to make a criminal complaint against Shine to get justice, to get closure, and stop him from abusing others. After all that time, we got nothing except more pain and misery. I must have been Hitler or some terrible abuser like Shine in the past. I met a solicitor a few weeks later, and he told me that McEnroy became the talk of the legal profession, for winning a case that everyone thought was unwinnable.

Chapter 18

Life without Simon

I don't know where I got the strength from, but I had to be strong for Wayne and Lee. I was very disappointed and could not be consoled, but I used all the mental strength I had to try not to think about Shine or the trial. I felt again that God was punishing me, and I couldn't figure out why. I didn't know how we had lost our case, but dwelling on it was doing me no good at all. I tried my best to not think about it, and when I did, I found ways to block it from my mind, at least temporarily. I had to get back to work so that I could pay for Simon's funeral. I had forced my grief into a box, but I don't think that it could have re-surfaced then. My head was full of crap from the trial, and all the ways I was stupid and a failure. There was no room for my grief amongst all my thoughts and feelings.

Thankfully I was able to pay Townley's in instalments for the funeral. I had paid them some already. I got a little job working in the bar of the rugby club for my brother, and that helped me with the rest. I was useless behind the bar because my head was not mine. I was never happy there but needs must, so I stayed as long as I could. In the end, my brother's contract with the rugby club was up, and I was out of work. I applied for jobs and took the first one I could get. It was on a management scheme in Homebase, and I was working out of their store in Santry. It was great for me because it allowed me to get stuck into something, I was comfortable doing, and keep my head occupied. There was plenty to do, and most of the people I met and worked with were friendly. It also allowed me to pay off the funeral bill bit by bit. I did not plan to stay in Homebase forever, but I still felt the need to prove myself to myself. I worked hard and did my best. I had no idea what I wanted to do with my degree and lacked confidence or self-esteem, so I did not see myself as suitable for any job vacancy I looked at. Even looking at vacancies brought me down that bit more, because I didn't feel I was good enough. It was also devastating because I could not make any decision concerning my personal life or to try to find a stable future or my rightful place in the world.

One day when driving up the motorway to Dublin, I got a phone call from Patricia Townley to tell me that there were only a few Euro left to pay for Simon's funeral. She told me that they were not going to request any further payments and would close my account. They were happy that we paid them just as we said we would, and Patricia wished us the best for the future. I thought that was very nice, and it pleased me to hear from them and to have the funeral fully paid for. I was more than pleased; I was delighted because I had not let Simon down this time, or anyone else for that matter.

One thing did bother me a lot since Simon died. Friends of Simon organised a benefit night to help pay for the funeral, and many people contributed. I did not attend as it was way too soon after the funeral, but I heard a lot of money was collected. I thought that was brilliant and would help a lot. Yet I never received a penny from that night, and neither did the funeral directors. Before Christmas 2003, I chased down the main organiser to ask about this. He convinced me that he called to our house to give it to me, in cash, but I wasn't home. So, he left it there for me. I believed him, because of the details he was able to give me, but I couldn't accept that this had happened. I dismissed it as much as I could because I could not deal with it at the time, and I did not want to annoy or anger those who had made contributions. I was annoyed with myself for not suggesting they gave the money directly to Townley's. I felt betrayed because the funds donated towards Simon's funeral was gone forever. A year later, it still bugged me, and I went to the Gardai, but they said there was nothing they could do because it was a family matter.

Homelife was still tough, and we found it hard to find some kind of normalcy, especially when I found out the benefit money was stolen. We pottered around as best as we could, never knowing what was around the corner and how we would deal with it. We were surviving and not really living. I can't say it was a happy home anymore, it was more like a home full of people who were just psychologically numb, probably much like a psychiatric ward. We drifted from day to day still devastated and not understanding Simon's passing. I was full of guilt for everything in my past, especially Simon's death and the failure to convict Shine. I had millions of questions in my head like what if I did this, what if I did that, why didn't I, why didn't Simon, and how I had let this happen. Even Patrick could not answer these questions for me or persuade me to let some of my guilt go. I convinced myself that Simon's passing was all my fault, and my guilt was justified. I did of course blame that next-door neighbour that raped Simon and his secondary school Principal, but as far as I was concerned, I had let it happen in the first place, and then did not deal with it properly. I had let Simon down in the worst way possible and deserved to be blamed and feel guilty. Bouts of anger were common in the house and often came out of the blue, especially when something suddenly reminded us of Simon and what happened to him. We were angry at those we felt were responsible, and we are mad at ourselves. I was furious, and most of that anger came from blaming others for what had happened to Simon.

I felt a sadness that came from the very depths of my soul, and one I thought would never go away.

Wayne was working, trying to find his place in the world. He had a couple of jobs, but I don't think he was ever happy in these jobs. I guess it was a means to an end and something to occupy his time. Lee was still at school, and Miss Clarke was now the Principal, and she kept him under her wing. He was still working in McPhail's and learning the trade, so to speak. He really loved working there and became a bit of a lady's man himself, and both school and work kept him occupied, and maybe even gave him some good moments and laughs. I could do nothing to lift the boy's mood and gloom and was even afraid if I did, I would be interfering and probably upset them even more. I started to keep my distance, watching and hoping that they would be okay and learn to have a new normal life. I prayed so hard for that.

My mistrust in politicians took a nasty turn that year. An affidavit was posted anonymously to me, from someone who was employed in the Lourdes Hospital. A local politician, Frank Godfrey, attended a meeting in 1999 with the then CEO of the Lourdes Hospital, about a matter not related to Shine. This affidavit was written in the offices of Robert D'Ore solicitors in Dublin. It was requested by a consultant O'Boyle in the hospital in the year 2000. The meeting was obviously heated because the CEO said to Godfrey "what do you want me to do? I just got rid of a paedophile" (referring to Shine). When I read this affidavit, I was astonished and forwarded it on to my solicitors at the time. What hurt and annoyed me was that Godfrey, as a supposed representative of the people, never brought this to the attention of the Gardai. I was convinced that if Godfrey had made a statement about what the CEO said, Shine would never have walked free. I could not understand how he had kept this quiet or why? I still can't, but every time I see him, I rage, and I make every effort to keep out of his way. I often wonder why he kept this to himself. I am no legal expert, but I could not see any way this evidence and the affidavit were not crucial.

I was out one night in Sarsfield's bar, a place I have been in only a handful of times. I was sitting at the bar with some friends, enjoying the craic. Then a woman came to talk to me. I recognised her as one of the jury members. She apologised for the decision to acquit Shine. She was trying to explain to me how one person on the jury influenced her and everyone else. I did not want to hear this, and I just stormed out of the building without saying a word. I thought that was very composed and brave of me because, what I thought of shouting at her, would not have been pretty or kind. I could not believe or understand how certain adults had allowed someone else to influence their decision on the guilt of Shine, and not argue their point of view. I thought about this and wondered what happened in the jury room when they agreed to acquit, or if some, or a majority might have thought he was guilty. Once again in life, I was lost and totally confused and felt more let down by our justice system. My friends thought I was lost too. They didn't see me run out of the pub.

As much as I wanted it to, the case against Shine would not go away. I attended meetings with the One in Four group, about some kind of appeal to the DPP. Professor Ivana Bakic from Trinity College Law School took an interest in the case and tried to see if we could appeal the decision to acquit Shine. I don't know why I even bothered to go, but it was probably because I did not want to let anyone down. I was sitting in the meeting, believing full well that there was nothing we could do and we were just wasting our time. I was thoroughly fed up and feeling more depressed. I was sorry I attended at all and promised myself I would not go again. The civil case was going forward, and maybe that was the only avenue of justice I had left. I grew more disinterested day by day because I just wanted the case and all the associated pain to just go away. I was trying to look after my family and trying to deal with my depression. I could feel myself drifting away from Valerie, not because of Simon, or the aftermath of his passing, but because of other things that had happened and I wasn't too unhappy about that.

Work was okay, but I had a bit of trouble with some of the cohort of new management that were in Santry for training. Over the years, I developed into a person that had no time for people who always wanted to put themselves first, and did not think of anyone else, except maybe to put them down. Many people tried to put me down and walk all over me, but I thought that I was too thick to let that happen, but in truth every time it happened, it hurt me. I just tried to get on with my work and kept out of their way. Deep down, was a very different situation. Every slight or criticism or comment aimed at me burned slowly through to my brain and then tried its very best to convince me it was all true. The more I thought about them, the more significant problems they became, and the more I started to believe them, the more I was reminded of what a useless failure I was.

I am not sure what happened next, because I was just existing day by day, trying to look after the boys and trying to do my job. It makes me sometimes wonder about how I was able to do a decent job in retail and make improvements when I could not look after myself properly. I could focus on work when I was there, but even the drive to and from Santry became a horror trip, because I was locked in a box with only my head for company, and no amount of loud music would stop the constant barrage of thoughts, failings, and criticisms. On many occasions, I drove to and from work and had absolutely no idea how. I could not recall the journey. I would just come 'awake' with a start and wonder where I was and how I got there. I was struggling again.

I was finding it impossible to cope with life. I was crying when I wasn't working, becoming isolated, and eventually, I ended up going back to see Doctor Neary. I cried like a baby when I got into his consulting room as if I had stored up a lake for this occasion. He let me cry for a while before he calmed me down. I hadn't stopped crying; it just wasn't flowing out anymore. He suggested I was experiencing a breakdown. I found out much later that it was because I had repressed my grief, and now it was exploding in my brain trying to get out. I learned, the hard way, that everyone, no matter who has to go through the grief process to come out the other end. So, I found myself starting to grieve again, and Simon's death seemed like it had just happened. Every emotion associated with my grief, like denial, disbelief, anger, blame, fear, worry, and sadness attacked me all at the same time. It was different from my 'normal' depression in many ways because it was all wrapped in loss and guilt.

On the other hand, it was very similar too, with the sadness, pain, feelings of uselessness, and being powerless to do anything about it. The doctor advised me to quit the job, in the hope that I would not have that to worry about too, which I did and never went back there again, even to visit. In truth, I don't think I would have been able to work with people and deal with customers every day. I just had to face up to my grief and let the whole process work its way through from start to finish. I was still seeing Patrick, and he concurred and tried to guide me through this process. Why, oh, why did I do everything wrong???

Being without a job had its own problems. I found it very difficult having nothing to do or focus on. I could potter around the house and the garden doing little jobs, but even that was often too much for me. If I made a mistake, missed or forgot something, I criticised and berated myself, as if I had done something horrible and that only made me feel a lot worse. There was no joy or even happiness in it anymore. Even my distraction ideas for beating depression did not work, and I did not want to leave the house at all or even go to the side of the house in case I saw someone. I could not sit and do nothing or relax all day. I have always found that very frustrating, and it just allowed my overthinking mind to take over. I could not decide what to do with myself from waking to the time I went to bed. When I was in this state, the only thing I could do was clean the house.

I felt the questions I had regarding Simon's suicide more than ever before. I needed some kind of answers, and I wanted them there and then. I started to research suicide, suicide bereavement, and anything else I could learn. It gave me something to do. I wasn't able to focus enough to read books, so I concentrated on articles I found on the internet and suicide bereavement websites. I quickly got very interested and found that I was learning something new. I emailed people and groups around the world with the questions I had about Simon's suicide, and I became more focused on this than anything else in my life at the time. I wrongly believed, of course, that I would find answers to the questions I had about Simon. I then started reading books and cross-referencing everything to get the truth. I started going to suicide bereavement courses in Ireland, Northern Ireland, and the UK and then attended suicide intervention and awareness courses. I took any suicide awareness course I could find online. The skills I learned at Trinity College were, at last, put to some good use, and I was comfortable working away, learning about suicide, and myself. That was far more than one of my usual distractions, but it was keeping my depression in check. It was far more important to me, and as I worked, I learned, and I focused on Simon, on suicide, and not on myself.

I started having ideas about using this information and knowledge to help others, and it was Wayne who suggested that I use all this research and facts to build a website to help people in our immediate area concerned or affected by suicide.

Lee sat his Leaving Certificate examinations in 2006 and done quite well and got on to a finance course at Dundalk College of Information Technology. He did not do brilliantly in his leaving but did not do poorly either; he just did what he had to do. Considering he was living life without his best friend and protector, I thought he did wonderfully well, especially as his heart was never really in it. I think he was more interested in the graduation night than any exams. He was still working in Mc Phails, but as a barman now, and I was very thankful that he had good friends there and in school. Wayne was working in a bank, but it was still a means to an end, and I was unsure what life had planned for him. He moved out to share a house with a few mates, but that did not last too long, because it was costly, and he missed the comforts and service at home.

He returned and got his room back and mostly looked after himself as much as he could. The boys seemed to be coping well enough, to me anyway, but I could not see inside their heads. They did not wear their hearts on their sleeve, like their Dad. I was still tremendously proud of them both and only wished the very best for them.

The best thing that happened for the boys, as far as I was concerned, was that they both started going out with lovely girls. I will admit that I think these girls did more to help Wayne and Lee with the loss of Simon than I ever did. I was just delighted that they had someone to help them deal with such a tragedy. They had someone to talk to, someone to lean on, and someone to rely on, and I was so happy for them. I was very fond of the two girls too. I did think that I started to see a change in them that indicated they were coming to terms with their lives, and I hoped it would continue, and it did. I was just drifting further and further away from Valerie.

Lee got the idea that because he liked McPhail's so much, he would not go to college but stay in the bar as a full-time barman. Who could blame him? McPhail's was the place to be, and he loved it there and made wonderful friends too. I did what I could to convince him to go to college and get a degree. I pointed out that he could still work in McPhail's. I did not think I got through to him, so when I got the chance, I went to meet with the owner of McPhail's and told him the story regarding Lee. He too was of the idea that Lee should go to college and promised me that he would have a word with him as soon as he could. He met Lee without saying anything about me, talked to him, and asked him about his future. He suggested his best option was going to college, and that he could have a job in McPhail's as long as he wanted. Lee went to college and kept working as a barman in McPhail's, and I was delighted with that.

My studies and research into suicide and depression taught me a lot about myself, my grieving process, and my depression. I was feeling good enough to finish counselling and take the massive step, for me anyway, of living my life without the safety net Patrick held for me. It was daunting though because I had been in therapy for about ten years in Ireland alone, and apart from a short break, was about to 'walk alone' for the first time in a decade. I was feeling good in myself, and I thought that I had beaten my depression again and for the last time. As I eventually emerged from the grieving process and my depression, I got a job in Dundalk, doing paperwork and accountancy in a factory. The job was right for me, and I got on well with everyone there, probably because my brother John was the engineer. I also enjoyed the fact that it was a nine-to-five Monday to Friday job. That gave me lots of free time to work on my research.

Chapter 19

Suicide Bereavement

I am happy to say that I did eventually manage to get through the grieving process, and I learned that we all have to go through this, even if we can put it off for a while. I still have terrible days when Simon's loss feels like it is fresh and recent, and the pain of missing him is much greater than usual. That usually occurs around his anniversary, his birthday, and Christmas, but can affect me at any time when something reminds me that he should be here with us. I find at times that I cannot get a picture of him in my mind without looking at a photo. I wish we had recorded much more of the boys growing up, especially when they were young, but that opportunity has passed, and there is nothing I can do about it now. I consciously try to make sure that Simon is around when we have any family event, and I would love to see him at these. I try to imagine him sitting or standing there. If I could even feel him around us, enjoying the craic, I might be reassured.

A neighbour once went to a psychic, and she was told that Simon watches over me all the time, but I just can't feel him there, and I have never seen any of those 'psychic' messages like a white feather. I do notice a robin from time to time, but I am bound to see some at some time. I wish I got a message from him, and I am kind of jealous when others say that they got one of these signs from Heaven. Maybe it's wrong to be asking, but I still need to be reassured that Simon does not blame me or hate me. That may sound stupid, but it is just the way I am, and I can't change who I am.

The one major factor that helped me get through the grieving process, and find a new normal life, was when I realised that there was no way I could possibly get the answers to all the questions I had about Simon. I could not tell precisely why Simon thought that suicide was his best and only option, but I learned enough to believe that he was in pain, couldn't face the future he envisioned for himself, and thought this was the only way to end the torture he lived with every day. He did what he thought, in his own irrational and illogical way, was the best for him and us. Simon never thought about or imagined the pain his death would cause because his upside-down thinking would not allow him to think about that, in case it would change his mind. To know and fully understand this does not fully explain what Simon thought when he made his plan or took all those tablets, but in a way, it does help to know he was not thinking straight. It also hurts like hell because it reminds me of all the questions I had. Such as 'why didn't he talk to me, or someone else?', 'what if I went to sit with him when I finished studying?', 'Why didn't I see he was in so much pain?', even though he was relaxed when I saw him that night. I have learned, way too late for Simon, that there is a period of calm between the time a plan is decided on and the suicide itself. It is like the person is happy with their decision and the act is just the end of the scheme. I can't verify this myself because I can't recall what I was thinking at these times. It does, however, explain why I felt that Simon was relaxed, and maybe even on the way up out of the lowest stage of his depression. There are millions of questions I have in my head that I cannot fully answer and I have to accept that the only way I will get full answers to these questions is when I die and hopefully get to Heaven and see Simon.

Understanding that has put me in a place where I am satisfied that I have all the possible answers I can get in this world. It was the one thing that allowed me to go through the grieving process and come out at the end, albeit into a new world, for me anyway. I still had all the other parts of the process to go through, and there were times when I felt I was going crazy (much more than usual). All the information I read, kind of indicates that the different emotions I would experience would all come in stages, but that is not what happened with me.

After Simon died, I was in complete shock and denial. I believe that the shock was a great thing to happen to me because, without it, my head would just have exploded. My thinking was numbed to such an extent that I might have been a zombie. I am glad that I was because I know that my brain could not take in the sudden loss of Simon, or the pain resulting from his suicide. In that sense, I am thankful for the shock I experienced, but as my mind was numb and isolated from reality, I could not accept that Simon had died. That is why I kept checking up on him when he was laid out in the casket. I was trying to make sure he was okay as if he was just having a rest. I was convinced that one of us, either him or me, would wake up from this horrible dream and everything would be fine. Even at the church and in the cemetery, I was still in a kind of denial that would not let me fully accept that Simon was indeed dead and buried.

When the days passed, all the evidence of Simon's suicide seeped very slowly through the barriers protecting my mind. The house became a lot quieter, and I started to believe and accept that Simon was indeed gone forever and that I would never see him again. I was still in shock, but the pain I felt deep in my heart and in my head was immense, and I struggled to come to terms with reality. The only pictures I could form in my mind was of him lying on the living room floor, or him in the coffin. He looked as cold as ice with no soul and no sign of that big smile he used to have. That was not how I wanted to see him or remember him, but it would not leave my head or let any other pictures in. I didn't or couldn't leave the house to face the cruel world or face anyone talking about Simon or offering their condolences. That would have just added to the pain, or so I believed. When the shock finally left me, I just sat down, bawling my eyes out. I was hurting badly, but the tears took some of the pain in my head with them, and I felt relieved somewhat when I cried, so I kept weeping. I was in bits physically for a couple of days after that, but that eased, and I was able to get some proper sleep.

Now it was time for the other emotions, like fear, anger, guilt, blame, shame, rejection, betrayal, and confusion to infect my brain. I had to remember that I still had two sons who I had to look after and try to keep safe. They were suffering too, and I am sorry to say, I doubt I was much help to them, even though I tried my best. I know that no one grieves the same way, over the same period, or even with the same intensity. Many of us try to put a lid on our grief so as not to offend anyone else or cause them more pain and sorrow. As for the boys, we kind of smothered them and was checking up on them every minute of the day. We were worried about them and wanted to keep them safe. That was the 'fear' part of the grieving process. Thankfully the boys spoke to us and asked us to loosen the leashes and let them live their own lives and promised us, they were safe and not thinking of suicide in any way shape, or form. I, for one, felt a whole lot better after this conversation and was delighted to let them live their lives, believing that they would talk to me if ever they had any dark thoughts. It was the best way to ease my fears.

I struggled with the anger I carried over Simon's suicide. Some of this was a rational response to the guilt I felt for letting Simon down and not being able to help him with his depression. My brain tried to assuage some of that anger by trying to find others to blame. That did me absolutely no good, as it did not relieve my rage at all. It just festered away in my mind, stopping me from moving through the grieving process. The problem with trying to blame others for what happened, and not being able to do anything about it, was that it just inflamed the anger that built up inside my mind like a volcano waiting to explode. I did not know it at the time, but all it did was deepen my grief and delay the possibility of getting through the grief process. The anger alone was trying to consume me, but I did not let it. It was only when I accepted that it was up to God to judge or punish all those I blamed, that I started to feel the anger dissipate. That was a real breakthrough for me and helped enormously in guiding me through the grieving process.

I also learned about blaming others and how it was just stoking up my anger and causing me to stay stuck in the same part of my grief process. The blame I had in my heart and my head was only hurting me, and maybe the boys. It was not hurting those I was angry with. It was a waste of my good time, and I started to believe that. I realised that it was not my responsibility to judge them, but God's. Now I was able to say the Our Father and mean every bit of it. I left Him to deal with those who had trespassed against

Simon and us. That too had a significant positive impact on me and helped me through my grieving process. I also found out through my research, that my situation, or my family situation, was not unique, and we were not going crazy. Many stories I read and many people who I communicated with showed me that our experience was the same or very similar to other people throughout the world. They had lost people to suicide and had never seen it coming, even though depression was a factor with most suicides. It was good for me to learn that the situation we found ourselves in with Simon, before and after his death, was unfortunately common throughout the world because it showed that I was not as stupid as I thought.

I don't think that I have ever got rid of the guilt I felt and still feel over Simon, but I have been able to use it to do a bit of good in the world. That's how I think about my guilt. That some good came out of it, so it is ok to live with. A lot of this guilt eased when I found out that many other people had lived through the same or similar situations. That helped me rethink my guilt, and I learned that it was not all my fault. I can live with my part in Simon's death.

I never blamed Simon for what he did or put us through. I understood what he had done and why, and learned much more. I never felt that Simon had betrayed us at all, yet I did feel kind of rejected that he did not feel he could trust me enough to talk to me on that fateful night. I could also see why he didn't. Simon watched me live through depression all his life, and I guess that he felt that he did not want to be a burden like I was. I couldn't blame Simon because I know he was not thinking rationally when he made his plan, and then took his life. I know that his thinking was upside-down, which made him believe that suicide was his best and only option. I can't blame him because he died as a result of a terrible illness.

I can't say that I was ever ashamed of what Simon did, but the way I felt in some people's company, made me think that others were ashamed for us and could not hide it. I never wanted their shame or pity, just maybe their understanding. I did what I always do; I avoided people who I felt were ashamed for us or awkward in my company. I did worry about Simon and the ideas and misconceptions about suicide being a murder, which is a mortal sin and excludes the sinner from Heaven. I got some relief when I learned that suicide was no longer viewed as a mortal sin by the church. I got a lot more comfort when I realised that suicide was almost always the result of a terrible illness, and I became convinced that no God would equate suicide with a murder. Simon's suicide was to relieve the pain and torture he lived with and could face no longer. I understand that, and I feel no shame for what he did.

I understand and believe that those who do take their own lives are not thinking straight when they make the decision. It's like their logic is turned upside down. We all have the instinct of survival, which we use to stop getting hurt or killed, but those deciding on suicide can just turn off this instinct as if it were a switch in the brain. The decision is based on 'fake news' about ourselves emanating from the dark depression festering in the mind and trying to control every aspect of our lives, even death. I am sure that Simon thought he was doing the right thing for himself and us.

He would not have to live in such terrible psychological pain anymore, and we would not be burdened by him ever again. I know he couldn't see anything past the act of suicide because once he did it, everything would be great for us. Maybe he thought he was putting himself in God's hands to be looked after and cured of his terrible depression. He probably could not see any way he would be back to being the happy-go-lucky boy that loved his life. That's the problem as far as he was concerned, everything he thought about was negative, except the suicide and the 'benefits' he believed his passing would bring for him and us.

Simon couldn't see that he was getting on well with a new counsellor and lots of positive things could have happened. Maybe he would not have gone back to school, or perhaps, with Caroline now in charge, he would have gone, finished his exams, and grew up surrounded by lots more friends. Surely, he would have many happy minutes, hours, and days and had a lot to offer in life. Simon was like me, he loved to be busy, and he could have got a career that he loved. I bet that he would have married, had children, and watched them grow into mini Simons or Simones. He could not see how many people he could have helped in life. I'm sure that if Simon and many of those who died by suicide, could have understood this, he and most of them might have reconsidered. I wish he did.

As I learned about suicide bereavement, I was dealing with my grief and finding ways to get closer to the end of the process. It did not end my pain or stop the grieving process immediately, but I believe that it made it a lot easier. I am sure that my studying helped me understand a little bit more and that too helped ease my pain. I eventually got through the grieving process because I believed that the last thing Simon wanted was to cause us any more pain. That took a long time to sink in, and I am still searching for reassurance from him. It helped a great deal when I stopped looking for the answers that did not exist in this world and realised that the anger and blame were hurting just one person – me! I still carry some of the guilt, but I can live with that. I wish that I had allowed myself to go through the grieving process when it happened instead of waiting until it exploded and gave me a mental breakdown. We learn from our mistakes.

The only problem I had with all this new-found knowledge was that I wished, for Simon's sake, that I had learned all this before he died.

Chapter 20

SOSAD

While I was working in EPC, I spent a lot of time re-reading and sorting all the information I had gathered during my research. I was still researching until I decided that I had enough information, and it was time to collate it all and try to work out what we needed for the new website. Working with Wayne and Lee, we decided that it should be like a signpost to anyone who had mental health questions, especially ones about suicide, and needed to know what to do or where to go. Wayne and Lee helped by checking and editing the pages I was writing for the site. Wayne was looking after all the computer and technical parts of the website, getting help when he got stuck. We had no idea what we were going to name the website until one day when he was reading something I wrote; he just said there is the name for the website. I could not see what he was talking about, but he pointed to a line that included the words "Save our Sons and Daughters" and pointed out the name SOSAD from the first letter in each word. We had our name, and we thought it was brilliant, and it was so apt.

I grew in confidence in the job and took over everything related to the audits in the factory. I did enjoy that, something I was responsible for because it gave me something to achieve. I took ownership of that, but my primary purpose in life was the SOSAD website and doing something to help people who had experienced and lived with suicide and depression. It was something good and helpful, and that pleased me tremendously.

The case against Shine rumbled on in the media, but I was not interested anymore. I got any breaking news or information from the sites on my phone, but generally, just read the headlines. I had stopped buying papers because I could not read or even look at any story of abuse, and the rest of the news just depressed me or annoyed me. I did not want to let any external factor influence me or give my depression any way to set itself in my brain, because I knew that could just be like adding fuel to the fire.

We launched the SOSAD website in December 2007, or instead, we let it go line, and we got one of the local newspapers to publish an article about it. We were happy with it, even if it was not as professional as many of the websites we looked at before. But it held useful, valuable information that we were sure would be of help to some people. I felt great about the whole thing. I thought we had achieved something remarkable. I knew that we would just have to keep an eye on the site every day. Other than that, we thought we had done our bit and turned the loss of Simon into something positive. It was based a lot on our family experiences and everything I had learned, and what we thought was missing. It was clear and straightforward to use, with easy to find information, and it was all done to try to help stop suicide and help other families live through what we experienced.

We had a decent enough Christmas in the house, but it was not the same, and never would be the same, without Simon. I was still retiring to the sitting room, and the telly after Christmas dinner was over, to sit and try and talk to Simon. I always went to the graveyard on Christmas morning and left a present for him. I would spend time in the weeks before Christmas cleaning the grave and making sure the plants and plant pots looked well. I was aware that I was trying to look after Simon now the way I should have looked after him when he was alive. I begged for his forgiveness and hoped to God that he had peace in his mind at last, with no more worries, no more depression or negative thoughts. I thought if he had this peace now, then he would be happy and that's all I wanted for him. The boys were getting older and didn't need me in their lives as much anymore. They were doing ok. Wayne still working and Lee in college and McPhail's, and they both still had their girlfriends who we had up Christmas day too, which made it a whole lot better.

It turned out to be the case that the SOSAD website was much busier than anyone expected, and it reached a lot of people who were affected by suicide or depression. While it was good news that the website was proving helpful, it was not useful enough. Many people got in touch with the boys and me, looking for help, information, or advice. They were ringing me at work, ringing me when I was at home, and even calling to the front door. We had created something good, but the support systems in place at the time were not good enough, or quick enough to respond to people's needs. There was, and probably still is, a serious lack of resources in their psychiatric divisions, and our Government did not seem to care about the terrible situation with depression and suicide in Ireland. Then there was the fact that many people just did not trust the HSE, or would not go anywhere near the psychiatric hospitals, because of the terrible stigma associated with them. Many people still called the psychiatric hospitals the 'madhouse' or the 'loony bin' etc. and no one wanted to be seen going to that place. I could understand that and why people didn't want to go anywhere near a HSE psychiatric facility.

Everyone who contacted us was in a desperate situation, and apart from advice and maybe a listening ear, we could give them very little help and support. That was not what we planned and not a pleasant situation to be in. For me, I was just letting people down and not helping them. I felt terrible, not being able to help the people who called after we had encouraged them to be brave and talk to someone. I felt like we were kind of fobbing them off by telling them to speak to their doctor or go to the hospital. Even that suggestion was deemed unhelpful because many of them had bad experiences with mental health services or had been waiting a long time to see a psychiatric professional. I don't know why I was so surprised because I had the same experiences with Simon. The system just couldn't cope with the demand and was letting people down, and it became clear to me that the timing of support available was just not good enough. When people in distress made the brave decision to talk to someone and seek help, they needed help there and then, and not months or years later. That is particularly true when someone is suicidal. It does not matter how much a person is at risk, as the situation can deteriorate in the blink of an eye. I was upset with myself for thinking I had done a good thing, when, in fact, I was just hurting people who came to me for help. However, I was not discouraged. I felt that it was up to me to solve this problem, which meant doing a lot more to help and support people. I realised that I needed it to talk this out with as many people as possible, starting with Wayne and Lee.

One of these people I spoke to put it to me clearly that I either had to drop SOSAD altogether or take it onto the next level. I knew what was needed, and I looked at it in economic terms. There was a considerable gap in the market, or the mental health support available locally. I wanted to fill in that gap, but if I were to do it properly, I would have to commit totally. The idea was based around helping people who may be suicidal, or those bereaved by suicide. Still, it soon became apparent that we should also aim to help people suffering from depression because if we didn't, they could well become suicidal themselves.

I took a long time thinking about what to do and listening to the advice I got from loads of people, including the local suicide resource officer in the HSE. I went on holiday to Rome with Valerie to get away for a while and see if there was anything left between Valerie and me. I also picked Rome so that I could go to the Vatican, not just to see it, but to find out where I stood with God. I had a super time, walking around seeing the sights, and I loved the Vatican. I even attended Mass and confessions in St Peter's, but I learned nothing to strengthen my faith. Valerie loved it too, but I could see how far I had drifted away from her.

Getting away and distracted by the beauty and majesty of Rome did clear my mind, and gave me plenty of time to reason about SOSAD. I made the decision that I was going to dedicate all my time to turning SOSAD from a simple website into a locally based support service, that would respond to people's needs when they needed it. I knew it would not be easy because I would need to learn about and plan for situations and people that were new to me. I also knew that I would need a lot of help and support. I was determined that I would not let people down and do my very best to help them as much as I could. I was no mental health expert or professional, but I could use my passion and skills to provide a much-needed support service for people in distress. I had some skills or knowledge in suicide interventions and suicide bereavement support, and I had a whole lot of experience with depression. I based a lot of our plans on my own experiences and the support I would have liked to see. As I did in retail, I planned so that SOSAD would meet or exceed the expectations of everyone who contacted us for support. I soon had the plan in place and was lucky enough to get some of those people who had advised and supported me, to agree to join the Board of Directors of the new charity we were going to form. Thankfully they all agreed. I was delighted that I had that team in place, but especially so because Wayne decided to sign up too. He always level-headed and direct and was great to bounce things off when we were working on the website. Lee was just too busy with college and work, and while he wanted to stay part of things, he didn't want to commit to anything and then let us down when College got in the way. I appreciated his honesty and knew that I could always rely on him if I needed to.

I was still working in EPC in Dundalk, spending most of my time getting ready for a substantial organisational audit that was due, but I was spending an increasing amount of time working on SOSAD stuff at work. Thankfully no one minded too much. I had decided to stay there until the audit was over and then leave in the early summer to dedicate all my time to opening a SOSAD counselling centre. I was feeling motivated like never before and felt the passion for something that I thought was being driven by Simon. There were no signs of my depression, and I was able to work and think with clarity. I learned that I was a lot smarter and effective when I let something process slowly through my brain before I looked for the answer.

The time for the big audit came, and I felt that we were ready. An audit team arrived from all over Europe and spent a week working through everything. We got through the audit successfully, and everyone was pleased with that and glad it was all over. When it was finished, I left work as planned. They held a big leaving party for me, and I was genuinely sorry to be leaving EPC and all my colleagues behind, but I was on a mission now, and nothing would stand in my way. I had more ups than downs on the journey, but every time I flagged or lost motivation, I was encouraged by the support of people around me. I was convinced I was doing the right thing and further encouraged because I thought that Simon was pushing me along and helping me set up something special.

I was back researching suicide and depression, but now I was looking into what people needed, and the best services around the world. We needed to know exactly what we wanted to offer and how we were going to accomplish this. My research and experience gave me the basis of a good plan based on what people needed. On top of that list, was having somebody, trained and helpful, available at any time, day or night, when people got the strength and courage to look for help. We needed to be able to help people who were at risk of suicide and all those who might be depressed, and keep them safe if they contacted us. We then needed to be able to meet them face to face as quickly as was possible and continue the suicide intervention, and continue keeping them safe. We wanted to put a safety net around the person using family and friends they could talk to if ever the urge to suicide or self-harm became unbearable. Keeping people safe, meant dealing with the issues that had them suicidal in the first place, and helping them and their coping skills, deal with the crisis in everyday life. That, of course, meant providing counselling and allowing this support to continue for as long as the client needed.

We had to find a way that would give us useful information on the clients' mental health, and I found some good and recognised assessments for depression and suicide online. They seemed to be very suitable for our needs. Every service we provided would have to be offered when the client wanted and when they were available, with no waiting lists, or long periods between first contact and the time of the first counselling appointment. It was clear that we needed a very safe and comfortable place for everyone to visit and get the support they needed. They had to feel welcomed, appreciated, and never judged, no matter the situation. The counsellors and anyone else who would be working in this new centre would have to be friendly, welcoming, and understanding of what our clients were going through. What we didn't want to do, was to be unavailable when someone contacted us for the first time, because we knew that people might be calling us, as the last option they tried before suicide. We needed to be there for them, and even if we missed a call, to ring back immediately and see what we could do to help, and maybe help someone stay alive. We did not want to make promises we couldn't keep, withhold our help and support to anyone, and we didn't want to be pushing clients out the door before they were ready. My studies had shown that this often led to the person becoming suicidal again, because they did not learn how to cope with life and the problems it throws at us every day. Now we had a plan of the services and support we needed to offer, and we were fully committed to getting this service up and running.

We found a suitable location and building on Trinity Street in Drogheda. It allowed us to have two counselling rooms, a kitchen and waiting room area, an office and a general reception/office area. It was close to the town centre, and the bus service, and it was easy to find. It was a single-use building with no other tenants. It seemed perfect. I decorated it and then went scouring the second -and shops for furniture and fittings. I was lucky to find decent stuff for the counselling rooms, the reception area, and office, but I ran out of money, and so I had to borrow to get what we needed for the kitchen, and then got the computers and printers on credit. I spent everything I had, but I didn't care. The SOSAD centre looked clean and welcoming, and the counselling rooms were comfortable and safe.

We needed volunteers, and I knew nothing would happen without them. Thankfully, the local newspapers were very supportive and ran articles about the new service opening in Drogheda, and always included our need for volunteers. We needed psychologists, counsellors, and people trained in suicide intervention to man the phones 24 hours a day. We needed admin support staff to keep everything together and to function correctly. We also looked for fundraisers to help us pay the bills and keep going. We had every member of the board make their contributions, in regards to their skills and experiences. We completed and submitted all the paperwork necessary to become a charity in Ireland. The number of forms involved was just a lesson in the way paperwork has become so crucial in the modern world. We would have to keep records of the clients, including, notes on any intervention or assessment, or maybe the person bereaved, and we had to keep them in a secure place. Thankfully, one of the counselling bodies in Ireland we were dealing with when setting up, suggested that the counsellors should look after all their counselling notes. We followed up on this excellent advice, which meant that the client's notes we kept, were not too big and could easily be stored away safely, and recovered if necessary.

In September 2008, with a lot of publicity in the local newspapers, SOSAD opened its first counselling Centre in Drogheda. We started with just a few volunteers and counsellors and immediately started getting calls. Most of these were from people asking about the service for themselves or someone they were concerned about. We were new, so had no track record, and people wanted to know a lot more about what we did before they put someone's life in our hands. I could fully understand that. It was very easy to make a mistake or say the wrong things, and we took that on board when talking to anyone, and thankfully, we never hurt or let anyone down. Not any that I know of anyway. From the very start, many of the calls we received were from people who were depressed, and the courage to make contact came to them at night. It was good for them and us that we had initiated the 24-hour phone support service from the start. It introduced many people to SOSAD and the support we offered.

We were lucky to have two counsellors offer their services with us immediately, and when someone accepted counselling, they did not have to wait. We had one psychologist when we opened first, and she looked after anyone who wanted support from us. She also took ownership of all the assessment and client paperwork, as well as the appropriate policies and procedures. The assessments were from America, and they gave us a good insight into a person's mental health, their level of suicide risk, and the severity of their depression. All this information was valuable in finding ways to keep the client safe, as well as assisting the counsellor and guiding the counselling sessions. It also helped us see how we could help them in practical ways too, like keeping in touch between sessions, talking to family or friends, with their permission of course, or finding other agencies that could help them with particular problems.

The first rule of SOSAD was to keep everyone safe, especially any person who was at a high risk of suicide. In those cases, with the client's permission, we involved family, or maybe a friend, in helping keep an eye on the client and keeping them safe at all times. It was like a safety net around each person with their family, making sure they didn't fall through it, and SOSAD always there to give help and support. We started with a couple of volunteers in the office doing admin work, looking after the phones during the day, making appointments, following up on people, and letting people in and out of the building. They were just as crucial to the well-being of all our clients as the counsellors and psychologists.

We also received calls from people who had lost someone they loved to suicide, and were looking to find ways to cope in their own lives. I became heavily involved in trying to help these people, and met with them and wanted to guide them through the grieving process. We started a regular suicide bereavement support group and were very fortunate to get two experienced facilitators. I was encouraged to attend because my experiences and insights might help others. Fr Iggy, the local and popular Augustinian priest, got involved too and did a lot to comfort and inspire those in attendance. Just like in the centre, we always had tea and coffee available for everyone to help put them at ease, or maybe relax a bit, and it always seemed to help.

We were helping people. I was doing quite a few suicide interventions and found someone experienced to help me with these. David was a great help in taking a load off my shoulders, but that did not last too long, because we just got busier and busier every day. The interventions were never easy because I never knew what was troubling someone until they told me, and sometimes, it was extremely difficult to get the whole story from the person. Still, I used the safety plan we had developed, and as often as possible, I got someone close to the client, involved. After every suicide intervention, I questioned myself to ensure that I did not let them down, but I still worried and hoped they would come in for an assessment and counselling. If they did, I was that bit happier that we were not letting them down.

Our website started receiving more hits than ever before, and to me, that just proved that people were checking us out before contacting us. Once we started getting busier, the number of clients grew exponentially, and I was spending a lot of my time recruiting and interviewing new counsellors, psychologists, admin staff, and people trained in suicide interventions. Thankfully we got plenty more volunteers, including another couple of lovely psychologists who were so amazed at the service we offered, that they worked almost full time in SOSAD. They were also able to recruit more psychologists to help share the load, and it meant that we had a psychologist available every day if someone needed their immediate support. Together we were able to work on improving and refining the client paperwork, as well as a secure computer database for the client's information. Everyone was involved in calling clients to check up on them and see how they were, and we developed a system where we text every client to remind them of their next appointment. That became a valued little service as many clients thanked us because they forgot about it, or thought it was the wrong day, which is not surprising considering their depression and different pressures confusing their minds. If we had only received a text or call reminding us about Simon's last appointment with his counsellor. Who knows what might have happened?

The follow-up calls were working a treat proving to be a great source of comfort and support for many of our clients, and in turn, this allowed them to trust us and rely on us even more. It seemed that the more people started to trust us, the more they recommended us to family and friends. With all the new volunteers, I had the time to start going round to schools, clubs, associations, etc. giving talks on SOSAD, suicide, and depression, and every time I gave it talk, we had a little surge in calls from new clients.

I was pleased in myself with no signs of depression either inside me or outwardly. I was as happy as I had been for many a year, and I had a real purpose in my life, and I was doing something to help others. I do think that I needed to have a worthwhile purpose in life, to keep a check on my depression, and have a kind of ordinary life. I could feel Simon motivating, encouraging, and pushing me along, especially when I got over-tired or questioned myself. I believed that SOSAD was my destiny, and I thought that it was a fitting legacy to Simon. I believed that if Simon was on my side, and helping SOSAD, then maybe God was helping me too. There was just no downside to having God helping me. I knew that I was not intelligent or smart enough to think about, plan, and start SOSAD without God and Simon's help. Neither would I have been able to keep it going and help more and more people every week. God and Simon were leading me and SOSAD, and I was just the driver, and I was pleased about that.

Lee celebrated his 21st the April after SOSAD opened and he decided that he just wanted a bit of a get together at home with a few mates and us. My baby was all grown up, and I wanted a special night for him. We got everything ready when the big day arrived. That evening we were shocked and delighted as a great crowd of his mates, turned out for him, and the house was packed. The kitchen and sitting room were stuffed, the smokers were all out the back garden. The stairs were full of people, and there was more out the front. It was brilliant, and I felt that Lee's mates were a lovely bunch of people. I was so glad that he had such good friends. I didn't talk to Lee all night. He was chatting away to everyone, laughing his head off, and having a great time. We chatted, laughed, and had the craic until Lee decided it was time for them to go to a night club. I wondered how he was going to manage to organise such a crowd, but they all took off in groups and walked downtown. Some of them stayed back and insisted that they help clear all the cans and bottles, food and glasses before they too headed off to catch up with Lee. It was a great night, and I was delighted for him.

Soon after that, I got involved in setting up a group to support the victims of Shine. While the idea of setting up a support group appealed to me, I was not sure I wanted to be a part of it. I was trying to keep all that crap out of my head, not find ways to push it back to the fore again. Yet I could never say no, so I went to the meetings when I could, but was more than happy on the odd occasion when something happened in SOSAD, and I had to go. We ended up setting up a helpline for people to call for help, information, or advice and we put the information and phone number in the local papers and on LMFM radio. The number we used at first was the SOSAD number, and I handled 70 calls from people abused by Shine in the first two days. I was shocked at the number of callers and their stories, and I thought that maybe Shine had abused hundreds of boys or perhaps even more. All the accounts I heard were very similar, but the biggest problem in my mind was that most of these callers were reluctant or would not contact the Gardai or the Hospital to make a complaint against Shine.

Some were just too embarrassed, and others did not believe that the system worked, and would only cause them more pain. I could relate to that, but I did not say it to any of them. I did not want to put them off looking for the justice I waited years for and didn't get. I tried my best to advise every caller to make a complaint at least to the hospital, and I suggested that maybe doing this would ease some of the pressures they were living under for years and years. I took the phone numbers and details of every caller, luckily enough, because some calls were cut off, and I was able to ring them back. Some calls were brief, with people just asking a few questions and not even able to talk about their experiences. Other calls went on for ages where victims of Shine described their abuse in detail and seemed to be very glad to get it off their chest at last, even if it was just over the phone. It helped them that I was a victim too, and many of them asked me about this before opening up to me. I could understand that making an effort to tell someone, and then not being understood, would just hurt an awful lot more. I hoped I was able to help those who called, and I worried for them, because many had never told anyone, but it had affected their lives terribly. I passed on all the names and details to the others in the group and recommended that they contact and keep in touch with all those other 'new' victims and give them someone to talk to, at least.

Soon after that, I left the group because I felt that being involved did not do my mental health any favours. I was terrified of doing anything that might awaken my depression and bring me down again. That two days taking all those calls burned my head from the inside out, but I was well aware that I could not help them with what they needed more than anything else, justice and closure. I also needed to concentrate and focus 100% on SOSAD. That was my life now, my calling, and as far as I thought, God's plan for me. A year or so later, another victim asked to meet me, which was not unusual because many victims came to me about their mental health. This man wanted me to set up a different group to represent the victims of Shine. He said he was speaking for many victims who felt let down by the support group. He asked me to help them set up a new group. I found that flattering, but I felt the warning signs banging in my head, telling me to stay away. After due consideration, I declined to help, and it was not an easy decision. I hated saying no to him and tried to explain that I was too busy with SOSAD and afraid for my own mental health. I don't know who was hurt more, him or me. I know I made the right decision, but refusing to help someone else does not sit well with me. I don't think they ever got the group started, and I am very sorry that I wasn't able to help.

One thing I did learn was that listening, and giving someone the time and space to say what's on their mind, without interruption, is on its own, a lot of help. It works a lot like the self-harm Simon used to relieve his pain, except there are no cuts, blood flows, or physical scars. It does

relieve some of the pressure in the mind and can help anyone think a bit more logically or rationally. We need that to
see that maybe suicide is not the only option for us. Having similar experiences helped me understand what others were going through, and I spoke plainly and clearly to
them about what they were experiencing. I told them no
lies or glib comments that might or might not help them,
and I made no promises. They all had some kind of life of
their own, and I had no idea what the future held for them.
Anything could happen to change their situation and level
of suicide risk. People hold on dearly to promises made
to them and feel very let down when the promise does not
materialise. It's like hope. It feels like being lied to or rejected and can push people over the edge. Helping people
with depression or thoughts of suicide is like walking a super high tightrope, and if mistakes occur, no matter how
small, it is the client who falls off the rope, and the consequences could be tragic. That is what we did not want
to happen ever. I can't say if I have ever saved anyone's
life, except maybe the boy in the pool in Mosney, and one
young girl I pulled out of the River Nanny, even though I
carried out hundreds of suicide interventions. These people just learned from me how to help themselves, and in
fact, saved their own lives.

I am not an empath, but I could feel another person's pain
and understand what they were going through. I worked
with them to find out the 'WHY'. In most cases, I learned
a lot about the issues that had them feeling so low. That

gave me ways to help or advise them on what support they needed. In most cases that involved getting properly assessed, where they could learn precisely what was afflicting them, and how we could help. In the cases where the suicide risk was very high, I tried to get them to the hospital and even accompanied them there. I would get family or trusted friends involved as soon as I had permission to and then ensured that SOSAD would follow up as often and as frequently as necessary. That seemed to work for everyone we tried to help, except for one client who took his own life. That devastated me and made me question everything we were doing, or whether I had made a mistake founding SOSAD. It was a difficult time, but not as bad as it was for his family and friends.

I carried out a lot of suicide interventions in the North East, and I was always pleased when I managed to help someone stay safe. One day I was asked to call to a house to visit a lady that I had met with a few times. She was unable to meet me at the centre, so I called to see her. When I got to her house, I knocked on the door, and her little boy answered. He took one long look at me, then shouted out at the top of his voice "Mam, the suicide man is here". I didn't know whether to laugh or cry.

I spoke to and tried to help many people who had lost someone close to suicide, again using my own experiences and what I had learned. A lot of the times, it was helpful for them if I let them talk about whatever was in their hearts and head. Then I tried to answer their questions as best as I could. Many questions were unanswerable, like my own questions for Simon, but I explained how these could not be answered on this earth, and that the relentless quest for these answers, just prolonged their grief. Mostly they needed someone to listen to their own story, and understand what they were going through, and then try to guide them through the grieving process. I felt it was essential to encourage them to call us when they needed to, rather than suffering in silence. I thought that they needed a safety net too, and felt it was a bit of comfort for them to have someone they could talk to when they needed it.

I was learning new skills to help me deal with people all the time, as well as building my confidence in the work we were doing. There were times that I thought I was not much help after I met someone, and I tried to understand why, and I was genuinely hurt and upset afterwards. On other occasions, I knew I had helped, and that gave me a fuzzy warm feeling that cheered me up and kept me motivated to keep going. Generally, though, once I had dealt with someone and put the safety plan in place, I was thinking about the next person or the people we could not or did not reach. I grew to hate hearing about suicides and questioned myself about why they had not given us a chance to try to save them. I know we couldn't help everyone, but my brain would not accept that, and I pushed everyone very hard to keep the awareness going. I enjoyed doing the bereavement work, but I always wished I was doing an intervention instead.

The Medical Council case against Shine was dragging on, with his legal team arguing in the High Court to try and stop the IMC Fitness to Practice Committee from investigating him. It was going nowhere except that Shine won his case in the High Court, but it was then immediately appealed to the Supreme Court. I was getting regular updates from those involved, much more than I got concerning my criminal case against Shine, but I just wasn't interested. It was dragging on forever and did not seem as important to me as the criminal case, and my search for justice and closure. The civil suit was drifting on like a long slow-moving stream, and I was not interested at all, again because of my mental health concerns and vulnerability. I still had to attend different psychiatrists for the case, and each time, I felt pretty depressed and useless for a few days, but luckily, I was able to come through it with no long-term depressive episode.

In SOSAD, I became aware of all the paperwork required to keep the charity going, and I was fearful that the charity could be closed if all the required paperwork was not fully up-to-date. We worked on a big manual of all the policies and procedures for SOSAD, and we tightened up on the data protection related to our clients. We reviewed the assessment paperwork we were using and decided we needed something better. Some of the psychologists got to work on this, and they found an assessment called the Core Evaluation, which we adopted and used as the basis of all assessments and assessment paperwork. It was ideal for the clients we were seeing and the issues they presented with. The psychologists preferred the new evaluation and found it much more user-friendly and informative. We always tried to update all the policies and procedures so that we exceeded the expectations of our clients and we worked to ensure that we were meeting or exceeding the standards required by the different regulatory bodies in Ireland.

The time passed very quickly in SOSAD and the number of clients we were helping each week rocketed. I had to move out of my office into the general office because we needed to convert the office into another counselling room. The two we had were just not able to cope with the demand. The numbers of volunteers we were lucky to have, increased just like the number of clients, and thankfully we were able to stick to our principles and not let anyone down. We surveyed 100 past clients, and 61 of them reported that their favourite part of the service was our follow-up calls and keeping in touch. We kept that up all the time with all clients, and always notified them of appointments by text. I learned so much about suicide and depression, as well as suicide bereavement. Mostly from talking to people affected, but also from going to courses and conferences. I felt though that the networking was essential for SOSAD, and I believed it would benefit the clients and we would learn to be better for them. One of the biggest mistakes I made in those early years, was when the infamous Paul Kelly from Console invited me to join a group in Dublin, the 3 Ts I think it was. I refused because I didn't feel that I could take on anything else. I should have joined, as I am sure that would have helped secure proper funding for the charity. I was always applying for funding, which we never got, despite promises and assurances from politicians and managers in the HSE.

No matter what happened to Paul and Console, I found him to be brilliantly helpful and supportive when we started SOSAD. He was always there for me when I had questions, and he came to Drogheda and spoke at the first SOSAD annual Mass for victims of suicide and their families. I know that Console got themselves in financial difficulties, and Paul used the charity's accounts as if they were his own. I was shocked when I heard the news, but as the story developed, I got mad and angry. Not at Paul, but the system and myself. The number of clients Console had in a year, at the time of all the trouble, was less than we had in SOSAD in a week, and they were getting millions in funding, and we couldn't get a cent. I could not figure out why this was the case but started to think that maybe 'my face didn't fit'.

We started having our annual Mass for all suicide victims in the Augustinian church, with Fr Iggy in charge, in 2009. It came from discussions in the bereavement support group. I was conscious that people bereaved felt kind of ignored by society following a suicide. It was, unfortunately, true that many of those that died, felt ignored by the system, and I wanted to show that no one who died by suicide should be ignored or forgotten. I wanted a special way to pray for and remember them, and give anyone that wanted to, a chance to join in. Maybe too, they would learn something that would help them with their grief. The first Mass was amazing and so beautiful. The church was packed, and people were standing in every bit of space they could find. Fr Iggy and Paul spoke brilliantly, the music was enchanting, and afterwards, many people congratulated us and thanked us for giving them such an opportunity. It was clear we had done the right thing, and the Mass became a fixture on the calendar. A couple of years later, we somehow got Kairos to film the Mass for live broadcast on RTE television. It was a lot of hard work and rehearsals, but it worked out so well that RTE received calls about the Mass. The musicians and singers involved, organised by Gerry Simpson, spent a full month rehearsing but it was well worth it, and again Iggy was just brilliant.

In 2008, it was Paul who put Yellow Asylum films in touch with me about a documentary series on suicide they were planning. I met them to hear of their plans, and they were keen that the Moroneys should take part. We had a family meeting about it, and Valerie, Wayne, and Lee were interested once they were assured that the crew would deal with us with sensitivity and understanding. Having met the team from Yellow Asylum films, we were sure that they knew what they were doing, and would handle us sensitively and professionally. I thought we would all get on well together when making the documentary. We even managed to persuade some of Simon's friends to participate, including Pat Clarke, and it was not long before filming started. They were in Drogheda for a week, and we did get on brilliantly with everyone. They were very sensitive to us and respectful and allowed us to dictate the pace of the filming. They filmed all over the house, interviewing us in our comfort zones, and getting us to talk openly and honestly with gentle encouragement and guidance. They interviewed Valerie and me together in the kitchen, and I honestly felt like an idiot. I was mumbling again and speaking before my brain kicked in. They filmed me shaving and driving the car, but thankfully these shots were edited out. They did the boys in their rooms, and they seemed happy with how it went. They filmed Simon's friends wherever it was comfortable for them. They had all their filming done by the end of the week, and we were sorry to see them leave. It was the first time the house had been busy for ages.

I was hoping that making the documentary would be in some way, therapeutic for each of us, and then maybe help other people who have lost someone to suicide. We did have fun, but at times, but it was tough to speak about Simon and what happened to him. It brought it all back to us, but it did not adversely affect any of us, even though we were glad when we didn't have to speak in front of the camera anymore. It was therapeutic; I think because we thought we were doing a bit of good.

The documentary series was shown on RTE 1 in early 2009. The documentary about Simon was the first in a series of 3 titled "I See a Darkness" and the other two in the series featured a suicide in Cobh, where my sister lives, and a story about a lady attempting suicide. I thought that we could show it somewhere when it was aired on RTE, and it would be an excellent way to promote SOSAD and the work we do. We booked the Westcourt Hotel and decided to have a question and answer session when it was over. I was delighted when the place filled up with people. I was very nervous because I thought I came across like a bumbling idiot. We had seen the documentary before because we had the right to change or delete any part of it if we so wished. I don't think we changed anything because it looked so good on the screen. When it started on the big screen, everyone was silent and watched intently. My stomach was churning around like a washing machine, thinking about what everyone in the Westcourt thought about it. I watched closely, but some parts just made me close my eyes and ears. Wayne and Lee spoke wonderfully, particularly Wayne, who was so articulate and precise, that I wished I could do that. I was so proud of them. Simon's friends, Pat, Michael, and Mandy, spoke wonderfully about him. I heard tales and stories I never knew about. Some of the things I learned, hurt me to my core, and I felt so sorry for all those who were very hurt by Simon's suicide. I was glad that Simon had them as friends.

I did find it very hard to watch, and even later, when we went on a college tour to discuss and raise awareness of suicide, I could not bear to watch the short clip they showed. I suppose it just brings back the loss of Simon as well as my guilt and my part in his suicide. I just can't let that go, but over the years, I have learned to cope with that and accept it for what it is. There is nothing I can do now to change it or stop Simon from taking his life. I believed that it was my guilt as well as Simon and God that kept me going and motivated me to do more. All in all, I thought showing the documentary in the Westcourt went very well, and we spent an hour answering questions when it was over. The questions were all outstanding, and Wayne stole the show with his brilliant replies.

Financially, SOSAD was doing ok. Despite never getting funding, it did not take a tremendous amount of money to keep SOSAD going. Many people did all they could, like organising fundraisers, or events, to help raise money and support SOSAD. I thought that if we got any funding, it would mean that we could expand to different places, and maybe be able to pay for psychologists or counsellors to take over the managing of SOSAD. That would have been a massive step for us, and I was sure it would improve the services we offered. Yet the funding never came. I didn't think finances were a problem because so many people worked on our behalf, raising what they could. The money seemed to be available when it was needed. I believed that Simon and God were in charge and would make sure we kept going.

I used to love the feeling on a Friday when it was clear that everything was done and there was nothing left to do for that week. All appointments for the next week were organised, all the paperwork was complete, and every follow-up call had been made. It was a feeling that everything was done and done correctly. That, to me, was an outstanding achievement, and then on a Friday night, I would go out for a few pints and a bit of a laugh. I used to drink in O'Casey's, or McPhail's. O'Casey's was my local and was always good for a chat, a bit of banter, and a laugh. I went to mc Phails because Lee worked there and because they had great bands. I loved the music and the craic, and I enjoyed seeing people having fun and being happy. I secretly wished that they would never need the services provided by SOSAD.

Chapter 21

Valerie

Valerie was my first, and probably only real love. When we got together back in the 70s, I found her to be kind and trustworthy, even if she was often very shy. She was easy to talk to, and I was always comfortable in her company. Once her shyness had eased, she was calm and relaxed as well as friendly, with any group of friends we came across. She was easy to love and fall in love with, and I was delighted and fortunate to have her as my wife.

She was a brilliant Mam to the boys when they were young, and they got the best love and care a mother could give. She looked after me when I was most affected by depression and suicide, and it is a fact that she saved my life on a couple of occasions. I would not be here now if she did not have the sense to get me professional support, especially after I attempted suicide. I will never forget that, even if I didn't show it or tell her. We did lots of things together, as a family and all got on wonderfully well.

I thought we were very happy when we got married and then lived in London. We loved each other's company and had three wonderful boys. The cause of most arguments in our house were the ones regarding my depression. I could never recall most of these, but I thought that Valerie was entitled to argue, considering what I was putting her through. The only other thing that bugged me was Valerie was often flippant about the cleaning. That's what I thought anyway, and I often disregarded that she always cooked the food, done the washing and ironing, and looked after the boys. I took on all the cleaning, tidying and maintenance jobs in the house. I got used to it and was glad to have something to do when I was depressed and stuck at home.

Nothing much in this regard changed when we came back to Ireland, but we were still strong together, and I still loved her dearly. I think the move home did affect her, mostly because she missed her own family. Her Dad, Paddy, had died in Drogheda when we lived in London, and a few years later her oldest Sister Anne, died too. I was always aware of how deeply she missed her Mam, but she was really hurt when her Dad, and then her big sister died. Outwardly at least, she seemed to be coping well enough, but she had a hard time, especially with anniversaries. I am sorry to say; I don't think I was much help to her at all. I believe that she missed her family in London even more after Anne died.

When I went back to education, and then college, she took on little jobs to help keep the house going. The boys were growing up fast, and it seemed that we stopped doing things together. I am to blame for much of that, as I put all my focus into my studies. It was just like when I was working. I neglected Valerie, but never realised that.

When we were living in London, a friend of ours, Billy Mooney, told me that Valerie was drinking vodka every day when I was not at home. I had seen no evidence of that and dismissed it as pure rubbish. I thought that Billy was taking the piss. Back home, I started to notice that it was getting harder and harder to get Valerie out of the pub if we went out for a few drinks. She always wanted another drink, and then another, and I was so annoyed with her. We did not go out too much at the time, so I did not dwell on it. Then one day, I decided to give the house a deep clean, and I found bottles of vodka everywhere. None of them was full, but neither were they empty. I found them in places in the kitchen, bedroom and under the stairs, that are generally not cleaned or tidied. I was disgusted, and we had a big row, and it was the first time I mentioned that she might have a problem with alcohol, but she was adamant she didn't. Of course, she blamed me, because I was too busy to spend time with her. She was right, but that, I feel, was when we started to drift apart.

Simon's death wrecked her, and I tried my best to look after her and the boys. It was not so easy for her to drink when I was home all the time, and I started doing all the shopping too. She was a great comfort to me then, and we seemed to be getting closer again, rather than drifting apart. I was glad I had her around after Simon died, and I think we helped each other. It did not bother me too much when I was busy doing lots of little jobs around the house, and she was sitting around most of the day. She had to grieve also and in her own way. I did think that Simon's passing did bring us closer together and thought that maybe we would continue like that forever.

Once I went back to work, and then working on SOSAD, things started to deteriorate once again. She was not part of or involved, with the setting up of SOSAD. She didn't want to know, but I think she was proud that we had done something positive from Simon's suicide. I organised counselling for her in SOSAD, but she missed so many of her appointments that I had to cancel them. It was her counsellor who suggested to me that Valerie had a problem with alcohol. I had no idea she was back drinking to such an extent, and I confronted her. She denied that she had a problem and promised she would stop. I believed her, and even started getting her to help out in SOSAD, but she let us down on far too many occasions, and I had to put a stop to that.

A couple of years after Simon died, Valerie had a heart attack and went to the hospital. The strange thing was that, when she felt unwell, she went outside, because she was hot. She sat on the wall, smoked a cigarette, and called for a taxi to take her to the hospital. She did not feel much pain, but when she got to the A&E, we discovered that she had a massive heart attack. Once she got settled, I went home to get her clothes and stuff for her hospital stay, and once again found lots of opened bottles of vodka, and even some wine. I was disgusted but did not say anything when I returned to the hospital. That was not the time. Once I went home, I went on a bigger vodka search, and I found a lot more. I felt it was an absolute waste when I poured them all down the sink, but I wanted every single drop of alcohol gone from the house.

When Valerie got home, we spoke about it, and she promised that she would not drink or bring home alcohol anymore. I did believe her and thought that the heart attack had given her a scare, and would help her keep her word. She was great for a while, and stuck to her word, but was soon back buying alcohol and hiding it from me. I carried out regular searches and was always pouring drink away, especially vodka. That went on and on, and every time I confronted her, I got apologies and promises. The more this went on, the less I believed her, and she would never admit she had a problem. She would be great for a while and then drift back to her drinking. I am sure that she thought I didn't know. It was not too long until she had a second heart attack, and that did not stop her drinking at all. She didn't go back to work after the heart attacks, which meant that she had nothing to do all day. I don't think that helped her at all.

I am not sure if confronting her about her drinking was the right approach, but I did try to help her get professional help, but she just would not admit that she had a problem, and therefore didn't need any help. I have asked her why she does it, but I have never received a straight answer. I guess that she is trying to medicate herself to help her cope with all the loss she has had in her life. I can understand that, but I know that there is nothing but more pain at the bottom of the bottle.

The longer this has all gone on, the more separated we became. Valerie's drinking has become a lot worse over the years, and it is tragic to watch. She can't just have a few drinks and then get some sleep. Once she starts, I don't think that she can stop. She stays up all night drinking, and I have seen her early the next day, still drinking and pissed out of her head. Eventually, she falls asleep, and there is not a sound from her all day, and I wonder if she is alive or dead.

One of the main issues I have with her drinking is the lies. I cannot believe a word from her mouth anymore. Another issue I have is watching her kill herself slowly but surely. It is like the slowest suicide ever. I hate to see her that way. Another problem I have is that she can get very abusive, and therefore hurtful when she is drinking. I just do all I can to ignore her and hope she goes away when she gets fed up. I know that these are the main reasons I have drifted away from her, and I guess that I just don't love her anymore. I can't believe or trust her, and that hurts me. I am very well aware that she gifted me three amazing Sons, and helped look after me when I was severely depressed, and I feel guilty about drifting away from her now. Yet I don't feel I have any choice, and I do want to live the rest of my life in peace. I hate her when she is drinking. She often goes somewhere at weekends for a few nights, and I am glad of the respite and happy that, for a while at least, I am not watching her kill herself slowly.

That, of course, is my view on our relationship, and Valerie might describe it entirely differently. It takes two to tango, and I am sure that she feels that I am as much to blame for the way our marriage is ending. I know that I am too. I have given up trying to save our relationship, and try to avoid her as much as I can. Once I went back to work, and then started working on SOSAD, I cut her out of my life completely. Anytime I tried to reignite the flame, I was left hurt or disappointed. I can honestly say, in hindsight, that I did not try hard enough. We are both to blame.

Chapter 22

Expansion

The big problem with SOSAD. as far as I was concerned, was that the geographical area we were covering was huge, taking in the whole of the North East of Ireland and sometimes Northern Ireland. I travelled wherever I was needed, especially when people could not get to SOSAD in Drogheda. I didn't mind all the travelling, but getting these people to attend for assessments or counselling was proving difficult. They lived too far away, or couldn't get a lift, or were just not comfortable travelling to a different town or county. Thankfully, some people in Navan were interested in opening a SOSAD centre there, and I viewed this as one answer to this particular problem. I was keen to expand SOSAD and reach more people. There already were some volunteers willing to help run the place like Marie and Carmel. That was a bonus, and they were sure that they would get all the volunteers we needed. Marie had lost her son to suicide, and she felt that she had to do something. She, like me, had an urge to do what she could to help prevent suicide.

It was hard finding a place that fitted my vision, but we ended up renting a house that was very close to the town centre. The location was good, and the house had plenty of rooms we could adapt to our needs. The layout of the house meant that the only way we could make it work was to turn the bedrooms upstairs into counselling rooms. That was new to me, and I was not sure that having counselling upstairs would work, but the ladies seemed happy with it. We cleaned it up, well they did all the work, and while it was not perfect, it was a safe and comfortable place for everyone. We had the official opening, and all went very well. It did not take too long to get busy because SOSAD already had a reputation there. As far as I was concerned SOSAD just extended its reach to more people who could do with our help. Marie and Carmel recruited enough volunteers to provide the right level of service and support, at least for these early months. I trained everyone as much as I could, and it was refreshing to see so many turn up for the training sessions. While we got all the counsellors and admin support volunteers we needed, we always had trouble getting psychologists there, and sometimes had to send one or two over from Drogheda to help out. All the volunteers were very keen to learn and start helping people as if I could turn them into psychologists overnight. I had to reign them in a bit, but it worked out fine. I showed them that everyone would be involved in the client's welfare, even if they were not counsellors or psychologists. Every volunteer was important in the work we did and would be helping clients in their own way.

I was right. All the volunteers were brilliant with the clients, and SOSAD Navan got busy quickly. I was thrilled with that but not so happy that they kind of ignored the paperwork. I tried to get them to keep all the client's notes up to date because I knew it would mean better support for every client. Any time I was there, I tried to help them get up to date and emphasised how important it was. It was a constant battle trying to get that fundamental goal right, and when we did get it right, I found that it had all fallen by the wayside, the next time I visited.

Apart from the continuous lack of psychologists, the only other problem, as far as I could see, was funding. I had paid for everything out of the funds we had in Drogheda, but we needed something to keep it going. As usual, when setting up, many local politicians promised us all the support we needed but ran away when we reminded them of this. We kept it going somehow and then support from locals, in the form of their own fund-raising, started to materialise and ease that pressure. It never fully supported SOSAD Navan, but SOSAD Drogheda had enough money to cover the shortfall. All in all, SOSAD Navan was a great success from the start and was going to make a positive impact in the Meath community.

SOSAD in Drogheda was open from 9 am to 9 pm Monday to Friday, and 9 am to 3 pm on Saturday, but we started to struggle to get all our new clients into counselling immediately. We were also recruiting new counsellors all the time, just to keep up with the demand. It was one hell of an adventure for me, but to be honest, I loved it. My favourite part of the job came to be the suicide bereavement work, and I was just delighted to be able to make a difference in someone's life. We had a super team of volunteers that were growing in number all the time, and I believe that everyone enjoyed being in SOSAD, even if it was tremendously difficult at times.

That year (2009), I was honoured to be given a civic award by the Mayor of Drogheda and the Drogheda Borough Council. I was flattered, and deep down, I felt it was undeserved as there was still a substantial local suicide problem, as well as too many people struggling with depression. I accepted the award on behalf of all the brilliant volunteers in SOSAD. That year also, we started planning to open a SOSAD centre in Dundalk. People from that part of Louth were crying out for local help and support, and they had a massive suicide problem. The issue of people from the Dundalk area coming to SOSAD for help and support and then missing appointments, often through no fault of their own, was still a big problem. Opening a SOSAD centre, there would surely help the community, and erase the non-attendance issue. As usual, I did my research, and Kathleen, the psychiatric nurse in the hospital, was the most wonderful resource and guide.

The turnover of volunteers in SOSAD was always a bit of a problem, except perhaps with counsellors. Thankfully they were more permanent because some of our clients needed counselling for a year or more, and it was always better for them if they had the same counsellor. The psychologists we had always seemed to move on. Many of them moved to jobs or careers that were what they hoped for. I was always delighted when they told me how working in SOSAD had helped their application and interviews. I was sad to see them leave SOSAD but happy that they were moving up in the world. Many of our admin and support volunteers moved on too, many of them choosing further education in the psychological or counselling profession. Volunteering in SOSAD had piqued their interest, and helped them decide that this part of the caring vocation was the one for them. I was thrilled for them too. It did mean a lot of recruiting and training but was always worth it because every volunteer helped enormously in keeping people safe and helping them with their depression.

Between 2009 and 2010, I was desperately searching for a new psychologist that would be able to spend a few days in SOSAD. As SOSAD expanded, my trips became more frequent, and I was doing a lot more awareness talks and bereavement work. I was afraid that SOSAD in Drogheda would suffer as a consequence. I needed someone to manage and organise all the psychologists, and the assessments and make sure that every new client was placed in counselling as quickly as possible. A young lady, Elaine G, got in contact one day out of the blue. I met her as soon as I could, and she started working in SOSAD soon after. She was a Godsend.

She took to her new role like a duck to water, and soon had a handle on the way we worked, our policies and procedures and all the necessary paperwork. She looked after all the psychologists, counsellors and clients, and turned out to be brilliant at the assessments and allocating the clients to the best counsellor for that particular case. She had graduated from UCD in Dublin, and although she was only in her 20s, she was very organised, and calm under pressure.

Elaine, the psychologist, was a quiet and reserved girl, who seldom spoke about her life outside SOSAD. So much so, that at times I thought she was shy, but I don't think she actually was. We could talk easily about SOSAD, but not much about anything else. To be honest, I found that quiet confidence a bit intimidating at times, and I never learned too much about her during the next five years.

Around the same time, another lady, another Elaine, joined us to help out in admin, and any other way she could. She was another Godsend, and I felt that Simon and God were playing their part and helping me whenever I needed it. She was so eager to learn, and I kept adding to the list of tasks I gave her. I was very keen on statistics, on everything to do with clients, like numbers of counselling appointments and cancellations, numbers of assessments, and the number of calls from people in distress. She took on these tasks, and looked after and coordinated all the other admin volunteers, as well as the suicide intervention officers. She helped the counsellors and psychologists whenever she could and took over the appointment's diary.

Elaine B was in her thirties and had a young Son. She had lost her brother, as well as some friends to suicide, and I guessed this was her motivation. I found her to be brilliant; she acted like a true professional and seemed to have been born for this work. She was open and friendly all the time, and thankfully, the two Elaine's got on very well together and became friends. That pleased me because I got the feeling the Elaine B had few or no real friends. It seemed to me that anytime she spoke about friends, she was referring to friends on social media and not friends she spent some time with.

She quickly became important to me, and I relied on her more and more as time went on. I felt that I would be lost without her. I liked being in her company because I found her so easy to get on with and because she was always reminding me of visits or talks, I had. She was managing my diary, too, as well as me at times. I needed that, and it was great to have someone cover for me when I was busy. She became like my right hand, guiding me all the time, and taking a lot of weight off my shoulders. I loved all my volunteers, but she was my favourite.

I consciously put a lot of effort into increasing our finances. When I was happy enough, I approached Elaine G and offered her a full-time permanent paid position as the coordinator of SOSAD Drogheda. It was nowhere near the proper rate for a qualified psychologist, but she accepted immediately. I needed that, as I was spending most of my time in other centres, going to meetings, meeting fund-raisers, or delivering awareness talks. She was doing a brilliant job, and while I wanted to reward her, I also wanted to try and ensure she stayed with SOSAD. I was thrilled she accepted and felt that SOSAD Drogheda was in excellent hands, plus she had Elaine B to help if needed.

With the money situation still favourable, and looking like it would always be enough for my plans, I decided to reward Elaine B too, but give her much more responsibility. Because of her situation with her son, and her having to look after him after school, I decided to offer her a paid permanent part-time position. It was the same hours she was already doing. I took her out the back yard of SOSAD, because it was the only unoccupied place in SOSAD that day, and offered her the position. I explained that I wanted her to take over the admin for the whole charity, and work with the other centres to ensure their paperwork was up to date. She accepted gleefully, and I could see how excited she was. I was very happy for her and delighted that she accepted my offer. I did not doubt that she would help the charity progress and be of even more helpful to me.

One thing I did keep up, was making sure Simon's grave looked presentable at all times, especially for his birthday, anniversary and Christmas. I would get deflated when the plants at the top of the grave would die off and the new season of plants was not yet available, because it didn't look its best. I attended the annual 'Blessings of the Graves' every year, even though I hated it because it was on Father's Day. I always accompanied Mam and Dad, but they spent most of the time at Gran's grave, and I was my own. I did not like that, and as I looked around at all the families together, I felt so isolated and alone and felt sorry for Simon. I could not wait to get out of there. Standing there on my own, year after year, had me overthinking again and one thing, in particular, bugged me and even upset me when I was vulnerable. It was about Simon being at peace. From the funeral on, I was told that he is at peace. That was a lot of comfort to me when I accepted it. Yet here we were at Cemetery Sunday, and many other occasions when I think about it, praying for peace for Simon and everyone else interred in the graveyard. If Simon got peace when he passed, why are we still praying for it now? My question was, is he at peace or not? This question still annoys me, but maybe this is just an indication of how my overthinking mind works, and to me anyway, everything is or should be 'black or white'.

While I was feeling ok nearly all the time, there were certain occasions in the calendar year that I had to be very careful about. The hardest for me was, and still is, Simon's anniversary. About a week before, I start to feel it coming like the world is about to end on the 10th. I can feel the sadness wash over me and seep into my brain. The guilt I always carry becomes more profound, and Simon's loss feels close to the loss I felt after he died. It is grieving all over again, but I have learned that it just happens and there is nothing I can do about it. After all, I know Simon deserves any time I think about him.

When the 11th comes, I am fine again, and the sadness, weariness, and most of the guilt just washes out of me as quickly as it seeped in. Simon's birthday somehow does not seem as bad, but it still hurts. I wonder about how we would be celebrating if he were still with us. Probably lots of crazy fun and he would be all excitable and happy. I wonder what he looks like now and I am reminded of a story I heard, after Simon died, of course. One Sunday, one of Valerie's relatives in Drogheda was getting their new baby baptised, and Simon went with his Mam. They went to the baptism and then went with all their relatives, to the pub. I have a photo of that day, and Simon was wearing his big. I can see that it was not fake. He looked happy and seemed to be enjoying himself. After the pub, Simon went off with some of his cousins. I think Valerie thought he went to get some food. Simon didn't go for a takeaway. Instead, he went to one of the local night clubs. When I found out, the first chance I got; I went to the nightclub to find out how they had let Simon in there in the first place. The bouncers were great about it and sat me down for a chat. They told me Simon had been going there for years and they never asked for ID because they thought Simon looked well over 21. They explained how he always seemed to be in good spirits and was never any trouble at all. He did not often go, just the odd time, and was always welcome. I honestly did not know whether to laugh or cry. Simon always wanted to be 21, and I loved the idea that here, and in the eyes of the bouncers, he was 21, and I'm sure he loved that. It didn't surprise me, because of his muscular, athletic build, but on the other hand what the hell was a 16-year-old doing in a nightclub, and how did he do it without me knowing? He must have been sneaking out after I went to bed, just like when he took my car. That brat!!!

The other time is Christmas. I miss Simon adding some form of hilarity and stupidity to the occasion, and I re-member his last Christmas when he spent every cent he had, on presents for us. They say time is a great healer and I don't agree with that at all. It's what you learn about yourself, in that time, that helps. I have learned to cope without Simon. His suicide meant we had to find a new normal without him. I learned so much about suicide that many of the questions I was asking have satisfactory answers. I realised that I had to go through the whole grieving process before I could live again. I learned that keeping hold of those hurtful emotions, like anger, for ex-ample, prevent any chance of living a natural life, which Simon wants, probably above anything else. I do still have that guilt, but it does not control me or stop me from living. It is there to remind me of the terrible mistakes I made and a reminder to never take anything for granted. I used it to motivate me in SOSAD and keep everything going, and to try my best never to let anyone down.

Over that couple of years, I went on holiday a couple of times with Valerie to Tenerife and Lanzarote. I was not trying to reignite anything; it was just that I was still married to her and didn't think that going away on my own was the right thing to do. They turned out to be a lot of hard work. On one occasion, when we were packed and ready to go, Valerie told me that someone had stolen her savings and she had nothing to bring with her. I didn't believe her, and we had a big argument, and I was still in a terrible mood when we got to the hotel in Tenerife. I had enough money though because I am not a big spender on holidays. I sucked it in and tried to have a good time and relax. Going on holidays like that, in the sun, with a nice walk nearby is the only way I could relax, recharge the batteries and go back to SOSAD fresh with a clear mind. Both holidays were a big let-down, as I didn't get to relax properly. I wanted to go for my walk along the seafront every morning and evening and then relax in the sun reading and listening to music all day. Valerie didn't want to go for a walk with me, and then wanted me to do stuff with her every day, and we only argued. As it happens, they were the last time we went on holiday together.

In April 2010, I finally received my medical records from the health service. Twenty-something pages, including the index and documentation about collating the data. I was dumbfounded and could not believe that these few pages covered my whole medical history. The first thing I wanted to sort out was the torn muscle versus the broken hip argument and sure enough, the few pages from my initial visit to Shine, my stay in hospital and visits to out-patients, referred to a fractured hip, or a tiny bone on the hip. I noticed that I was admitted for immobilisation because I had an "avulsion of the right inferior iliac spine". I looked up the exact problem and did not see how that warranted a two-week stay in the hospital, and being confined to bed for most of that time. That describes a fracture of a small bone on my hip. It is usually caused by some sudden force on it and not kicking a ball. There was no sign of the x-ray in my notes. I can't find anywhere on the internet that recommends immobilisation for an "avulsion of the right inferior iliac spine". As far as I am concerned, my medical records make no sense to me. Recovery was much easier and did not warrant a hospital stay. It wasn't who had altered my records, but how he had done it, and why did he remove lots of other stuff from the records, that he had no involvement with, as far as I was concerned. If it wasn't Shine, then I was sure it was someone doing it at his request. I was sure they were tampered with and absolutely positive that I was in hospital in 1975 for a torn thigh muscle in my right leg. I knew that is what I was treated for, yet that is not what my medical records say. I received the broken hip in the crash in 1979 and remembered the bent steering wheel that did the damage. It was no wonder I got confused and frustrated on the witness stand.

I checked the rest of my 'records' and could not believe all the stuff that was missing. The stay in Dundalk hospital after the car crash was not included. If that wasn't in my records, what crash was Mc Enroy referring to, and trying to accuse me of? Was I losing my mind? I felt like I barely existed, and it was all some kind of dream. Nearly half of the pages I received refer to an endoscopy years later. I remember visits to the hospital that I have no records for, like the two different times I split my head open, or the time I fell off the trailer delivering potatoes. I wallowed in pity and anger for a few days and then decided to try to forget about it. It was in the past and no good to me anyway, and I was not going to upset myself chasing up the rest of my records, or trying to get them corrected. I was angry because I was thinking about O'Boyle and the Gardai and wondering how they made sense of my records. I questioned how they matched my statement to my medical records, or if they ever bothered. Then I thought they would have to care first. I decided to let it all go, and because of SOSAD and the work we were doing, I managed to do that, which in itself was unusual for me.

Later that year, I was invited to the REHAB awards night and dinner in the Crowne Plaza Hotel in Dundalk and urged to attend. I did not speak to anyone in REHAB because Elaine B had taken the calls and passed the message on to me. I did not know what the REHAB awards were, but I agreed to go. Someone else had arranged for me to give a talk in Virginia in Cavan that same evening. Not wanting to let anyone down, I was sure that I could give the speech in Cavan and then go to Dundalk and just be a little late. That day I got delayed in SOSAD and rushed home to grab something to eat, have a shower, and get changed. When in the shower, I slipped and fell out onto the floor. The toilet had stopped my fall, and the lower part of my back was in absolute agony. I couldn't move and had to call out for help. Valerie and Wayne heard my cries, and even with them, it took me an age to get off the floor. I was in so much pain. They got me into my bedroom, and I managed to dry myself and put some clothes on. Every move seemed to make the ache worse, but I eventually managed to get down the stairs and into the sitting room. I sat on the sofa, but could not find a position that did not cause me more pain. I knew that I was not going to be able to go to the hospital, so we called the Doctor-on-Call. It was not too long until a doctor came to the house. He suggested that I had damaged my kidneys and some ribs, but he could not be sure. He advised me that I would have to go to the hospital for x-rays and treatment. He also suggested that I leave it until early Saturday morning because casualty would just be too busy and there was nowhere, I could wait in any comfort. He gave me injections for the pain and went on his way, but we had to call him back later that night, as I was in pure agony. He did come back and gave me Ketamine, I think, and even with that, the pain would not ease.

I knew I was going nowhere, so we contacted the people in Virginia to apologise and try to explain how a toilet had disabled me. I don't think they believed us. Then we rang the Crowne Plaza, and they definitely did not believe us, but what could I do. I still felt terrible for letting people down, but I was helpless. Later that night, I was still trying to find a place on the sofa that did not hurt so much when the phone rang. It was Fr Iggy, and he was at the awards night in Dundalk. We talked about what happened, but I don't think that he believed me either. Then he told me that I had won the REHAB Louth Person of the Year award, and he was delighted to have accepted the award on my behalf. Now it was my turn to think he was lying, or at least taking the piss out of me. Eventually, he convinced me he was ringing with the good news, and I was utterly shocked. I had no idea I was nominated for any award, and no one had mentioned this to me. I thanked Iggy and told Valerie and Wayne; Lee was at work. I was chuffed but sorry I was not able to go and thank everyone myself, but I knew Iggy would have done a brilliant job. Again though, I felt it was undeserved, like getting an award for finishing a marathon, at the halfway mark. I had only done a bit, and there was a lot more I could do.

I called an ambulance at 7 am the next morning, and it quickly arrived and conveyed me to the hospital, where I was given plenty more drugs for the pain and told I had cracked a couple of ribs and damaged my kidneys. It was the kidneys that were causing most of my agony, and it would just take time for them to heal. I was glad I did not have to stay in the hospital. I don't like that place and went home to recover. A few days later, Paul, the photographer with the Drogheda Independent, called up to give me my award and take some photos for the paper and REHAB. I still couldn't sit properly, and he took the piss out of me big time. He told me how they all laughed in the hotel in Dundalk when they heard why I was not there, and he loved telling me all about it. Talk about a terrible bedside manner.

We opened SOSAD in Dundalk that year. It was a small old house, but all we could afford to rent, but it would serve our purposes until we got established, and then we would look for somewhere more suitable. We cleaned it up as much as we could and decorated it. The counselling rooms were upstairs and did look comfortable and safe. I had met a lovely girl one day called Davina when I was up in DKiT. She had just finished studying there and earned her degree. I thought she would be brilliant for us, and asked her if she would volunteer and get SOSAD in Dundalk up and running. She agreed, at least until she found a paid job for herself. Davina was as good as I hoped, and I was amazed at the level of support we got from the people in Dundalk and surrounding areas. She soon had plenty of volunteers, had them all trained, and she organised everything the way it was supposed to be.

From the start, SOSAD Dundalk had lots of calls for bereavement support, which was not surprising considering the vast number of suicides there. I was happy to be able to help these people and offer them all our support. I made sure that they had the contact details for Dundalk and encouraged them to call if they had any concerns or worries. I was glad that we seemed to be helping others from the beginning. The one issue I couldn't figure out in Dundalk was that although we were organising plenty of interventions and assessments, not many wanted to continue into counselling. It was like they were helped somewhat and then thought they would be ok on their own. It was strange and continued over the years there. As far as I was concerned though, we had extended our reach and would now be properly able to help and support those that found it too difficult to travel to and from Drogheda.

Lee graduated from DKiT, and I went with him for his graduation ceremony, and I was as proud as punch. I couldn't wait for his name to be called so that I could see him get his certificate. When he was called and got his cert, I wanted to roar and shout, but I stayed quiet with a big stupid grin on my face. I felt like I had received the degree, not him, and I was so happy for him. I know he did what he could all through college, but I guessed it must have been tough for him. He had his girlfriend and was still working in McPhail's. How he managed to study, work, and spend time with Sarah Jane, I had no idea. I know he preferred to be with Sarah Jane or in McPhail's rather than studying.

He soon landed a full-time position in International Financial Services (IFS) which was located just a few minutes away from us. IFS is a back-office type of operation for State Street International. Lee had to learn all their financial procedures and find his place in the new job, but he navigated his way through it easily enough. He made lots of new friends there and tried to keep working in McPhail's, but he couldn't keep that up for long. It was a wrench for him leaving McPhail's, but he still kept in touch with all his mates from there, so all was not lost.

Soon after he started his new job, he moved to live with Sarah Jane. It was her late Gran's house in Clogherhead and was a lovely, warm house. The house had been re-built and decorated and looked just amazing. Everything seemed to be on the up and up for Lee, and I could not have been happier for him. We were invited out to see it, and Valerie came with me. We took it all in and were very impressed with everything. It looked like a super home for the two of them, and they both seemed very happy. After the first visit, I did not call out too much because again, I was afraid of interfering in their lives, and to be honest, I did not know what to say. That amazed me. I could talk to anyone for ages about SOSAD, suicide, and depression, but found it hard to have a normal conversation with any-one, even Wayne and Lee. I dreaded not having anything to say and ending up with those long silences, which were not comfortable at all. I did not know how to talk about or share what I was thinking or felt.

When Lee moved out, Valerie left my bed to sleep in the empty room, using some excuse about moving out to let me sleep properly. I did not believe a word she said, but

I was happy that I had my room to myself. I didn't care why she had moved out. I made one mistake, though. I made a little home office in the bedroom, which I thought was great, and in many ways, it was. Four or more of us were sharing the one office in SOSAD, and it was difficult for any of us to get some peace, or get some work done. I was able to get a lot of work done at home and slowly but surely, I began to spend all the time I was not in SOSAD, up in my new workstation working away and not taking any kind of a decent break.

SOSAD Drogheda was now dealing with over 100 clients a week and nearly the same number of volunteers. We were starting to get stuck for rooms for assessments and counselling. Luckily one of the counselling rooms was quite big, and we were able to divide that up into two new counselling rooms. That helped ease the pressure. We had four counselling rooms in Drogheda now, able to handle all our clients more comfortably, for a while at least. We started to notice that we were getting new clients from Dublin and the Fingal area and some even travelling from South Dublin. We were just happy we could help. It was evident that SOSAD would work brilliantly with one or more centres in Dublin, but when I researched it, I found that we just did not have the money needed to set up in the Dublin area. Maybe I thought, we could look at opening in Dublin again if we ever got funding.

I was spending much of my time 'on the road' giving talks on SOSAD, suicide, and depression. I enjoyed that, especially when I thought that I got my message and points across. There were many points of view about what to say to teens at the time. I had, with the help of some psychologists, developed talks around depression, suicide, and suicide bereavement. It was honest and sometimes brutal and geared towards helping the listener. It was always very well received. There would not be a sound, except my voice, in the classrooms and halls when I spoke, and I felt they understood what I was trying to teach them. The best reception was always in the schools and colleges I visited. They were the age group most affected by suicide at that time. They genuinely wanted to know more about this 'suicide' that was in many cases affecting their homes, friends, and school mates, and I didn't think they needed anyone pussyfooting around the truth. It really seemed to work for them, and many of them came to SOSAD for help and support and even advice afterwards. I was doing a bit of good in this horrible world.

The talks I gave on suicide included the definition as well as an accurate description of what suicide was, as I have spoken about elsewhere. I spoke about the causes and how anyone could get thoughts of suicide. I talked about the importance of talking to somebody if ever they felt suicidal and reminded them of the consequences if they didn't. I spoke about depression and how it grows and affects people. I described it as an illness that anyone can get, just like the flu. I told them about the various and many symptoms and the real danger of not telling anyone. I always spoke about the fact that seeking help early would mean that they could be treated before the depression became too severe. I told them about the numbers affected by depression, and the numbers dying by suicide. I paid particular attention to the age group I was talking to, and where that group stood in the ratings. I tried to speak to them as if it was a one-to-one session and often added parts of my own story to emphasise a point. When I talked about suicide bereavement, I concentrated on the many aspects of the grieving process. I described many of them and how they seemed to attack us all at once. I spoke about my own experiences a lot and tried to show them how best to navigate through this grieving process. I reminded everyone that we are all different, and therefore, we all grieve in different ways, and not at the same pace. I just tried to guide bereaved people as well as those who wanted to help anyone bereaved by suicide.

Once, I visited a school in Drogheda and gave my usual talk on suicide and depression. One of the students asked me questions that set my alarm bells ringing. To me, it was like he already had a suicide plan. After the talk, I made sure I caught his attention and tried to talk to him, but he insisted he was in a hurry to get to his next class. I handed him the SOSAD information and details and told him that I understood that he didn't want to talk there and then, but asked him to consider giving us a call when he wanted, and he could even ask for me if that was easier for him. I was glad I had included my belief that no matter how suicidal a person might be, there is always that little spark of life trying to keep us alive. I spoke to one of his teachers about my concerns and asked her to keep an eye on him. A few days later, I happened to be in SOSAD when the phone rang. Elaine B answered and immediately threw the phone at me, beckoning me to take the call. That was unusual as she was excellent on the phone, and this was not like her at all. When I got the phone to my ear, I just said, as calmly as I could, "Hi, It's Peter here, how can I help you". He replied, as calm as you like "I am standing on a wall, beside the river, and I am going to jump in. What can you do about it"? I knew I was in trouble, not only by what he said but by the way, he seemed very calm and collected about his situation. It was like he had made his plan and was happy with his decision, and was about to jump when that little spark of life reminded him of SOSAD. I told him that I was going to get him off that wall then away from the river and we would meet and have a chat. He answered back, and that is all I wanted to hear at that stage. He wanted to know "how" but I veered him away from that by asking for his name, so I knew what to call him. When he told me and said he knew me, I asked him how. He told me that I had given a talk in his school a few days earlier. He was still talking, so I asked him what he thought about it. He told me that much of it made sense, but other parts were rubbish. I didn't argue but asked him what he thought about that spark of life I mentioned. He replied that he didn't believe that, and I asked him if it could have been that spark that made him call. He hesitated, and I thought he was thinking hard. While he was thinking, I suggested that he get off the wall so that I would feel more comfortable talking to him. He kind of objected at first, but I reminded him, that he could always climb back up on the wall if he wanted, so he got down.

I was so relieved, but now I had to get him away from the river altogether. We talked more about the parts of my talk that made sense to him and how they related to him, and I started to learn a lot about why he had considered suicide. The more I learned about him, the more I was able to help him. We began to play a 'game' where I managed to get him further away from the river and closer to SOSAD every time I made sense or helped him a little bit. I got him away from the river, then across the road, then up the road, and so on until I heard him say. I'm at the front door". I was at the door in a second and welcomed him in. It was that same boy from school. We went into the kitchen, had coffees, and chatted for ages, sometimes about what he was going through, and other times about his interests and friends. We talked about anything at all. I was just trying to help him relax and find out any little detail that for him was a 'reason to live'. I had already learned all the reasons why he thought suicide was his best or only option, and I was trying to turn all his 'negatives' into 'positives'. Sometimes I was getting somewhere, and then I wasn't, but overall, I calmed him down, and he agreed to go for an assessment. I told him it would help him and us, understand a lot more about himself. We were lucky that Elaine G was available and she looked after him. While he was assessed, I got his family involved and up to date, and one of his relations came in to be with him and take him home and keep him safe. I did this with his full permission because we discussed what we were going to do in detail before he went with the psychologist. We always did that. We involved every client in every decision about their mental health. I think this kind of helped them believe they were more in control of themselves and what was going to happen. Once he was assessed and had a long helpful chat with the psychologist, he agreed to go into counselling, and he left the building looking much better than when he arrived. I was delighted for him.

In 2011, I was honoured to be asked to be the Grand Marshall of the St Patrick's Day Parade, in Drogheda and Dundalk. They were both at the same time, so I couldn't do both. I picked Drogheda because they asked me first and I had already agreed to do it when the people from Dundalk got in touch. When the big day arrived, I had my best suit on with a big sash and had Wayne and Gerry Simpson accompany me. We walked through the town at the head of the parade, and I was unsure about what I should be doing. I was waving and grinning like a Cheshire cat with all the cream, but felt silly and thought that I was doing it all wrong. I made an effort to wave to or connect with many of the kids on the route as I felt more comfortable doing that.

The crowds were truly massive, and the atmosphere was brilliant. We often had to stop and wait because the part of the parade behind us was too far back. It was organised chaos, that was slowly snaking around the town with lots of different music and noise. When we got to the viewing stand where all the 'guests' or modern-day Pharisees were seated, I smiled through gritted teeth at most of them but was genuinely happy to see some others I liked and trusted. We continued through the crowds, stopping and starting, and it was great to see so many enjoying the spectacle, especially the younger generation. They all looked so happy to be there, and that cheered me up. We got to the end on the Quays, and the boys left me, and I felt right a right idiot standing there on my own waving every float and group to the end line. Later I had to go to the reception and say a few words, which I was able to manage no problem, but then I found it very difficult to talk to the people individually or get more involved like I was supposed to. I just did not feel comfortable enough. I did get a laugh, though when Marie, a committee member, caught a local politician trying to steal a couple of bottles of wine from the reception. I just laughed, and it reaffirmed my idea that politicians all looked after themselves as much as possible, before even thinking of the community they were supposed to represent. I did enjoy the honour of being invited to be the Grand Marshall, and I did enjoy the parade. I was just over-thinking again, and every time I did that, I got depressed. What was wrong with me?

Wayne went to Maynooth in 2011 to study astrophysics and suddenly seemed at peace with the world. I was happy for him but not sure where he was going to get a career from that, in Ireland anyway. He was working part-time in the local Specsavers to support himself through college. He drove to Maynooth and back every day, and he found a shortcut, on county roads and lanes, which avoided most of the heavy traffic. He immediately got stuck into his studies as if he was born for it, and he made lots of new friends too. Sometimes he told me what he was doing or studying, but I was utterly lost after half a second and had no idea what he was talking about. I just learned that as well as the science parts of his course there were lots of very tough maths. He was able for it, but he even had to admit that there were a couple in his classes that were just geniuses. At least he had them to contact if ever he got stuck. I gave a few of my talks to the students there, and while I enjoyed going up to see him in his university, I often felt as though I was 'invading his space' and was careful not to interfere in his life. I had done enough damage.

SOSAD in Cavan opened in 2011 and what a let-down that was for me. I had been in Cavan a few times giving talks and was asked why SOSAD did not have a centre in that area. Some politicians were close to demanding that we open there. I did my research and found that Cavan had one of the highest suicide rates in the country. I found that the rural quieter parts had a huge problem related to loneliness, uselessness, and hopelessness. I also learned that many older adults were struggling while not wanting to be a burden on anyone. So, they were keeping all their problems to themselves. Eventually, they were not able to cope anymore, and suicide often followed. The urban parts of Cavan had just as bad a problem with suicide, but here it was the younger generation that was affected most.

I got some funds together, found a suitable location and building, and then tried to recruit volunteers. The house was very close to the town centre, and again the counselling rooms were upstairs. Despite all the talks I had delivered in Cavan and all the people and politicians who had made so many promises to me, we found it hard to get counsellors and admin volunteers, and impossible to find psychologists. We were not deterred, and started training the counsellors who were willing, and had the time, in our assessment procedures and that kept us going. We were lucky to get enough people who would operate the phones at night and do what they could to keep people safe or let them know how SOSAD could help. It was the most challenging opening so far, but as time passed, more volunteers signed up, and many more people called looking for help and support. It was slow progress but worth every bit of it.

That Christmas, Lee bought me a present that changed my life, and maybe even saved it. Lee and Sarah Jane arrived early that morning. I knew they were coming up for their breakfast. I was in the sitting room, and he told me to close my eyes and to have an open mind. I had no idea what he was talking about, but he repeated it and reminded me to keep my eyes closed. I did what I was told. There was talking and whispering, and I just thought it was something to do with my present. It had to be. What else could be causing such a fuss? I heard everyone gathering in the sitting room, but I did not hear any parcels or packaging moving at all. Then he told me to open my eyes, and when I did, sitting in front of me on the floor, was a tiny puppy. It was looking lovingly up at me, and it looked so beautiful. Her lovely brown eyes looked as if they were from a cartoon. She was mostly white but had a beautiful shade of brown over one side of her face and her ears. I picked it up gently because it was so small and looked almost fragile. I found out it was a female mini Jack Russell and was born that September. She was beautiful and took to me straight away.

The boys had often asked if they could get a dog, but I refused because I knew I would end up looking after it. This was different. This was my new baby, and I welcomed this new responsibility with all my heart. I promised I would look after her properly. She was lively, friendly and all excited, and I was too. They had also bought the basics, like food and bowls, etc., to keep me going for a few days until I could get to the pet shop. I was all set up. Then we all shared our presents, which was so brilliant and my baby found a new toy - wrapping paper.

It was the best present I ever received, even though the boys have given me some great gifts over the years. On Father's Day, after Simon died, they bought me a new pool cue. It was terrific, and I still use it now, but I have to keep it at home because others found it so good that they adopted it and used it whenever they could. I would have to go looking for it every time I wanted to play a game of pool. They also bought me new TVs, streaming boxes, and all the accessories and while they were all brilliant, they will never match my new baby.

Later that Christmas morning, we all went to my Mother's house, and I took her along. I had just received her, and I wasn't going to leave her so soon. She was a big hit with everyone, especially my nephews and nieces and I asked them to pick a suitable name for her. Everyone got involved, and because it was Christmas, we settled on Holly. She could not stop playing with everyone and made us all laugh. Later at home after Christmas dinner, I retired to the sitting room to talk to Simon, and I took my new buddy with me. She explored every inch of the sitting room and played with anything that she could find before coming over to me, wanting to be lifted. When I picked her up, she spent a while trying to find the most comfortable position for herself and settled on that space between my thighs. She was already comfortable with me, and it felt so right sitting there with her, talking to Simon and watching TV.

A couple of months later, I went on holiday to Fuerteventura on my own. Winter was coming to an end, and I thought it was a great time to go away. As the holiday grew closer, I got more excited and was looking forward to the break. I went to the bank to withdraw my savings to pay for the holiday and give myself some spending money. When I got there, I had nothing in my account. I got talking to the staff in the bank, and they told me that €600 had been withdrawn twice in the previous two weeks from an ATM close to where I live. I thought that the machine had made a mistake or the only other possibility was that my card was skimmed. Maybe I could get my money back and go and enjoy the holiday. I soon learned that the ATM did not make a mistake, and my card was not skimmed. My card was used in the middle of the night, on both occasions. It was not the bank's fault, and I would not be getting my money back. I was devastated and had no idea what I could do. I went to the police station and made a complaint, and they sent someone up to the house to talk to Valerie, and she just admitted it, without the slightest guilt or shame. The cops were useless then as they saw it as a family matter, and I knew I would never see that money again. I had to go back to the bank with the crime number and get my card, and associated numbers changed. All this when I was supposed to be packing and flying off early the next morning.

There would be no holiday now. Later I was talking to my Mam, and she asked about my credit card. I only used that for emergencies and had forgotten all about it. I knew where I had it in my bedroom, and went and found it straight away. The holiday was back on, and I started packing. Holly kept jumping into the case as if she was coming with me. I did regret not being able to take her.

Every time I am on one of those lovely walks along the seafront, I always think of her and wish she was with me there. She would love it.

Despite all the drama, I had a lovely relaxing holiday on my own. I got plenty of sun, lots of walking and read a few books. I relaxed like never before and felt fresher and motivated when I got back. I did not mind being on my own. I was alone but not lonely. I was, for once, able to chat easily with anyone I met and that too helped me relax and enjoy the holiday.

Sometime later, I think, I was driving somewhere when I got a phone call from the solicitors representing us in the civil case against Shine. I can't remember the name of the solicitors because they had changed a few times. I didn't know why or who authorised the move to new legal representatives, and I didn't care. The case had started many years before against Shine, the Lourdes hospital, and the North East Health board. Somewhere along the way, the Lourdes and NEHB were dropped, and I don't know why. Maybe I had been told and forgot about it, or perhaps it happened, and I didn't notice. I couldn't understand what happened, but I was afraid to dwell on it.

I was told there was an offer of settlement made and accepting the offer was recommended, so I did just that. It was a lot of money as far as I was concerned, yet was a pittance compared to what people were awarded for slander, and barely matched what people got for a broken finger at the time. I simply could not make sense of that, but I also thought that this finally was the very end to this whole sorry mess. It was not long until my over-thinking took over, and I started to regret having accepted the offer. Although it was in some way, the closure I wanted so much, it was not the closure I craved. I felt that I did not get the justice I thought I would get almost 20 years previously, and although Shine was not working as a doctor anymore, that I was aware of, he could still be abusing boys. I could not imagine paedophiles just giving up and stopping that which gave them so much pleasure. I wondered and worried that Shine was still at it, maybe at his home or somewhere else. If he was, we had failed those 'new' victims and that hurt. I was overwhelmed with the realisation that I had hurt myself and my family for nothing at all, except a little bit of money. I felt like I had sold out on everything I had tried to do. I did not get justice at all, and the only closure I got felt more like a payoff.

I had to fight like crazy to keep going, and thankfully SOSAD kept me busy, and like my distractions of old, kept my depression at bay. I thought that at least the case was all over now, and I would never be bothered by it again. I also started to believe that with this case finished for me, then maybe my depression would be kept in check for evermore too. How wrong I was.

I sometimes never learn my lessons from the past. I had given a talk in a parish hall in Drumconrath, and afterwards, the whole group wanted SOSAD to open in their locality. It was in the rural part of Meath and Cavan, and I thought it was the logical next step. I made more enquiries and was sure a small centre in that area was warranted and needed. I checked back regularly with the church group and told them of the importance of having plenty of volunteers. They seemed to be very enthusiastic, and I thought that getting the volunteers we needed would be no problem. I found a place that was suitable and very well situated in Kingscourt, a town in the middle of this whole country area.

When I signed the lease and got the keys, I organised a group from Drumconrath, and anyone else they could rope in, to clean the building and make it ready for use. I was so disappointed when only three people turned up to help. I didn't know it then, but that was an indication of what was going to happen there. From that day only one person was of any real help. She was dedicated and willing, but I think she got fed up trying to get others involved. Many said they would, but didn't show up when requested. I was trying to help to get the volunteers we needed. We did get a few, but then suddenly they were gone. There were many different 'clicks' in the area that did not get on with anyone in another group. When I thought we had the volunteers we needed to open, even if it was just on a part-time basis, I learned that many of the volunteers would not be starting at all. It was demoralising and painful for me, but I started something and wanted to see it through, so I kept pushing on. Eventually, we did get enough volunteers to open on a part-time basis, and use other branches to cover the phones when it was closed. I was sure then, that like Cavan, it would be a slow process. I kept pushing on, but no one was contacting the centre for help, and I found out that SOSAD was not always open when it should have been. Volunteers would just not turn up or lacked interest and motivation because they did not believe they were helping anyone. I could understand that, and over time I also learned that no one was calling because of some of the people involved. It was a disaster, but it still took me a long time to realise that there was nothing I could do about it. I was reluctant to admit failure and close it down but didn't know what else I could do.

Eventually, someone suggested I move it to Carrickmacross, a town, not too far away in Monaghan. It was a bigger town, and it seemed like the answer to my problems. But the move didn't change much at all. We found a building that was suitable but not ideal. We got a few more volunteers involved, which was great, but we had just moved all the problems from Kingscourt to Carrickmacross. People still did not want to use SOSAD because of some of the people involved. I wanted SOSAD to be an asset to the community and needed our reputation to grow so that more people would learn to trust SOSAD.

I even had to go to court over the lease in Kingscourt. The owner wanted the whole four years and nine months of the tenancy agreement fully paid, and would not entertain any offer I made to her. I offered six months, and then a year's rent to her, but she would not budge, and so we ended up in court. The same court that Shine and Mc Enroy had flattered and deceived us all years before. Thankfully the solicitors argued and settled on a pay-off outside the court itself and my appearance in that room full of terrible memories was brief and we ended up only having to pay the six months, which was my first offer. That was the only time anything worked out for me in Kingscourt.

Being in that courthouse again was genuinely horrible, not only from all the memories which plagued me, but because I felt very uncomfortable and troubled just being there, and I could not wait to get out. I was sweating as if I was on trial for murder, or something just as horrible and evil. I imagined I would be sent away to the dirtiest dankest prison cell my little mind could picture. I was not in control of myself at all, and my over-thinking had a field day playing with my thoughts and emotions. I was delighted to get out when it was all over and content to have the rent in Kingscourt sorted, and maybe I could put that place and the disaster that unfolded, out of my mind forever.

The people in Monaghan, like in the Kingscourt area, needed SOSAD and the help and support we provided. Yet, because of the people and personalities involved, it never took off properly. A few more people did make contact looking for help, but most avoided the place like it was cursed. We did manage to get some decent volunteers but nowhere near enough, and again the centre was often closed when it should have been opened. I even got dragged into some sort of Garda investigation into one of our volunteers, and nothing was going right. The policies and procedures were not put in place at all, and nothing was working as it should. Going there just hurt me, and I remember how terrible I used to feel when I was driving to Carrickmacross. I had to do something. I knew that starting again from scratch was the best option. But I was concerned about telling the volunteers that they were no longer needed.

I did just that, in the nicest possible way, saying we were going to try something new because what we were doing there was just not working. I reminded them that many people did not like, trust or want anything to do SOSAD. That meant that SOSAD was excluding many of the people from Monaghan who needed our support. I also talked about the Garda investigation being something that could be very damaging to SOSAD and insisted that we could not be involved in any way. The whole reputation of SOSAD was at stake. So, we just closed it for a while. It was my failure. I should have spent a lot more time in my research, before opening in Kingscourt. If I had known about the problems we were going to have, I would have driven away as fast as I could. I should have remembered that people are brilliant at saying how good they are and how much they can help, only to disappear when they are needed.

We found a new team for SOSAD Carrickmacross and got everything organised as best as we could. We trained everyone in their new roles and re-opened. I was happier with having enough volunteers and having the correct structures, and I hoped but did not believe that everything would work out as planned. I wanted SOSAD Carrickmacross to make a difference in the community. I spent a lot of time there helping out at awareness events and doing talks about SOSAD, but it still seemed different in some way, and I did not know why. The number of new clients there increased very slowly, which was good, and the number of volunteers increased too except for psychologists. They were non-existent in Monaghan or just unwilling to join us, but we got by with the help of a two, who were just fantastic. We just had to arrange all assessments for when these were available. It did sometimes break one of the golden rules in SOSAD, of getting people assessed as soon as they were available, but there was nothing else we could do.

The spectre of the 'old' crew in SOSAD Kingscourt and Carrickmacross would still not go away. Some people would not come near us because of their association with SOSAD. There was, though, a gradual increase in people looking for suicide bereavement support, and I was delighted to be able to help. There was no one trained or experienced in suicide bereavement in SOSAD Monaghan. So, it was down to me. I was also happy to 'keep in touch' with the bereavement work, as I had become occupied with all the SOSAD branches and all the admin work required and necessary to keep us ahead of the game. I liked trying to help people and was particularly happy with myself when I knew or learned I had helped.

SOSAD Carrickmacross did grow and become a part of the community, but it never got anywhere near the number of clients or volunteers it should have. It was miles better than in those 'dark old days', but something was still not right, and I couldn't figure it out. I kept visiting, offering whatever help and support I could, and kept giving my talks to raise awareness and the profile of SOSAD. It did help, a bit, but I was spending too many evenings there giving speeches, or attending events, that I started to feel weary. All my work was beginning to take its toll on me, but I thought it was just a blip, and I would feel better soon.

There was a lot of excitement in SOSAD though as I had somehow convinced Shane Horgan, the Leinster, and Ireland rugby player, to join us as our patron. Shane was from Bellewstown, not far from Drogheda, and had attended my old secondary school. We met in Bewley's café in Dublin and had a long chat. I found him to be charming, very bright, and tremendously interested in SOSAD and the work we were doing. He was particularly interested in teens and how suicide was affecting and very dangerous to this age group. He happily agreed to become the Patron of SOSAD. I was delighted to have him with us but had to research a patron's role when I got home.

He was brilliant for the charity and raising awareness of SOSAD. Lee had organised a Christmas Dinner Dance for SOSAD and Shane was invited. He came along, brought the Heineken Cup trophy, and happily posed for photographs with everyone, and talked to everyone in attendance. We carried that fund-raising event on for a few years, and Shane always turned up looking dapper and pleased to be with us. He was so approachable and easy to talk to for everyone he met. We were running a big fashion show as a fund-raiser those years too and Shane was there when he was not away playing rugby or training. Shane worked on his own on trying to get the Government interested and involved in a national awareness strategy for teens, aimed mostly at the schools. Still, as with the Pharisees of old, he got lots of promises and good intentions but got nowhere. Shane even had to organise two tickets for the Heineken Cup final one year for a minister, with the promise of some progress in his quest. He secured the tickets, but I had to arrange delivery to Leinster House because the minister would not collect them. Shane never heard from the minister again, and I felt he was somewhat deflated by all the brick walls he met when trying to do some good for our teens. I'm sure he would have found it easier scoring ten tries in a Heineken Cup final.

My problem was exactly that – my problem. Shane returned every single call I made to him. I could never catch him at the right time. I was aware of how he was super for

SOSAD, but I became increasingly aware that I was unsure of how I should be dealing with Shane and how I should be helping him. My crazy brain had me convinced that because I was of no use to Shane, I was no good to him. It grew harder and harder even to call him to say Hi or ask him something. These feelings of inadequacy, usefulness, and helplessness only increased when I guessed he was struggling with his efforts to reach the teens of Ireland, and make them more aware of the dangers of suicide. Shane did get very ill and end up in a hospital with a serious illness. I did phone him to say I was thinking of him but then was kind of afraid to ring him and interfere with his recovery. As time passed, Shane retired from rugby and moved to London, and his connection to SOSAD was over. I had failed Shane, even though I had made plenty of promises to myself that I would never let anyone down. He still got us connected to the official Leinster Rugby Supporter's Association, who were of great help and support when he left, but I doubt that I made any kind of a decent impression with them either.

We did open a sixth branch in Tullamore too. That was out of our comfort zone. I spoke at lots of meetings there and again was almost begged to open a centre there. The more discussions and chats we had; the more people expressed an interest in joining up if we had a SOSAD in their community. I wanted to believe all the promises made by potential volunteers and local politicians and community leaders. I was wary though and decided that we should recruit first and make the decision on opening there when we see what volunteers we have. I had learned my lessons, to a point, and I was pleasantly surprised at the number and calibre of the volunteers we signed up. They were all hugely enthusiastic, and with their help, we found a very suitable building in an excellent location. We decided to go ahead and open a SOSAD centre there. We signed the lease and had the building cleaned up and decorated in no time. It was in an excellent location, very close to the town centre. The layout of the building meant that we had one counselling room downstairs and two upstairs. That worked out well, and we were not forcing anyone up the stairs when they were not able to. I was there a lot, helping train all the new volunteers. I got the two Elaines to come to Tullamore for the day, and we trained a whole lot of volunteers in groups. Elaine G trained the psychologists, Elaine B trained all the admin staff, and I trained all the intervention volunteers and inducted the counsellors. It was a very long day, but it all worked out brilliantly.

The new volunteers were all very keen to learn and get started helping others. Their enthusiasm was motivating me to do my very best for them, and I enjoyed my frequent trips down there. It also went a long way to mitigate the disaster I had with Kingscourt. SOSAD Tullamore started slowly but steadily and gradually, more and more people and community groups got in touch, looking for some sort of help and support. Becoming an essential and trusted member of the community so quickly helped keep the volunteers focused and motivated them to do more. It was great to see. I helped out whenever I could and carried on giving my talks wherever I was invited and helped Mags, the branch coordinator, whenever she needed some. Mags was a real 'people' person and was able to keep everything going just as it should, but was not afraid to ring for help if she got stuck.

It was not without its problems, nothing ever is, but the big problem there was the issue of funding. No matter what they tried, nothing was ever the success it should have been. Of course, the local Pharisees were of no help, even when we pleaded with them for some support. The local suicide resource officer was no help and was one of these people who looked down on me, and I didn't like her from the start. At the time, the service and support we offered, in terms of our response times, waiting lists (we had none), and the way we connected and helped others, was something the HSE could only ever dream of. Yet she was questioning us on every aspect of our operation and then doubting or not believing our answers. Anyone from another community group I asked, agreed she was like that as a person and that she may have felt ignored when the idea of opening in Tullamore first came to us, and we didn't contact her and ask for her 'permission'. It was true that for once I did not make contact with the local suicide resource officer when planning to open in Tullamore, but that was because everything I heard about her, put me off.

Funding was a concern for me, but it was countered by the fact that SOSAD Tullamore was starting to make a positive impact and was helping make a difference in people's lives. SOSAD Drogheda was paying nearly all the bills for Tullamore, just as we had done for all the other centres. That, I knew, was not sustainable. SOSAD Tullamore needed to find a way to support itself. Overall, I was pleased with SOSAD Tullamore, the volunteers, and the positive buzz about the place, and I got involved in the fund-raising and looking for financial support. We did get some donations in, but nowhere near enough to keep Tullamore open. Even when other people or groups got involved and did their own fund-raising events, the turnout was far less than expected, and the funds raised barely covered any costs associated with the event. At least they didn't lose any money, but it was a growing concern. Once again, I did not know what to do about this, and the extra travelling involved was making me feel a lot more tired. I just kept thinking that things would ease off for me, and I would soon be back to normal.

Chapter 23

Depressed again

By 2013, SOSAD Drogheda was helping 200 clients every week, with over 100 volunteers, and it was getting increasingly difficult to accommodate everyone. Every volunteer was working on top of someone else, and there was nowhere to add more space. I asked the landlord if we could have the upstairs of the building as well as downstairs. He told me that could not happen. We had to do something, and the only option left to us was to move to a bigger building. I started searching and found a lovely old building, with plenty of rooms, and I invited the two Elaines, members of the Board as well as Wayne and Lee, to have a look and get their opinions and suggestions. It was used as a solicitor's office before but had been left empty for years. It was hard for everyone to see how we could clean it up and convert it to what we needed, but straight away, I could see the potential and what I wanted in every room. I could see how we could have five counselling rooms, a reception, a waiting area, a small kitchen for volunteers. Two other rooms could be multi-purpose and used as two offices for small meetings, training, and even counselling sessions or assessments if required. There was also a big safe room that was ideal for all the client's paperwork we had to keep. It was close to the town centre and simple to find. It was on Magdalene Street, just across the road from where the cattle market used to be.

We signed the lease, and although the rent was much more expensive than Trinity Street. I thought it was worth it. We launched a big appeal for paint, furniture, and funding, and once again, we were indebted to the people of Drogheda and the surrounding areas. Many local businesses got involved and donated paint, furniture, pictures, plants and lots of other useful items. Many local people, including my mother, contributed everything from new chairs, to plants and photos for the walls. We applied for funding to help with the move and ESB Electric Aid and the Hospital Saturday Fund awarded us two grants that paid for all the new computers and printers we needed. When all that money was gone, I paid for everything else. After all the people of Drogheda had shown how generous they were, so I thought I would do the same. I just wanted to make the whole centre look as perfect as I envisioned.

We got a big crew of volunteers to help clean and decorate the place, and even with such a willing bunch of workers, it took nearly two months to get the building ready to open. When the work was all finished, I was amazed and delighted with how the place looked, especially all the counselling rooms which looked like counselling rooms should. We had timed it perfectly to have the official opening during World Suicide Prevention week in September. I got my Mam and Dad to do the honours, and they were thrilled with themselves. We had a good crowd of guests come along and see the new centre. The local newspapers sent journalists and photographers, and I thought we needed all the coverage we could get to show locals where the new centre was. I was absolutely delighted and very proud showing different people around and everyone seemed to be incredibly impressed with the whole set up. It was precisely what SOSAD needed, and all the clients had no problem with the move and found the new building to be welcoming, clean, and comfortable, and that was all that mattered.

We put the main entrance down a little laneway so that our clients knew that no one could see them enter. That was still a big problem for many of our clients, because of the terrible stigma associated with mental health, and because people just felt safer when no one knew their business. I had to pinch myself when I went through all the accounts and found that the whole relocation, even though it did cost a fortune, did not cost SOSAD too much. Almost everything was donated, given in grants, or paid for with money received from fund-raising. It was just a tremendous effort by the local community, and I was overwhelmed by their generosity.

Somewhere in all this chaos, Wayne had split from Michelle and Lee had split from Sarah Jane. Lee moved in to share with one of his friends. Wayne was still at home. I did not know why both couples had separated and did not ask. I still did not want to interfere, and I felt it was none of my business. I felt too that if they wanted to tell me, they would. I did feel genuinely sorry for them and the girls too. I found them both to be lovely, and I was always happy to see them. The best times in the Moroney household, after Simon passed, was when it was busy with Lee, Sarah Jane, and Michelle calling in all the time. I remember even joking about getting a sign-in board at the front door, so I could track everyone who was in the house. I definitely missed that, and the place became somewhat lonelier, but at least I had Holly, who did her best to make sure that I did not feel that it was quieter.

The joy I felt in SOSAD did not last, however. The two Elaines went to a friend's house one night and had a bit of a session. I don't know exactly what happened, but apparently, Elaine B was drunk and said some truly awful things about Elaine G. I have no idea what was said and I never found out what it was. I thought it would all die down, but it didn't and caused a new atmosphere of tension and bitterness in SOSAD. They had been good friends and worked exceptionally well together and were a great help to me and SOSAD. They were a tremendous support to every client or volunteer that crossed their paths. I tried to find out more and try to solve the problem by taking each girl on a separate trip in the car, where we could speak in absolute privacy, but that got me nowhere at all. Neither of them would tell me what happened, but I did understand that whatever was said was very cruel and offensive. I could see that Elaine G was very hurt by what was said. Both Elaines wanted the other sacked and Elaine G, who was the branch psychologist, withdrew and isolated herself upstairs as often as she could. She still tried her best to be professional when dealing with others, but the close bond she had with the other Elaine was gone. I kept trying to talk to her and get her motivated again with no luck. I even bought her a big bunch of flowers which just ended up in the bin. She was angry with Elaine B but annoyed with me because I did not sack the other Elaine. I could see that she felt offended and wanted something done, but I thought that I could do nothing more because it happened outside SOSAD, and I didn't know what was said in the first place.

Why Elaine B wanted the other Elaine sacked I don't know. She was the one that caused the offence, as I believed, and had therefore started this whole problem. I knew that Elaine G was very quiet, and often thought she was sensitive. So I understood why she was hurting so much. On the other hand, Elaine B did not seem to be bothered, and I did not see that she was hurting in any way. I thought that she was angry and she became very moody. I don't know why she was angry but thought that some of it was directed at me because I did not sack the psychologist Elaine. I saw a different side of her that I never saw before and I didn't like it. I could not figure out what was going on in her head at all. I didn't know why she didn't just apologise for what she said, or why she was in such a mood in the months before Christmas.

The problem would just not go away until Christmas, after another bit of trouble, Elaine G left. I was devastated that she was gone. She looked after and coordinated all the volunteer psychologists and managed all their assessments and allocated new clients to the most suitable counsellor. She had been excellent in her work, and we were fortunate to have her, but she perceived the problem with Elaine B as being so terrible that she had to leave. Maybe she was upset that I did not fire Elaine B. I was so sorry that she was gone, but I was disappointed with myself because I was not able to help her and solve the situation when it started in September. I felt so guilty and hurt that I went missing for the day and did not want to talk to anyone. Lots of people were looking for me, maybe in case I did something stupid, and they were relieved when they found me. After that, I tried so hard to put it behind me. I treated Elaine B the same as always because I trusted her, and never thought any more about her involvement in the trouble, even though I should have been wary. She though was delighted she had 'won' and had new energy and enthusiasm about her when we opened after Christmas.

We were lucky enough to replace Elaine G with someone who had been in the charity for years and knew what the position entailed. She was the perfect fit for the job, but it did take her a while to get used to how busy SOSAD Drogheda was. Carmel had been a volunteer in SOSAD Navan and was smart, very friendly, and easy to get on with. She knew all the policies and procedures, so I did not have to go through them with her. I think Carmel loved her new job and was very keen to do her very best. I even laughed to myself at times when I saw her running around like a headless chicken, but she never complained. She wanted to look after everyone and even 'mother' them if that was what was needed. She settled in very quickly into her new role, and even though I had interviewed a few candidates, I knew I made the right decision. I was happy for her and glad for myself. SOSAD Drogheda was in excellent hands.

Elaine B was happy with her too, but while they became friends, they were never as close as the two Elaine's were. I thought Elaine was back to her best, and I still relied on her managing much of what I did from day to day. The atmosphere in SOSAD was right again, and everyone seemed happy. Everything, as far as I was concerned, seemed to be under control and the centre was running as smoothly and efficiently as ever it was. It was a great place to visit as a client, or as a volunteer, and I felt that all our efforts were very worthwhile.

We were always working to improve the service and support we offered all clients and callers. We organised a training course on suicide bereavement support for

SOSAD volunteers, and many signed up from the different SOSAD centres. We held the training sessions in the Westcourt Hotel, on Saturdays, and everyone thought that it was hugely helpful and were eager to put their new knowledge to good use. I thought it was beneficial and informative and I was glad that we had arranged the course. It gave us all a lot of new skills and knowledge to use when dealing with bereaved people, as well as the confidence to face up to what were always tricky and traumatic sessions. In support of this new training, we began working on new suicide bereavement support packs, that would help us and any bereaved people we met.

We also included a new online training and information course as part of the induction into SOSAD, and every new volunteer, no matter whether they were psychologists or admin support, had to take this course and pass it before starting. We set up new training manuals for all volunteers and kept the policies and procedures up to date. Everything settled down nicely. Everyone got on with their work, and SOSAD was busier than ever before, helping more and more people. I felt that almost everything was running smoothly, and I often wondered what could possibly go wrong.

I didn't have long to wonder. A new volunteer was very keen to learn every aspect of the job. She was quite overbearing at times, but I think that she just wanted to be doing more work. There was no problem between her and Elaine at first, but then things started to go wrong. Elaine was getting paranoid that the new volunteer was looking to take over her job and position in SOSAD. That never entered my mind, and when Elaine said it to me, I told her so. I reminded her that she was like my right hand in SOSAD, looking after me, and helping out in so many ways. I said that I would be lost without her. For whatever reason, Elaine did not seem to accept this. She grew to resent the new volunteer and cause a bit of friction in SOSAD. I didn't know what to do. The resentment continued, until after a big argument between them, the volunteer left. I felt sorry that she had gone as I thought she had great potential and a very caring attitude, but again I didn't question or consider Elaine's involvement in this spat. I felt that she was the one that held all the administration in SOSAD together, as well as me at times, and never imagined that she might be the problem or part of it. I could not see past how great she was for me and SOSAD. I was happy that as far as SOSAD was concerned, it was all peaceful again with an excellent atmosphere.

Everything at home was the same as before. Wayne was studying away and working in Specsavers. Valerie and I just drifted further and further apart, while still living in the same house. I ended up getting an order of protection from the courts because Valerie attacked me and tried to strangle me with a cord. I called the Gardai, and they told me to get an order of protection, to ensure my safety, and give them something to act on if she attacked me again. I am sure I went to court, but I just can't remember. I very vaguely remember being in a closed-session court in Dundalk, but I can only guess that it was for the protection order. The only good thing about this whole sorry mess was that I did not lash out at her again. I was obviously struggling at the time if I can't remember such a critical event, but at least I had SOSAD to distract me.

Lee started dating a lovely new girl, Shauna, who he met at work. He found the work he was doing unrelenting and stressful, but he seemed to be able to cope. It was not too long before he and Shauna rented an apartment in Grange Rath, and it was a lovely place for the two of them. I only visited them on the very odd occasion, mostly when invited, because I still had the same feelings about interfering, or maybe not being welcome at an inconvenient time. I cared deeply about Wayne and Lee but could not show it. I am sure that they must have felt that I didn't care, or was spending every moment I had in SOSAD, just to ignore them. Every time I had the idea of calling to see Lee and Shauna, my stupid crazy brain convinced me not to go. My mind made me think of every excuse under the sun until I accepted one or more of the excuses I made up and did not go. Then as time went by, the longer I did not visit, the harder it became to actually go.

I didn't realise it at the time, but my depression was growing in strength, and beginning to influence my thoughts again. I have no idea why it started to come back at this time, and the only possible candidate is the protection order or maybe the struggle to keep SOSAD going. I tried my

433

very best to avoid any confrontation with Valerie, but that was impossible with both of us sharing the same house. On top of that, I am useless at arguments. My brain does not work fast enough, and I don't know what to say, until much later when the row is well over, and it is far too late to say anything of use. So, I tried to avoid any confrontation at all and kept away from Valerie as much as I could. The more depressed I was, the more I hurt I felt after any little disagreement with Valerie, and any name she called me, seemed to upset me more than usual.

Most of the Board of Directors of SOSAD had been there since the very beginning. They were always there to help when required, and were great at advising me when I needed it. They worked best as individual members willing to do whatever they could for SOSAD, especially in their fields of knowledge and experience. We had our regular board meetings, but it was more like me telling them what was going on. I was always asking for their advice and input, even though I had often made my mind before we met. It had worked so well in the past, but now I was having second thoughts. I was starting to have doubts about many things, and the Board was one of these. How the Board developed was my fault. I managed everything in SOSAD and didn't let them run the charity as a productive board of directors should. I thought that now was the time we should look at everything to do with governance and try to make the necessary changes to bring SOSAD to a new level and help ease my workload.

I knew I was struggling and wanted to give some of my responsibilities to the Board. I was hoping that it would stop me sliding back down my well to Hell. I was a real hands-on type of guy and wanted to know and be part of every aspect of SOSAD. It was hard to give that up, but I had a feeling I wasn't coping anymore, and I was afraid I would drag the whole charity down with me. I wasn't doing much work with clients anymore except for suicide bereavement work and helping out when challenging cases challenged the psychologists and counsellors. I was still doing my talks everywhere I could, and pushing the updated policies and procedures as well as the new training format and paperwork. I felt it was my responsibility to look after and take care of all 'my' coordinators and volunteers. They were like my second family, and I wanted to support them in any way I could.

I did all the accounts for each branch, as well as forecasts, budgets, and reports and I grew increasingly concerned about the lack of any kind of funding in Tullamore. I was not able to use Drogheda funds anymore to support Tullamore, and could not move accounts from elsewhere. I had encouraged each coordinator to become responsible for their own finances, even though I still paid all the bills. I gave them monthly bank reports about every cent lodged into their accounts, as well as everything paid out. They all knew exactly what was in the bank, and therefore what funding they needed, to keep open for the year. None of them had the funds to support Tullamore as well as themselves. I don't know how we kept it open, but we did. Yet

I was feeling increasingly troubled, and again had no answer.

When I had processed the idea of a new Board of Directors, I felt that I needed to make sure that they had everything they needed, including rules and regulations, best practices, and maybe a guide to help them improve the charity. We started working on the governance structure, following the guidelines set by the Charity Regulator. I spent a few months ensuring every aspect of SOSAD met or exceeded the recommendations and action plans set out in the governance 'manual'. When I finished the preparation work, I carried out an audit of every SOSAD 'department', and while I found the results to be satisfactory, I became aware of all the work needed to be positive we were operating to the rules and regulations.

Maybe because of this, the Board members realised that this would mean a lot more work and involvement for some of them. Some knew that they would not have the time or energy to commit to this new plan and informed me that they could not continue. I was disappointed for sure, but I knew that they were all genuinely invested in SOSAD and were honest enough to tell me that they would not like to continue and then let the charity down. Nobody wanted that. I was sad at the significant upheaval coming and was only 'hoping' that we could find a new Board of Directors that would take SOSAD to the next level. I wasn't going to hold my breath.

I went to plenty of fund-raising events for SOSAD. I didn't mind that, as it allowed me to thank those that had organised the event. I knew the hard work they had put into the fund-raiser and then trying to get as many people as possible turn up. I also guessed that many were very anxious before the event, hoping that all their efforts were not in vain. I wanted to thank them no matter what, and give them an idea of what their hard-earned money was going. I liked going to these nights out, but around this time, I started to have trouble keeping my good face on. I was tired and weary. The kind of tiredness I only get when my depression starts to influence me and tries to control my thoughts and emotions. I pretended again, to look like I was doing brilliant and having a great life, but that only added to the tiredness. It's like my acting mind goes around carrying my depressed mind, and it weighs a ton.

I felt sorry for Tullamore because they were still getting busier, which meant they were helping more and more people while having no money. I had tried everything I could to rectify this with no success. More worryingly for me at the time is the difficulties caused by a former volunteer in Tullamore. She had overstepped her boundaries and was spoken to. She left SOSAD but continued a social media war with SOSAD for months until she eventually stopped. That affected everyone involved in Tullamore and hurt me in so many ways. I did not know how to stop her and protect the SOSAD reputation, and that made me feel useless.

IN TWO MINDS:

I let all these problems and more fester in my head and feed my depression. It was growing in influence all the time, and I was slipping down that well. I am not saying that I heard voices, I never did, but depression influenced my emotions and somehow convinced me to do things the 'depression' way, and not the way I would typically do it. I don't even know which is the 'normal' way for me, but I think it has become the depression way.

Chapter 24

Love

SOSAD just kept getting busier and busier with more people coming to us for help and support, and as time went on, I got more and more depressed. I knew what was happening to me, but I refused to accept that my depression was gaining strength, and increasing its hold over my mind. I thought that I had beaten the worst of it and would never slip down the well again. I was trying to force myself to believe that it was just some bad days that everyone gets. I was lying again, to myself. I was too thick and stubborn once again. I believed that SOSAD was my destiny, as well as Simon's legacy, and surely God and Simon would not let my depression regain control. Once again, I was a fraud, but the person I was fooling was myself. Once again, I did not heed what was happening to me, and allowed it to grow and gain influence within me, and drag me further down me well to Hell.

In SOSAD, I was trying to look after everyone and everything. I was trying to make sure that everyone in SOSAD was coping with the increasing caseload and associated paperwork. We were updating the policies and procedures so that we would be able to evolve to a computer-based system to manage SOSAD and every client. I was trying to run the charity as best as I could, and not let anyone down-ever. I tried to guide, influence, and support every SOSAD centre as much as I possibly could, and visit them at least every two weeks. We had to recruit continuously, especially for counsellors and psychologists, and then induct every new volunteer, and train them in the SOSAD policies and procedures. I always tried my best to be available to help, support, and advise everyone in SOSAD, especially the branch coordinators. I was delighted to be able to help them in any way I could. I was not working a lot with clients directly, but I wanted to be available to help with the very high-risk cases or to help devise a safety plan for someone. I was working with clients bereaved by suicide, and some who were bereaved by a different kind of loss, and trying to train volunteers at the same time. I had to try to keep everyone motivated to keep giving our unique level of care to each client. I also planned and prepared for all the Board meetings and general meetings, while still trying to network as much as I could. I never refused an invitation to deliver a talk on suicide, depression, or suicide bereavement. I always thought they were crucial in reaching out to other people in the community. I was doing far too much myself, but I knew it was for a great cause, and I believed that I still had Simon and God supporting me.

I was doing all the financial work, including budgeting, reporting, the accounts, and paying the bills as well as trying to manage the fund-raising for Drogheda. I was trying to organise our fundraising events like the SOSAD 5K and hoping that they would be a success and help get us on a sounder financial footing. Nothing we tried, seemed to work. I was applying for funding everywhere I could but not with any success. For the first time since we launched SOSAD, the finances became a real problem. Fund-raising was down, and I struggled to pay the bills each month. I started to fear for the future and was worried that we might lose SOSAD. I couldn't bear the thought of that because SOSAD was Simon's legacy and it was a crucial means of help and support to more than 500 people a week. How could I let Simon and all these people down? I funded SOSAD myself, out of my own money for 4 or 5 months, and ensured that the few paid staff we had, got their salaries. All the necessary bills, like rent, electricity, and phones, were covered. I did not want to damage the excellent reputation SOSAD had built up. I could not understand why funding had dried up, but I thought that maybe the substantial fund-raising effort we had to move SOSAD, had maybe dried up a lot of our goodwill. I even approached some of the local Pharisees (ministers) begging for financial support, or even something to get us through this challenging period. They just said how great SOSAD was, promised a lot, and delivered nothing.

One of the most enjoyable parts of being in SOSAD for me was the regular coordinator's meetings, especially when we all went to a local hotel afterwards for something to eat and a few drinks. I loved us all being together, and I thought it was an excellent way for us all to bond and have a bit of a laugh. Around this time, we had one of our meetings in Drogheda and then went to the Westcourt Hotel. While there, we were all sitting together talking and enjoying each other's company, except Elaine, who sat with her head bowed all night looking at her phone. I tried to involve her on many occasions, and I noticed others trying as well but still, she kept on her phone, basically ignoring us all. I was mad at her, and I thought she was so rude, but I said nothing. She suddenly jumped up, put her big smile on, and said she was going. It was the first time she had said a word to anyone in the Westcourt. Even after she was gone, I found it hard to control my rage and enjoy the craic. The next morning, I texted her and told her I was disgusted by her behaviour, and I thought she had acted disgracefully. I was still mad at her. She complained to the Board, who got us all together with her step Dad along to help her. The complaint about my texts was put to me, and I agreed that I could have handled it much better. The next part of her complaint shook me to the core.

I had told Elaine months before, that I loved her for the way she looked after me in SOSAD, for taking lots of pressure off me, as well as all she was doing for SOSAD. She was sitting on a small sofa in my office, and I just told her. I genuinely meant that and thought she was like a brilliant personal secretary. I remember even talking to one of the psychologists about it, and how I thought Elaine was helping me through a tough time. I felt that I was lucky to have her and that she meant a lot to me. Now she was complaining about this, inferring that there was something sexual in it and that she felt very uncomfortable about the whole episode. I felt hurt and betrayed by her accusations, and I remember thinking that she had shown no signs of being uneasy at the time, or since. She didn't seem to be uneasy or anxious in any way when she worked at the other computer in my office, and even though we chatted all the time, she never said anything to me about having any problems.

The Board was patient, and we all talked for ages, but we were getting nowhere. It seemed that nothing we could do satisfied Elaine. I think that we all grew exhausted and weary with the lack of progress and I asked to speak to Elaine on my own. The two of us went to my office, and I tried to explain what I meant when I said that I loved her. She wasn't interested. I asked her if I had ever said anything indicating that I had any other interest in her. She agreed that I never did. I asked her why was she bringing all this up now, and she replied that she was upset when I sent her that text. I told her that I was sorry for the way I dealt with the situation, but that I still thought she acted disgracefully. I apologised for the way I handled the situation. This conversation went on for a while until eventually, Elaine said she was okay. I told her that she should know that she could talk to me anytime and asked her to tell me if she ever felt uncomfortable again. I said that I was sorry if she got the wrong impression when I said to her that I loved her. We went back to the group and told them the issue was resolved, and they were all happy with that. Later on, that night, when thinking about what happened, I got the feeling that Elaine was not satisfied at all, and just told me what I wanted to hear, so that she could get out. I felt that she was right to complain about how I handled the situation, but could not understand why she added in a complaint about me loving her. Elaine didn't seem satisfied with my apologies, and I had no idea what she wanted to gain from the complaints. Our relationship was never the same after that, but I still thought she was great at her job, and as far as I thought anyway, our working relationship was not strained but just ok. Whether I could trust her was a different matter.

All of this just made me feel a lot more depressed, so I went back to Doctor Neary with my tail between my legs. That, to me, was another time I had failed myself and having to go back to the doctor showed me how useless I was. He suggested that I was suffering from burnout, and that had worsened my depression. He insisted that I take some time, weeks not days he said, away from SOSAD. I reluctantly agreed and tried to organise plenty of cover while I was away. Christine, the coordinator in Cavan, was able to look after all the other centres and Drogheda worked fine without me. Christine was a lovely person, and I thought that we got along very well. She was brilliant at her job, and I knew that she was one of the best coordinators in SOSAD. I knew SOSAD was in good hands.

Yet I felt lost without SOSAD, and I could not relax at home. I started to paint the house but got no therapeutic benefit from it. I was unable to work through the painting properly and rushed through every bit of it as if I was trying to get it finished before the house fell down. I couldn't help myself or calm myself enough to take my time. In truth, the time off did me no good, because I did not let it. I just wanted to get back to SOSAD as quickly as I could. I was fidgety and irritable all the time, and even though I did get lots of sleep, I still felt tired and drained. I admit that I felt ashamed that I had to take time off work, and I felt the need to get back to work to prove that I was fine, even though I was severely depressed. SOSAD was a part of me, and I found it very difficult to be disconnected somehow from my charity.

I went back to SOSAD after less than two months, but I was probably even more depressed than I was when I took time off. I tried my best to show I was back to my best. I lied to everyone about how I felt and how the time off had been brilliant for me. Going back did give me a focus and a little bit of a boost, but it did not last long. I should never have gone back so soon. I should have given myself time to strengthen myself and my mental health and deal with

445

my depression. Hindsight is not always a great thing, and patience is not one of my virtues.

A local barrister came to me and talked about how much he admired SOSAD and asked how he could help. I didn't know how I could use him and his skill set, but he kept getting in touch with me, and an idea grew in my head. The idea of revamping the Board of Directors came back to me, and I thought that Ronan the Barrister was another answer to my prayers. I got him into SOSAD to do a few shifts and help out with the admin, just so that he could understand what SOSAD did. Ronan did seem a bit lost, but he didn't run away, so I asked him if he would consider becoming the new Chairperson of the Board of Directors. I explained what my plan for the new Board was and how he would have to recruit new board members and build a new Board. He was delighted and readily accepted, and I started planning for the AGM to vote him and any new volunteers onto the new Board. Something was bugging me about Ronan though, but I could not put my finger on it. I didn't overthink about it because I thought if Ronan could work half as good as he talked, SOSAD would be in good hands, and I would have a lot less to do. I planned not to get too involved in the new Board as I wanted them to find their own way, come up with their own ideas, and not be too bogged down by me. The new Board of Directors was elected at the AGM with Ronan as the chairperson. I had finished getting us compliant with all the national governance requirements, and the new Board was the last step.

I got all the paperwork and governance documents ready and made packs for each member of the Board. At their first meeting, I handed them out and then left them to examine all the rules and regulations and discuss how they wanted to proceed. I felt like I had just dumped all this on them, but I was way too tired to hang around, and I guessed that they would contact me if they needed anything.

I was still struggling to cope with my workload and was very concerned about the finances. I was stressed because I felt that I had to finish everything as soon as I started. I replied to all emails and messages as soon as I received them, but that was because I thought that was just good manners, I was constantly checking all the statistics and information for SOSAD to make sure that all clients were looked after properly. I was still delivering talks whenever requested and driving up and down the country. I was visiting the other centres trying to make sure that the coordinators and volunteers were coping. I tried to help out whenever and wherever I could. I helped out in Drogheda, which was by far the busiest centre we had. We were still working on the new bereavement pack and establishing new bereavement support teams for each branch. I was looking after everyone, except myself, and I was struggling to cope. I realised that, but instead of stopping, I kept going. The more I pushed, the more inadequate I felt. I thought that I couldn't do anything right and that I was a fraud, again.

All this pressure and my worries just deepened my depression. My sleeping patterns became very irregular, and I was waking up at all hours of the early morning. I was never able to get back to sleep. I often found myself working in SOSAD at 4 in the morning, usually on SOSAD paperwork. When I was not able to focus on that, I did some painting or cleaning. I had to do something to try to stop the terror and misery building up in my brain. I started to feel that I had deceived everyone in SOSAD, and everyone who had ever supported us in any way. I imagined that I was going to be found out very soon, probably by the new Board or by the closing of SOSAD because of the lack of finances.

Any confidence in my abilities and self-esteem left me like rats leaving a sinking ship. I became very anxious about meeting anyone, so I avoided it as much as I could. I did not want to see any clients, in case they looked at me and saw what a fraud I was. I did not want to meet or talk to volunteers, because I would just let them down, and they too would see what a failure I was. I was still acting and lying like a professional and feeling guilty whenever I got home. I knew I wasn't functioning properly at work, but Christine and Carmel in Drogheda were covering for me. Yet I kept pushing on, trying to keep SOSAD open.

The financial situation got so desperate that I asked Hubert in the Drogheda Independent if he would do an article about SOSAD to see if that would give our finances a boost. I was thinking about showing how it cost a little over €100,000 per year to run the six SOSAD centres, and how any little bit of funding would go a long way. I was sure that a little financial boost would take some of the pressure off me. As part of the appeal, I wanted to give a rough breakdown of the costs. I had no problem revealing my salary, but I was concerned about how the branch coordinators would feel. I emailed them all for their opinions, thoughts and advice. They all replied, except Elaine, but from their replies, I saw that they were concerned and uncomfortable with this plan, so I had to come up with a different one.

That afternoon, Ronan called in to see me. I was in my office, and he joined me there, and we chatted for a while. He then told me he had received a complaint about my plan to reveal the breakdown of the costs in my newspaper article. I asked him who had complained, but he would not tell me. It was easy to work out because I had emailed everyone who got back to me and told them I would come up with something different. I didn't know why Elaine was going behind my back like this. All she had to do was reply to me, or even chat with Carmel. I was fuming and exploded like a volcano. I told him that that plan had changed and showed the emails informing the coordinators. He was trying to calm me down, but I was not having that at all. I wondered and asked why she had not come to Carmel or me. She had no basis for a complaint, as I was just looking for everyone's approval.

I admit now that my reaction was way over the top, but I was livid with Elaine and felt betrayed once again.

I didn't forget about what she did or stop wondering what her game was, but I put a considerable amount of my focus on the 5K we had coming up and our event for World Suicide Prevention Day on the 10th of September. I forced myself to do everything I could to make the 5k a great success and help get us out of this financial hole we found ourselves in. At the same time, I was putting the finishing touches on our new suicide bereavement pack that we could launch on World Suicide Prevention Day.

The 5k that year was on the 9th of September, and plenty of volunteers turned up to help. The start and finishing lines were outside the Aura Leisure centre. The pre-registration figures were not as good as in previous years, and I was very disappointed. We had put a lot more work into promoting the 5 K this year, but the registrations were down. That was very disappointing, and I thought that the event was not going to be saving of the charity, I hoped it would be. I was hoping for a big turn out on the night, but the weather was not on our side. It was miserable and wet. I knew that would not encourage the crowd I wanted. It seemed to me that everything I touched turned to crap.

A decent amount of people did turn out in the end, but not as many as I hoped. I put my good face on, making sure everything was working as it should and thanking everyone for their support. I was running around like a headless chicken, relying on the volunteers to do their bit. In the midst of all this, I noticed that Elaine was just standing on her own, doing nothing to help. Elaine had arranged to sit with and work at the same table as one of the other volunteers. When Elaine arrived, she found that another volunteer had taken her place. She stood with a huff on her like a 13-year-old. I noticed and asked her to look after the money for the night, and keep it safe, and went back to my job as a headless chicken. I didn't think about it anymore because I thought she would do it.

When the 5k started, one of the volunteers came to me, asking about the money. It was left in two cash boxes on one of the tables. There was no sign of Elaine, and she had not bothered to look after it at all. I wanted to find her and say something, but I didn't. She did not help out tidying up and getting the water and fruit ready for the runners' return. She was standing on her own, and I could see she was fuming, so I left her alone. When all the runners came back, I said hello to as many people as possible. When they went home, we started cleaning up and packing everything in my car. Elaine stood away from us, just watching. She was no help at all. I think she was further enraged when no one offered her a lift home. I certainly didn't, and I was always the one who gave her a lift if she needed it.

Later on, I decided that I did not want her to be miserable looking and unhelpful the next day at our event for World Suicide Prevention Day. I text her saying she didn't need to come on Saturday. I was careful and polite, remembering the time I text her before, and she complained. She wasn't having it, and it turned into a massive argument by text. I eventually told her that I didn't want her to spoil our event and upset the other volunteers as she had at the 5k. Elaine was acting worse than any spoilt brat, and I did not want to be anywhere near her. Eventually, I got my point across.

That Saturday, we had a lovely day and launched our new Suicide Bereavement pack. We had plenty of visitors to SOSAD Drogheda, and many volunteers were there to help. There was a fantastic atmosphere, and I thought that everyone was happy to be there. We got plenty of praise for the bereavement pack and its contents, and I got a little boost from that. I had counted all the money raised from the 5K, and while it was helpful, it would not last long. It was nowhere near what I hoped for. The atmosphere and the support were just what I needed. Many visitors took some of the new bereavement packs, and I thought that was a start in making them available to the wider community. I was glad that Elaine was not there, especially if she was in the same foul mood.

On the Tuesday after that, I was nearing Tullamore, when I rang SOSAD and asked Elaine to move her stuff out of my office. I did not explain but didn't want her working that close to me anymore. Carmel answered the phone to me and passed it on to Elaine. She usually worked at reception, but when she wanted to do a bit of work in peace, she used the other workstation in my office. Up until now, I had been happy with that arrangement. As far as I was concerned, the reception was her place of work. The other computer in my office was for the psychologists, to give them somewhere quiet to write up all their notes. I used to think that I was good at 'feeling' how others felt, and reading body language, and up until the complaint to Ronan, I did not see that Elaine had any problem with me. After that complaint, I could see that both of us were a bit uneasy when we were in the office together, but she still used my office, even when there were other work stations available. Now I was not sure what to think of Elaine. I thought she was childish and stupid on Friday night, and I was not sure that I would be comfortable with her working in the same office anymore. I was afraid that I would tell her how I felt and end up having a huge argument, and probably another complaint.

On Tuesday afternoon, I took a phone call from Ronan asking to meet me that evening, and I agreed. Ronan and two other directors came in together, and we met in the little staff room. They told me that Elaine had made another complaint. She complained that I stopped her attending the event on Saturday, and forced her out of my office. She said she had put a lot of work into the day and the bereavement pack. I tried to explain how her only involvement in the whole thing was suggesting that we get the sandwiches in a local café. That was her only contribution, and I was disgusted that she was lying about her involvement. I explained why I took this decision and that I just didn't want her anywhere near me or SOSAD on Saturday. She could have turned the milk sour. I explained the text messages between us and showed them my phone and texts. I was getting more annoyed by the second, but when they told me that Elaine complained that I had roared and shouted at her on the phone and told her to 'fuck off' out of my office, I could not control myself anymore. I am afraid that I reacted very angrily and with little or no dignity. I felt betrayed again, and I was hurt by the accusations and lies put to me. I tried to explain the phone conversation with Elaine and how I did not shout or swear. I told them how Carmel was with Elaine in reception when I rang because it was Carmel who answered the phone and passed it to Elaine. I explained that Carmel would know if I had been shouting or swearing. I thought that somehow, even with the rage of the Hulk, I managed to answer the complaints, and hoped that would be the end of this mess. I knew I still had Elaine to deal with, and I wanted to get to the bottom of all this and find out what was bugging her.

A couple of days later, I was in SOSAD and trying my best to get some work done. I wasn't succeeding. The compliant and Elaine would not leave my thinking. I could not figure out why Elaine was acting like this, and I was thinking about her previous complaints and her sudden issue about loving her. I knew there was something behind all this, but I could not figure out what. I even thought that Elaine might have thought that there was something between us, and I was going to ask her out. I thought that maybe she was upset because I didn't. I know this sounds stupid, but my brain was working as hard as it could, to try to find out what had Elaine acting like this. I was still livid with her, but I wanted to get to the bottom of this.

I wanted to find out what was really going on. I went to reception and asked the volunteer where Elaine was. She told me Elaine was busy at that moment and I asked her to let Elaine know I wanted to talk with her. I went back to my office to wait. I soon got a call from Ronan, telling me not to speak to Elaine, even after I explained what I wanted to do. The rage was back, and I was so mad that I made a bit of a show of myself by banging the kitchen cabinet doors when I could not find the coffee. I had to go home before I did something I would have regretted later.

The following Sunday, I got an email from Ronan with Elaine's complaints attached. They were hand-written on four sheets of paper. When I read them, I could see that they had changed. They looked like entirely different complaints. There was no mention of me swearing and shouting at her, which I thought was good. Instead, she brought back the objection about me telling her I loved her and that I was texting her outside working hours. I was mad that she was bringing the 'love' thing up again, especially as I thought that it had been dealt with by the last Board of Directors. I remembered that she said she was okay with it after I explained everything, even though I did not think she was. I was also mad at her complaint about texting her. We both text each other on a semi-regular basis as friends do. I did text her on many occasions before her second complaint, and she texts me too. I used to check in with her to see how she was or enquire about something I knew she had happening in her life. I thought I was a friend of hers and I looked on her as a dear friend. She did not mention that we often text each other in her written complaint.

I read through the complaints a few times but did not give my head any time to let it process in my mind. I replied straight away, even though I was mad. I replied in writing to the complaints and thought it was such bullshit. That's one of the things that caused me so much trouble. I felt that it was easy to see that her complaints had changed drastically and thought that surely anyone with half a brain cell would see this for what it was. A load of crap. The other thing that bugged me was why Elaine was doing all this. What was she at, and what did she want? I had no answers. I was overthinking again and imagining the worst. I wondered why the Board allowed the complaints after they changed so much. I started to think that maybe they were using them as the basis for something else, like maybe getting me out of SOSAD. It seemed very plausible to me. I thought that they were either stupid to let these complaints continue, or very smart using them to get rid of me. I didn't believe they were stupid.

That week, Stephen invited me down to the pub to talk. When I got there, he handed me a letter telling me I was suspended. The letter said it was because of my behaviour when I was slamming kitchen doors. I was furious and started wondering where all this was going, and what I was supposed to do. They did not let me talk to Elaine and then used my actions and lousy behaviour against me. Maybe the suspension was justified, but it just strengthened my view that there was a lot more going on.

A few days later, I was invited to attend a meeting in SOSAD at 8 pm. I was extremely anxious about the whole thing, and my depression was dancing around my head as if it had won the grand prize-me. I was in SOSAD but could not just sit there and wait until 8 pm, so I went for a walk around the town. I was passing St Peter's church and noticed that Mass was starting. I went into the church to pray for this to go away and asked God, and every saint I could think of, to help take this burden away. I got back to SOSAD in plenty of time for eight o clock. I had to wait until ten past nine until I was called. My anxieties and worries grew to annoyance and anger for having to wait for so long, and that just fed to the fury building up inside me.

When I got into the room, I saw the whole Board of Directors waiting there for me, with their chairs all around the room. They were sitting towards the empty chair in the room, where I supposed I was to sit. I was not told that I would be meeting the whole Board. Nor was I advised to bring anyone, so I was on my own, and that was a huge mistake. I did not think that I would need someone to support me because I thought we were just going to have a chat about the whole thing. The people in the room were not welcoming or friendly. I took my chair, facing everyone and Ronan started talking. He told me he was recording this investigation into the complaints made by Elaine, and I began to take my pen and notepad out. He roared at me for even trying to write things down because he was recording it. I needed my notes to help me remember what was said, and I was glad I did because when Ronan eventually stopped talking, I had a long list of bullet points.

What happened next is much of a blur, but I remember how I felt. I was just abused and bullied for the next hour and a half. I was told I was useless and that no one in the charity liked me or had any time for me. I was a sexual predator and had ruined the charity, and it would be better off without me. I was shocked at first then could not believe what I was hearing. I looked to the people around me, and I thought to myself, that they all knew me. I thought they knew that I was not the person there were describing. Yet they continued. I was raging, and I tried to defend myself, but it was very hard trying to get my point across when everyone was shouting insults at me. I could not believe how vicious everyone was to me, and my head could not work out why this was happening. I did not agree with anything they said, and when the meeting calmed down, they were telling me what I should do. I was too furious to do what they asked of me, and I would not relent. The meeting ended with nothing achieved or resolved, and I left them.

When I left, I thought about what I could remember. I wondered why this had turned into such a mess. Maybe the Board were right, and I was useless and a liability to SOSAD. Perhaps I was a sexual predator and deserved everything I got. I was angry at the way I was treated and could not understand why they had decided to attack me as they did. They had a long meeting before they called me, so I thought that the abuse was part of their plan. Maybe I was right. Maybe, I thought, they were using the complaints to get rid of me. I was depressed enough before. Now the Board of Directors and Elaine were jumping all over me forcing me down the well.

It wasn't too long before some of the Directors phoned me and they apologised for being so rough with me at the meeting. I wasn't too pleased to hear from them and too thick to accept their apologies. I didn't understand why they did it, so I was not able to process it. I was still angry about the way they treated me and felt that it was so unfair. They told me that all I had to do was apologise to Elaine for saying I loved her and all this would go away. They admitted that they knew the complaints were a farce, but they had to be seen to have done something. I had to think long and hard about this and was not inclined to apologise again to Elaine for something that I felt I had nothing to apologise for. I thought if I apologised, she would keep complaining and I would have to keep apologising. I was not willing to do that. I had apologised in front of Elaine, her step Dad and the old Board of Directors, and that didn't solve anything. I tried to talk to Stephen, who had been on the Board since the very beginning, to see if he could help me make sense of the situation, but he was of no help at all. He just wanted me to say sorry too. I was very disappointed with Elaine and the Board, but I thought Stephen was a good friend of mine. I was in real trouble when I contacted him and expected better advice and maybe some support or understanding. Once again, I felt let down.

I had a holiday booked, which I thought was lucky and perfect timing. I went on holiday to Caleta De Fuste, but it was the worst holiday I ever had. I could not get all the crap out of my head, even when I was on my long walks. I couldn't read at all, because I could not concentrate on the stories, and I just could not relax. Before I went on holiday, I had suggested to the Board that maybe I would apologise, but I needed to think a bit more, before deciding. I knew everyone thought that an apology would make all this go away. Then again, I thought that would be the wrong thing to do, even if it got rid of this problem. It seemed like it was hiding a hand grenade under the floorboards. One day someone was going to step on the floor, and the grenade would explode. My conscience or core values would not let me do that because it would just be like lying. I decided against making any kind of

apology to Elaine, and I felt kind of satisfied with my decision. I knew it would prolong the mess in SOSAD, which
by now was having a very negative effect on everyone. I
just hoped that this could be resolved differently. I did not
even wait to come home to tell the Board of my decision.
I contacted them from Fuerteventura. They were furious
with me, but I was sticking to my principles, even though
I had massive doubts myself.

Once I got home, it was back to work in SOSAD, but I
might as well have been lost in space. I was like the walking dead, going through the motions, avoiding Elaine altogether, with the aura of the complaints hanging over me,
like the dark cloud of depression that occupied my mind.
I couldn't shake the feeling that no one in SOSAD even
liked me, and I was getting more and more depressed. As
always, I tried my best not to show it, but it was becoming
more apparent, and I started to worry and felt ashamed
of myself. I felt humiliated because I knew that I had not
handled myself with any dignity since this latest batch
of complaints. I was mad with myself for having trusted
Elaine so much and for being so stupid to think that she
was the future of SOSAD in Drogheda. I used to believe
that she too was a part of SOSAD, and would be there forever. I used to think that I was training her up in every
aspect of SOSAD so that she would be able to manage it
one day.

I think that one of the most significant issues back then
was that I could not understand what Elaine was doing or

why. I had no idea what she wanted, and I started to believe that she didn't really want an apology. Yet I had no ideas. Because I could not understand what was going on, I couldn't process it. When I couldn't process it, it stayed on my mind annoying the hell out of me. I retreated to the safety of my home and tried to work from there whenever I could, and was happy to visit the other centres and stay away from Drogheda. The driving I did then was furious, and I am fortunate not to have killed myself or someone else. We often joked in work about how terrible I must have been in my past life, but now, with the whole world against me, I thought that I must have been Hitler, Vlad the Impaler before that, and then Emperor Nero of Rome. I believed that all my 'punishment' was justified.

As the days dragged past, there seemed to be no progress with the complaints at all. I talked to Ronan a few times about it, but the more I spoke to him, the more I believed he was just lying to me. Nothing he promised ever happened, and when he told me that he did not believe a word of any of Elaine's complaints, I still didn't believe him. Eventually, just before Christmas, I was told that a mediator had been appointed to deal with the complaints. I thought that we were heading for mediation and I, for once, since this whole mess started, thought an end was now in sight. I received a call from this mediator that December and tried to impress on her my desire to get this done as quickly as possible so that we could all move on, and hopefully, I might start to feel better within myself.

I have no idea what happened that Christmas at all. I just can't remember anything from that whole period. I know that I worked Christmas day covering the phones for SOSAD as I always did, and spent St Stephen's day following up on any calls and writing up the necessary notes and call information. I can't remember anything else at all. I was back at the bottom of my well again, and it harmed my ability to function as a person. I felt that no one on the Board believed a word I had said about the complaints. I tried to reassure myself by thinking that I had told the absolute truth at all times, and hopefully, that would mean something. I don't think my brain would allow me to accept that.

It didn't help either that I completely fell out with the Board of Directors, and would not even talk to them any-more. I knew Ronan was lying to me every time I spoke to him. He was always telling myself, Carmel, and Christine something completely different, as if we never chatted with one another. That annoyed and frustrated me, and made me question everything, which just made me feel worse about myself. I was lucky to have Christine and Carmel on my side and the go-between between the Board and me. They told me of anything that was happening, which to me, was nothing.

When all this was happening, Wayne graduated from Maynooth, and I went with him for the graduation ceremony. We went on his route and arrived very early. We just walked around the campus, and he was showing me where he went to classes and anything else of interest. Then crowds of people started arriving, and I guessed that the ceremony would be happening soon. He told me to go ahead and get a seat while he went off to his assigned place. The security was strict at the door and checked everyone's invite before allowing them into the hall. By the time I got in, I was lucky to find a seat, but it was miles away from the stage. I could see it if I strained and stretched myself to the tallest, I could be. Soon, I saw Wayne in the parade of graduates and thought he looked very academic. After the usual long speeches, the ceremony began, but I still had to wait for ages for his name to be called. I was hoping he was not as nervous as I was. When I heard the name Wayne Moroney, I got all excited and stood to make sure I could see him receive his certificate. I did take a photo, but he was so far away that it was awful. After the ceremony, everyone left the hall and assembled outside. I met some of his college buddies, and it was nice to put faces on some of the names I had heard from time to time. He had told me that others would not be there as they had moved abroad to study. He was chatting to everyone he met while I stood back like his minder. I was delighted to see Andrew Towell there, and I had someone to talk too. His daughter had graduated also. I enjoyed the day, and it gave me something to be cheerful about. I was delighted for Wayne and so proud of him. He went on to do his Masters, something about the physics of climate change and I thought that was a good move for him. It seemed to me that he enjoyed being in college, and it gave him something to focus on. It, in turn, brought back the Wayne we knew before Simon died. He was still living at home, and I wished the very best for him and hoped that either his degree or his Masters would lead to a promising career.

When all this was happening, Valerie took me to court for maintenance. I was astonished because I paid all the household bills. I did not want to give her more money because I knew she would just use it for more vodka. I paid all the household bills, including the rent, but she was paying for the broadband. I was doing all the cleaning and maintenance work in the house and paying for everything I needed. I spoke with a solicitor. She did not think Valerie had a case, and when I was notified of the date, I told my solicitor. She told me she would not be available that day and would get the case adjourned. I believed her and why wouldn't I. Yet when the day came, I was in SOSAD and Valerie phoned me to say my name had already been called in the court. She was there, and I was not. I ran to the court and called the solicitors on the way. The solicitor was not there, but her secretary got someone else to represent me. She spoke to me for a total of 1 minute before I was called again. I did not get to say a word, and a minute later, I was told to pay Valerie €50 a week for maintenance. I had no idea what happened, or why I was forced to pay Valerie when I was already paying for everything. I find it hard to trust any lawyer anymore after my stupid solicitor let me down. This case did further strain whatever relationship I had with Valerie, and I just stopped talking to her.

Lee was living happily now with Shauna, as far as I could tell, but we did not see much of each other, mostly my fault. I missed him but could not convince myself to go and visit or even call him. He was still working in IFS and living in the apartment in Grange Rath, and I was delighted every time he and Shauna called to the house. I wanted to get to know her a lot better, but deep down, I didn't know what to say to her, or how to talk to her properly, so I learned very little. Lee did seem to be happy, though, and I was delighted for him, even if I could not say it or show it.

I was working all kinds of crazy hours in SOSAD, but not too much in Drogheda, except when I worked from home. Mostly it was very early in the morning when I could not sleep. I found that trying to get back to sleep was soul-destroying and getting up was easier. Elaine was still coming in every day, but most days, I did not even see her. I kept well away from her. There was no communication between us at all. She had isolated herself in the office upstairs. She was still dependent on her Mam or step Dad to drive her to and from SOSAD every day, but they had stopped dropping in to say hello when picking her up. Her 'revenge' on me was taking its toll on her too. She was not engaging with anyone in the charity like she used to. I could not see if she was doing any work at all. Nevertheless, I left her to it and wished that the mediation would happen sooner rather than later.

It was the last Friday in February 2017 at about 5 pm, when I got an email from the 'mediator' with a password protected document attached. When I rang the number I was given, I got the password, and I opened the file. The first thing I noticed was that it was an investigation, not mediation, that was happening. I had no idea that the mediation I was promised had turned into an investigation. I was positive that I didn't know, but I started wondering if I had been told and forgot all about it. I didn't know what to think. I was stunned. Then I noticed that the complaint was 84 pages long. It was about one complaint per page. What had started has two complaints the previous September, then changed to two different ones a week later had now morphed into roughly 84 complaints. I had no idea how that happened, or why it was allowed to happen. I thought that it couldn't be real, but then I started thinking that this was a sure way to get rid of me. I could think of no other reason why this was happening. The Board was not stupid, I thought, they were trying to be smart.

I printed off the 84 pages and almost cried my heart out, but Carmel was with me, and I managed to control the tears but not the shock and rage at what I was looking at. Once that was done, I decided to take them home to read. Over the weekend, I managed to read only ten pages. I could not read anymore. It seemed that she turned every little thing we ever did into a complaint, like visiting her in the hospital was inappropriate, and invading her space one day when she was in reception. She complained again about the swearing and shouting at her in

September. I could not believe what I was reading, and I could not imagine how any person with any kind of sense could believe any of this rubbish. Surely anyone with any functioning brain cells, let alone a trained mediator/investigator, would see how ridiculous this all was. I thought I was depressed before, but now I had found a whole new low, and I had no one to talk it out with.

The investigator had scheduled a meeting with me for 10.00 am in the D hotel the following Wednesday. I got there early and found the room we were supposed to be in. I was on my own again, when I should have had someone with me. I never thought about that, as I was in such a state. I was trying to remain calm and think positively. I tried to believe that we would go through this, and then it would be all over. I was tense, overly anxious, and when I found the room was empty, my mind reacted badly. The investigator was not around, and it was past 10.00 am. My anxiety grew like a mushroom cloud after a nuclear explosion, and I couldn't even sit on the chair outside the room. I paced and paced, got a coffee, and paced some more, inside and outside the hotel. Eventually at 10.35 am she arrived and I got the barest hint of an apology. We got started, and she asked if I had read the complaints and I told her that I had just read ten pages and could not read anymore, no matter how often I tried. She asked if I wanted to re-schedule, but I said I would prefer to continue and get it over with. I thought that once I answered all the questions, I would be free from all this at last, but it wasn't too long until I lost this little bit of positive wishful thinking.

I thought the woman in front of me was very unprofessional in being so late and not offering any kind of sincere apology, just a grunt. She was amateurish with her method of questioning me. She reminded me of Chief Wiggum in The Simpsons. She would ask one question about a complaint and then go back to the time I told Elaine I loved her over and over again. I told her time and time again exactly what happened. I answered the other questions as best as I could, but there were specific allegations that I found impossible to answer because I couldn't recall them. I couldn't give a straight answer to something that didn't happen. Yet as I responded to a question, she returned to the love thing again making, what I thought at the time, the dumbest and laziest attempt to get me to slip up. I didn't. I lost my head with her and told her so. I asked her, rather forcibly, to stop asking about that. I told her that as far as I was concerned, that was dealt with by the previous Board. I also pointed out that it was not on the original complaint. She was having none of it. No matter how many times I answered, she would not be satisfied. All she wanted me to say was that I loved Elaine and had some kind of dirty affair with her.

But the worse was still to come. Elaine complained that I had tried to get her to go with me to a hotel in Swords. Why Swords, I thought. I wondered if there was a hotel in Swords. We don't have a SOSAD there, so why would I want to go to Swords. I had no idea what was going on at all anymore, and I still couldn't accept that this was happening. I wanted to know about the original complaint and why they had grown to eighty-four pages without telling me until the previous Friday. I had no idea what was going on and was very angry and frustrated, but she would not answer any of my questions, saying that it was not down to her. Yet years later, I found out that it was her that had allowed Elaine to make the 84 complaints, and the Board later endorsed this, well after my interview. I could not work out why this was allowed because I believed that it was very unfair and shouldn't have been allowed.

I managed to get through the whole day of questions and accusations, and she told me that she had several witnesses to talk to, and she would make her report and findings to the Board. I wasn't going to hold my breath. I called Ronan and arranged to meet him in the lounge of Stephen's bar, which was closed during the week. Stephen was behind the bar when I got there, and I was kind of glad that it wasn't just Ronan and me. I told them about the interrogation I had just endured and asked about the investigator. I told him that I found her to be unprofessional and that I did not like her because of the way she treated me. She was one of those people who think they are perfect when they are far from it. She spent one year in the Workplace Relations Commission and thought she knew it all, so she could do what she liked. She interviewed me like I was guilty of being alive, and the most horrible person ever. She did not like me, and she showed it in every word she spoke to me, every little change in her body language, and the way she was unflinching in her opinion. Ronan told me she was not who they wanted, but she was all the Board could find at short notice. That just made me madder, and I wanted to know what was short notice about the six months of misery and accusations I had just endured. I wanted to know why they had accepted the only person they could find. Maybe my thoughts about her were accurate. He tried to reassure me that everything would work out fine. They had to go through the proper procedure, but he said the Board thought it was a load of bullshit. I wish I had recorded that, but I didn't. That didn't appease me. I said that I was concerned because Elaine threw so much shit at me, and some of it would stick. I told them about the complaint of trying to get Elaine to a hotel in Swords. Now Ronan was visibly taken aback, and he told me not to worry, and it would all be sorted soon. I was drinking pints like they were necessary to keep alive, but I still couldn't believe a word Ronan was saying to me. I even offered to resign from SOSAD there and then but he wasn't having it. I was glad when he left, but I wasn't feeling any better.

A month or so later, I received the investigator's report containing all the witness evidence. I was delighted to see, in every single aspect, that all the witnesses had said the same as me in every detail they were asked about. I clung to that like a lifebelt in an ocean. Surely now the investigator would see that I was telling the truth. But my hope soon disappeared. There was maybe one witness who could help with the most serious complaint of me trying to get Elaine into a hotel room. Yet this investigator made only one attempt to contact this witness but did not reach her and left it at that. Only one try at getting someone who could help with the most outrageous complaint. Despite this, she found that this complaint was valid. I could not understand this. She said that her findings were based on the balance of probabilities, but then she added that it was her view that I did indeed try to get Elaine into that room. That, to me, were two completely different things. I could see that she was judging me based on her opinion and not anything else. I hoped the Board would see it that way too, but then again, maybe they had a different plan.

Once I had read that, I didn't bother reading much more. That was a grave accusation I was accused of with no evidence whatsoever. I thought that reading any more was a waste of time. I was also not in much control of myself and reading what I read made me feel a lot worse. I found it ridiculous, as too many of her findings were based on her opinion or her view. She even ignored what the witnesses said. She did not deal with the facts and seemed to accept every single word Elaine said.

The week before Easter, Carmel came to me saying that Elaine was taking two weeks holiday. I replied that she couldn't take her holiday without proper notice. I wanted to make sure that everything concerning Elaine was done 'by the book' and give her nothing else to complain about. The following Monday Elaine did not show up for work, and later she sent in a medical cert. She was off sick and never returned to SOSAD, and that was fine with me.

A while later, I was invited by the Board to a meeting to discuss the report. I accepted and then found out that it was a disciplinary interview. I went along, not knowing what to expect. I again stated my case that the investigator was unprofessional and unfit to deal with this matter. My pleas fell on deaf ears until I raised my concern about the sexual harassment complaint. I pointed out that the investigator made only one attempt to contact a witness who might have insight into this matter. It was apparent none of them had a clue what I was talking about, as they all wanted to know what page that was on. I was disgusted with them, but not surprised. It just verified that they had no idea what they were doing, and there was another objective at play here. I let them all read and digest this part of the report, and they agreed with me that the investigator's failure to contact this witness was poor judgement and unprofessional. The interview was adjourned to allow them to get the investigator to carry out her investigation properly and contact this witness.

There were a few minor issues that I was found guilty of, and I agreed with the findings myself, but I did not let them know this. They were all little things that had happened over the last five years. The 'Love' thing though had not gone away, and the investigator found that, or more accurately 'in her opinion', I was guilty of sexual harassment. I was again on my own at this hearing, and I have no idea why. In hindsight, I should have had someone to help me because I was not in any state of mind to be representing myself, and although there was no bullying this time, I felt I was being manipulated.

I was in bits mentally, at the bottom of the well, and the only force keeping me going and possibility alive, was the urge to defend myself and the truth, no matter the opposition and challenges. I had been praying furiously to God and Jesus, Mary, and anyone else I could, for help. I knew that I had told the truth all the time and that they should be able to help me out of this mess. Yet they just seemed to let it rumble on. I felt I had no one to turn to except God, but I didn't think he was listening to me anymore. I began to think that maybe I had used up all his good favour when he kept me alive and that I had lost his support now. I was indeed on my own and stopped going to Mass or praying at night because I felt it was a waste of time. It wasn't long before my depression was pointing out the horrible life I had. I had lost a Son, was crippled with depression, had been sexually abused, suffered from blood clots, and had type 2 diabetes. I was battling to save SOSAD, Simon's legacy, and that was going to be taken away from me. There was nothing I could do to stop that. That was not God testing me anymore; it was just punishment for something. I did not know what. I would have to fight this on my own, but I did get Carmel and Christine to accompany me when I went to any more interviews.

The investigator did get hold of the witness, and then she concluded that there was no evidence that I had tried to get Elaine into a hotel room and that complaint was dropped. Soon after that, I was called to another meeting with just 3 of the directors, and I had Christine and Carmel with me. During this interview, the focus was entirely on the time I told Elaine I loved her. I was asked about it for 4 or 5 times. I answered as I always had and tried to emphasise, that yes, I said it, yes, I meant it, but not in any romantic way. I tried to tell them that I did nothing before or after that to suggest that I wanted to get romantically involved with Elaine. It was heated, and I was getting fed up with the same questions time and time again. I did not feel that they were listening to me, and I had no idea what they wanted me to say.

Then one of the Directors got up, called the interview silly and a waste of time. He said that he had always known there was a closeness between Elaine and me, and everyone was aware of this, but he didn't believe that it was any more than love for a close friend. He then added that I had been asked the same questions so many times over the previous years and had given the same answer, and still they were asking it over and over again. He said he couldn't take part in this witch hunt anymore and then he walked out. We all stopped and took a break. There was nothing else I could say and felt that at last someone had listened to what I said and was aware of how stupid this whole investigation was. I felt humiliated by the entire experience. I don't think I have ever used the word 'love' since, except to Holly.

After the little break, I tried to continue, but I was in a rage smothered with disbelief, hurt, and confusion. When the complaint about love came up again, I lost it and walked out. I just could not answer them. I had given the same answer time after time, but they were asking as if it was the first time it was ever mentioned. I left because I felt that I could not control the rage in me, and went before I lost control. I wanted all this over and done with. I tried my very best to take part and answer honestly, but I didn't want the interview to erupt into a big shouting match. I was better off doing what I did.

A few days later, I contacted the two Directors and apologised and told them I was trying my best; it was late at night, and I just was not able to sit there and not explode. They said they understood and we agreed to reschedule. The next meeting was all a blur like I was there in body only. I had been ashamed of how I acted at the last meeting and fully intended to be more professional this time around. I was not in a rage or even angry this time. It was like I was indifferent to the whole thing, or resigned to the thought that whatever I said would make no difference to the proceedings at all. I know I had Christine and

Carmel with me but have no idea if we spoke at all or what we talked about.

In September, almost exactly two years after the complaints were made, I was at work on a Tuesday morning when Carmel arrived at about 8.30 am. I went to say hello and greet her outside the front door, which I often did. When she saw me, she started crying and asking me why I was there. That was strange, but everything in SOSAD seemed weird at the time, but Carmel was obviously weeping for a reason, and I did not know what that was. She then told me the Board had a meeting the night before and after that Ronan had phoned her to tell her I was sacked. Wow!! That was some news, but it did not sink in at all. She told me that Ronan said he would email me. I was stunned so much that I did not react in any way. I didn't explode or cry. If anything, I just felt let down by those around me. I said my goodbyes to Carmel and went home, but there was no email from Ronan. Typical Ronan I thought, said he would do something, and then not do it. I kept an eye on my emails and at 10.05 am I got the email from Ronan saying my contract had been terminated for gross misconduct, specifically bullying and harassment. I had no idea what bullying and harassment they were referring to. In all the meetings I had with the Board, bullying and harassment was not discussed, so I had no idea where they got this from. I was never asked a single question about bullying, not was the word harassment ever used. Maybe they viewed telling Elaine that I loved her as harassment, but other than that, I have no idea what they meant by harassment and bullying.

I had the right to appeal, but I felt that no one had listened to or believed a word I had said over the last two years and thought that the appeal would be no different. I still could not accept or understand how two complaints, turned in something else when written down, and then into a whole book of complaints. Nor could I figure out why this was allowed at all. I was unbelievably hurt at losing the charity I had built up and more importantly, Simon's legacy. Somewhere deep in my mind, maybe in the darkest part, I was glad it was all over at last. I was not able to think for myself and was numb to everything that was happening. It was a bit like the shock I experienced when Simon died.

I had been attending Dr Neary regularly about my depression, and when I spoke to him, he advised against making any decisions in the state I was in, and that just made me put any thoughts of the appeal out of my head. I needed to hear that because I could not decide on whether to consider an appeal or not. The last two years had been torture for me but maybe now that I was sacked, the pain and misery I lived with, would ease off.

Chapter 25

Message from Simon

It was two days later, on Thursday, when I noticed I still had my keys to SOSAD, so I went there to give them back. I did not go in but phoned Carmel, and she met me outside. I gave her the keys, and we were chatting when I noticed the locks were changed. I mentioned this to Carmel, and she told me that they were replaced soon after I left. So now, I was seen as a criminal, if they thought they had to change the locks. I felt like that anyway. What kind of a person did the Board think I was? I went home, and Valerie was moaning at me, reminding me of how I stupidly lost the charity and Simon's legacy. It wasn't an argument, just her venting. I don't know for sure what happened to me then. I remember what I did, but it was like I was watching someone else instead of me.

I was calm and went upstairs and cleaned my bedroom and made the bed. I had a shower and changed into some decent clothes. I got a sharp blade from the shed, and put it on the bedside locker, and lay down on the top of the bed. Everything was clean and tidy, and it was ready. I got a load of tablets ready, especially the new sleeping tablets Dr Neary had me on. I text Christine and Carmel to tell them I was leaving this cruel world. I was sure that anything they would do to help me, would be too late with the number of tablets I had. Texting them was just a loose end I had to clear up. I took them all in a few swallows and washed them down with water. I lay on the bed waiting for the tablets to put me to sleep for the very last time but had the blade ready in case nothing happened.

I had the plan for a while, but my 'spark of life' was somehow stopping me from carrying out the suicide. Even after I was sacked, that spark kept me alive, but the changing of the locks, the thoughts of what the Board thought of me, as well as Valerie moaning about me losing Simon's legacy, was too much too bear. They were the straws that broke and took me with them. I lost any will I had to live. The 'spark of Life' was smothered out. Now my suicide plan was all I had left in the world.

As I lay there, I had a thought, and I was sure it came from Simon. I looked at his photo, and the belief grew a lot stronger. He was telling me to look at the pictures of Wayne and Lee, and think about them, and what my suicide would do to them. I did look at their photo, and that spark of life kicked in and told me I was making a huge mistake. I suddenly remembered the aftermath of

Simon's suicide and the pain and devastation. I did not want to inflict that on the boys again, no matter how bad I felt. I shouted at Valerie to call an ambulance, and she came up to the room, and I told her what I did. She called 999, and the ambulance arrived soon after. I thought at the time that I was still ok, but the paramedics put a rush on after doing some tests on me, and I was soon in the Lourdes accident and emergency unit. I remember seeing my Mam and Dad there, along with Carmel and Ilona from SOSAD. Valerie must have told them. I was examined immediately and put into a room and given a charcoal drink, and then nothing. I conked out, and the next thing I remember was when I woke up a couple of days later in the intensive care unit in Navan hospital. Lee was there with me, and the nurse came over to talk to me and remove various pipes and tubes. She told me that I was sent there because there were no intensive care beds in Drogheda. I knew by the look of the room that I was not in Drogheda. I felt that I had put all the doctors and nurses, as well as Wayne and Lee, to all this trouble for nothing. She explained how my organs had shut down, and I had to be resuscitated in the Lourdes, and monitored in intensive care until I woke up. I felt like such an idiot because the one time I had changed my mind, and didn't want to die, I had almost succeeded.

I felt absolutely nothing when I was unconscious. I had no vision of Heaven or anything like that, and my past life did not flash before me. I remember nothing at all, but maybe that is precisely what we feel and remember when we die.

Lee was thrilled and very relieved when I woke up, and he was asking me questions like a quick-fire quiz master. I answered as best as I could, but I didn't mention that the 'message' from Simon and the thoughts of him and Wayne, had kept me alive. For once, after a suicide attempt, I was glad I survived and had failed in my most recent effort.

After the doctors came and checked me out, they told me that I could go back to Drogheda to the Psychiatric Unit, not to the General Hospital. I noticed this but did not say anything about it. Lee offered to drive me instead of waiting for an ambulance. The doctors agreed, and Lee drove me to the Psychiatric Unit in Drogheda. It was dark when we got there, and I was seen relatively quickly by a psychiatrist. That in itself surprised me. I was glad because I wanted to get out of there as soon as possible. After the introductions, the doctor told me that they were admitting me and had a bed ready for me. There was no way I wanted to stay in a psychiatric hospital. I did not wish to suicide at that time, and I did not want to be in a psychiatric ward. I felt that I would lose that spark of life if I were admitted and surrounded by people with their horrible feelings and experiences. I imagined that I would not feel comfortable or safe there, and I was afraid that once they got me in, I would never get out. I truly believed that they would find so much wrong with my mental health, that they would deem it to be unsafe to let me out. I also felt that they, like everyone else in my past, according to my thinking, would just let me down, and I was not able for that. I could not trust them as I should have.

I knew that it was strange that I had forgotten all about Wayne and Lee, Holly, and my whole family for that matter when I decided to leave this cruel world, but I was glad that Simon reminded me just in time. Any later and I would not be here now. I probably would have been totally unresponsive by the time I got to the hospital and unable to be resuscitated. I would be dead, and that would put the boys and my family through the same horrible grief all over again. I was sure that I was safe from suicide then because I was able to think about the boys and all we had been through when Simon died. I didn't want to put them through that again. My only regret this time was the scare I must have given them, and I must have brought the thoughts of Simon's suicide back into sharp focus for them. I felt very sorry and guilty about that.

The doctor spent over an hour assessing me and still trying to get me admitted for my own good. I took part in the assessment and answered all the questions as honestly and truthfully as I could, but I would not agree to be admitted. Lee got annoyed and even angry with me, but I still would not budge. They were both trying to get me to stay in the hospital. But once again, I was too thick and stubborn to relent. I felt sorry to be putting Lee through this, but all I wanted was my own bed and to go home to Holly. When the assessment was over the psychiatrist told Lee and me that I was at a very high risk of suicide, and I could understand that. They both suggested that only having Valerie at home was not enough to protect me, in case I did something to harm myself. I was so stubborn, and maybe stupid, and eventually, the doctor relented and allowed me to go home. She arranged for the psychiatric home team to visit me every couple of days. Lee drove me home in a huff that I could feel burning in him, but I was going to prove it to him that I could look after myself, and Wayne would be there when he was not working.

The home visits I got proved to be a blessing, even if they still tried to convince me to go into the hospital. With their guidance and support, I was able to manage my day and got to visit the Consultant Psychiatrist who put me on the list for counselling. I was glad of the visits because it gave me someone to talk to, and because Valerie, despite all her promises, would go missing for days at a time. I explained why to the Psychiatric nurse, and she grew more concerned and pushed for me to go into the hospital. I disagreed because I thought that I was lucky I escaped there in the first place and was not going back.

I was not 'better' in any way, and I felt so guilty for putting everyone through what must have been a very worrying and traumatic time. I was thrilled to get visits from Mam, Dad, and my family, but I was acting and lying again. I lied about feeling much better in myself when I felt like shit. The only things I was kind of happy with were that I did not die and did not go into the psychiatric hospital. I did have a bit more fight in me to take on my depression, but I wasn't very good at that. Some of the people in SOSAD got in touch, which was very nice, but some stopped when SOSAD rang asking me to visit a bereaved family and have a chat with them, and I refused. I hated doing that, but I could hardly look after myself, let alone another grieving family. I was shocked that they did not consider my mental health when they decided to contact me and ask me to talk to this other family. On top of that, I was recently sacked, wasn't I, or had I just imagined the whole episode? I was confused again.

In time the psychiatric home visits stopped, and I was on my own again. That was hard, and it was when I really started isolating myself and only left the house if it was necessary, or to visit Mam and Dad as usual on a Sunday morning. I tried to keep occupied cleaning and doing odd jobs around the house. I lived in my own world of uselessness and pain and was ashamed of what I did. I was still angry with Elaine and the Board of SOSAD but mostly because I had lost Simon's legacy. I searched for jobs to do where no one could see what I was doing and 'judge' me as I imagined. I spent a lot of time in the graveyard working on Simon's grave. I was pleased with myself when it was all finished, and I thought that he was ready for Christmas. I even spent time doing my Granny's grave in the freezing cold. I worked hard at cleaning and renewing the headstone and all the stonework. When I was finished, it looked almost like new. That cheered me up a bit.

I was content working in the graveyard because there was no one else around. I did not want my anxieties or fears to grow. I went up there to work, chat with Simon and my Granny, and look after them at the same time.

I was a wreck, and I started to believe that living with depression was my real destiny, not SOSAD as I had thought for so long. I would just have to get used to it. No one could help me except myself, and I definitely could not do myself any good. The promised counselling never materialised, but the Psychiatrist did organise a proper assessment. Over the 6 or 7 seven sessions, severe depression was confirmed, and I was told I was a schizoid. Schizoid is a personality disorder, characterized by a lack of interest in social relationships, a tendency toward a solitary or sheltered lifestyle, secretiveness, emotional coldness, detachment, and apathy. That confirmed what I am, even if I had to look it up myself after being told.

Believe it or not, I got more depressed, and the psychiatrist organised a social worker for me because, as he told me later, he thought he would never see me again. He thought I would die because I was so depressed and in so much mental pain. I was having lots of thoughts of suicide, some of them for painfully long periods, but I always looked to the photos of Wayne, Simon, and Lee, and that eased the urge to suicide. I often looked at a picture of Simon or went to the graveyard and asked him why had he saved me. Was my destiny to live in pain all my life, or was there something I did not know about?

The social worker was very helpful, but in the end, she could not help too much. Valerie was a massive problem in my life, and there was nothing she or I could do about it. Talking to her and the psychologist was a great help in letting me get things off my chest. When these sessions were over, I wished that I would get counselling, to at least help me relieve my pain, and maybe strengthen my coping skills. I was alive to some extent, but my overthinking was on overtime, and it just became harder to think and act rationally. It was extremely difficult to function or even manage my day properly. I would wake up stressed and anxious, and I tried to get something positive done every day, no matter how small and inconsequential it seemed. Getting something finished was a boost to my mental health and a little personal score against my depression.

Chapter 26

Holly

Not only has Holly been the best Christmas present I ever received, but she has been my lifesaver too. She is often the only one I can speak to, and even though I doubt she is even listening to me; I imagine she is. It is just like the way I talked to the boys when they were asleep. Most times, I am just explaining what I am doing or trying to do or talking to her about what she is doing. She has become my baby, and I chat to her like no one else. Holly is a little mini Jack Russel that is so full of energy and life that I cannot keep up with her. I just wish I could transfer some of that energy from her into me.

I don't know how she does it, but she always seems to know when I am taking her out for a walk. She waits for me behind the kitchen door, and she gets so excited every time. She jumps around me like a bouncing ball until I get the harness on her. I often tell her that she is acting like she never gets out, but she does look delighted. Then she heads for the front door all excited waiting for me to open the door. When I do, she bolts out like a missile from a launcher, but then stops and waits to make sure I am following. I do try to get her out early every morning because I prefer to go when I get up before thinking about it. She loves going down to St Dominic's Park where I can let her off the leash, so she can run and sniff her way through all the grass. That is how she explores her world, and I feel that it is good for her. I do have to keep watch though, because she will try to eat anything she finds, and I don't know if that would be good for her. She can often dart off to a place where I can't see her, and if she found an exciting smell, she will ignore my calls until I find her.

She loves to meet other dogs and say hello, and often gets very excited and runs around like she just got engaged. I think that meeting other dogs makes her walk complete. Sometimes we don't meet any other dogs on our walk, and I can tell that Holly is not as happy as when she does get meet and nuzzle up to other dogs. Holly also gets on well with a neighbour's cat. At first, she did not know what to do when this cat did not run away from her. Now, they just nuzzle each other if they meet. Even though I sometimes don't want to go out, the walk does me some good, and always excites Holly. I can't be in any hurry when taking her out, as she wants to sniff and cover as much ground as possible and leaves her scent in about 20 places on every walk. I imagine she is just letting other dogs know that she was there too.

In Two Minds:

I take Holly out every day, because she loves it, and seeing her happy, makes me happier. The walk does loosen
up my aches and pains from sleeping and pumps a bit
more of the 'good stuff' into my brain, to help me ne-
gotiate the day ahead more easily. Almost every time I
take her out, I get to laugh at her antics, especially the
way she gallops on the grass at speed when I pretend to
try to catch her. Sometimes she looks like a mini racehorse galloping towards me, with her harness looking like
a saddle. She sometimes chases the pigeons and seagulls
in the park, but I watch closely as some of the gulls are
bigger than her. I can see how happy that makes her and I
would hate to take that pleasure away from her. She walks
around the park, like she owns it, and has to welcome
every other dog as part of her official duty. She doesn't
mind humans either but is always a bit wary when she
first meets someone. If she knows them, she lies on her
back so that she can get her belly rubbed. That is more of
a demand from her, rather than a request, but she loves it
nonetheless. She is very nosey and stops to stare at people
who are close by, even when she is on her lead. One day
she walked head-first into a wall because she was staring at someone, and not looking where she was going. I
laughed, but she was not impressed. She loves it when
buses, trucks, and tractors pass by on the road. She has to
stop and stare, except when the air brakes make a sound,
which startles her. While she is always very enthusiastic,
heading towards the park, sometimes she is not as keen
on the way home. She does come to me when I call her

after a moment or two. Holly has to finish what she is doing first, and then waits a bit so that I know that she is the boss. I let her stop on some patches of grass on the walk, but not them all. As I've told her many times, if I stopped every time she wanted to stop, I would never get home. She always thanks me after a walk with a big kiss, but I think she might just be manipulating me into giving her a good rub, especially where her harness was.

Interestingly, she can fall way behind me in the park or football fields, but she can only go a small distance ahead of me before she stops to see where I am. Then she waits until I catch up to her. I often wonder why she does that. Maybe she is just keeping an eye on me and minding me properly. I do need to focus on her every time we go out. She walks in front of me and can get kicked. She wants to roll around in shit when I'm not looking at her. She needs looking after just like I do. Generally, though she is excellent to be with when we go out, and strangely never barks on our walks. Other dogs can be jumping around being playful and barking, but she never barks back. It is an entirely different story at home or in the garden. She thinks that she owns the place, and works hard to protect us, and bark at every cat or bird she sees, to tell them to stay away. She barks at any noise she hears and at anyone outside who is talking and not involving her.

I am deeply sorry to say that during the worse spells of my depression, I didn't take Holly for her walk at all. Then I felt very guilty, and instead of getting a boost from the 'good stuff', the guilt made me feel so sorry for Holly and even more remorseful. It is not that I don't want to take her out and give her reasons to be happy; I owe her far more than that. It is just that some days, wild horses would not be able to pull me out of the house. Those are the days when my depression is in charge. Then there are the days that I feel so tired and drained, often for no logical reason, that I find it difficult to even walk up the stairs. Every part of me aches, and I just cannot raise the energy or motivation to get myself and her ready to go out. I hate those days, and even though I try to spend more time playing with Holly, I feel I have let her down. It's funny how I can't think of how beneficial these walks are for Holly and me when I am at my worst.

I have spoilt Holly so much that she now thinks that she is the Princess of the house and I am her servant. She demands to play every time we are together until I either play with her or move somewhere else. Somehow, she got the idea that every time I start to do a bit of work, especially in the garden, I want to play with her. She will persist until I start throwing her toy for her to chase while trying to work. The problem is that she has so much energy, that she would play all day if she could, and it is tough to get her to sit and rest. Sometimes, I can calm her down by giving her a rub down or a nice scratching, and other times, I just give her a treat. She wants to be with me all the time and most of the time she is great company for me. I feel flattered that anyone wants to spend time with me. I try to be strict with her when there is a game on TV that I want to watch. I try to get her to rest or be quiet. Sometimes it works, and other times, I am just wasting my time. I either have to play with her or send her out to the kitchen. It is lovely, though when she is quiet or restful, and her favourite place to rest is still lying between my legs. She has taken control of one of the sitting room chairs, and always makes sure she gets there first if we have visitors. She doesn't want anyone else sitting there.

She can be a moody little bitch too, especially after I tell her off for something. If I tell her off in the park, then I almost have to drag her all the way home. She just does not cooperate with me and pulls back on the lead all the way home. If I don't let her out the back, she tries to lick her way through the patio doors. If I get her to stop that she goes into her bed, and growls at anyone that comes near her. Every time I think I am winning our 'who is the boss' argument, she ups the stakes and reminds me she is in charge, and not me. She owns her bed and sometimes is grumpy when I go near her in the morning, and she wants to sleep. She delivers that low growl that tells me to stay away and leave her alone. She owns her bowls and eats when she wants to. I tried putting her food out for an hour in the morning and evening, but she did not touch it. She likes it left on the floor until she is ready, and it is available any time she feels hungry. She loves the wet food I give her for dinner, or even some of the potatoes, gravy, or rice I make for her. Then she stuffs it down her throat in seconds and licks the sheen off the bowl.

IN TWO MINDS:

I know by the way she eats if she is not feeling very well and I pay special attention to her. I look out for any time she gets sick or has a particularly nasty poo. Thankfully I only had to take her to the vets once when she was ill. She knows where the vets are, and will not walk down or up that road. She plants herself on the ground, and I would have to scrape her feet along the path if I tried to move her. On the odd occasion we are walking on that road, she stops, and I have to carry her past the vets.

She can be a little devil too. I had to change all the fencing in the garden because she chewed away all the old shiplap fencing. She even chewed away a big sleeper I had and a garden seat I made. Thankfully I got her to stop doing that. The fencing now is made up of wooden planks, with no ends sticking out, so she can't get a grip with her teeth. Now with nothing to chew on, she licks the pebble-dashed wall, and it is an awful job trying to get her to stop. She does this when I turn on the cooker, dishwasher, or washing machines and makes noises like she is eating the wall. She eats all her 'blankies' and often gets herself trapped in the holes, and I have to rescue her. She gets so excited when I free her that you would think I just pulled her from the river. She can be a bit crazy. Still, I don't know where I would be without her.

Holly loves her comfort and is always dragging her blankets to wherever she wants to be. In the summer, when the sun is shining on us, she will position her blankets in a nice, sunny, warm spot and lie in the sun, as I do on holidays. In the winter, when I have the wood stove on, she drags them into the sitting room and places them in front of the fire, so that she is very comfortable as she warms that belly of hers. I do get a bit jealous because she behaves like she doesn't have a care in the world, and I wish I could be like that. Yet as smart as I think she is getting her blankets moved, she will not drag them back to her bed. I have asked and encouraged her a million times, and she just looks at me as if that was my job and not hers. She will not do any tricks or even shake hands, no matter how many times I bribe or try to train her. She looks at me as if I am stupid to think she would make a fool of herself. I didn't teach her properly when I got her, and anytime I try now just seems to be a waste of time. Holly does what Holly wants and nothing else.

I almost lost her once, and I thought my heart would burst. It was on a Saturday, and I decided to take her with me to SOSAD because there would be no one else at work that day. It was a lovely day, and I decided to walk down. In the park, she ran to jump on a wall, couldn't stop and ended up in the river. I was getting in to help her when Fiona, a friend from years ago, came along and told it was too dangerous. There were rocks and things on the river bed that we couldn't see with the dirty water. She said that I would fall and break my neck or drown. Holly was paddling like crazy to stay afloat and looking at me, pleading for help but I could not reach her. I called 999 and got the Coast Guard who said they would be there soon.

I prayed for her safety and called on Simon to help too. Holly was treading water like crazy, and I had never taken her swimming. She does not like water. I think Holly got fed up swimming with nowhere to go and decided to swim to the centre of the river. I watched in horror, fully expecting her to sink at any moment, but somehow, she changed her mind, and turned herself around and swam back to the wall. I was so relieved, but I still could not find any way to get to her and get her out of the water. Holly was finding it hard to keep paddling like she was, and I was not sure if she would last much longer. I was doing all I could do. I was talking to her encouraging her to keep paddling, but every time she looked at me, I could see the desperation in her eyes. She looked like she did not understand why I was not helping her. That was terrible for poor Holly. Soon after that, I noticed the Coast Guard launch a boat across the river, and they soon arrived and picked Holly out of the water. I don't think I was ever so happy to see someone in my life. They came close to the river bank and handed her to me. I was absolutely relieved and thankful to the Coast Guard and Simon for saving Holly, and I wrapped her in my jumper and put her under my coat and ran all the way home. I rang the vets, and they told me what I should do. I put Holly in a warm bath and then put her lying in front of the stove to heat her and dry her out.

I do worry about Holly and whether she is happy. Just like I worry about the boys. I got Holly neutered when she was old enough, but now I worry that was the wrong thing to do. I feel that becoming a parent was the best thing that ever happened to me and has contributed to most of the happiness I have ever had. Yet I worry that I have taken that opportunity away from Holly. I feel so sorry and guilty about that. Yet I know that I am a person that worries far too much.

She soon recovered and wanted to play, and it was hard trying to keep her in front of the fire to dry. I sat with her, and she stayed there quietly when I was beside her, and she got warm and dry very quickly. She was fine, and that was a fortunate escape for her and me. Her exuberance for life is something I am jealous of, and I sometimes cannot decide who is minding who. I do see some of Simon's personality traits in her, like her friendliness, wild spirit, and cheek, and I like that. Even when I tell her that she's 'a good girl', I get this look from her, which sometimes reminds me of Simon when he used to answer 'whatever' with that big grin on his face. She looks at me like she is saying 'whatever' and that she knows right well that she is a good girl, and I don't need to tell her. After all, she is the boss, and I should know my place.

There are times when I think that she is the only friend I have in life, and while that makes me sad, I also feel blessed that I have her to give me some times of happiness. She can even comfort me at times, especially when she lies with me in the sitting room. If I didn't have her, I would probably never get any exercise and get that boost of serotonin that helps me through the day. Taking her for

497

a walk can help with my overthinking because she needs to looking after all the time. In other words, my focus turns from myself and my problems to looking after Holly and making sure she is safe, especially since the river incident. I did read a psychiatric article from America that discussed how looking after a baby or a dog was great for one's mental health, and I can fully endorse that. They need your complete focus and can help you forget your issues for a time—the best kind of distraction.

What a present she was. I owe Holly my life. She is my lifesaver.

Chapter 27

Schizoid

It was very tough for me after I was sacked from SOSAD. I felt a part of me was taken away, and I didn't know how to cope. My depression didn't ease as I had hoped. I felt very depressed and dead inside. Nothing mattered to me. I didn't think about suicide, mostly because of Wayne and Lee and partly because the thoughts did not enter my mind.

Lee and Shauna went to live in the Cayman Islands in 2018, and I was sad to see them go but delighted for them at the same time. They had chosen a place that is very far away but with much better weather and an excellent chance to save for their future. I was happy to see that they were thinking ahead and had a good plan and prospects. Once they were happy, I was pleased for them. In 2019 they got engaged in New York and then came home to celebrate with us and we had a great time, even me. They planned to get married this year but had to postpone it to 2021 with the restrictions around the coronavirus. I haven't seen them for over a year now, and I miss that, but I am glad they are doing well. I want so much to look forward to the wedding, yet I can't seem to get my mind to wake up to the fact that it something I dearly want and should be crazily excited about. That annoys me, and I can find no way to feel 'normal' about the whole thing, even if this might be one of the best days of my life.

Wayne got a decent job working for Twitter in Dublin. He did sometimes come home looking stressed and frustrated, but I think he enjoys his work. He has his responsibilities and works with people from all over the world. Sometimes he gets to travel to different parts of America and Asia. He was always moaning when he has to travel to San Francisco or the Philippines, but I think that he secretly enjoyed the travel and meeting people he works with every day. He did not go out much as he was saving hard for a deposit on a new house. So, he stayed in his room almost all the time he was home, playing computer games and only emerging to get something to eat or drink.

I was also diagnosed with Type 1 diabetes and am now on insulin. I was type 2 since shortly after Simon died. Failing to keep my sugar levels under control was another kick in the teeth for me. I had failed myself, and I was so disappointed. I felt too that I had let my doctor and diabetic nurse down by not being able to keep my sugar levels under control. My insulin dosage has doubled, in small increments, since then, and I seem to manage my blood sugars better at the moment. Except that is, when I go on my binges. From time to time, especially when feeling more stressed than usual, I tend to eat a lot of lovely treats like buns and biscuits, that contain far too much sugar for me. It is comforting, but I always dread looking at my sugar levels the next morning. The high sugar levels in my blood make me feel guilty and eradicate all the good I felt stuffing my face.

My brother Michael rang me in November 2017 and told me that Shine was convicted of indecent assault on two males. I was kind of happy with that, but mostly I was just annoyed and disappointed. We had failed at our trial or were failed by the system, and this seemed to me to be a completely different trial, regarding other boys. The only parts the same was that it was the same Mr Shine, and the same forms of sexual abuse (I imagined). I didn't look at any of the news reports about his conviction. I didn't want to hurt myself any more. In truth, I was despondent, perhaps sadder than usual, and I did not deal with it properly. It just pushed me further down that well.

In 2018, my consultant psychiatrist was very worried about me, as I was that depressed. He organised a proper psychological assessment for me, and thankfully I did not have to wait too long. I found that helpful, but it was over far too soon for me. That's when I learned that I was a schizoid, as well as suffering from depression. The diagnosis did not help me at the time, but I could see how the schizoid diagnosis fitted me perfectly. Yet I was still worryingly depressed, so the consultant arranged for me to meet with a social worker because there were no counsellors available. I found her to be lovely, and all the talking I did, helped me get through the week. Again, that was over too soon, but I was lucky in that I was still seeing the psychiatrist, and my saviour, Dr Neary, and they were keeping me going.

It was a horrible time to be alive, and I had no purpose in life anymore, after I lost SOSAD. I had all my old symptoms of depression, and I isolated myself as much as I possibly could. I only left the house to visit Mam and Dad, or to go to the shops or doctor's appointments, or to take Holly out. My diabetic nurse even noticed how bad I was on one of my visits to her, and she was trying to encourage me to look after myself. She was saying how brilliant I was looking after others who were depressed or suicidal, and I should use that to look after myself. I didn't have the heart to tell her how useless I was at that. Mostly though, that two years is a blur for me, and I don't want to think about it anyway. It is just too sad and painful.

My relationship with Valerie is over, yet we still live in the same house. I hate watching or hearing her, going on one of her binges. I do worry about her too, especially on the days she stays in bed all day after a drinking session. On these days, she can sleep all day, and I often wonder if she is dead or not. I never go into her room to check on her, but listen out for any movement, or to hear her snore, before I can relax. I have gone through the scenario of finding her dead, so often that I could do it now in my sleep. I dread the nights when she patrols the house like a noisy ghost. I wake up every time I hear her in the kitchen because she has often left all the lights on, the fridge open, and on some occasions, left the cooker on. I am afraid that one night, she will burn the house down. I don't say anything about this, and I try not to argue with her at all, because it just upsets me, and I still have trouble finding the right thing to say. I sometimes get annoyed cleaning the house because a lot of the time I am cleaning up after her, and she does not lift a finger to help. I don't know how she can stay in her room all day, watching TV and doing nothing at all, except drinking.

In 2018, I was broke and told Valerie that I was not able to pay her €50 weekly maintenance. As ever, I thought I would feel better and get a hold of my depression sooner rather than later. I never had much patience. I explained to her that I was broke and could not afford to pay for her maintenance anymore. I also explained that I would indeed feel better soon and then get a job. Then I would be able to resume paying her maintenance. She was happy with that but did not offer to help me pay the household bills.

After I was sacked, I got in touch with a solicitor in Dublin. I went to meet him, and we spoke about what happened for about half an hour. I had all the paperwork I kept from the investigation and passed it over to him. All I wanted was the money SOSAD owed me and to find out why SOSAD sacked me. I wanted to know what bullying and harassment I was dismissed over. SOSAD owed me holiday pay and the money I had paid 'Linked In' on my credit card, for ads recruiting counsellors. I had been in touch a few times by letter which were utterly ignored. I asked Christine to help me out, and she tried her best, but still, they would not give me what was due. They said that they could not find my contract. I had put it in my office with the others, but they said it was not there. I let Christine know that it was the SOSAD accountants that had drawn up my contract, and they would have the original. I don't know if they contacted the accountants, but I did not get paid. It seemed like they were not satisfied with sacking me and just wanted to draw out my pain as much as they could.

I eventually got my case in front of the Workplace Relations Commission in 2019, but it didn't get very far. The adjudicator had worked with the investigator, so she adjourned the hearing. I was delighted because I was with a barrister and solicitor, while there were about 15 people from SOSAD. I tried not looking at them, but I wondered why there were so many. I did see Christine, and she came to say hello after, but Ronan called her back to the group. He did not like me talking to her. We spoke later on the phone, and she told me that she had to be there and that she hated every second of it. She had no idea why she was included and wasn't too happy about it.

A few months later, the case had a new adjudicator and a new date. I went again on my own and was represented by a barrister and solicitor. I had met them the previous time but not before that or any time since. They had a huge file that I had seen before. It contained every little detail from the start of the complaints made against me. It was huge. I was very nervous and anxious but hoped it would proceed so that it would be over forever. There were only four people from SOSAD with their legal representative. I heard that it was because the WRC could not accommodate as many as the last time. Before we started, the barrister asked me some last-minute questions, and I reminded him that all I wanted was the money I was due and the exact reasons why I was sacked. He asked what SOSAD owed me, and I told him about €8000. We were called to a small room upstairs, and we all sat around a big table.

Once we started, it was SOSAD who were taking up all the time. Each one from Ronan, to the secretary and the investigator, took forever. They took so long that I was not sure what point they were trying to make. I sat as quietly as I could but had to get up and leave a few times because of the lies I heard. I did learn that it was the investigator who decided to examine the 84 pages of complaints against me and not the Board. I don't know why she was able or allowed to do that, but then again, having spent just one day in her presence, I shouldn't be surprised. She acted like she knew it all, and took on the 84 complaints, without consulting the Board. I wanted my barrister to question her on this, and I was glad when he did. Then I wished he hadn't. She would not reply with a straight answer, and we all got lost, and my barrister dropped it. I wanted to know if what she did was legal but never found out.

The Secretary did let slip that they were trying to get me out of SOSAD for two years. I still don't know why maybe my face didn't fit or something like that. He never said why, and my barrister just let it pass as if it was inconsequential. It was important to me. I would have loved to know if the complaints were just an excuse to force me out of SOSAD. I wondered why they had dragged their investigation out over two years. None of the matters I deemed as critical was mentioned at all. I wanted to know why Ronan had told me the complaints were bullshit, and then I was sacked supposedly over the same complaints. I wanted to know if the investigator made her findings on her opinion of me. I thought she had, but she was not questioned on that.

I sat there all day, with a break for lunch, and I was getting bored and fed up. I felt that SOSAD was avoiding the main issues and distracting the adjudicator just like McEnroy had done years previously. Nevertheless, I thought that it was apparent to see and hoped the man deciding on this would see that too. At about 5 pm, I was asked a few questions. The first being why I didn't appeal the decision to sack me. I told them that I was not in any mental state to make a decision. I added that I had no confidence in any appeal because I thought that no one would believe me. I had told the truth before, and no one listened. I was asked a couple more questions about why I didn't appeal later, and I felt terrible trying to tell them about my depression. It didn't matter, though as everyone seemed tired and just wanted to get home. Then the adjudicator said that he would examine all the evidence and let me know their decision. Then it was all over.

Despite being in the room all day, my barrister never mentioned the money I was owed, nor the reasons why I was sacked. When I said it to him later, he said he forgot. Is it any wonder I have no faith in the legal profession? They had let me down again. I thought that the case was simple, but these professionals did it their way, and the whole day was full of convoluted arguments that I had no interest in. I didn't get any of the money until months later when I asked Christine to try to get it for me. Thankfully she managed to get the Board to offer me something, not what was due, and I accepted, just to cut the last piece of string binding me to SOSAD.

When the WRC wrote to me, they said that my case against SOSAD had failed. I wasn't surprised or shocked. As far as I could see, we made no case at all and didn't deserve to win. It was more about the technicalities of what happened rather than what actually happened. I didn't find out why I was sacked, whether it was planned as the Secretary said, or not. I got no answers, but I was just glad it was all over.

IN TWO MINDS:

Early in 2019 Shine was convicted again, and it passed me by as if it never happened. It was months later when I learned of the second conviction, or even that there was another trial. The only thing that pleased me this time was that I had not known it was happening. If I did, it might have brought back thoughts of my own abuse, or worse, thoughts about my criminal case and his acquittal. When I heard about it, it was all over, and he was sentenced to four years in jail. I was indifferent to all the news, yet still disappointed with myself, for having put us all through such misery.

Wayne bought a new house in 2019 but only got the keys this year. I am delighted for him and glad he has his place to call home. I was able to help him by stripping out the whole house, and then painting and decorating all the rooms. I was thrilled to be able to do something to help and happy that I did not make a mess of it. I took my time and enjoyed myself, but I noticed that I enjoyed it more when he was not around. Nothing against Wayne, but I have become comfortable working on my own, and I don't like anyone looking at me or passing comments on my work until it is finished. Working in Wayne's house was the first time, apart from holidays, that I was away from my own house for long periods. Any time I was in his place, I had an urge to go home, and I noticed that I had the same notion on other occasions. There is never any reason for me to rush home, but I think it might be the only place my mind feels safe. Other than that, I don't know why I should get these feelings, but at least I am aware of them now and can prepare myself if I leave the house.

I never did feel well enough or have any confidence or self-esteem, so I never did go back to work. In 2018, I was summoned to court over non-payment of court-mandated maintenance. Valerie never mentioned anything about this until I got the summons. I couldn't believe what she was doing at first, but then I accepted that I did not even know her anymore. I guessed that all that mattered to her was money and vodka. I attended court on my own and was represented by a solicitor. I still wasn't sure if I trusted any solicitor, but I did not think I had enough confidence to express myself. At one stage, my solicitor came and told me that Valerie wanted the arrears all paid to her that day. I could not afford that as it was €1200 and I didn't think it was fair. I disagreed so we had to wait until the end of the day until our case was called. That old rage was back, and I fought like crazy to control myself. In the court this time, I thought I was calm and controlled, and I ended up doing most of the talking, simply because the judge was directing her questions at me. I explained that I had stopped paying the maintenance with Valerie's agreement, which Valerie tried to deny. The judge explained that I should have gone to court and got the maintenance stopped, and I was sorry that I didn't. The judge looked at the supporting documentation on our finances and expenditures and asked why Valerie was getting maintenance in the first place if I was paying all the household bills. I tried to explain, but the more I talked about it, the more ridiculous it sounded. I wanted to blame the solicitor who had let me down, but didn't, as she was sitting close by.

The judge though was patient with me. After a bit more discussion, the judge explained that I had to pay the back maintenance owed because it was court-mandated, even if it was unjust. The judge asked me if I could pay her back €50 per month. Valerie's solicitor intervened and asked for a lump sum that day, but the judge dismissed that. I agreed to pay what I owed in monthly payments. I was happy with that, and then the judge cancelled the original order for maintenance, and I was thrilled with that. Valerie was not too pleased leaving the court, and I was over the moon with that.

I believe that the SOSAD Board disintegrated about a year after they sacked me and all they achieved was to drive a massive wedge between themselves and the staff and volunteers who run SOSAD. They didn't listen to or heed the coordinators or volunteers, and it was the charity that suffered. That is so sad. It does add some credence to the idea that they were just there to get me out of SOSAD. I don't believe that the complaints should have been allowed to proceed in the first place. I don't understand why the Board made me suffer terribly for two years. But I hope they know the damage they did to SOSAD and me.

Chapter 28

The Final Chapter

I have been so lucky in life so far and very fortunate to still have my life, and I need to focus on that, along with Wayne, and the future Mr and Mrs Lee Moroney. I am always nervous about the wedding, but I am trying to prepare myself to be a good Dad and to enjoy it as I should, with no acting. I have no idea how or why I am still alive, but I am glad that I am and happy that I am so useless at suicide. I believe that I am alive for a reason, but I don't know what that is, yet!

I don't hate Shine, the rapist, Elaine, the Board of Directors of SOSAD, or anyone else, but I am trying to put my faith into whatever God has planned as punishment. Maybe Karma will play a part. I certainly hope so, but again it is entirely out of my control. The thoughts that Shine was eventually found guilty and put in jail does help a little. He cannot abuse anyone from there, but it is not the justice or closure I had hoped for. Karma eventually got him. I seldom think of Simon's rapist, and I have not seen her since she moved away. I have not seen her boyfriend either, but I often wish the rumours about them being threatened and forced to move out were true. I still think I should have beat him up when I had the chance. It doesn't matter if I was sent to prison because I did not have much of a life anyway. Then, I would not have founded SOSAD, which is terrible, but would not have lost it, which is good.

I think the whole row with Elaine has caused me to have serious trust issues after I thought she was like my right hand. I loved her as a dear friend. I have kept lots of secrets about her and her Mam, that she told me in confidence, as a friend would. I am not sure if I can ever trust anyone anymore. I have seen Elaine a couple of times when I was walking Holly, but I kept well away, in case she had more lies to tell about me. I am glad I do have Holly with me, because I genuinely fear that she could easily report me for rape, or attacking her. I wouldn't put it past her. She is capable of anything. I don't want to go through all that shit again. I still don't hate her. I see her as a thirty-something-year-old woman who behaves like a 13-year-old. This kind of explains her complaints about me, and is all I want to know. I am sorry we lost our friendship over something stupid, but I am happy and safer knowing that she is not in my life anymore.

I have no idea what I should do about my medical records. I don't want to get involved in chasing them up and trying to get an accurate copy. I don't think I could face all the red tape and hassle. I believe the hospital, or Shine, tried to erase my existence, and I am delighted that they failed. I am still here, and maybe that upsets Shine, and that pleases me. I find it hard to believe how the Gardai handled my complaint. I don't understand what happened, but I know that being accused of collusion did not help me. I believe I was right when I thought that the Gardai involved had no experience in sexual assaults of this nature and therefore didn't help the case. I try not to think about the justice system and all the ways it failed me. It is too depressing. I just hope that the Gardai are properly trained now, and the justice system is not so cruel to the victims.

I don't hate Valerie either, but I have no love left for her at all. I do hate watching her kill herself slowly with drink and cigarettes. When she goes on her binges, she does not eat or even have a cup of tea for days on end and then moans about not feeling well. She still smokes, especially when drinking, after living through two heart attacks. I am still waiting, ready for the day she does not wake up. In May this year, when we had beautiful lovely weather, I was working in the back garden. I was putting a new concrete top on the flower bed walls. Valerie came out and lay on her sun lounger. It was before 10.00 am, and she was extremely drunk. She was still drinking.

I tried to ignore her, but she kept phoning her friends while videoing me. She was saying what a c... I was, and an idiot and many other names. I got mad, and I couldn't stop what I was doing because the concrete would dry. I did the only thing I could think of. I called the Gardai. They arrived a few minutes later, and even though they spoke to both of us, they did nothing, and Valerie was still calling me a c... when they were leaving. I finished what I was doing as quickly as I could and went inside. I washed and got changed and went to make myself a coffee. When I got to the kitchen, I saw that Valerie had fallen over and was lying on my freshly laid concrete. She was snoring her head off. I left her there, but I was fuming as she had ruined all the work I did. She stayed there like that until 5 pm when she came into the house and went upstairs. I hoped that she had hurt herself.

The next week the gardai called and I wasn't expecting that. They were just following up on their call from Friday. Valerie was away for the weekend, and I told them so and gave them her phone number. Later that day, different Gardai called, and I wondered what was going on. They told me that Valerie had secured a protection order because of the terrible mental abuse she had to endure, and because I would not let her use the kitchen or the garden. I was the one who was mentally abused over the last few years, not her. I asked the Garda how I was able to stop her using any room in the house, and told him about the incident last Friday in the garden. He was aware of that, and he suggested the Valerie was just 'covering her ass'. I agreed with that, and the garda explained the rules to me.

I have applied to get this protection order discharged, but I am still waiting, and will not get to court until December. As the Garda explained, if Valerie made any other complaint against me, I would be arrested. I don't know how that can be right or fair, and it is hard living with the threat of arrest for nothing except lies.

I don't talk or engage with Valerie, and I am sure that watching her kill herself slowly, is no good for my mental health. She was in hospital recently for a burst appendix and then for pneumonia and other complications. That did not stop her drinking. Still, we live together in the same house, and when she is not drinking, everything is calm. She can be polite and friendly, and I sometimes find that strange. I wonder if she is looking for something of me, and I am often right. I just can't trust her anymore. She goes out to visit a friend on Thursdays and then she goes off for the weekend to stay with someone. She pays no attention to the COVID-19 19 rules. I don't mind, as then she is away from me, and I don't have to worry about her.

I find that I have no real passion for anything left, and I miss that. I was a very passionate person, and I wore my heart on my sleeve, as they say. I was incredibly fanatical about SOSAD and every single person helping out, or looking for help and support. Now it seems I lost my passion altogether or left it in SOSAD. I always felt emotionally involved and passionate about the jobs I had in my life. Perhaps far more than I should have, but I couldn't help myself. I can't get passionate about anything in my life at present, no matter how hard I try. I miss the passion that used to motivate me and keep me going. It was able to keep my depression at bay on many occasions. I miss being emotionally involved in life, but not the heartache. I guess this is my schizoid personality disorder, which numbs me from the very essence of life. I do hope that maybe my passion will return in the future and help me feel alive, but I won't hold my breath.

I am not sure what I would do if ever I got the opportunity to go back to SOSAD. Some days I think that I would love to return because I know that I still have a lot to contribute. I know that I could fix up the damage caused by the directors and get everyone focused on helping others. On other days I think that I am better off away from it altogether. Yet SOSAD is Simon's legacy, and I poured more than blood, sweat and tears into it, and it still feels like part of me. I don't know what I would do. I know that I did not behave correctly or with dignity after all the complaints started. I feel ashamed of the way I acted, and I don't want to use my depression as an excuse. I should have looked for legal advice straight away and had someone represent me at all the meetings I had with the Board. My mental health would probably have been much better if I had taken a lengthy period off work when the doctor told me too. But it is way too late to learn that now, and they are just more regrets to add to my long list and other facts about my life that I don't want to dwell on.

I can't say if this is the final chapter of my life, but I would like to think that it is not. I don't hope for a better future because then I won't be let down or disappointed. I feel my depression is mild at this moment, and that means that I can just function enough every day to survive. I still follow my routine every morning when I get up, and the walk always helps me, as well as Holly. Walking Holly every day has been brilliant for me, and I find that I can say hello or chat to people much easier than before. I am fighting my depression every day, and I am holding my own. That is brilliant for me. I know my distractions will never cure me of my depression, but they do help keep me at a functional level. I have learned to avoid thinking because that stops me doing what I want to do when I want to do it. If I start thinking about something I am going to do, my mind will try to convince me not to do it. It will pour lots of reasons why I should not try anything because it still wants me on my own, doing nothing, so that it can gain more control. I don't want that.

The more I do every day, the less chance I give to my depression. I remind myself always that there is some good to come for me, and I have to look after Holly and Simon's grave. I have learned that I need to have something to hold onto, just to keep going. I have Lee's wedding to look forward to, and that alone helps me in so many ways. It is another 'reason to live' for me. It is also why I am working in the garden and the house so that our home is comfortable and inviting for them when they come home. I cannot wait to see him and Shauna walk down the aisle to the altar and see the two of them become one. All this works for me and allows me to live close enough to a normal life.

I do sometimes dream of living in Caleta De Fuste, at least for the winter months. I would only go if I could take Holly with me. I am sure she would love it, and she does not seem to be bothered by the heat. I would have to be in the right state of mind with an exit plan because I know that I cannot go without my depression. I would need to have something to do to help me keep it at bay, but I am sure that the great weather, the lovely walks and the chance to explore, would be brilliant distractions. I am fed up with checking the weather forecast here before doing anything, and I am sick of that cold, windy weather that we seem to get too much of here in Ireland. Retiring to Caleta de Fuste is even lovely to daydream about, and even that can keep a lid on my depressed thoughts. Maybe someday this might happen.

I never did get the counselling that I was promised, and now that I am feeling much better, I am not sure that I would want to start now and open that box of snakes. I have somehow managed to get myself out of the severest stage of depression, and don't want to go back to that Hell anymore. Maybe counselling is exactly what I need to sort out my core values and strengthen my coping skills. I will think about that if counselling is ever offered.

I am still not sure where I am with God, or if I am still part of His plan. I am back praying again, but not attending Mass, yet. I like to think about Mary and Joseph and pray to them, even if it is just to remind them that I am still alive, and ask them to check in on Simon. I think that all the confusion, doubts, and questions I have about my faith have muddied the waters between Heaven and me, and what I felt about God is wrong and maybe stupid. I have been having this sneaking suspicion that God, with Simon's help, has been guiding me and helping me write this book. I can accept that because I don't think that I could have written this on my own. Just like SOSAD, but maybe not as strong this time. I think they might be doing the work and I am just the pilot. I do want a relationship with GOD, but I fear that will not happen until I find the peace of mind I crave.

I do know that the only person who can help me through this is me. I am still searching for the peace I have longed for all my adult life, but I have to beat this depression to have any chance of that. My distraction tactics have worked well for me, but I have to keep trying. Otherwise, I will sink a lot faster than a rock in the ocean. This book has been washing around in my brain for years. I had hoped that it would be therapeutic for me, but it turned out to be more traumatic. The biggest problem I had was that I have no self-belief. That meant going over every paragraph time and time again, but I feel happier now that I am finished at last. It has taken a whole lot of my physical and mental energy, and I am not surprised that I feel so drained. Maybe now I can build up some of the psychological and physical strength I need to survive.

IN TWO MINDS:

I would also like to go back to work, to become a value to society again. I am not sure that anyone would hire me with my history of depression. I don't think I would employ myself, so I have been putting together the first draft of a business plan, and I fully intend to see that through, when I get the confidence to do so. It is okay writing in private, but a lot harder for me to share it with others, or contact the suppliers that make my business plan viable. I do think that it is a great idea that will be a very positive benefit to our environment, but I will just have to wait and see how it pans out. Other than that, I have no plans for the future, and I am trying to live day by day. I want to be able to keep living like that.

Writing this book, is in itself, a purpose for me, and I believe that this has helped me in my war against my depression. I needed to have something positive to focus on, and it has worked for me. It has allowed me to block out all the nasty, negative thoughts and ideas that would have infected my mind if I had no purpose.

I love my boys, who are grown men by now, and I miss Simon terribly, just like I miss Lee living so far away. I still wonder about Simon and what he looks like now. Unfortunately, I cannot imagine what he looks like at all, so that is just another thing I will have to wait before I can see for myself. Maybe I will find a way to be able to chat with Wayne and Lee and be a good part of their lives, for once. I would love to learn more about Shauna and have a great relationship with her too. I want to be able to feel that love in my heart, and mean it when I say I love them. I can't wait until I have some grandchildren that I can love and spoil. I think that will help me make up for being a terrible father. I would love to feel and experience other emotions, like joy and happiness, and have the courage I need, to keep some kind of control over my depression. I want to keep fighting for my life and never want to start to believe that suicide is my best and only option ever again. I want to live, and I would love to find some peace.

About the Author

Peter Moroney

Is a father to three boys. He earned an Honour's Degree in Business and Economics from Trinity College, Dublin in 2003. Peter enjoys keeping busy, holidays in Caleta de Fuste and he loves being a daddy to Holly, a mini Jack Russell.

Contacts

Website: www.intwominds.ie

G mail: inwomindsmemoir@gmail.com

Address: 50 Rowan Heights, Marley's Lane, Drogheda. Co. Louth. A92 A66R

Facebook: facebook.com/petermoroney.773/

Twitter: @InTwoMinds

Instagram: Instagram.com/pppmoroney/

Printed in Great Britain
by Amazon

61738745R00302